Optimal Trading Strategies

Quantitative Approaches for Managing Market Impact and Trading Risk

Robert Kissell and Morton Glantz

with special contribution by
Roberto Malamut, Ph.D.
Foreword by
Neil Chriss, Ph.D.

AMACOM

American Management Association

New York • Atlanta • Boston • Chicago • Kansas City • San Francisco • Washington, D.C.
Brussels • Mexico City • Tokyo • Toronto

Special discounts on bulk quantities of AMACOM books are available to corporations, professional associations, and other organizations. For details, contact Special Sales Department, AMACOM, a division of American Management Association 1601 Broadway, New York, NY 10019.
Tel.: 212-903-8316. Fax: 212-903-8083.
Web site: www.amanet.org

This publication is designed to provide accurate and authoritative information in regard to the subject matter covered. It is sold with the understanding that the publisher is not engaged in rendering legal, accounting, or other professional service. If legal advice or other expert assistance is required, the services of a competent professional person should be sought.

Library of Congress Cataloging-in-Publication Data

Kissell, Robert, 1967-
   Optimal trading strategies : quantitative approaches for managing market impact and trading risk / Robert Kissell and Morton Glantz ; with special contribution by Roberto Malamut.
        p. cm.
Includes bibliographical references and index.
   ISBN 0-8144-0724-2
 1. Stocks. 2. Investments. I. Glantz, Morton. II. Malamut, Roberto, 1965- III. Title.

HG4661.K47 2003
332.64'2--dc21

                                                              2002155973

Printing number

10 9 8 7 6 5 4 3 2

To our wives Felise and Maryann—
Who offered encouragement, love, and support
during the writing of this book

And to our parents—
Who provided guidance and direction over the years

CONTENTS

FOREWORD

Financial decision-making focuses on the relationship between risk and return and in the case of investing we make decisions that optimally balance the total risk of a portfolio with its expected return. We seek to maximize return or minimize risk while holding the other constant. This way of looking at the world—pioneered by Markowitz and culminating in the Capital Asset Pricing Model of Sharpe, Lintner and Mossin—gives fundamental insights into the types of portfolios that investors will optimally hold. But these theories, while telling us a great deal about what individuals should *hold*, say nothing about how to *acquire* them. This is where *Optimal Trading Strategies* enters the picture.

For an individual investor the problem of how to acquire a particular stock is hardly a problem at all. The trading volumes that a typical individual investor produces hardly require creative problem solving, so much so that we could readily compare an individual investor's trading activity to spitting in the ocean. On the other hand, institutional investors are often too big to be overlooked by the market and therefore they should worry—and indeed do worry—about the costs of acquiring portfolio positions and selling out of them. These costs—transaction costs—comprise a great deal of the topics and analysis in this book.

For institutional investors trading into and out of portfolios is not a harmless activity—entering the market changes the market, and therefore the decision to buy or sell a security must include the potential price movements—the transaction costs—associated with the trade. In simple terms, if I forecast that a stock will rise from 100 to 103 in the next two weeks but if in acquiring the position I will move the market so that I pay 101 on average instead of 100, then my true expected gain on the investment is closer to 2% than the original 3% forecast I made. The movement of the price from 100 to 101 in the act of buying it is called *slippage* and forms part of the transaction costs associated with the trade. This important concept underpins a host of important topics covered in this book—transaction cost modeling, pre-trade portfolio analysis and optimal trading strategies among them.

For some time now, sell side Wall Street firms have offered institutional investors the service of *portfolio* or *program* trading wherein a trading desk trades a portfolio of stocks on behalf of a client—the premise being that the brokerage firm will supply expertise in trade analysis, minimization of slippage and perhaps also assume some or all of the risk in executing the transaction. The aim of a portfolio trader is simple in principle: buy into or sell out of the portfolio position with the least amount of slippage. The problem is balancing two forces that fundamentally oppose one another in providing an easy solution to the problem. To see this note that if trading causes slippage, then an obvious preventative step to take would be to trade more slowly. Slow down the rate of trading and reduce the magnitude of slippage—that is, reduce the cause that is producing the effect. This does work, but in slowing down trading one introduces the second and very important force: market risk.

Take the simple example buying a single stock whose price in the market is presently 100. If I need to buy a lot of the stock, I might drive the price of the stock up so that the average cost becomes 101 or 102. If I slow down trading by breaking up the big trade into a number of smaller trades in some way, I might be able to reduce the amount by which I push the market price. But in waiting to trade, the price of the stock will almost certainly move irrespective of my reduced presence in the market, *and the price might move in the opposite direction I want it to*. By how much it moves and in what direction it moves is a mystery to most over very short time horizons, but that it will move is not in dispute. We can summarize all of this simply: *when it comes to trading, you are dammed if you do and dammed if you don't.*

Do trade and push the market.
Don't trade and the market pushes you.

Pushing the market costs you because prices move against you—if you buy, the stock becomes more expensive as you trade, if you sell buyers pay less. On the other hand, if you don't trade the market may move against you too. You don't know for sure that it will, but the possibility exists and this is what we mean by market risk.

Thus, the decision of how fast to trade—for example in acquiring a portfolio—depends on what balance we wish to strike between the transaction costs and market risk. The decision of how fast to trade boils down to choosing a path along which to trade—in the case of buying a portfolio this is simply all of the intermediate steps along the way from not owning the portfolio to owning it fully. This is a simple qualitative description of the problem, but it captures most of its salient features.

The quantitative description of the problem goes further. It shows that most trading paths are simply not worth considering at all. They are not optimal. They take on too much risk relative to their cost or cost too much relative to their risk. The quantitative approach demonstrates conclusively that among all possible paths to acquiring a portfolio certain paths *are* optimal—for their given level of risk they have the minimum cost or vice versa.

Now, if we think of the trading path as a strategy for acquiring a portfolio—or for that matter selling one—then we can replace *trading path* with the *trading strategy* and we arrive at the central idea behind this theory and behind the title of this book. To buy or sell a portfolio requires a trading strategy and a framework for understanding which strategies are *good* and which are not, and this naturally leads to a host of questions most of which are discussed, analyzed, and answered in the chapters herein.

One interesting feature of the work is that it leads naturally to the notion of an *efficient frontier* of trading strategies, language that Rob Almgren and I purposefully borrowed from Markowitz' portfolio selection and the Capital Asset Pricing Model. This idea, which turns out to be remarkably useful as a way of understanding the relative merits of different trading strategies, works in complete analogy to the Capital Asset Pricing Model. Each strategy has a certain transaction cost and a certain risk. If you plot all strategies on a graph then what one finds is that they form a parabola like shape and only those strategies on the boundary of that shape are optimal. We call this the efficient frontier.

What I have just described forms the core of my own research in this topic with my collaborator Robert Almgren, and it is discussed and expanded upon at great length in this terrific new book. For one thing, to make use of this framework—to understand institutional trading at all—requires understanding how to model and measure the relationship between the size of transactions and the amount they push markets—*transaction costs.* Understanding transaction costs is critical to evaluating investment performance and trading performance—no institutional money manager can afford *not* to understand transaction costs. I would say that if one sliced out everything from this book except the work on transaction costs it would still be an important contribution to the literature and well worth its price.

But the authors further and give a complete description of optimal trading strategies and a discussion of the principal bid business, a subject that has been of considerable interest to me for some time. In fact, I met the first author of this volume, Robert Kissell, at a conference at Columbia University in 2001 where we each, unbeknownst to the other, were presenting original research on the question of how to mathematically model this business. Finally, the last three chapters should be of interest to any institutional investor concerned at all about evaluating broker performance.

This book covers a broad stretch of material from the institutionally important and practical to the particular and mathematical. Any time a subject arises out of a mathematically intensive theory applied to a practical problem, the set of potential beneficiaries generally outnumbers those with the mathematical training to study the original work in its entirety. Therefore when a work comes along such as this book that carefully develops and explains the theory and its conclusions while remaining fully grounded in the important practical details, it should not be overlooked by anyone wishing to advance their knowledge.

Neil A. Chriss
Managing Director of Quantitative Strategies
S.A.C. Capital Management

PREFACE

The goal of *Optimal Trading Strategies* is to formulate a mathematical approach to address those questions and issues that arise during the implementation phase of the investment cycle—namely, a quantitative framework to identify, measure, and estimate transaction costs. In this book we introduce proper mathematical techniques to forecast market impact cost and timing risk associated with trading strategies. The techniques provide investors with the means to analyze the trade-off between cost and risk and evaluate alternative strategies to determine the strategy most appropriate for the fund, and ultimately achieve best execution.

Every day investors are faced with choices pertaining to implementing investment decisions. Hence, they need to understand the cost consequences of their decisions and portfolio returns. Numerous studies have shown that transaction costs typically comprise the largest quantity of fund tracking error. Thus, improving fund returns can be accomplished by exercising proper transaction cost management control.

Up until now, most financial research and literature has focused on the investment decisions: asset allocation, stock selection, portfolio construction, risk management, performance attribution analysis, an so on. An abundant quantity of literature and commentary focuses on the decision-making process (e.g., equities, bonds, cash, derivative products) as well as ample graduate courses, texts, seminars, and conferences. Furthermore, an array of investment-related decision models have been thoroughly studied, tested, modified, and revised. This provides the proper decision-making tools for managers to specify an appropriate portfolio. However, the same level of research is missing from the implementation decision phase of the investment cycle. There is a missing link in the investment cycle tying the investment decision to execution. Investors have numerous questions regarding implementation but relatively little information on how to evaluate implementation decisions. For example, some of the concerns of managers and traders include the following questions: What will this trade cost? How do we estimate trading costs? How long should execution take (minutes, hours, days, weeks)? How should the order be sliced? Should we choose an agency transaction or a principal bid? How do we evaluate alternative strategies—trade aggressively or passively? What trading strategy should we employ? How do we measure performance? How do I select a broker?

Optimal Trading Strategies addresses the deficiencies surrounding transaction cost analysis and implementation decision making. We present appropriate methodology, framework, and decision-making models to manage transaction costs through all phases of the investment cycle. We present cutting-edge techniques to develop optimal trading strategies, risk aversion, price improvement, and best execution. We show how Almgren and Chriss' efficient trading frontier (ETF) can be used to develop appropriate trading strategies as well as measure best execution. We introduce the concept of a capital trade line (CTL) as a means of further improving the cost profile of a strategy as well as the development of mixed trading strategies that consist of an allocation between agency and principal. We introduce the concept of the economic fair value (FV) for a principal bid from the perspective of investors. Additionally, we focus on developing a post-trade measurement process that can be used to measure trading costs and fairly assess execution performance. Finally, we present techniques for incorporating transaction cost management directly into all phases of the investment cycle to achieve best execution strategies, preserve asset value, and increase portfolio returns.

It has often been said that there is no CAPM or Black-Scholes available for investors to evaluate the implementation of the decision. Our goal is to bridge the gap between portfolio selection and implementation.

ACKNOWLEDGMENTS

There are several people who have provided significant comments and contributions and without their help the writing of this book would not have been possible. Roberto Malamut provided major insight into the real meaning of the concerns and issues encountered by investors, brokers, and traders. His problem-solving ability, quantitative knowledge, and immense insight of optimization techniques played a major role in the formulation and development of much of the framework presented. We would also like to thank him for his contributions to Chapter 12, Advanced Trading Techniques. Alexis Kirke played a key role in the early development of much of the underlying theory and quantitative process that led to the development of the ideas and concepts presented in this book. Neil Chriss and Robert Almgren pioneered much of the early research in the field. Their contributions have created new disciplines and focus areas within the financial sciences. They provided extremely helpful comments along the way. Without their leading edge work, transaction cost analysis and trading cost estimation could not be at the stage it is today. The Almgren and Chriss efficient trading frontier will truly revolutionize financial decision-making for years to come. Robert Ferstenberg provided helpful guidance and suggestions throughout the writing of this book.

Throughout the writing of this book there were many individuals who provided significant ongoing research and helpful suggestions in many of the areas we discuss. Agustin Leon, senior quantitative analyst at Ivy Asset Management, played a major role in the formulation of the theory and performance testing used in our intraday trading risk approach, ultimately leading to our preferred hybrid covariance matrix. Pierre Miasnikof provided much of the statistical knowledge and expertise in developing the quantitative approaches for estimating market impact and evaluating alternative trading strategies. James Poserina, researcher extraordinaire, provided the necessary research support and data needs that ultimately made the writing of this book possible.

We also wish to thank some very special quantitative analysts and colleagues who have shared their knowledge and provided helpful comments throughout the writing of the book. They are: Kevin Byrne, Richard Dixon, Edward Dockery, Sean Fitzgerald, Alaric Fontenot, Scott Kravatz, Christopher Kwiakowski, Gerry Milligan, Bill O'Shea, James Rubenstein, and Regina Tsirkel. We hope that we have provided as much to them as they have to us.

INTRODUCTION

Chapter 1—Transaction Costs provides an introduction to financial transaction costs. Here we differentiate between "measuring" and "estimating" costs. The chapter provides a thorough investigation of the true goal of implementation (e.g., preserving asset value), and provides a working definition of "best execution" that can be used by all market participants to develop appropriate execution strategies ex-ante and measure performance ex-post. This chapter provides insight into how transaction costs affect each phase of the investment cycle. We conclude with a recommended transaction cost management approach to reduce cost and ultimately increase returns.

Chapter 2—Unbundled Transaction Components Cost provides a thorough investigation into the natural components of transaction cost, namely, commissions, taxes, fees, spreads, delay, price appreciation, market impact, timing risk, and opportunity cost. In this chapter we distinguish between a visible and non-transparent cost and also between a fixed and variable transaction cost. We expand on the implementation shortfall methodology so that we can better identify and classify our costs based on where and when they arise during the investment cycle. We conclude with an introduction to the formulation approach for estimating trading costs, that is, those variable non-transparent transaction costs that arise during execution.

Chapter 3—Pre-Trade Analysis presents the reader with the appropriate framework for conducting a pre-trade evaluation. We emphasize the appropriate statistics to gain a quick and thorough understanding of the trade list. We present the necessary data to estimate trading costs and timing risk as well as develop optimal trading strategies. We depict how the list should be viewed and analyzed using graphs and tables. This chapter introduces the reader to the intraday trading behavior of stocks and presents a framework for determining the stability of these patterns. This chapter examines in detail the intraday trading patterns for volume and price volatility and presents estimation techniques for forecasting daily volume, volatility, and price movement. Trading risk and risk decomposition is thoroughly investigated from a trading standpoint. This chapter also distinguishes between what constitutes trading difficulty and what constitutes a costly trade. The work presented in this chapter serves as the building blocks for our market impact and transaction cost estimation model.

Chapter 4—Price Appreciation provides the reader with a detailed description of price appreciation. Price appreciation, also referred to as the price trend, stock alpha, or drift term, is the natural price movement in the stocks. It is how the stock would move in a perfectly efficient market without any uncertainty or noise. The chapter discusses the basics of traditional price evaluation models, for example, fundamental and technical analysis. It continues with a description of the appropriate forecasting techniques for estimating trading costs. We discuss the linear, percentage returns, and growth price evolution models. The chapter concludes with the derivation of trading cost estimates for price appreciation.

Chapter 5—Market Impact provides the reader with a definition and detailed description of market impact. Market impact is the price movement in the stock caused by the particular trade or order. It is caused by the liquidity demands and information leakage of the order. In this chapter we describe the market impact cost through usage of supply and demand curves and distinguish between temporary and permanent impact. We provide a mathematical description of market impact cost using price trajectories. Lastly, as a means of gaining insight into the market impact cost function, we compare and contrast investor trading costs to the dealer function.

Chapter 6—Timing Risk provides a definition of and a detailed description of timing risk. Timing risk is the uncertainty surrounding trading cost estimates. It consists of price volatility and fluctuations in intraday volume profiles. In this chapter we investigate some of the more common volatility forecasting models, HMA, EWMA, GARCH, and so on. We then continue with an investigation of risk models, namely, single and multiple factor models and provide a review of fundamental, macro, and statistical models as a means to gain insight into stock covariance and correlation. We conclude the chapter with the development of a short-term intraday risk model that is a hybrid of a short-term volatility forecast and longer-term correlation model.

Chapter 7—Opportunity Cost discusses the opportunity cost of an order. Opportunity cost is the foregone profit or loss of not being able to fully implement an investment decision. It arises either because there is insufficient stock liquidity or adverse price movement. In this chapter we provide the methodology to identify and determine the cause of opportunity cost as well as introduce the process to estimate opportunity cost ex-ante based on price appreciation and permanent market impact. We conclude the chapter with a comparison of opportunity cost to timing risk since the two are often confused.

Chapter 8—The Holy Grail of Market Impact focuses on the development of a market impact model. We introduce statistical techniques to uncover the more important factors of market impact. The approach used to estimate market impact of a trading strategy is a price trajectory model, which under the right set of assumptions simplifies to a simple cost allocation methodology. This process is based on an instantaneous market impact cost I*. The chapter also provides advantages and disadvantages of different market impact modeling techniques and concludes with a set of examples to reinforce the concepts presented in the chapter.

Chapter 9—Optimal Trading Strategies presents the framework for developing an optimal trading strategy by incorporating each of the unbundled non-transparent trading cost components. We provide the methodology to determining the strategy most appropriate to meet the goals and objectives of the fund, namely, risk aversion strategies and price improvement. We incorporate the estimation techniques from the previous chapters and develop a variation of mean-variance optimization to determine an optimal trading strategy that has the lowest amount of cost for a given quantity of risk and the least risk for a given level of cost. We discuss the concepts of efficient trading frontier, the capital trade line, and mixed strategies consisting of both agency and principal. This chapter shows how the usage of statistical theory and probability distributions can be used to evaluate alternative trading strategies, compare agency executions to principal bid transactions, and ultimately lead to better implementation decisions.

Chapter 10—Principal Bid Transactions introduces the reader to the principal bid transaction. A principal bid, also known as a risk bid or capital commitment is a transaction where brokers provide investors with guaranteed execution of the trade list at the market prices at a specific point in time (usually the close). For this service investors are charged a premium. In this transaction, all risk is transferred to brokers, hence the principal bid premium is in part to compensate brokers for their work in executing the list, the costs incurred, and in part for the risk acquired. The principal bid premium is usually higher than the commission charge of an agency execution since it is only intended to compensate brokers for the work involved in trading the list. The chapter discusses different execution strategies to maximize expected profit as well as maximize the probability of achieving a profit, that is, bid improvement strategies. The chapter concludes with an investigation of the fair value to charge for execution from the point of view of investors and based solely on the characteristics of the trade list.

Chapter 11—VWAP Trading Strategies provides a thorough investigation of VWAP trading strategies. We provide a complete decomposition of the VWAP distribution and show how investors can determine the appropriate order slicing scheme to minimize deviation from VWAP. We introduce the reader to the concept of VWAP convergence to evaluate the advantages and disadvantages of completing the order early and VWAP tilt strategies for those investors seeking to improve the likelihood of executing at a price more favorably than VWAP. In addition to providing insight into the VWAP statistic we show investors how one can improve the VWAP cost profile though use of the ETF and careful planning of the execution strategy.

Chapter 12—Advanced Trading Techniques presents statistical techniques for conducting advanced trading analysis. Preceding chapters focus on deriving a framework for estimating trading costs and developing optimal strategies. The framework provided, however, consists of a complex optimization problem not likely to be solved quickly enough to be to be beneficial to traders. Traders typically require solutions in a matter of minutes; anything longer may not be useful. We provide appropriate transformations, simplifications, and numerical approximations to achieve optimization convergence in minutes rather than hours, days, or more. Here we also discuss the proper means for incorporating opportunity cost and limit orders into the optimization formulation. We conclude with a modeling methodology to perform a program-block separation, that is, a separation of the good risk (i.e., shares that contribute to risk reduction through diversification and hedging) from the bad risk (i.e., those shares that add incremental risk to the list). Subsequently, this separation serves as the basic foundation for structuring crossing orders to minimize the potential risk exposure.

Chapter 13—Post-Trade Analysis provides a formal discussion of post-trade analysis. We introduce an expanded implementation shortfall formulation that better accounts for all of the transaction cost components associated with an agency execution. Subsequently, we introduce a variation of the implementation shortfall for measuring costs associated with a principal bid transaction. This chapter pays special attention to making a distinction between measuring actual execution costs and evaluating execution performance. We address the limitations and shortcomings of the common benchmark comparison approach as a performance measure. We introduce an improved metric, the relative performance measure (RPM), which is more consistent and stable because it allows one to make comparisons across stocks and across days. The chapter concludes with a recommended approach for measuring best execution that consists of evaluating each and every decision made throughout the implementation phase of the investment cycle. This includes evaluation of the specified implementation strategy, cost estimates adjusted for actual market conditions (ex-ante), evaluation of traders'/brokers' ability to achieve fair market prices, and evaluation of trader/broker decisions causing deviation from the specified strategy. The process also includes a means to measure the performance of the executing principal broker for principal bid transactions.

CHAPTER ONE

Transaction Costs

MONEY MANAGERS CONSISTENTLY UNDERPERFORM THEIR paper portfolio benchmarks, some by as much as 2 to 3% annually. One contributing factor to the underperformance is transaction costs associated with implementing investment decisions. The implementation of a financial decision is not free. It has an associated cost and usually results in reduced portfolio returns. If managers do not properly manage these costs during all phases of the investment cycle, many of the fund's superior investments will become only moderately profitable and other higher-quality investments will become unprofitable. This means simply that managers need to be more proactive in managing transaction costs in order to achieve their benchmark and provide investors with competitive portfolio returns. Well-developed methods are available to manage and reduce costs throughout all stages of the investment cycle. However, most of this work has not been adequately disseminated throughout the industry. We provide quantitative techniques; define the quantitative framework for estimating, analyzing, and managing these costs; and offer appropriate metrics for measuring costs and evaluating performance, all of which will result in lower transaction costs and higher portfolio returns.

Managers who ignore transaction costs in the planning process or apply inappropriate techniques to estimate and/or measure these costs can easily underperform their return bogeys. Financial markets are highly competitive and success is often determined by only a few basis points. Therefore, ineffective cost management can be detrimental to performance. It can cause funds to lose value and ultimately managers to lose investors.

Introduction to Transaction Cost Consequences

Consider the following scenario. Managers A and B are close friends who attended the same university and began their careers at the same prestigious Wall Street firm. It was at that firm that they received identical training and learned the same research and modeling techniques. The two friends cultivated the same "correct" outlook. They were the elite of the firm. After establishing themselves at the firm and earning a loyal following, they left to set up their own money management funds. Money quickly poured in.

Both managers consistently achieved superior returns for their clients. However, manager A outperformed manager B, sometimes by as much as 50 bp per quarter. Word of manager A's dominance spread through the industry. Manager A began receiving a larger inflow of investment dollars resulting in more assets and higher management revenues, though their management fee was identical. Manager A was perceived the better manager even though both invested in and held identical portfolios (which was not known to one another at the time).

After several years of managing funds, the two friends met for dinner to catch up on their lives. They spoke of the old times in college and business school, and even of the long hours for little pay at the firm early in their careers. They spoke of their families, and their love of sports and the arts. After awhile, the conversation turned to business. Both realized that they still shared identical views of the economy and financial markets, and even held identical portfolios. Astonishing—but more astonishing, manager A consistently outperformed his old colleague, B.

Manager B was perplexed and put forth the question: "We have the same training and knowledge, identical views, and we even invest in the same stocks at the same time. Your returns are consistently higher than mine. Why?" Manager A, beaming, sipping his cognac replied, "Transaction costs, transaction costs, transaction costs."

Do Transaction Costs Have to Exist?

The earliest investigation of transaction costs and their effect on the profitability of a firm is traced to Ronald Coase in his essay, "The Nature of the Firm," *Econometrica,* 1937. In that article, Coase studied and evaluated the comparative costs of organizing transactions through the market as opposed to within the firm itself. He conjectured that associated transaction costs play a major role in influencing an investment firm's size, strength, and comparative advantage. His work provided a framework for more effectively analyzing economic and business decisions vis-à-vis transaction costs. No small matter, Coase's seminal work led to the 1991 Nobel prize in economics.

The relationship between Coase's economic transaction costs and our financial transaction costs involves the information content of investment

decisions and negotiation skills of traders. Coase understood that to determine fair market prices for goods or services one needs to understand all
relevant issues surrounding the transaction: market dynamics, supply and
demand, competitive pricing and, certainly, transaction costs. Without this
knowledge we can be reasonably certain that fair prices will elude us in the
marketplace. Transaction cost is a necessary price of doing business and a
vital component if one is to correctly determine an investment vehicle's
fair market price.

Transaction Costs in the Equity Markets

In the equity markets, transaction costs refer to costs incurred while implementing an investment decision. They consist of all costs required to facilitate the transaction, including the price "sweetener" required to attract
counterparties into the market.[1] This consists of the price premium paid
above the decision price for a buy order and/or the required price discount
offered below the decision price for a sell order. Transaction costs surface
during the implementation of the investment decision, which makes investment decisions more expensive, and in turn reduces the financial gains of
the portfolio. Transaction costs negate much of the effort put forth by managers and analysts in uncovering superior investment opportunities. Portfolio managers claim that transaction costs are around 1% for a typical
transaction and can often be as high as 2 to 3% for some large orders in
adverse market conditions and/or in illiquid stocks. It is no wonder then
that most managers underperform the market. Managers many times refer
to this underperformance as portfolio slippage. They claim it is a market
phenomenon and cannot be avoided. But this belief is far from the truth. As
we show throughout the book, there are many actions managers and
traders can take to avoid these high costs. In fact, the majority of the costs
should be avoided entirely.

Empirical Evidence of Transaction Costs in the United States

One of the leading transaction cost consultants in the industry is the
Plexus Group. They provide total transaction cost consulting, cost measurement services and broker performance evaluation as well as investment advise. They have measured the total implementation cost of some
transactions[2] to be on average 87bp for listed and 134bp for Nasdaq
stocks. Further, they found that these costs could amount to as much as

---

1. *Sweetener* is the term Robert Schwartz used in *Reshaping the Equity Markets* to refer to the
premium required to attract additional sellers into the market or the discount required to
attract additional sellers into the market.
2. Source: Plexus Group, November 2001. We have defined total transaction cost to be the
sum of execution costs, delay costs, and commissions.

Figure 1.1. U.S. Transaction Cost

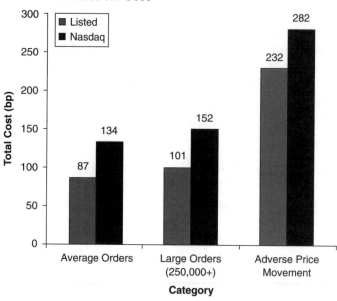

230bp to 280bp in times of adverse market conditions. This is shown in Figure 1.1. For further evidence regarding trading costs see Bessenbinder and Kauffman (1997), Bessenbinder (1998), Bomowitz, Glen, and Madhavan (1999), Jones and Lipson (1997), or Keim and Madhavan (1997) and Conrad (2001). Also, O'Hara (1995) provides in-depth discussion of previous works.

Empirical Evidence of Transaction Costs in Global Markets

High transaction costs are not exclusive to U.S. financial markets. It is even more prevalent in many of the global markets. Figure 1.2 depicts the average transaction costs in global markets.[3] As reported in this figure the average cost across countries is 132bp. The largest implementation costs are incurred in Germany, UK, and Hong Kong. This means that on average, global investors lose 1.3% of each investment dollar due to transaction costs. Further, it could amount to an even larger amount in adverse market conditions and in illiquid stocks.

It is small wonder that the United States has the lowest average total implementation cost. U.S. managers seem most aware of these costs and have become very proactive in developing strategies to reduce and manage these costs.

3. Source: Myners Report, Plexus Group. We have added an average delay cost of 52bp to the costs reported in the Myners report because we are interested in the total implementation cost whereas they are only reporting commission costs and execution costs.

Figure 1.2.   Transaction Costs in Global Markets

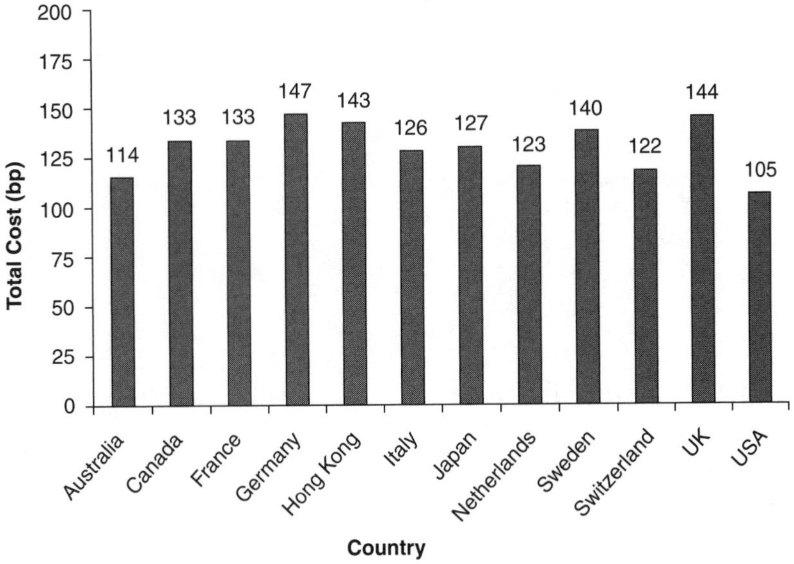

When Do Transaction Costs Arise?

Transaction costs arise during all phases of the investment cycle and affect every financial decision we make. It is the fiduciary responsibility of plan sponsors, managers, traders, and brokers to exercise transaction cost control so yields on investment portfolios do not suffer. Insufficient transaction controls can result in misallocation of funds, inefficient stock selection and portfolio construction, inappropriate implementation strategies, incorrect broker selection, and overall poor execution.

Investment Cycle

The financial investment cycle consists primarily of four stages: asset allocation, portfolio construction, execution services, and portfolio attribution. Transaction costs affect the decision in each and every phase. Transaction costs throughout all phases of the investment cycle have been discussed by Wagner (1999, 2000, 2001), Hill (2000, 2001), Rubenfeld (2000), for example. A brief discussion of these consequences follows.

Asset Allocation

Asset allocation is the process of distributing investment dollars across various investment classes as a means of diversifying risk and targeting a specified level of portfolio return. The more traditional asset classes consist of cash, bonds, and stock. But more recently, other alternative investment classes such as commodities, futures and derivatives, real estate, private

Figure 1.3.   Investment Cycle

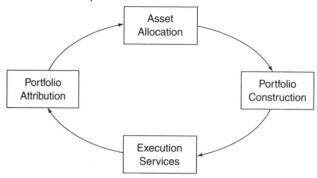

equities, hedge funds, oil and gas, and timber have become more conventional. But regardless of the investment class, transaction costs have a significant effect on overall portfolio returns. If they are not considered in the asset allocation planning process, they will lead to a misallocation of funds and cause portfolios to underperform their targeted returns.

Portfolio Construction

The portfolio construction phase of the investment cycle consists primarily of specifying the exact instruments to purchase or sell in each asset class, for example, bonds and stocks. In the construction of an equity portfolio, managers often need to decide upon different categories of stocks such as large cap, mid cap, or small cap; different sectors; or even the decision of growth or value stocks. In any regard, stocks are selected based on their expected return and associated risk. If transaction costs are not incorporated into the investment decision, the result could be an inefficient portfolio mix caused by an inaccurate assessment of return. Transaction costs play a very important role in the actual stock returns and need to be considered in the portfolio construction phase of the investment cycle.

Execution Services

The execution services phase of the investment cycle consists of the actual implementation of the investment decision. This phase, which is also referred to as the implementation phase or trading phase, involves making decisions regarding how, when, and where to buy and/or sell stocks. Decision makers have the responsibility of evaluating all potential trading options to determine the best method of implementing the specified trade list. They need to decide upon the appropriate trading strategy (aggressive or passive), the appropriate trading option (principal or agency), the appropriate trading venue (traditional broker, ECN, or crossing system), and finally, the broker who will execute the trade. Since this phase is the most involved with actual trading of an order, decision makers need to exert careful cost control. Subsequent chapters are dedicated to the evaluation of these implementation alternatives.

Portfolio Attribution

Portfolio attribution involves measuring fund performance and determining reasons for missing the targeted level of return (either higher or lower). It also helps differentiate between superior stock selection and pure luck. For implementations, portfolio attribution (or alternatively post-trade analysis) refers to the measurement of transaction costs and assessment of broker/trader performance. The goal is identical to that of portfolio returns—to measure costs to improve future decisions and distinguish between exceptional broker/trader performance and luck. In the industry, there are many consulting firms that provide traditional portfolio attribution services. However, far fewer firms specialize in transaction cost post-trade analysis.

Many funds subscribe to post-trade measurement services as a means of satisfying mandates by plan sponsors or investors but do not use the information for improving portfolio returns. This creates another unnecessary performance drag on the fund; these investors would be better off if the fund did not subscribe to the services at all. Very often, information is not incorporated into the fund's planning process because performance measurement techniques employed by these services are deficient; they do not correctly distinguish between measuring a transaction cost and assessing execution performance. Thus, the analyses do not distinguish skill and luck. In Chapter 13 we address these issues.

Transaction Cost Examples

In presence of transaction costs the expected return and future value of an investment is calculated as follows:

$$E[r(t)] = (1 - TC) \cdot (1 + r)^t - 1 \tag{1.1}$$

$$FV[M(t)] = M \cdot (1 - TC) \cdot (1 + r)^t \tag{1.2}$$

where,
$M(0)$ = current market value of the investment
$FV[M(t)]$ = future value of the investment at time t
r = return per period of time t
$r(t)$ = cumulative return at time t
TC = transaction cost
t = period of time

Example 1: Cost Calculation. Compute the associated transaction cost of a buy order for 100,000 shares of ABC if the price at the beginning of trading

Table 1.1

Asset Class	Expected Return	Transaction Cost
Bonds	5%	50bp
Stocks	15%	75bp

was \$50/share, the average execution price was \$50.25/share, and all shares were executed.

$$TC(\$) = 100,000 \text{ shares} \cdot \$50.25 - 100,000 \text{ shares} \cdot \$50.00 = \$25,000$$

$$TC(\$/\text{share}) = \frac{\$25,000}{100,000 \text{ share}} = \$0.25/\text{shares}$$

$$TC(bp) = \frac{\$25,000}{\$5,000,000} \cdot 10^4 bp = 50bp$$

Example 2: Asset Allocation. A manager is directed by the plan sponsors to allocate \$1 million between stocks and bonds in order to achieve an expected return of $R^* = 10\%$ over the next year. Using data in Table 1.1 compute the allocation between stocks and bonds.

Let,

p = percentage invested in stocks
$(1 - p)$ = percentage invested in bonds

Then the allocation between stocks and bonds is calculated as follows:

$$p \cdot M \cdot (1 - TC_S) \cdot (1 + r_S)^t + (1 - p) \cdot M \cdot (1 - TC_B) \cdot (1 + r_B)^t = M \cdot (1 + R^*)$$
$$p \cdot \$1M \cdot (1 - 0.0075) \cdot (1.15) + (1 - p) \cdot \$1M \cdot (1 - 0.0075) \cdot (1.05) = \$1M \cdot (1.10)$$
$$p = 57.18\%, (1 - p) = 42.82\%$$

The manager needs to invest \$571,800 in stocks and \$428,200 in bonds to expect a return of 10%. If transaction costs were not considered in this example, it would lead to an allocation of 50% stocks and 50% bonds, which would yield a return less than the required 10%.

Table 1.2

Stock	Expected Return	Transaction Cost
ABC	10%	75bp
XYZ	9.8%	40bp

Table 1.3

Stock	Expected Return	Transaction Cost
ABC	11%	250bp
XYZ	10%	50bp

Example 3: Portfolio Construction. An analyst is asked by the money manager to evaluate two investment alternatives. Using data in Table 1.2 compute the better alternative if the holding period will be at least three years.

$$E[r(t)] = (1 - TC) \cdot (1 + r)^t - 1$$
$$E(r_{ABC} \mid t = 3) = (1 - 0.0075) \cdot (1 + 0.10)^3 - 1 = 32.10\%$$
$$E(r_{XYZ} \mid t = 3) = (1 - 0.0040) \cdot (1 + 0.098)^3 - 1 = 31.85\%$$

Thus for a three-year holding period ABC is the more attractive investment choice even though it has a higher transaction cost. However, if the holding period were not three years, XYZ would likely have been the better alternative.

Example 4: Holding Period. A manager needs to decide which is the more attractive investment choice, but does not know exactly the length of the holding period. Using data in Table 1.3 compute the breakeven time when the investments would have the same value. This is determined by solving for t in the following equation:

$$E[r_{ABC}(t)] = E[r_{XYZ}(t)]$$
$$(1 - .025) \cdot (1 + 0.11)^t - 1 = (1 - .0050) \cdot (1 + 0.10)^t - 1$$
$$975 \cdot (1 + 11\%)^t = .995 \cdot (1 + 10\%)^t$$
$$t = \frac{-0.02031}{-0.00905} = 2.24 \text{ years}$$

Thus, if the manager believes the holding period for the investment will be 2.24 years or longer, they should invest in ABC. If it is believed the

Figure 1.4.   Expected Investment Values

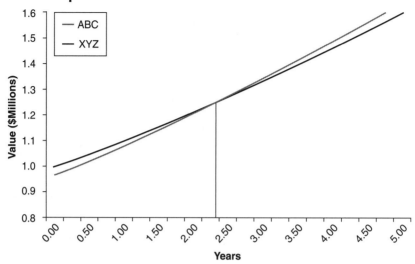

holding period will be less than 2.24 years, they should invest in XYZ. This is illustrated graphically in Figure 1.4.

Example 5: TCM Program.   An active fund with $1 billion dollars under management is contemplating a transaction cost management program. A conservative estimate of the program savings is estimated to be 20% of current costs. If the fund experiences annual turnover of 125% and currently experiences transaction costs of 100bp, how much is this program expected to improve portfolio returns annual?

This is determined as follows:

Let,
S_1 = the annual cost in dollars without the program
S_2 = the annual cost in dollars with the program

The annual cost to the portfolio is estimated as follows:

$S = M \cdot \text{Turnover\%} \cdot TC$

Then the savings of the program is determined as follows:

S_1 = $1 billion $\cdot$ 125% $\cdot$ 100bp = $12.5 million
S_2 = $1 billion $\cdot$ 125% $\cdot$ 80bp = $10.0 million

This program is expected to save $2.5 million annual in transaction costs. Therefore, even if the fund hires one or two analysts to focus solely

Figure 1.5. Transaction Costs Pyramid

on transaction cost analysis, the savings will more than outweigh the incremental expense of administering the program.

While these examples may appear overly simplified, incorporation of transaction costs in the investment decision phase is often absent. The omission of transaction costs typically results in a misallocation of investment dollars, higher costs, and lower portfolio returns.

Transaction Cost Components

In total there are nine different cost components. They are broker commissions, exchange fees, taxes, bid-ask spread, investment delay, price appreciation, market impact, timing risk, and opportunity cost. They each adversely affect portfolio returns in different ways and in various degrees. As mentioned, transaction costs are either visible or hidden. It is the hidden costs that make up the largest percentage of total transaction costs and visible costs that make up the smallest percentage of total transaction costs.

We describe these transaction costs as a pyramid[4] with the most visible costs on the top (e.g., they can be seen from a distance) and the least transparent costs shown on the bottom (e.g., they can only be seen up close). This analogy provides a very nice illustration regarding the visibility and associated cost consequences of transactions. It is depicted in Figure 1.5.

---

4. Plexus has historically illustrated these transaction costs as an iceberg with the most visible and least costly components shown above the waterline and the least visible and most costly components shown below the waterline.

In this figure, the cost components most visible from a distance are those costs that contribute the least to the total transaction cost. Costs least visible (non-transparent) from a distance contribute most to total transaction costs. Fortunately, these non-transparent cost components provide the greatest opportunity for cost reduction. Skilled managers and/or traders can add value to the investment cycle and reduce portfolio slippage by effectively managing these costs. Unfortunately, the cost reduction of one non-transparent cost is typically at the expense of another non-transparent cost. Therefore, traders need to understand all costs and how they interact with one another. For example, as we reduce market impact by trading more passively we expose the fund to a greater risk. As we trade more aggressively we reduce risk but increase market impact. It is not possible to reduce all cost simultaneously. Proper transaction cost management requires careful balancing of all costs.

What Exactly Are Transaction Costs?

Transaction costs are costs associated with implementing business decisions that are incremental to the cost of goods or services purchased or sold. In economic terms, transaction costs refer to costs paid by buyers and not received by sellers and/or paid by sellers but not received by buyers. Transaction costs consist of both fixed and variable costs, and transparent (visible) and non-transparent (hidden) costs. Fixed components are those costs that are independent of the actual implementation strategy. And variable costs are those costs that do indeed depend on the implementation strategy. Thus, variable costs can be controlled and reduced during implementation. Visible costs are those costs whose structure is known in advance (such as commission fee or tax rate). Non-transparent costs are those costs whose amount or structure is not known in advance (such as market impact); thus, structures must be inferred or estimated from market observations. Overall, it is the variable non-transparent costs that account for the largest percentage of transaction costs.

Law of Supply and Demand

Hidden or non-transparent transaction costs often arise due to the buying or selling pressure exerted into the market by prospective buyers or sellers. These charges can represent the highest percent of total transaction cost. If they are not properly quantified and managed, they can cause an otherwise profitable business deal to go bad.

The effect of non-transparent transaction costs can be illustrated through the law of supply and demand. As you demand more of a good or service, you push the price up and pay a premium on top of the purchase price to attract additional suppliers of the good or service into the market. As you supply more of a good or service, you create a surplus and need to offer it to the market at a discounted price in order to attract additional buyers.

Figure 1.6. Supply–Demand Equilibrium

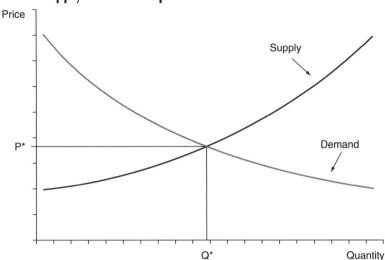

The law of supply and demand plays a dominant role in determining the market price of securities. As market participants demand a higher quantity of shares, they must offer the market at a higher price in order to attract an adequate number of sellers. The equilibrium price of the good or service is thus determined by the price where the supply is equal to the demand of the good or service (see Figure 1.6). In this figure, the quantity demanded is equal to the quantity supplied Q^*. As market participants wish to sell quantities of shares into the market they must discount the price in order to attract additional buyers into the market. That is $P < P^*$. As market participants wish to buy quantities of shares they must offer a premium to attract additional sellers into the market, thus, $P > P^*$.

Liquidity Demander

A liquidity demander is an investor who actively pursues execution of investment decisions. This transaction may consist of either the purchase or sale of a stock or trade list. The term *demand* refers to the investor's execution requirement: either stock acquisition in exchange for cash or receipt of cash in exchange for stock. Participants demand that counterparties enter the market so they can complete their transactions. In most cases it is the buy-side investor who takes on the role of liquidity-demander because they are required to implement an investment decision. But the role of liquidity demander is not limited to only buy-side investors. The sell-side also at times takes on the role of liquidity demander as a means of balancing inventory of stocks. For example, suppose that over the course of the day a broker-dealer accumulates a short position in a stock that exposes the firm to a large amount of market risk and potential large losses if adverse price

Figure 1.7. Liquidity Demander Cost Curve

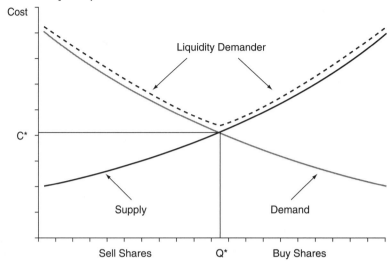

movement occurs. To correct this, the broker-dealer will enter the market to buy stock to offset the short position and balance inventory. This action may require the broker-dealer to pay a premium for the shares. Conversely, if broker-dealers become too long in a position they will enter the market with the investment objective of selling the shares to balance their inventory even if it requires them to offer the shares at a discounted price. In either case, the broker-dealer is actively pursuing the execution of an investment decision and is classified as a liquidity demander.

In Figure 1.7 we depict the liquidity-demander cost curve. Notice how the cost to investors is always on the upper envelope of the supply-demand curve. If investors upset equilibrium by entering a buy or sell order, there will be associated adverse price movement resulting in an incremental cost.

Liquidity Supplier

Liquidity suppliers, specialists, market makers, broker-dealers, and many hedge funds are market participants willing to transact with the market-place but only at their specified price or better. They differ from liquidity demanders in that they do not need to implement defined investment objectives, but are willing to transact at their specified target prices or better. Their goal is to earn a trading profit by charging a premium for their liquidity and only transacting at their specified prices or better. The role of liquidity supplier is not limited to the sell-side. Buy-side investors can also take on the role of a liquidity supplier, but at a substantial risk to the fund. For example, consider an investor who has just had an inflow of cash and needs to invest those dollars in some specified index fund. This investor can for a period of time presume the role of liquidity supplier by only executing orders when prices fall within some specified range. Market prices may not fall within a specified price range over time and investors may be forced to execute at substantially less favorable prices. Also, liquidity demanders still incur market impact in this case although it is not observed. Liquidity demanders need to pay careful attention to their trading strategy selection before taking on the role of liquidity supplier.

Measuring Versus Estimating Transaction Costs

It is important that investors understand the difference between *cost measurement* and *cost estimation*. Cost measurement occurs after trades have been executed, for example, ex-post. Cost estimation, on the other hand, is completed prior to actual trading of the list, for example, ex-ante. There is a large difference between measuring cost ex-post and estimating transaction costs "pretrade." Transaction costs are measured as the difference between the execution price and the market price at the time of the investment decision. The result of this measure is a single point value (e.g., $5,000, $0.10/share, or 50bp). Unfortunately, it is not possible to isolate and identify each cost component (except for possibly the fixed cost components). For example, it is not possible to determine the quantity of cost attributable to market impact, price appreciation, or the buying and selling pressure of other market participants. But it is possible to identify the source of these costs as trading related.

Transaction costs are "estimated" or "forecasted" as a probabilistic distribution consisting of a mean or expected cost and a risk parameter and are dependent upon a specified trading strategy. A transaction cost estimate is not provided as a single point estimate. Providing cost estimates as a distribution of costs (e.g., the normal distribution) provides a better representation and a complete picture of potential costs. These statistical distributions serve as the basis for evaluating alternative strategies and determining the strategy most appropriate for the fund. The estimation of transaction costs also differs from the measurement of transaction costs in that the estimation is based upon cost components, namely, price appreciation, market impact, and timing risk. While it is not possible to isolate and identify the exact cause of the transaction cost (e.g., market impact), ex-post, it is necessary to forecast these costs based upon the individual cost components. Estimation requires an entirely different methodology than measurement.

Measuring Costs

Accurate measurement of transaction costs is essential for quality decision making. It provides information regarding the exact implementation cost of the decision to allow managers to assess the true profitability of their investment decision. It also provides the basis to assess the accuracy of the investment and transaction cost estimation models. They serve as a building block for implementation models to evaluate alternative execution strategies. Finally, these costs serve as the basis for assessing implementation performance.

The proper technique for measuring transaction costs is the implementation shortfall (IS) methodology formulated by Perold (1988). The IS metric is defined as the difference between the actual portfolio return and its paper return benchmark and accounts for *all portfolio costs* except for the management fees. An improvement to this methodology is one that categorizes costs following the IS methodology and distinguishes Wagner's delay cost component. This expanded IS equation is:

$$IS(\$) = \underbrace{X(P_d - P_0)}_{Delay\ Cost} + \underbrace{\sum x_j p_j - \sum x_j p_0}_{Trading\ Cost} + \underbrace{(X - \sum x_j)(P_n - P_0)}_{Opportunity\ Cost} + Visible \quad (1.3)$$

where,

X = total shares
x_j = shares executed in the jth transaction
P_0 = stock price at the beginning of trading
P_d = the decision price
P_n = price at the end of trading
p_j = price of the jth transaction
Visible = visible cost components of commission, spreads, taxes, and fees
and,

$$X, x_j = \begin{cases} > 0\ indicates & Buy\ order \\ < 0\ indicates & Sell\ order \end{cases}$$

It is important to note here that opportunity cost of unexecuted shares consists of an investment-related (delay) and trading-related component. Further discussion occurs in Chapter 2, Unbundled Transaction Cost Components, and again in Chapter 13, Post-Trade Analysis. The illustration of our IS equation decomposes cost components into their non-transparent and visible components. This representation provides better identification of non-transparent transaction costs based on where and when they arise (e.g., delay, trading or execution, and opportunity) and offers necessary insight in proper transaction cost measurement techniques. This is an ongoing theme throughout the text.

Evaluating Performance

A consequence of cost measurement is performance evaluation and is intended to assess how well traders and/or brokers perform while executing the list. Performance measurement allows us to determine the traders and brokers most capable of trading various types of orders, sectors, and/or markets. Having this information on hand will allow us to select the broker who is best suited to trade a particular list. It also allows the fund to reduce the delay cost of implementation because there should not be any hesitation in determining the best broker for the execution.

The preferred approach for measuring performance is one that relies on a relative performance measure (Kissell 1998). This technique compares the execution of the order to the rest of the market activity. In this case, rather than providing a numeric value that is difficult to interpret, a percentile ranking score is used. For example, a score of 90% indicates that the performance was better than 90% of all other activity in the market, 60% indicates that the performance was better than 60% of all other activity in the market, and so on. This allows easy comparison across stocks, across days, across markets, and we do not run into any problems with the symmetry of trading performance. Performance measurement techniques will be presented in Chapter 13, Post-Trade Analysis.

Estimating Costs

Transaction cost estimation takes place before the commencement of trading. The most influential factors are order size, side, volatility, intraday volume patterns, sector, and the specified trading strategy. Cost estimation is performed to provide traders with associated cost and risk estimates for various trading strategies. Because cost estimates consist of a cost and risk estimate for a particular strategy, it is not possible to provide a cost estimate as a single value, for example, 50bp. Instead, traders estimate transaction costs as a range or distribution of costs, for example, 50bp ± 25bp, that pertain to a specified trading strategy. Estimating costs in this manner proves to be a very valuable tool. It allows investors to evaluate alternative implementation strategies, compare an agency execution to a principal bid transaction, and assess the likelihood of executing better than some specified price or within some specified amount of time. Finally, it provides the basis for investors to develop optimal trading strategies that minimize cost subject to a specified level of risk and maximize opportunity for price improvement.

Our discussion of the proper analytical framework for estimating transaction costs concentrates on the variable non-transparent trading-related transaction costs because these are the costs investors can control during implementation. Cost estimation is based on the following price trajectory formulation:

$$p_t = p_{t-1} + \mu_t + \kappa_t + \varepsilon_t \qquad (1.2)$$

where,
p_t = price of the tth trade
μ_t = natural price appreciation from time t-1 to t
κ_t = market impact of the tth trade
ε_t = price volatility, with, $\varepsilon_t \sim N(0,\sigma^2)$

The price trajectory shown above is a simplified version of reality. It does not distinguish between temporary and permanent market impact nor does it account for the dissipation of temporary impact over time. It is introduced here to demonstrate that accurate cost estimation begins with an understanding of non-transparent trading related transaction costs, namely, price appreciation, market impact, and timing risk. This formulation is shown again in Chapter Two, Unbundled Transaction Cost Components, and is fully developed in Chapter Eight, The Holy Grail of Market Impact.

Traders Dilemma

During the implementation of a trade list, traders endure conflicting objectives. If traders execute too aggressive they incur high market impact costs. If execution is too passive, traders are exposed to significant timing risk that could result in even higher trading costs due to adverse price movement. Traders should balance the trade-off between cost and risk, and determine an optimal balancing point consistent with fund goals. The set of conflicting objectives is known as "the trader's dilemma."

The computation of this equilibrium point, that is, the trade schedule that balances these conflicting costs, represents a real challenge. The framework we use to resolve the traders dilemma surfaces as this book's major focus.

Best Execution

Best execution means many things to many people. But it can be categorized as price, time, and size factors (Figure 1.8).[5] For example, value and passive investors are concerned with price improvement and preservation of asset value. Growth and momentum investors require immediacy. Still others, such as block traders and large mutual funds, require liquidity or size enhancement.

Indeed, though the term *best execution* is somewhat vague, we propose a definition intended to serve as a guideline for achieving best execution:

> Best execution is the process of managing transaction costs throughout all phases of the investment cycle to ensure that the portfolio realizes its highest returns possible. During implementation, best execution requires estimating costs and evaluating strategies to determine the strategy that best maximizes the likelihood of preserving asset value based upon the goals and objectives

5. The concept of price, size, and time as components or best execution was presented at the University of Amsterdam (Kissell, 2000).

Figure 1.8.

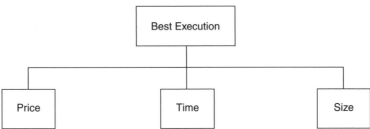

of the fund. Subsequently, it requires traders/brokers to continuously adapt to ever changing market conditions to ensure the likelihood of preservation of asset value is always maximized.

The best execution maximizes the possibilities of achieving cost reduction and/or price improvement within a specified risk tolerance or price level (fund objectives). It is unreasonable to expect trades to always occur at the best market prices or to always have orders executed to completion. There are times when a best execution strategy will cause trades to occur at unfavorable prices or cause residual shares unexecuted at the end of trading. However, a best execution strategy and proper guidelines will ensure that these occurrences become atypical events. More often than not, the prescribed best execution strategy ensures complete execution at fair market prices, and more importantly within cost and price guidelines specified by managers. Only if a strategy provides the best opportunity to achieve one's implementtion goal can it be considered a best execution strategy.

Goal of Implementation

The goal of investment research is pretty well accepted as the quest to uncover stocks most likely to achieve superior returns. However, when it comes to implementation of investment decisions there are conflicting views regarding execution goals. Some market participants believe the goal is to achieve the VWAP price because it represents a measure of fairness. Some believe the goal is to achieve the closing price if that is the price that funds are valued. Still others believe that the goal is to achieve the opening price or some other decision price benchmark. Finally, there are those participants who believe the goal of implementation is to execute better than some specified price. All of these differing opinions can result in some very conflicting implementation strategies. But the one commonality across all views is that preservation of asset value is vitally important. That is, we want to ensure that the new portfolio value is as close to the original portfolio value as possible.

The goal of implementation is to preserve asset value.

Thus we can state the goal of implementation as to minimize the difference between the average execution price P_{avg} and the decision price at the time of the investment decision P_d. This is formulated mathematically as:

$$Min \quad \varphi = |P_{avg} - P_d|$$

or as a more desirable mathematical function:

$$Min \quad \varphi = (P_{avg} - P_d)^2$$

The value of φ, however, cannot be described as a single value cost estimate because it is a function of random market prices P_t making itself a random variable. Therefore, φ is best described as a distribution with an expected cost and risk term. What makes matters difficult for investors here is that these terms are competing with one another. As one term is reduced the other term increases. To best preserve asset value (or achieve any implementation objective for that matter) both distribution parameters need to be considered when developing the implementation strategy. With this in mind, we find three potential decision-making criteria incorporating cost and risk terms that can be used by investors to develop an appropriate implementation strategy. They are 1) Minimize Cost, 2) Balance the Tradeoff between Cost and Risk, and 3) Price Improvement.

Goal 1: Minimize Cost

The first criterion is to minimize costs within some acceptable level of risk. This quantity of risk may be specified by the firm, i.e., maximum allowable risk exposure, or may correspond to the level of risk from the investment model. This goal is formulated mathematically as:

Min: *Cost*

subject to: *Risk* $\leq \mathfrak{R}^*$

where $\mathfrak{R}^*$ is the maximum allowable quantity of risk exposure specified by the firm

Goal 2: Balance the Tradeoff between Cost and Risk

The second criterion is to balance the tradeoff between cost and risk. It is often preferred by investors who are unsure of a proper maximum level of risk exposure, but have a preference to the amount of risk they will accept for a corresponding decrease in cost. This goal is formulated mathematically as:

$$Min: \quad Cost + \lambda \cdot Risk$$

where λ is the risk aversion factor that represents the investor's desired level of tradeoff between cost and risk. For example, a level of $\lambda = 1$ generally indicates investors who are equally concerned about cost and risk.

Goal 3: Price Improvement

Price improvement is the criterion used by investors who desire a strategy that maximizes chances a trade list better than some specified cost. This criterion is often selected by participants seeking to maximize short-term returns or investors seeking to maximize their chances of executing better than a principal bid. It is formulated mathematically as follows:

$$Max: \quad Probability(Cost \leq C^*)$$

where C^* is the maximum acceptable transaction cost. In a way, C^* represents an upper bound on the average cost of the order.

Reasons Supporting Using the Decision Price as the Transaction Cost Benchmark

Preservation of asset value as an implementation goal requires the use of the stock price at the time of the investment decision P_d as the benchmark price because this is the price that defines the initial value of the trade portfolio. Furthermore, P_d represents the price used in the manager's investment model (e.g., portfolio optimizer, fundamental or technical analysis system, etc.). It is essential that managers keep their transaction cost benchmark price consistent with those prices used to derive the investment decision, otherwise, an inappropriate portfolio mix will result. In instances where prices are not used to derive the investment portfolio, such as with passive index funds, it is still imperative to use the market prices at the time of the investment decision if one wishes to preserve asset value.

Investors who are still not sold on preservation of asset value as a goal of implementation or are required to minimize costs compared to a different benchmark price for whatever reason can still employ our techniques. Our framework can be easily expanded to develop an appropriate implementation strategy for the specific needs of a fund. Investors only need to substitute our benchmark price P_d with their desired benchmark price P_b and compute corresponding cost and risk functions. This may require some rewriting of the mathematical equations and reformulation of the objective function. We ensure that the techniques presented here once fully understood can be easily adapted to a vast majority of implementation needs. For those goals that are beyond the scope presented here our framework will still serve as a starting point and foundation for those models.

Transaction Cost Management Process

Transaction cost management is the process of achieving best execution. It consists of evaluating transaction costs in order to develop an appropriate execution strategy, a three-step process that should be carried out before, during, and after implementation of investment decisions. Variations of alternative transaction cost management programs have been presented by Wagner (1999, 2000, 2001), Kissell (2000), Jenkins (2000), and Bradley (2000).

Step I: Investment Decision

Transaction cost management begins with the investment decision. This allows more appropriate asset class allocation and allows managers to improve screening and select lower cost and higher return stocks in the portfolio construction phase.

Step II: Implementation—Estimate Costs and Evaluate Strategies

Managers and traders should work closely during implementation in order to determine accurate cost and risk estimates for the list and investigate alternative implementation strategies.

Prior to trading, perform pre-trade analysis to gain an understanding of trading list characteristics, for example, screen for liquidity, volatility/risk, price trends and momentum, as well as summarize by sector, capitalization, and market. Stock specific cost and risk estimates alert managers to orders not likely to be absorbed by the market within their target prices. This allows managers the opportunity to revise the size of the order prior to trading and reduce if not eliminate opportunity cost. Managers and traders will work together to determine an "optimal" or "rational" trading decision to meet the goals of the fund such as one that best manages the trade-off between cost and risk or maximizes the opportunity for price improvement. This analysis also allows the fair comparison between agency execution and principal bid transaction.

Additionally, pre-trade analysis provides the necessary data for trader/broker selection. In conjunction with Step III, managers will have on hand a detailed account of how their brokers performed in the past with lists of similar characteristics. This allows managers/traders to make a quick selection of the broker most capable of executing the specified trade list and reduces the delay cost of trade.

Finally, a proper transaction cost management process continuously monitors market conditions and costs throughout the day and allows traders to react to ever changing market conditions by modifying trading strategy in real time. Traders will trade aggressively to take advantage of available liquidity or passively to keep from incurring incremental market impact. This allows managers to increase order sizes to take advantage of better market prices and reduce orders when the market prices have become too unfavorable.

Step III: Perform Post-Trade Evaluation

Post-trade analysis consists of assessing the quality of the implementation of the investment decision. Most typically, post-trade analysis consists of measuring actual transaction costs and evaluating broker/trader performance. But it additionally needs to evaluate the actual execution decision of managers to ensure that it was in the best interest of investors. Costs need to be evaluated to understand where and why they occurred. This will provide insight into the credibility of the estimation model and ensure better future cost estimates that can be incorporated back into the investment decision and implementation phases. Post-trade analysis also needs to be carried out so that managers can evaluate the effectiveness of brokers/traders implementing the trade. They need to determine if brokers/traders caused the fund to incur any unnecessary costs or risk and as a means of separating skill from luck. That is, it will determine who is really adding value into the process. Finally, post-trade analysis also provides valuable information regarding who is more capable of trading what types of orders. Continuous evaluation of broker/trader performance will provide managers with sufficient information to allow them to assess the strength and weakness of each, and more appropriately select brokers/traders for future trades based on stocks, lists, sectors, markets, capitalization, market conditions, and so on.

Transaction cost management is the process of achieving best execution and should be followed throughout every step of the investment cycle. The remainder of the book focuses primarily on Step II: Implementation— Estimate Costs and Evaluate Trading Strategies—because it offers the most opportunity for transaction cost savings.

CHAPTER TWO

Unbundled Transaction Cost Components

TRANSACTION COSTS ARE INCURRED DURING implementation of business decisions. In economic terms they are defined as costs paid by buyers not received by sellers, and/or costs paid by sellers not received by buyers. In equity markets, however, financial transaction costs represent costs incremental to the decision price. Financial transaction costs consist of fixed and variable components and also separate into visible and hidden (non-transparent) fees. Unbundled transaction cost components consist of nine components: commissions, taxes, fees, spreads, delay cost, price appreciation, market impact, timing risk, and opportunity cost.

Our categorization of transaction costs is more in-depth than currently presented in industry literature. But this level of detail is necessary for proper transaction cost measurement and estimation techniques. The categorization serves as the foundation for our transaction cost framework and is defined as follows:

Fixed Costs: Fixed transaction costs are those costs that are not dependent upon market prices or trading strategy. Fixed costs cannot be effectively controlled through a specified implementation strategy. These costs are completely known in advance. Fixed costs make up a very small percentage of transaction costs.

Variable Costs: Variable transaction costs are those costs that are determined from the actual market prices and dependent upon the trading strategy. They will vary based on the actual implementation of an investment decision. Investors can effectively manage variable costs through a carefully specified execution strategy. Variable costs account for a very large percentage of total transaction costs. Plan sponsors, money managers, traders, and brokers can add a considerable amount of value to the implementation process simply by controlling variable transaction costs.

Visible Costs: Visible (transparent) transaction costs are those components whose cost or fee structure is either known exactly in advance or is easily measurable from actual market data. It is also possible to isolate the cost attribution for each visible cost component. For example, commissions are known prior to trading and spread costs can be measured from market data. Visible costs account for a very small percentage of total transaction cost.

Non-Transparent Costs: Non-transparent (hidden) transaction costs are those components whose cost structures are not readily known or observable from actual market data. For example, market impact cost is not readily observable from market data because price evolution can only be observed either with or without the order. Thus, it is difficult to predetermine the cost consequence from market impact. Investors, therefore, must estimate these cost structures and parameters using statistical inference or other estimation techniques. Hidden costs account for the largest percentage of total transaction cost. Fortunately, they provide the greatest opportunity to improve execution quality and add value to the investment process via careful selection of execution strategy. If these costs are not properly quantified, controlled, and contained they can cause an otherwise profitable business opportunity to sour.

Unbundled Transaction Costs

Managers and traders should understand each distinct cost component by first unbundling transaction costs into their natural constituents. There are nine distinct components.[1] The unbundling of transaction costs is not a new concept. It has been suggested by many over the years. For example, see Ferstenberg (2000), Hill (2000, 2001), ITG (2000), and Wagner (1988, 1993). They are defined as:

Table 2.1. Unbundled Transaction Costs

	Fixed	Variable
Visible	Commission Fees	Spreads Taxes
Non-Transparent	n/a	Delay Cost Price Appreciation Market Impact Timing Risk Opportunity Cost

1. There have been many academics and practitioners who have over years provided industry with an incomplete listing of transaction costs. We, however, have performed a thorough examination of transaction costs and provide a complete, unbiased, unbundled list of transaction costs.

In Table 2.1 we categorize each of the nine transaction cost components as fixed or variable and visible or non-transparent. As shown in the table, the majority of costs categorize as non-transparent and variable. This is both good and bad news for investors. Good news because costs are primarily variable; they can be managed during implementation resulting in lower transaction costs and higher portfolio returns. Traders who practice transaction cost management add value to the process. Unfortunately, the cost structure is unknown. Thus, investors should estimate these costs via statistical inference and other modeling techniques. To the extent that quantitative modeling is accurate, investors will be able to reduce costs.

1. Commissions

Commissions are payment made to broker-dealers for executing trades. They are generally expressed on a per share basis (e.g., cents per share) or based on total transaction dollar amount (e.g., some basis point of transaction value). While commission charges are known in advance, they do vary from broker to broker. At times, they may vary based on difficulty of trade where easier trades receive a lower rate and trades that are more difficult are charged a higher rate. Commission is a fixed and visible transaction cost component.

2. Fees

Fees charged during execution include ticket charge assessed by floor brokers on exchange, clearing and settlement costs, and SEC fees. Often investors see these fees bundled into commissions charged by executing brokers. These fees are a fixed and visible transaction cost component.

3. Taxes

Taxes are a levy assessed to funds based on realized earnings. Tax rates vary by type of return. For example, capital gains, long-term earnings, dividends, and short-term profits tax at different rates. Funds with higher returns are assessed higher total tax amounts. Taxes are visible and variable cost components—visible because tax rates are known in advance and variable because the execution price dictates the cost quantity.

4. Spreads

Spread cost is the difference between best offer (ask) and best bid price. It is intended to compensate broker-dealers for matching buyers with sellers, and for risks of holding long or short positions waiting for additional buyers or sellers. Spreads represent a round-trip cost of transacting; however, this is only true for small orders. Spread costs are visible and variable transaction cost components—visible because they can be measured at any point in time, variable since spread cost varies throughout the day and can be greatly affected through implementation strategies. For example, micro pricing strategies along with a combination of market and limit orders affect spread costs incurred by investors.

5. Delay Cost

Delay cost represents loss in investment value between the time managers make investment decision P_d and the time traders release orders to the market P_0. Since managers more often buy stocks on the rise and sell falling stocks, delays in order submissions to market result in less favorable prices and higher costs. Delay costs often result because traders hesitate in releasing orders to the market because of uncertainty regarding "capable" brokers. Delay cost is a variable cost component because it is dependent upon strategy. Orders released to the market immediately will incur relatively little delay cost while investors hesitation can be quite costly. Plexus Group has estimated these costs average 62bp per decision.[2] Delay cost may also arise due to a jump in market prices from the prior night's close to the open. In these cases the delay cost is beyond the control of investors and is a phenomenon of non-continuous trading. Without a transaction cost management process, these costs cause a drag on performance; however, with fiduciary oversight this cost significantly reduces or is eliminated.

Example: Delay Cost. A fund manager discovers an undervalued stock that is currently trading in market at a price of $50 and instructs the trader to buy 250,000 shares. The trader looks for the most capable broker to handle the order. However, by the time the trader chooses a broker and submits the buy order the price has risen to $50.25 per share. In this case, the trader's hesitation cost the fund $0.25 per share or 50 basis points.

6. Price Appreciation

Price appreciation represents natural price movement of stock. It is how stock prices would evolve in a market without any uncertainty. Price appreciation is also referred to as the price trend. It represents cost (savings) associated with buying stock in a rising (falling) market or selling (buying) stock in a falling (rising) market. On average, price appreciation represents a cost to funds because managers typically buy stocks that are rising and sell stocks that are falling. Price appreciation is dependent on expected stock trends and implementation strategies. Price appreciation is a non-transparent variable transaction cost component.

Example: Price Appreciation. A manager decides to buy 250,000 shares of XYZ currently trading at $50/share and expected to increase 20% annually. Therefore, the stock will likely move at $0.04/share or 8bp per day. If the trader were to buy 50,000 shares a day over the next five days, he or she would expect to pay an average price of $50.08 per share. Total price appreciation transaction cost is $.08/share or 16bp.

2. *Institutional Investor,* Transaction Costs: A Cutting-Edge Guide to Best Execution, Spring 2001.

7. Market Impact

Market impact represents movement in stock prices caused by particular trades or orders. Market impact is one of the most costly transaction cost components and always causes adverse price movement—a drag on portfolio returns. Market impact costs arise from either liquidity demands of investors and/or the information content of the trade signaling that the stock is under/overvalued. Market impact causes investors to pay premiums to complete buy orders and offer price discounts to finalize a sell order. Market impact cost depends on size of order, stock volatility, side of transaction, prevailing market conditions over trading horizon, and specified implementation strategy. Market impact is a non-transparent variable transaction cost component.

Example: Market Impact. A trader receives a buy order for 50,000 shares of ABC. Market quotes, however, only show 1,000 at the best ask and another 5,000 shares total in the limit order book (e.g., 2,000 shares at $50.25, 3,000 shares at $50.50, and 4,000 shares at $50.75). The trader can only execute 1,000 shares at the best available price and another 9,000 shares at higher prices for an average price of $50.50/share on only 10,000 shares. To attract additional liquidity into the market, traders need to offer price premium, hence, incurring market impact cost. This cost stems from the trader's liquidity demand and causes an imbalance in market supply-demand equilibrium. Liquidity demands are an example of temporary market impact.

A trader receives a buy order for 250,000 shares of XYZ. Inadvertently, an order quantity enters the market and signals the stock is undervalued. Investors who currently own stock are no longer willing to sell shares at current market prices. Instead, they require a markup on the current price to transact at the stock's fair value. Information signaling an under- or overvalued stock that causes a market correction is an example of permanent market impact.

8. Timing Risk

Timing risk cost component refers to uncertainty surrounding the order's exact transaction cost. It is due to uncertainty associated with stock price movement and prevailing market conditions and volume patterns at time of transaction. Timing risk is also commonly referred to as volatility or execution risk of list, but this definition is incomplete. Execution cost uncertainty is also dependent upon actual market volumes and intraday trading profiles of stock. Timing risk is a non-transparent variable transparent cost component.

Example: Timing Risk. Timing risk of a stock or list accounts for potential unexpected price movement. If a stock is currently trading at a price of $50, we can be reasonably sure that it will be trading between $49.50 and $50.50 over the next few hours. However, we do not have the same amount of certainty that after two days the price will wedge between $49.50 and $50.50. A more realistic price range is likely to be between $48.00 and $52.00. When investors execute orders over time, the price likely becomes more or less expensive. Assume trader A receives a buy order for 100,000 shares of ABC and decides to trade the list passively by slicing the order over several days. If the price moves in favor of the trader, he or she will receive a better price than expected—worse if the price moves away. Traders usually execute orders following a prescribed strategy where the order is sliced and traded in different intervals over the day. During higher market volume traders will incur less market impact costs. During less liquidity traders will generally incur higher market impact costs.

9. Opportunity Cost

Opportunity cost represents the forgone profit of not being able to implement investment decisions. It represents the cost of not being able to complete an order. The reason is usually due to insufficient liquidity in the market, or prices moving away too quickly. Since managers typically buy stocks that are rising and sell stocks that are falling, the inability to fully execute a decision results in a missed profiting opportunity. It is a cost to the fund resulting in diminished portfolio returns. Opportunity cost is a non-transparent variable transaction cost component.

Example: Opportunity Cost.   A manager discovers an undervalued stock currently trading at $50 per share and instructs a trader to buy 250,000 shares. The trader executes the order using a slicing strategy in order to minimize market impact but is only able to buy 200,000 shares by the end of day. At that time, the price increases to $51 and is no longer undervalued and the manager cancels the remaining shares. Opportunity cost of not executing the remaining 50,000 shares at $50 is $1/share or a total of $50,000.

Transaction Cost Classification System

Transaction costs fall into three categories: investment related, trading related, and opportunity cost (see Figure 2.1).

Investment-Related Costs

Investment-related transaction costs include manageable costs during the investment decision phase of the investment cycle—taxes and delay cost. While taxes are indeed dependent upon actual execution costs, thus vari-

Figure 2.1. Transaction Cost Classification

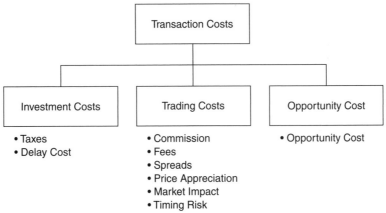

able, the tax rate is known in advance and is a visible transaction cost component. Taxes are a very complicated issue and best if incorporated in the investment decision process. Delay cost is a non-transparent variable transaction cost component and is more of a penalty associated with indecisiveness and waiting to trade. This cost exists mainly because there is a lack of communication between managers and traders in specifying implementation goals of investment decisions.

The longer it takes for traders and managers to resolve proper implementation objectives, the more potential there is for price movement making investment decisions more costly. One reason hesitation occurs is that traders are often not provided with proper analytics to determine an appropriate trading strategy for trade lists or are unable to quickly assess the broker best suited to execute investment decisions. Therefore, traders often spend valuable time investigating how lists should be implemented and the broker(s) or trading venue to use. The easiest means to reduce delay cost is for managers and traders to work closely so traders understand managers' true implementation objective. Furthermore, traders should be equipped with proper implementation decision tools and performance measurement systems to rapidly evaluate costs and strategies as well as determine the broker to select for execution of the list.

Trading-Related Costs

The second classification of transaction costs is trading-related costs. Trading-related transaction cost components comprise the largest subset of transaction costs. These costs include those that arise during implementation of investment decisions and can be effectively managed during proper execution of the list. While these costs cannot be eliminated, they can be dramatically reduced via a trading strategy that best meets the goals and objectives of the fund. These costs consist of both fixed and variable costs and visible and non-transparent costs. The associated trading-related costs of commission, fees, and spread can be further categorized as trading service cost components and are intended to compensate executing brokers for work involved in trading a position, locating liquidity, negotiating prices, and clearing and settlement. Non-transparent variable cost components consist of price appreciation, market impact, and timing risk. Traders can affect cost and risk of implementation through actual trading strategies. For example, price appreciation and timing risk are minimized via implementation with an aggressive trading strategy. Market impact, however, is highest with an aggressive strategy and lowest with a passive strategy. Therefore, traders should balance trade-off between these cost components. The result will certainly improve portfolio returns. Trading costs are dependent upon trade list, order size and liquidity, volatility, market conditions and intraday patterns, and volume correlation across all names in the list, and specified implementation strategy. The majority of this book focuses on developing a quantitative framework to manage and reduce non-transparent variable trading-related costs and develop appropriate strategies to meet goals and objectives of funds to achieve best execution.

Opportunity Cost

The third classification of transaction costs is opportunity cost. Opportunity cost is in one way an investment-related cost and in another way a trading-related cost. It is an investment-related cost whenever managers specify orders too large to be absorbed without producing adverse price movements. It is a trading-related cost whenever traders force unnecessary market impact. Opportunity cost arises because traders are unwilling to transact at existing market prices or because of insufficient market liquidity. The best way to reduce opportunity cost is for managers and traders to work together to determine if the market can readily absorb order sizes within the specified price range of managers. This requires proper pre-trade analysis and cost estimation of the trade list. If managers determine that the market cannot readily absorb the desired quantity of shares, managers can modify the order to one that can be easily absorbed by the market and then invest surplus funds in the next most attractive investment vehicle. The net result is reduced opportunity cost and increased portfolio returns. Throughout the book we provide quantitative techniques to help managers and traders deal with opportunity cost.

Transaction Cost Formulation

The classification of transaction costs using the previously described classification scheme allows us to formulate transaction cost as follows:

$$
TC = \left\langle \begin{array}{c} \text{Taxes} \\ \text{Delay Cost} \end{array} \right\rangle + \left\langle \begin{array}{c} \text{Commissions} \\ \text{Fees} \\ \text{Spreads} \\ \text{Price Appreciation} \\ \text{Market Impact} \\ \text{Timing Risk} \end{array} \right\rangle + \left\langle \text{Opportunity Cost} \right\rangle \quad (2.1)
$$

$$
\underbrace{\phantom{\text{Taxes Delay}}}_{\text{Investment–Related}} \qquad \underbrace{\phantom{\text{Commissions Fees Spreads}}}_{\text{Trading–Related}} \qquad \underbrace{\phantom{\text{Opp}}}_{\text{Opportunity Cost}}
$$

Combining our unbundled cost categorization with our cost classification allows us to formulate transaction costs as follows:

$$
TC = \underbrace{\left\langle \text{Delay Cost} \right\rangle}_{\text{Investment–Related}} + \underbrace{\left\langle \begin{array}{c} \text{Price Appreciation} \\ \text{Market Impact} \\ \text{Timing Risk} \end{array} \right\rangle}_{\text{Trading–Related}} + \underbrace{\left\langle \text{Opportunity Cost} \right\rangle}_{\text{Opportunity Cost}} + \underbrace{\left\langle \begin{array}{c} \text{Tax} \\ \text{Commissions} \\ \text{Fees} \\ \text{Spreads} \end{array} \right\rangle}_{\text{Visible Costs}} \quad (2.2)
$$

$$
\underbrace{\phantom{\text{Delay Cost Price Appreciation Market Impact Timing Risk Opportunity Cost}}}_{\text{Non–Transparent Costs}}
$$

This formulation provides the basis for our transaction cost measurement and transaction cost estimation framework.

Cost Measurement

The measurement of transaction costs can be written following Perold's implementation shortfall measure where we distinguish these non-transparent costs as investment, trading, and opportunity cost as follows:

$$
TC(\$) = \underbrace{X(P_d - P_0)}_{\text{Investment Related}} + \underbrace{\sum x_j P_j - \sum x_j P_0}_{\text{Trading Related}} + \underbrace{(X - \sum x_j)(P_n - P_0)}_{\text{Trading Related}} + Visible \quad (2.3)
$$

$$
\underbrace{}_{\text{Non–Transparent Cost Components}}
$$

where,

X = total number of shares, $X > 0$ indicates a buy, and $X < 0$ indicates a sell

x_j = number of shares executed in j^{th} trade

$\sum x_j$ = total number of shares executed

$X - \sum x_j$ = number of unexecuted shares

P_d = manager's decision price

P_0 = stock price when order was released to market

p_j = price of jth trade

P_n = stock price at end of trading

$Visible$ = visible costs of commission, fees, taxes and spreads

In the previous notation we adhere to the pricing scheme suggested by Perold in that the prices for P_d, P_0, and P_n are taken as the midpoint of the bid-ask spread at the corresponding time. Therefore, spread cost is included in the trading related component. The price of the trade p_j, however, is taken at its exact transaction price. The specification of the IS in the preceding format allows us to distinguish those non-transparent transaction cost components from visible cost components. This classification scheme is essential for understanding transaction costs and later for developing estimation methodologies.

Discussion on Components

The investment-related cost classification is measured as the change in the value of the portfolio between the time managers make the investment decision and the time traders are prepared to trade.[3] This is computed simply as the number of shares in the order multiplied by the price change, that is, $X \cdot (P_d - P_0)$. In the majority of situations, managers purchase stocks that are rising, and sell stocks that are falling. Thus, the associated delay reflects a cost to the fund. This component constitutes a substantial cost and their estimates show the cost to be in the order of 30–50bp per transaction. However, as traders practice proper transaction cost management, the time between the decision time t_d and order release time t_0 becomes small causing the delay cost to become effectively zero, that is, $P_d - P_0 \to 0$ as $t_d - t_0 \to 0$.

The trading-related cost classification φ is measured as the difference between the total transaction dollars and the value of that number of shares evaluated at the price of order release P_0, that is, $\varphi = \Sigma x_j p_j - \Sigma x_j P_0$. Since the price of order release P_0 is evaluated at the midpoint of the bid-ask spread, the spread cost is already included in the trading cost calculation and does not need to be incorporated as its own separate component. The trading-related cost comprises the greatest quantity of transaction cost but can be effectively reduced if proper transaction cost management techniques are put into effect. These techniques will be thoroughly discussed in subsequent sections.

The opportunity cost classification represents the missed profiting opportunity that results from not being able to completely implement investment decisions. It is measured as the number of unexecuted shares multiplied by the price change between the time of order release P_0 and the price at the end of trading P_n. This measure is intended to represent the change in portfolio value that is not enjoyed by funds. The cost of unexe-

---

3. The time the order is released to the market is considered the time at which the trader is prepared to execute the order and has decided upon the appropriate trading venue and broker. This time is not literally the time at which the trader begins executing the trade because many times the trader makes a conscience decision to hold off on the execution for one reason or another. It is extremely difficult to accurately identify investment-related and trading-related cost when t_0 is not properly recorded.

cuted shares over the entire implementation horizon t_d to t_n can be decomposed as:

$$O.C. = (X - \sum x_i)(P_n - P_d) = \underbrace{(X - \sum x_i)(P_d - P_0)}_{Investment\ Related} + \underbrace{(X - \sum x_i)(P_n - P_0)}_{Trading\ Related}.$$

Thus, managers identify opportunity cost as investment related and trading related. Since managers typically buy stocks that are rising and sell stocks that are falling (as well as exert an imbalance in the market supply-demand equilibrium of the stock causing adverse price movement), this component generally reflects a cost to investors. It is quite possible to effectively reduce opportunity cost to zero through proper transaction cost management techniques; there the gap between investment decisions and order release should ultimately be minimal. Trading-related opportunity cost exists because of inadequate liquidity conditions and/or substantial adverse price movement. But if managers and traders work together they could assess liquidity conditions and estimate execution costs to determine the appropriate order size that can be readily absorbed by the market. Within managers' specified price range the number of unexecuted shares will effectively fall to zero. Thus, $O.C. \rightarrow 0$ since $X - \sum x_j \rightarrow 0$.

The visible cost classification consists of commissions, spreads, taxes, and any other fee charged to investors (e.g., ticket charge, clearing and settlement fee). Many times, however, brokers bundle these fixed costs (visible excluding spreads and taxes) into the commission rate charged by the broker and investors never see the costs. For the most part, these visible costs represent the smallest portion of the total transaction cost and cannot be affected or controlled by proper transaction cost management practices (i.e., selection of implementation strategy).

Cost Estimation

What Will a List Cost to Trade?

That is the $64,000 question. It is one of the most commonly asked questions during the implementation phase of the investment cycle and one that we are asked repeatedly. As we will show, the solution and framework required to answer this question are not as difficult as many would like us to believe. However, this requires a complete knowledge and understanding of the associated costs. In short, there is no simple, single answer. The cost of any transaction is dependent upon many factors such as order size, volatility, correlation between names, market conditions, intraday volume patterns, and selected trading strategy.

Cost Estimation: Brief Introduction

Our discussion of the proper analytical framework for estimating transaction costs and developing and evaluating appropriate trading strategies focuses on the non-transparent variable trading-related transaction costs since these are the costs that can be controlled during implementation. Subsequently, these pre-trade transaction costs will be appropriately referred to as trading costs. In short, the pre-trade costs are estimated based on the following price trajectory formulation:

$$p_t = p_{t-1} + \mu_t + \kappa_t + \varepsilon_t \qquad (2.4)$$

where,

p_t = price of the tth trade
μ_t = natural price appreciation from time t-1 to t
κ_t = market impact of the tth trade
ε_t = price volatility, with, $\varepsilon_t \sim N(0, \sigma^2)$

As mentioned in Chapter One, Transaction Costs, this price trajectory formulation is a simplification of reality because it does not distinguish between temporary and permanent market impact nor account for the dissipation of temporary impact over time. It is shown here to demonstrate the need for a complete understanding of the non-transparent trading related transaction costs, namely, price appreciation, market impact, and timing risk.

Therefore, in order to estimate costs we first need to determine the cost structure for price appreciation, market impact, and our timing risk. The remainder of the text is dedicated primarily to examining and evaluating trading cost components of the investment cycle and to answer concerns and issues of those implementing the trading decision. More specifically, we thoroughly examine each cost component in order to gain insight into its mechanics and provide the means for measuring and forecasting each cost component based on a specified strategy. We also discuss methods for reducing opportunity cost before and during the implementation cycle. This, however, can only be accomplished after a complete understanding of the trading costs. Then we provide a quantitative framework for determining an "optimal trading strategy." This strategy minimizes trading costs for a specified level of risk. This, of course, is developed in a way to find the most appropriate strategy for the fund and the one that best meets its investment goals and objectives.

A trading cost:

▲ is Measured as the difference between the execution price and the price at the time of order entry

▲ is Estimated as a distribution of costs that consists of an expected cost and a risk parameter, not as a single cost estimate

▲ is Dependent upon the size and volatility of the order, the correlation of price movement across all names in the trade list, and the actual market conditions over the trading period

▲ "corresponds" to a specific trading strategy

CHAPTER THREE

Pre-Trade Analysis

PRE-TRADE ANALYSIS PROVIDES DETAILED DESCRIPTION of stock trading characteristics including liquidity, prices, risk, and summary groupings across capitalization, sectors, markets, exchanges, and so forth. It is intended to provide useful information to traders to improve execution quality. Pre-trade provides insight into the trade list that can be employed as a feedback loop between managers and traders, funds and brokers. Pre-trade provides information needed to select brokers and solicit principal bids. The pre-trade report is the first step of implementation helps to determine the difficulty level of executing a list or order. Many factors influence the difficulty in trading an order—order size, stock volatility, price trend, and market capitalization. From a trader's perspective, even more important factors include consistency of daily volume profiles and intraday trading patterns—trading volume over the course of the day and period fluctuation. One technique for minimizing transaction costs is to trade passively over multiple periods, which should reduce market impact. However, this requires traders to become knowledgeable of the volume likely to trade on the day and in each period, and how it will vary. Only then can traders successfully react to changing conditions and adjust trading strategy in an appropriate manner.

Before implementing an investment decision, traders need to perform pre-trade analysis to help them assess trading difficulty, estimate trading costs and risk, and help in the development of a profitable trading strategy.

Current State of Pre-Trade Analysis Systems

The majority of pre-trade analytics have evolved from similar ones used on the investment decision side. These techniques combine portfolio management statistics with basic trading characteristics such as liquidity, volatility, spreads, and price. These systems are useful in providing high-level portfolio information that facilitates discussions between managers and traders, and between funds and brokers, but they are usually not comprehensive enough to handle some of the problems traders face during implementation. Shortcomings of many existing hybrid pre-trade analysis systems take account of the following:

1. Much of the information included in pre-trade reports is borrowed from the investment decision side and contains large amounts of information that has little significance in improving execution quality.
2. Traders tend to feel obligated to discuss this information with fund managers, often wasting time deliberating over issues having little to do with implementation.
3. The information overload diverts attention from mainstream issues that actually reduce transaction costs.
4. Traders may draw false conclusions about the list and make incorrect decisions (for example, how and when to execute an order).
5. The fund will likely incur higher transaction costs. Current procedures are often a detriment to best execution.

What Does a Pre-Trade Report Need to Include?

A well-structured pre-trade analysis system:

1. Incorporates the order list, associated trading statistics, and company fundamentals
2. Provides information to evaluate alternative implementation strategies, compare an agency execution to a principal bid transaction, evaluate the opportunity cost of the list, and help select the broker most capable of executing the list
3. Allows managers and traders to prescreen for difficult names or costly executions due to insufficient liquidity, adverse price movement, unstable trading patterns, and/or high market impact and timing risk
4. Provides opportunities to reduce associated opportunity cost and develop rational trading strategies
5. Provides insight into trading risk.

Pre-trade analytical systems ease the way through the implementation phase of the list and help traders achieve best execution. The compiled

Figure 3.1. Pre-Trade Analytics

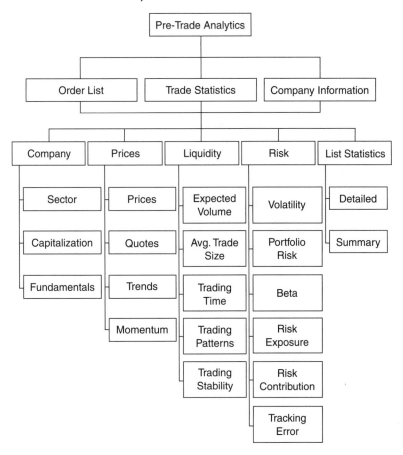

data of a pre-trade report fit into four statistical categories: company specific, prices, liquidity, and risk. The pre-trade report combines the information in these four categories and produces detailed stock reports and list summaries (see Figure 3.1).

Company Information

Sector Groupings

One of the more common grouping methodologies for stocks is their major economic line of business or more commonly their business sector. Money managers use economic sectors as the basis for investment decisions (e.g., a technology fund) and to diversify (hedge) market risk. Nevertheless, traders find sector groupings attractive because price movement of stocks in identical sectors is highly correlated. Therefore, traders are capable of gaining valuable insight into the risk characteristics and risk decomposition

Figure 3.2.   Sector Breakdown

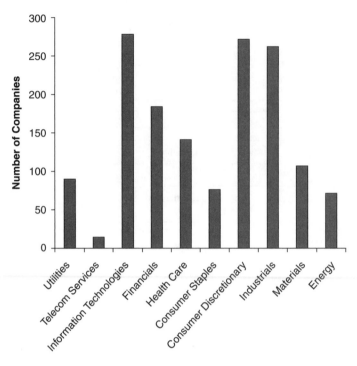

of the trade list by surveying the sector groupings. Depending upon the data source used there are usually around ten economic stock groupings. Stocks in each respective sector break out further into industry and sub-industry groupings. Industry and sub-industry groupings play an important role in helping managers construct the portfolio, but they typically do not provide traders with additional information they can use to develop trading strategies. Hence, pre-trade reports typically do not describe the company's business activity any more specifically than its sector level. Figure 3.2 provides a depiction of the number of firms in each sector for those stocks that comprised the S&P 1500 index as of January 2002.

Market Capitalization

Market capitalization denotes company value and is equal to the stock price multiplied by number of shares outstanding. Another means of grouping stocks is based on size or market capitalization: large, mid, and small cap (although some managers insist on a fourth category, micro cap stocks). Stocks with similar market capitalization exhibit comparable trading statistics and trading patterns. Larger capitalization stocks are associated with smaller spreads, lower volatility, higher liquidity, lower cost, and less risk. Smaller capitalization stocks are associated with larger spreads, higher volatility, reduced liquidity, and thus higher trading costs combined with additional timing risk. Hence, investors who are risk

Figure 3.3. S&P 1500 Stocks (as of January 2002)

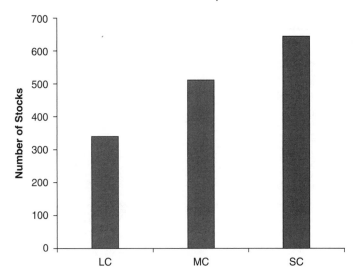

averse often invest in the large cap blue chip names because of lower price fluctuations and less market risk.

Market Capitalization Categorization

There is no standard industry definition for categorizing stocks into market capitalization categories. Standard & Poors breaks down stock indices into large cap (the S&P 500), mid cap (the S&P 400), and small cap (S&P 600). However, prices fluctuate, and because the S&P does not continuously revise their indices, we sometimes find stocks in one index carrying a higher market capitalization than stocks listed in a larger capitalization index. For example, S&P 400 index stocks may exhibit market capitalization greater than stocks listed in the S&P 500 index.

We prefer a genus calling for three categories: market capitalization greater than $5 billion—large cap stocks; between $1 and $5 billion—mid cap stocks; less than $1 billion—small cap stocks. The three categories complement the S&P large cap index (stocks in the $5 billion market cap range). Figure 3.3 shows the number of S&P 1500 stocks that fall into each of our market cap groupings.

The Plexus Group uses another similar classification scheme. Differences between these methods are summarized here:

- ▲ The Plexus Group categorizes large cap stocks as stocks with market capitalization of $10 billion. Mid caps are classified as stocks with market capitalization between $1 billion and $10 billion and small cap stocks as those with market capitalization less than $1 billion.
- ▲ The difference between these two methodologies results in the number of companies designated as large and mid cap stocks.

Market

The pre-trade report identifies each stock based on its listing. U.S. stocks are listed either on a listed exchange such as the NYSE or AMEX, or on the Nasdaq. Similar to sector groupings and market capitalization categories, numerous studies show commonality of costs and trading patterns across stocks in the same market. For example, the NYSE is typically associated with lower spread costs than the Nasdaq market.

Country

For global trade lists, the pre-trade report should incorporate a country designation that classifies groupings by country. This allows managers and traders to review their investment strategy and select brokers based on performance, country to country. Stocks originating in the same country exhibit similar trading statistics, for example, returns, risk, and cost.

Fundamentals

Fundamental data deals with financial health and more specifically, a firm's value (intrinsic value is a fundamental concept and springs from long-term growth projections). Analysts incorporate company financials along with valuation attributes: management strength, economic outlook, sector strength, and a host of specifics including dividends and future target prices. Portfolio managers rely on fundamental data to develop long-term investment objectives and construct stock portfolios.

Traders employ alternative fundamentals to help them understand characteristics of the trade list. Firms with similar basics exhibit parallel trading characteristics: price returns, volatility, liquidity, and to some extent trading patterns. For example, firms exhibiting high price-to-earnings (P/E) and high price-to-book (P/B) ratios are momentum growth stocks. These stocks are highly reactive to news making them subject to rapid price advancement or declines, and sporadic periods of high and low liquidity pools. These securities often experience rapid price jumps with little or no trading volume. Stocks with lower P/E and P/B ratios are value stocks and are characteristically less volatile. These stocks adhere to more stable and consistent trading patterns. Traders with a trade list consisting of a large concentration of growth stocks will need to exercise more care and judgment during implementation than traders with a large concentration of value stocks because of the potential erratic trading behavior of the growth names.

Index Constituent

Another important piece of information pertaining directly to the trade list is if any names are a constituent of a stock index. If so, these stocks are subject to potential rapid price movement with high periods of liquidity preceding index reconstitution date and portfolio rebalancing. When the weighting of a stock in an index changes, there are associated periods of increased trading activity and rapid price movement. Managers required to hold those stocks in their portfolio cause excessive buying and selling pressure. Empirical evidence shows a spike in price for those stocks added to an index, or whose index weights increased (and a price drop for those stocks deleted from the index or whose index weights decreased). Often, this price movement is followed by a price reversion immediately after reconstitution day. In fact, numerous studies observe this phenomenon with the Russell indices at the time of the annual reconstitution at the end of June. Traders aware of these occurrences and familiar with buying and selling pressure exerted on stocks during an index reconstitution or rebalancing are better able to develop effective implementation strategies. Furthermore, these traders add value and improve portfolio returns by exploiting price discrepancies that occur during these times. The potential for trading profits exists during times of index reconstitution and portfolio rebalancing.

Prices

Market Prices

Market prices are often stated as the last trade price or in terms of current market quotes. The last trade price serves as a historical measure, not as the sole predictor of prevailing market conditions. Usually the last trade and current market quotes are close, but differ if there are quick movements in prices or adjustments in the limit order book. Such differences usually occur when stocks lack quote liquidity or when orders convey valuable information to the market regarding future transaction intentions of investors.

With reference to market quotes, there are two frames of thought regarding the correct way to state the price of the stock. The first is to state the current market price as the ask for buy orders and the bid for sell orders. The second is to quote the current price of the stock as the midpoint of the best bid and offer. Then, the incremental amount to this price represents the trading cost of the transaction. This quote has the appealing feature that it provides a single market price for all others, buys and sells, and for all order sizes. However, the trading cost for each order will vary based on its size and side.

Thus, we proceed by defining the current price of a security to be the midpoint of the best bid and ask price in the market. That is:

$$Price = \frac{Best\ Ask\ Price + Best\ Bid\ Price}{2} \tag{3.1}$$

Quotes

Market quotes consist of prices and quantities that prospective buyers and sellers are willing to transact in the market. These are all the orders contained in the limit order book for the stock. It is important for traders to have access to the full universe of market quotes. This includes quotes from exchanges, market makers, broker-dealers, investors, electronic communications networks (ECN), alternative trading system (ATS) and crossing systems. Pre-trade systems should provide traders with the full spectrum of public quotations consisting of prices and quantities. Further, these systems need to provide the venue of the posting as well as cumulative volumes at each price to assist traders in routing orders to the lowest cost destination. Further, pre-trade systems should be capable of deriving the cumulative public limit order book using all available public market information. This provides traders with the best possible representation of market prices and current liquidity.

Spreads

As mentioned previously, the spread cost of a stock is the difference in price between the best bid and best ask and represents the cost of a round-trip transaction in the stock. While this is theoretically correct only when the order size is less than or equal to the quantity displayed on the best bid and ask, the spread cost gives somewhat of an indication of the trading difficulty and risk of the stock. Those stocks with lower spread costs are generally the less difficult and less risky names to trade and those stocks with higher spread costs are generally the more difficult and more risky names to trade. Spread costs are usually expressed in basis points so that spreads can be easily compared across stocks of different prices. For example, without any other information we cannot accurately assess the trading difficulty associated with two stocks if all we know is that they each have a spread cost of \$0.10/share. However, if one stock has a price of \$10/share and the other has a price of \$50/share, then their spread costs in basis points are 100bp and 20bp respectively. Hence, it is likely that the stock with a spread cost of 100bp will be more difficult to execute than the stock with a spread cost of 20bp.

We compute the spread cost as follows:

$$\text{Spread(\$/share)} = \text{Best Ask Price} - \text{Best Bid Price} \qquad \text{(3.2)}$$

$$\text{Spread(bp)} = \frac{\text{Best Ask} - \text{Best Bid}}{\text{Price}} * 10^4 \text{bp}$$

Price Trends

As with any process, there is always a need to have insight regarding the recent activity or performance. This is especially true in financial markets where informed investors or traders have potential for extraordinary gains with solid knowledge of price behavior. Hence, before implementation, traders assess and gauge recent price performance of stocks in the trade list. Is performance news related, market driven, or based on excess buying or selling pressure?

To assess recent activity we measure the historical price change or simply price returns over a period. In order to determine a reason behind the previous activity, analysts review news on the company, compare the price movement to the market and sector index, and attempt to gain insight into excess demand and supply of the stock using technical indicators. While there seems to be a never-ending set of technical indicators, we are not advocating their use to predict future returns, but rather to gain an understanding of previous activity. For example, a stock might have trended upwards during the last week without any news on the company.

Price Change

The price movement of a stock refers to its historical price change over a period such as the last month, week, or day. For example, an n-day price trend is derived using the previous closing price of the stock and the closing price n days previous. It calculates as follows:

$$r_n = \left(\frac{P_t}{P_{t-n}} - 1 \right) * 100\% \tag{3.3}$$

Relative Strength

The relative strength of a stock is a comparison of its recent price movement to some benchmark index such as the S&P 500 or the sector index. A statistic greater than one indicates that the price has outperformed the index while a statistic less than one indicates that the price has underperformed the index. It is calculated as follows:

$$RS_n = \frac{r_{in}}{r_{bn}} \tag{3.4}$$

where r_{in} is the n-period return of the stock and r_{bn} is the n-period return of the benchmark index.

Buying-Selling Indicators

Multitudes of technical indicators focus on measuring the imbalance in buying and selling pressure in an issue. While these indicators provide insight into the future returns of stocks, we only propose their use to gain understanding of causes for recent movement, not for predicting future returns. Investors should perform a thorough analysis of any technical indicator before using it to make buy and sell decisions. Some of the more useful technical indicators for gaining insight into recent buying and selling activity are the relative strength index (RSI) (J. Welles Wilder 1978), stock stochastics (Dr. George Lane 1950s), On Balance Volume, and Williams %R (Larry Williams). For a thorough introduction to technical indicators see *New Concepts in Technical Trading* (J. Welles Wilder) or Technical Analysis from A to Z (Achelis, 1995).

Momentum

Stock momentum provides us with an estimate of future price movement. We refer to price momentum as the excess movement compared to its price appreciation. The statistic provides traders with insight into the future excess price movement above or below its anticipated trend so they can plan an implementation strategy. For example, if the stock price trends upwards, traders benefit by executing buy orders early and sell orders later to take advantage of better prices. If the stock price trends down, traders execute buy orders later and sell orders earlier to take advantage of better prices.

Estimation of the momentum term is more difficult than simply measuring past performance and price movement. While many traders use historical movement as an indication of future prices, the measure often leads to disappointing results. Additionally, often traders and analysts incorrectly state the difficulty of a trade based on some historical price movement. The belief here is that the trend will continue to persist. If the price has been trending upwards, buy orders will be more expensive and sell orders less expensive; if the price of the stock has been trending downward, buy orders will be less expensive and sell orders more expensive. Analysts have found that previous price trends are not good forecasts of future trends.

Short-term stock alphas are proprietary and usually not shared. In fact, all market participants should be cautious of information supporting short-term price movement provided by research shops. If someone has an accurate short-term prediction model, he or she will likely keep the information confidential. In addition, some may try to create a stir in the market by providing price movement projections for a position they already hold in order to offset the positions at a future period in time at a better price.

A method used to project price movement based on recent activity is a qualitative momentum measure that helps determine the likelihood a recent trend will continue. Rather than calculating a numeric value for the momentum statistic, a set of qualitative measures such as trending, neutral, or reversing can be derived.

The trending indicator defines a stock that exhibits patterns or trends that occur statistically more often than would be observed in a random process. It indicates that the historical movement is more likely to continue. A neutral indicator refers to a stock whose historical pattern or trend is indistinguishable from that of a random process. A reversing stock is a stock with patterns or trends that occurr statistically less often than a random process. This indicates that the historical trend is more likely to reverse than continue. While this approach is not perfect, it provides traders with those names that are likely to be more and less costly due to future price trends.

The qualitative momentum measure can best be determined based on the following expression:

$$\text{Prob}(E[r_{t+1}] > 0 \mid \Omega_t) \tag{3.5}$$

where, $E[r_{t+1}]$ is the expected return in the next period and Ω_t is the set of the most recent stock performance at the current time or alternatively as:

$$\text{Prob}(E[r_t] > E(\mu_t) \mid \Omega_t) \tag{3.6}$$

where $E(\mu_t)$ is the anticipated natural price appreciation.

For true momentum phenomena to exist there needs to be some dependence between future returns and previous returns. Hence, analysts only need to test for data independence. The more common techniques consist of an *n*-period serial correlation lag and the "runs test" for determining the persistence of trends. Some of the more recent techniques consist of computing the Hurst exponent H for a fractal process. If H=1/2 then the data is believed to be random, if H>1/2 then there is long-term dependence in the data, and if H<1/2 then there is a reversing trend. For further information on estimating the Hurst exponent see Hurst (1951), Mandelbrot (1982, 1997), Hastings and Suguria (1987), Hastings and Kissell (1997), and Peters (1994, 1996).

Range

The range of the stock is the difference between its high and low price on the day and is intended to provide traders with insight into the potential total price movement over a day.

$$\text{Range} = \text{High} - \text{Low} \tag{3.7}$$

The range measure serves as a descriptor of price volatility and as a measure of the potential profit by buying at the low and selling at the high.

Trading Range

The trading range metric is expressed as a percentage of the midpoint of the high and low prices calculated as follows:

$$Range_1 = \frac{p_{high} - p_{low}}{\frac{1}{2}(p_{high} + p_{low})} \tag{3.8}$$

Traders use the trading range measure as a comparison of volatility across stocks. Those stocks with a higher trading range are more risky and those stocks with a smaller range less risky. The range measure does differ from the volatility measure in that it shows the total size of the trading intervals, whereas volatility measures the amount of dispersion around a price trend. The trading range of the stock is used as an indication of a potential shift of the volatility paradigm of a stock making the stock either less or more volatile. This is determined by borrowing the relationship between the range and standard deviation commonly used in statistical quality control.

Profit Range

Expressing the range as a percentage of the low price provides a measure of the maximum profit opportunity for the stock. That is, the profit range:

$$Range_2 = \frac{P_{high} - P_{low}}{P_{low}} \tag{3.9}$$

This measure provides insight into the profit potential of the stock achievable through buying at the low and selling at the high, or alternatively selling (short) at the high and buying at the low. The reason behind this is that the low price, not the midpoint, represents the price that investors purchase the stock, and the profit amount is the difference between the high and low prices. Traders capable of correctly timing the market can use the profit range to gain insight into the likely trading profit of a stock as well as screen for those stocks that provide the highest opportunity for profitability.

Liquidity

Market liquidity statistics provide information regarding the concentration of order flow in a stock and the market's ability to quickly execute large blocks of stock with little or no price movement. A liquid market allows an investor to quickly execute substantial quantities of stock without adversely affecting its price or incurring a cost. However, an illiquid market causes investors to pay a high premium to quickly execute a large buy order and to provide a discount to quickly execute a large sell order.

The size of an order is expressed as the percentage of the trading volume for the stock. This allows for easy comparison of orders across different stocks. It is difficult to compare the size of two orders using only the total share amounts because each order size is in effect a function of its respective market volume. For example, it is not possible to compare the relative size of a 100,000-share order in ABC and a 50,000-share order in XYZ from the order sizes alone. However, if we know that the 100,000 share order of ABC represents 5% of the day's volume and the 50,000 share order of XYZ represents 30% of the day's volume, then we can conclude that the order in XYZ is larger than that in ABC.

Table 3.1. Order Size and Difficulty Level

Order Size	Difficulty Level
0–5%	Easy: one day
5–15%	Relatively Easy: one day with some work
15–25%	Difficult: may require multiple days
25%+	Very Difficult: recommend multiple days

Expressing the order as a percentage of trading volume also allows traders to quickly screen the list for what might be difficult trades. A general rule of thumb pertaining to difficulty of executing orders is that orders < 5% of Average Daily Volume (ADV) can be easily absorbed by the market over the course of a day without much price impact. Orders between 5 and 15% of ADV can be traded during the course of a day but with some work. Orders between 15 and 25% of ADV are difficult trades to execute and will require effort from traders to locate liquidity pools, negotiate prices, and minimize information leakage pertaining to their trading intentions. In addition, depending upon actual market conditions, these orders may or may not be absorbable by the market over the course of the day. Orders in excess of 25% of ADV are extremely difficult to execute on a single day and incur a high transaction cost if they are forced. Orders of this size should be executed over multiple days in order to minimize price impact of the order (see Table 3.1). However, this approach does come with an increase in timing risk (trader's dilemma).

Average Daily Volume

The most common technique used in the industry for forecasting the expected daily trading volume in a stock is the historical average daily trading volume in the stock over some time such as the previous 30 days. This calculation is as follows:

$$ADV_t = \frac{1}{30} \sum_{i=1}^{30} V_{t-i} \tag{3.10}$$

where V_{t-i} represents the total traded volume i days previous. For example, $i = 1$ refers to the previous day, $i = 2$ refers to two day ago, etc. Some industry practitioners prefer the median as opposed to the mean as an indication of expected volume. Mathematically, the 30-day median is computed as:

$$\hat{V}_{Median} = \frac{1}{2}(V_{15} + V_{16}) \tag{3.11}$$

where V_n denotes the nth highest volume day.

Figure 3.4.   Daily Trading Volumes S&P 1500 Stocks Jan 2000–Dec 2001

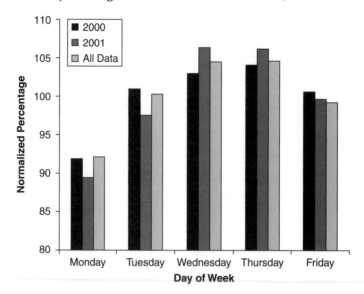

Day of Week Effect

There exists a day of week effect associated with daily trading volumes. An analysis of traded volume for those stocks that comprised the S&P 1500 (as of January 2002) showed a weekly pattern. The results of that analysis found a day of week effect in market volumes. The traded volume in stocks on Monday (92%) is below the daily average. Wednesday and Thursday were the highest volume days at 104% of the daily average. The daily volumes for these stocks on Tuesdays and Fridays were at the daily average (e.g., 100%). Repeating the analysis for each year further validated this observation (see Figure 3.4).

These results improve the forecast of daily trading volumes. For example, if we let $I(day)$ be an indicator function specifying the day's historical percentage of the average daily volume where $I(day)$ is defined as follows:

$$I(day) = \begin{cases} 0.92 & \text{if Mon} \\ 1.00 & \text{if Tue} \\ 1.04 & \text{if Wed} \\ 1.04 & \text{if Thur} \\ 1.00 & \text{if Fri} \end{cases}$$

Then, the improved daily volume forecast using the ADV and median respectively is computed as:

$$V_t = I(day) \cdot ADV = I(day) \cdot \frac{1}{30} \sum_{i=1}^{30} V_{t-i} \tag{3.12}$$

Figure 3.5. Trade Size Distribution

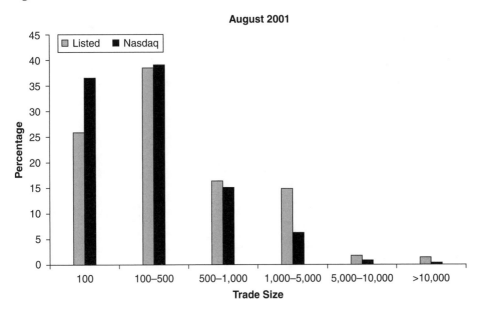

Average Trade Size

Average trade size is determined as the mean of all market trades over a historical period such as the last couple of days or last week. The calculation used to compute the average trade size of a stock is the usual mean calculation and works out as follows:

$$Avg \ Trade \ Size = \frac{1}{n} \sum_{i=1}^{n} shares_i$$

where n equals the total number of market trades in the stock over some historical period such as the last day, week, or month. Insight into the average trade sizes alerts traders to what the market is most capable of absorbing. Traders then execute in similar size trades as a means to minimize information leakage and market impact cost.

Figure 3.5 provides a summary of the percentage of executions that occur at different trade sizes for listed and Nasdaq for those stocks that comprised the S&P 1500 index. The vast majority of trades occur at relatively smaller sizes of 100 shares and 100–500 shares.

Intraday Trading Patterns

Stocks trade more frequently at the open and close than during midday. In fact, if we plotted the intraday trading patterns over the course of the day, we find they typically follow a u-shaped pattern. Good traders exploit this

Figure 3.6. Intraday Volume Profile

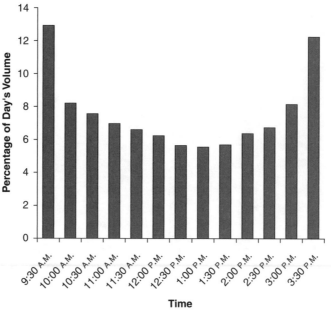

by slicing a large order into smaller pieces and executing those slices during times of maximum liquidity where they are most capable of absorbing the incremental volume, thereby minimizing information leakage and reducing transaction costs. Intraday trading volumes are usually computed by segmenting the day into trading periods and then calculating the percentage of the day's total volume that traded in each period. The most common segmentation groupings are the fifteen-minute and half-hour intervals, although many high-frequency traders prefer five- and even one-minute periods. Figure 3.6 shows the average intraday trading pattern for the universe of S&P 1500 stocks during August 2001. Observe the u-shaped pattern with increased volume levels at the open and close.

Daily Trading Stability

Statistically, we can describe the degree of uncertainty associated with an estimated parameter θ as the coefficient of variation (CV). It is intended to provide traders with insight regarding the difficulty and work required to execute an order. It does not necessarily give insight into the expected cost of the order. Mathematically, this formula measures the quantity of variance surrounding the expected value of the parameter. This value is then divided by the expected parameter to express it as a fraction. The CV for any estimated parameter is as follows:

$$CV = \frac{E[(\theta - E(\theta))^2]^{1/2}}{E(\theta)} = \frac{\sigma(\theta)}{E(\theta)}$$

The CV for the ADV liquidity statistic is computed as follows:

$$CV(ADV) = \frac{\sigma(ADV)}{ADV} \qquad (3.13)$$

where

$$\sigma(ADV) = E[(v - ADV)^2]^{1/2} = \frac{1}{n}\sqrt{\sum_{i=1}^{n}(V_i - ADV_i)^2} \qquad (3.14)$$

In terms of trading, it is more difficult to execute an order with a high CV, primarily because a high CV requires traders to remain focused and reactive to market conditions and be proactive in their negotiations for better prices. Trading an order with a low CV allows traders to focus primarily on the proactive role of negotiating the better prices. It is likely the CV will be a new and unintuitive measure of trading difficulty for traders and managers. However, if used as a comparative measure it will yield valuable insight surrounding the typical trading patterns of the stock even to junior traders. For example, most traders have good intuition for how a listed large cap security trades. However, it is difficult to explain how a Nasdaq small cap stock trades in comparison. If we know that listed large cap stocks have a daily CV of 50% and that Nasdaq small cap stocks have a CV of 75%, we can easily determine that there is 50% less certainty surrounding the expectations for the Nasdaq stock. Further, if a mid cap stock has a CV of 20% we can expect it to trade much more regularly and much less sporadically than even an average listed large cap stock because its CV is lower. This indicates that it has a more stable trading pattern and further implies that it is an easier stock to trade.

Intraday Trading Stability

Ideally, traders want to execute orders at times of maximum liquidity when the market is most capable of absorbing additional order flow and the potential for adverse price movement is the least. Unfortunately, there is also uncertainty surrounding the amount of volume in each trading period. As we know by now, implementation decisions need to incorporate the stability of trading patterns, otherwise incorrect conclusions can and will cause funds to incur higher costs and/or more risk than necessary. While intraday trading patterns follow a u-shaped pattern, uncertainty surrounds trading volume in any period (see Figure 3.7).

It is possible for a stock to have an unstable inter-day volume estimate but stable intraday profiles. This means that while we do not know exactly how much volume will trade on any given day, we do know how that amount will trade through the day as a percentage of its daily volume. For these stocks, traders could quickly assess the expected total day volume

Figure 3.7.   Intraday Volume Stability

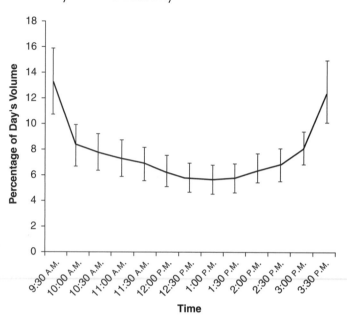

simply by observing the volumes in the first few periods of the day. Traders could then quickly adjust the prescribed strategy based on market conditions. Similarly, it is quite possible for a stock to have stable daily estimates but unstable intraday profiles. This means that we do indeed have a good estimate of the total amount of volume that will trade over the entire day but we do not know how it will trade throughout the day. Traders could observe the stock's trading behavior over the morning then make educated inferences regarding expected volume profiles over the next half day. The worse case scenario for traders is for a stock to have a high daily CV and associated unstable intraday patterns. The best case, of course, is for the stock to have a low daily CV and stable trading patterns making trading patterns predictable and requiring little work.

Comparison of Trading Difficulty to Trading Cost

A misnomer in the industry is that orders with high trading costs are the more difficult orders to trade. While there is correlation between trading difficulty and trading cost, it is not necessarily true that high trading cost orders will be difficult orders to trade.

We define a difficult execution as a stock with unstable trading patterns. These are the difficult names to trade because it requires traders to locate liquidity, negotiate prices, as well as monitor and adapt to the ever-changing market conditions. The difficult names to trade are those stocks with unstable market conditions because prevailing market conditions are not easy to forecast. These stocks require traders to adapt the execution strategy often throughout the day to accommodate higher and lower periods of liquidity and volatility. It is feasible for a high cost order to be a relatively easy trade and a low cost order to be a difficult trade. Trading difficulty is a function of the amount of work required to execute the order and the overall need for traders to adjust to changing market conditions and make modifications to the specified trading strategies. Those orders that do not require intervention from traders, other than for locating liquidity and negotiating prices, are the easier executions. Those orders that require additional intervention such as adjusting strategy based upon changing market conditions are the more difficult executions.

Easy executions are those stocks with a high degree of trading stability. These are the names where traders can forecast prevailing market conditions and focus energy on locating liquidity and negotiating prices. A large order in a low volatile stock with stable trading patterns is an easier position to execute than a smaller order in a high volatility stock with unstable trading patterns. However, for a same-sized order, stocks with more unstable trading patterns will incur a higher trading cost than stocks with more stable trading patterns. The more difficult trades are those stocks that require traders to adapt to changing market conditions and make ongoing decisions regarding trading strategy as well as locate liquidity and negotiate prices.

Estimated Trading Time

This statistic indicates the time it will take to execute an order following a specified strategy defined by the participation rate (trading rate). Here, the strategy is typically stated as a percentage of volume, for example, by trading at a rate equal to 10% or 20%. Thus, for any order X with average daily volume ADV we can compute estimated trading time in average days t^* if the order were executed at a rate α. The calculation is:

$$t^* = \frac{X/ADV}{\alpha} = \frac{X}{\alpha \cdot ADV} \tag{3.15}$$

For example, suppose a trader has an order of 100,000 shares in a stock with ADV equal to 1 million shares. If the trader executes the order at a rate of 10% and 20% the expected amount of time in normal market conditions to complete the order is:

$$t^*(\alpha = 10\%) = \frac{100,000}{0.10 \cdot 1,000,000} = 1 \; day$$

$$t^*(\alpha = 20\%) = \frac{100,000}{0.20 \cdot 1,000,000} = \frac{1}{2} \; day$$

This statistic is useful for managers and traders to estimate the amount of time to complete execution, especially considering that in most cases the order is executed at a rate of $10\% \leq \alpha \leq 25\%$.

Traders could improve upon the expected trading time estimate by making an adjustment to the ADV to account for cyclic patterns and the day of week effect.

Risk

To investors and managers risk refers to potential decrease in the value of a stock, portfolio, or some other investment vehicle, over some period. However, risk as it is defined in the literature pertains to uncertainty in price movement over some period, either increasing or decreasing. Having accurate risk estimates on hand provides managers with a more complete representation of potential future gains or losses by proving ranges around expected values rather than simply a single future value estimate. Managers can use this information to develop estimates regarding the likelihood that the value of the portfolio will be higher or lower than some specified value at some time in the future, that is, VaR analysis. Risk statistics also provide managers with valuable insight into risk composition of the portfolio in order to facilitate risk reduction through diversification and hedging schemes to better managing risk and ultimately have more certainty surrounding future portfolio values. Further, these estimates may also serve as the basis behind investment decisions such as in the case of minimizing tracking error or in constructing a portfolio so that its associated risk does not exceed a specified level.

Risk estimates are equally important during implementation because they provide realistic expectations of potential cash exchange—cash outlay for purchase or cash redemption. Risk estimates are a means of providing the complete picture behind the actual cost of implementing an investment decision. Traders who exercise proper trading risk oversight should not be surprised by the actual cost of implementation. In addition to providing traders with ranges surrounding expected trading costs, risk measures are used to shed valuable insight into the risk decomposition of the trade list. This information allows traders to make more appropriate implementation decisions that reduce total execution cost of the list. Different list characteristics require different means of implementation. These risk measures provide traders with necessary data to analyze the most appropriate execution strategy for a given list.

Traders use risk measurement statistics to determine what stocks or groups of stock are contributing risk to the trade portfolio rather than reducing risk through diversification. They can then develop techniques to efficiently offset this risk and lower transaction costs. This information allows traders to determine orders to execute aggressively or passively.

Furthermore, risk statistics and characteristics of a trade list should serve as the basis for developing crossing strategies as well as allocating a trade list between agency and principal execution. The appropriate risk statistics for traders and how they can be used to better develop an implementation plan is described next.

Most financial literature computes volatility and risk using stock weights and the variance-covariance matrix expressed in price returns. This representation was developed for money managers whose primary concern is a long-term horizon. Traders, however, are more concerned with the risk of a trade list over a very short horizon so expressing risk in terms of $/share has a much greater meaning. From a computation standpoint, units expressed in $/share is also preferred because it reduces much of the computation complexity. It provides opportunity to use residual shares rather than residual weights in calculations and it is extremely powerful in performing multi-period optimizations. All subsequent risk calculations, hence, will be expressed in $/share.

Stock Volatility

The most common measure of stock volatility is the standard deviation of price returns. As mentioned, for trading purposes it is more meaningful to express volatility in units of $/share rather than in returns. Money managers speak in terms of returns, but traders speak in terms $/share. Unfortunately, computing volatility using price change (i.e., $\Delta p_t = p_t - p_{t-1}$, where p_t is the closing price on day t) violates some fundamental properties of statistics.[1] Namely,

    i.   is not stationary
    ii.   is bounded below
    iii. not normally distributed

To correct for these statistical violations we derive volatility using either price returns r or natural log of price returns g then convert into $/share.

Price returns r and natural log of price returns g is calculated as follows:

$$r_t = \frac{p_t - p_{t-1}}{p_{t-1}} = \frac{p_t}{p_{t-1}} - 1 \tag{3.16}$$

$$g_t = \ln\left(\frac{p_t}{p_{t-1}}\right) = \ln(p_t) - \ln(p_{t-1}) \tag{3.17}$$

---

1. For a complete discussion of statistical violations as well as advantages and disadvantages between r and g see Chriss (1997), Elton and Gruber (1995), Francis (1991), or Hull (1997).

The actual selection of r or g does not matter much for our purposes because $r_t \cong g_t = (1 + r_t)$ for reasonable daily returns, e.g., $-0.20 \leq r \leq 0.20$. Further, daily price returns in excess of 20% are most often the consequence of news, information, or a crash. Analysts are encouraged to investigate extreme value functions for these possibilities. Our immediate needs require a volatility measure for normal or expected market conditions. The statistic g, however, does have an appealing advantage over r because it is an additive function (see Hull, 1997). But for simplicity we continue to use r because it has a more intuitive meaning.

Price returns volatility is calculated as follows:[2]

$$\sigma(r) = \sqrt{E[(r - E(r))^2]} = \sqrt{\frac{1}{n-1} \sum_{j=1}^{n} \left(r_j - E(r)\right)^2} \qquad (3.18)$$

where r_j denotes the price return on the jth previous day.[3]

Price returns volatility is converted into \$/share as follows:

First,

$$r_t = \frac{p_t - p_{t-1}}{p_{t-1}} \cong \frac{p_t - p_{t-1}}{\overline{p}} = \frac{1}{\overline{p}}(p_t - p_{t-1}) = \frac{1}{\overline{p}} \Delta p_t \qquad (3.19)$$

providing $\overline{p}$ is not too different from each p_t. This is indeed a reasonable expectation for short time periods.

Second,

$$\sigma(r) = \sigma^2 \left(\frac{p_t - p_{t-1}}{p_{t-1}}\right) \cong \sigma^2 \left(\frac{1}{\overline{p}} \Delta p_t\right) = \frac{1}{\overline{p}^2} \sigma^2(\Delta p_t) \qquad (3.20)$$

since $\overline{p}$ is a constant.

Third, for short time periods (e.g., ≤ 3 to 5 days), and with $E(r) \leq 50\%$ annual and $\sigma(r) \leq 75\%$ annual we can substitute the current stock price p_0 for $\overline{p}$ with negligible loss of accuracy. This yields

$$\sigma^2(r) \cong \frac{1}{p_0^2} \sigma^2(\Delta p_t) \qquad (3.21)$$

2. A divisor of $(n-1)$ is used to provide an unbiased estimate of volatility. For more information on unbiased estimators see DeGroot (1989), Meyer (1970), or Brickel and Doksum (1977), Greene (2000), or Mittelhammer, Judge, and Miller (2000).
3. In Chapter 6, Timing Risk, we provide an improved methodology for estimating future volatility.

While this approximation holds for the shorter horizons that are of interest to traders (e.g., minutes, hours, days, or even up to a couple of weeks) it is not an appropriate approximation for longer time horizons that are of interest to managers.

Finally, variance $\sigma^2(\Delta p)$ and volatility $\sigma(\Delta p)$ expressed in \$/share is:

$$\sigma^2(\Delta p_t) \cong p_0^2 \sigma^2(r) \tag{3.22}$$

$$\sigma(\Delta p_t) \cong \sqrt{p_0^2 \sigma^2(r)} = p_0 \sigma(r) \tag{3.23}$$

Following this formulation, the total dollar variance volatility of the order is:

$$\sigma_\$^2(x) \cong x^2 p_0^2 \sigma^2(r) \tag{3.24}$$

$$\sigma_\$(x) \cong \sqrt{x^2 p_0^2 \sigma^2(r)} = x p_0 \sigma(r) \tag{3.25}$$

Relationship Between Range and Standard Deviation

There is a statistical relationship between the trading range and the standard deviation for small sample sizes (e.g., $n \leq 15$). This is:

$$\hat{\sigma} \cong \frac{Range}{\sqrt{n}} \tag{3.26}$$

This relationship is used in statistical quality control but can also be applied to financial situations to gain quick insight into potential shifts in the volatility paradigm. Traders can assess market conditions by computing the average range over two different times, for example, the previous five days, and the five days before that. If the average range for the more recent period is statistically different from the average range for the previous period, it is likely that the volatility of the stock has changed. A higher more recent range measure indicates a more risky stock and a lower more recent range measure indicates a less risky stock. The same can also be determined for the stock market as a whole.

Covariance

Covariance is a statistical measure of the co-movement of two random variables. In finance, covariance represents a measure of the common movement of stock returns. The covariance measure is extremely important for computing portfolio risk, beta, and risk exposure.

Mathematically the covariance of returns of two stocks i and j is:

$$Cov(r_i, r_j) = E[(r_i - E(r_i))(r_j - E(rj))] = E(r_i r_j) - E(r_i)E(r_j)$$

This expression is converted into \$/share following the same approximation methodology used for individual stock volatility and is as follows:

$$Cov(r_i, r_j) = E(r_i r_j) - E(r_i)E(r_j)$$

$$= E\left(\frac{p_{i,t} - p_{i,t-1}}{p_{i,t-1}} \cdot \frac{p_{j,t} - p_{j,t-1}}{p_{j,t-1}}\right) - E\left(\frac{p_{i,t} - p_{i,t-1}}{p_{i,t-1}}\right) \cdot E\left(\frac{p_{j,t} - p_{j,t-1}}{p_{j,t-1}}\right)$$

$$\cong \frac{1}{\bar{p}_i} \cdot \frac{1}{\bar{p}_j}(E(\Delta p_i \Delta p_j) - E(\Delta p_i) \cdot E(\Delta p_j))$$

$$\cong \frac{1}{p_i} \cdot \frac{1}{p_j} Cov(\Delta p_i, \Delta p_j)$$

where p_i and p_j are the current prices for i and j respectively.

Therefore, the covariance of stock prices expressed in \$/share is:

$$Cov(\Delta p_i, \Delta p_j) \cong p_i p_j Cov(r_i, r_j) \tag{3.27}$$

This can also be computed from individual stock volatilities and the correlation coefficient ρ_{ij} as follows:

$$Cov(\Delta p_i, \Delta p_j) \cong p_i p_j \cdot \rho_{ij} \sigma(r_i)\sigma(r_j) \tag{3.28}$$

since, $Cov(r_i, r_j) = \rho_{ij}\sigma(r_i)\sigma(r_j)$

The covariance in dollars for two orders x_i and x_j is computed as follows:

$$Cov(x_i \Delta p_i, x_j \Delta p_j) \cong x_i p_{i0} \cdot x_j p_{j0} \cdot Cov(r_i, r_j) \tag{3.29}$$

It is now possible to compute the covariance matrix C in \$/share from the covariance matrix of returns C_r as follows:

$$C = DC_r D$$

where D is the diagonal matrix of current stock prices, that is,

$$D = \begin{bmatrix} p_1 & 0 & \cdots & 0 \\ 0 & p_2 & 0 & 0 \\ \vdots & 0 & \ddots & \vdots \\ 0 & 0 & \cdots & p_m \end{bmatrix}$$

The covariance between a trade list X and a benchmark index Y is most typically computed using the dollar weights and covariance matrix expressed in returns as follows:

$$Cov(r_x, r_y) = w_x^t C_r w_y$$

where,

w_{ix} is the signed dollar weight of the ith stock in X

w_{iy} is the signed dollar weight of the ith stock in Y

$$w_{ix} = \frac{x_i p_i}{\sum |x_i| p_i} = \frac{x_i p_i}{V_x}$$

$$w_{iy} = \frac{y_i p_i}{\sum |y_i| p_i} = \frac{y_i p_i}{V_y}$$

V_x is the total absolute dollar value of the trade list X

V_y is the total absolute dollar value of the benchmark index Y

Then,

$$w_x^t C_r w_y = \left(\frac{x_1 p_1}{V_x} \cdots \frac{x_m p_m}{V_x} \right) C_r \begin{pmatrix} \dfrac{y_1 p_1}{V_y} \\ \vdots \\ \dfrac{y_m p_m}{V_y} \end{pmatrix}$$

$$= \frac{1}{V_x} (X_1 \ X_2 \ \cdots \ x_m) \begin{pmatrix} p_1 & 0 & \cdots & 0 \\ 0 & p_2 & 0 & 0 \\ \vdots & 0 & \ddots & \vdots \\ 0 & 0 & \cdots & p_m \end{pmatrix} C_r \begin{pmatrix} p_1 & 0 & \cdots & 0 \\ 0 & p_2 & 0 & 0 \\ \vdots & 0 & \ddots & \vdots \\ 0 & 0 & \cdots & p_m \end{pmatrix} \begin{pmatrix} y_1 \\ y_2 \\ \vdots \\ y_m \end{pmatrix} \frac{1}{V_y}$$

$$= \frac{1}{V_x} X^t DC_r DY \frac{1}{V_y}$$

$$= \frac{1}{V_x} \frac{1}{V_y} X^t CY$$

yielding,

$$w_x^t C_r w_y = \frac{1}{V_x} \frac{1}{V_y} X^t CY \tag{3.30}$$

The total dollar covariance between a trade list X and a benchmark index Y is computed from the covariance matrix expressed in $/share as follows:

$$X^t C Y = V_x V_y w_x^t C_r w_y \qquad (3.31)$$

A final note on the covariance between a trade list X and any benchmark index Y is that it is imperative that each vector X and Y be the same size and contain the same stock in the same order. That is, stock x_i and y_i need to represent the number of shares of i in X and Y respectively. That is:

x_i or $y_i > 0$ represents a buy order or long the stock
x_i or $y_i < 0$ represents a sell order or long the stock
x_i or $y_i = 0$ indicates that the trade list or benchmark index does not
    contain shares of stock i.

Portfolio Risk

The trade portfolio represents the collection of all buy and sell orders in the list. Portfolio risk, hence, refers to the uncertainty in price movement for this collection of names. Portfolio risk is also referred to as trade list risk, basket risk, or program risk, and it is a function of individual stock volatility and the covariance of price movement across all pairs of names in the list. This is shown as follows:

Let R_x represent the dollar weighted average return for the trade portfolio, that is,

$$R_x = \sum_{i=1}^{n} w_i r_i$$

where w_i and r_i represents the dollar weight and expected return of stock i respectively. Then, portfolio risk is calculated as follows:

$$\sigma(R_x) = \sqrt{E[(R_x - E(R_x))^2]}$$

which yields,

$$\sigma(R_x) = \sqrt{E[(\sum_{i=1}^{n} w_i r_i - E(\sum_{i=1}^{n} w_i r_i))^2]}$$

and after some algebraic manipulation we find:

$$\sigma(R_x) = \sqrt{\sum_{i=1}^{n} \sum_{j=1}^{n} w_i w_j \sigma_{ij}(r)}$$

where

$$\sigma_{ij}(r) = Cov(r_i, r_j)$$
$$\sigma_{ii}(r) = \sigma_i^2(r_i) = Var(r_i)$$

Using our approximations for stock volatility and covariance from above we compute the total dollar portfolio variance $\sigma_\$^2(X)$ and total dollar portfolio risk $\sigma_\$(X)$ using the covariance matrix C in \$/share as follows:

$$\sigma_\$^2(X) = V_x V_x w_x^t Crw_x = X^T CX \qquad (3.32)$$

So,

$$\sigma_\$(X) = \sqrt{X^T CX} \qquad (3.33)$$

Trade Schedule Risk

Trade schedule risk differs from portfolio risk in that the trade schedule constitutes a shrinking portfolio over the trading horizon. In each subsequent period the trade portfolio will be different. Traditional portfolio risk calculation scales risk for the appropriate time period based on the assumption that the portfolio holdings will not change. When holdings change the scaling property is no longer a valid, risk needs to be computed in each period.

When we consider a trade schedule it can be thought of as a portfolio of holdings that changes from one period to the next, thus, its associated risk needs to be computed for each period. This process is discussed next.

The statistical property where volatility scales with the square root of time is derived from the following:

$$\sigma(\Delta p(t)) = \sqrt{\sum_{j=1}^{t} \sigma^2(\Delta p_j)} = \sqrt{\sigma^2(\Delta p) + \cdots + \sigma^2(\Delta p)} = \sqrt{t \cdot \sigma^2(\Delta p)} = \sqrt{t} \cdot \sigma(\Delta p)$$

Following this we find the total dollar variance for an order X held over n-periods to be:

$$\sigma_\$^2(x) = \sum_{j=1}^{n} \sigma^2(x\Delta p) = \sum_{j=1}^{n} x^2\sigma^2(\Delta p) = x^2\sigma^2(\Delta p) + \cdots + x^2\sigma^2(\Delta p) = n \cdot x^2 \cdot \sigma^2(\Delta p)$$

And the total dollar risk is:

$$\sigma_\$(x) = \sqrt{nx^2\sigma^2(\Delta p)} = \sqrt{n} \cdot x \cdot \sigma(\Delta p)$$

This formulation provides the necessary insight into computing the risk of a trade list. Suppose that an order X is executed over n-periods but that the number of shares in each period is changing due to trading. If we represent the number of residual shares remaining in the order in period j as R_j the total dollar risk of the trade schedule is computed in a similar fashion to portfolio risk. That is:

$$\sigma_\$^2(X) = \sum_{j=1}^{n} \sigma^2(R_j \Delta p) = \sum_{j=1}^{n} R_j^2 \sigma^2(\Delta p) \tag{3.34}$$

thus,

$$\sigma_\$(X) = \sqrt{\sum_{j=1}^{n} R_j^2 \sigma^2(\Delta p)} \tag{3.35}$$

From this we find the total dollar risk of a trade schedule x_k for a list of stock executed over n-periods is:

$$\sigma_\$^2(X_k) = \sum_{i=1}^{m} \sum_{k=1}^{m} \sum_{j=1}^{m} R_{ij} R_{kj} Cov(\Delta p_i, \Delta pk)$$

where,
R_{ij}= residual shares of stock i in period j
$R_{ij} R_{kj} = R_{ij}^2$ and $Cov(\Delta p_i, \Delta p_k) = Var(\Delta p_i)$ for $i = k$

The total dollar risk of a trade schedule x_k can be computed using matrix notation as follows:

$$\sigma_\$^2(x_k) = \sum_{j=1}^{n} R_j^T C R_j \tag{3.36}$$

and

$$\sigma_\$(x_k) = \sqrt{\sum_{j=1}^{n} R_j^T C R_j} \tag{3.37}$$

where C is the covariance matrix expressed in \$/share.

Correlation Coefficient ρ

The correlation coefficient ρ is a measure of the strength of the linear relationship between two variables. In finance, it is used to measure the relationship of price movement between two stocks or between the trade list and a benchmark index such as the S&P 500, Russell 2000, or a sector index. The correlation coefficient is a measure that lies between −1 and 1, that is,

$-1 \leq \rho \leq 1$. A correlation of $\rho = 1$ between two variables indicates that the variables are in perfect sync with one another, and a correlation of $\rho = -1$ indicates that the two variables move perfectly in opposite directions.

The correlation between two stocks i and j is calculated as follows:

$$\rho_{ij} = \frac{Cov(r_i, r_j)}{\sigma(r_i) \cdot \sigma(r_j)} = \frac{Cov(\Delta p_i, \Delta p_j)}{\sigma(\Delta p_i) \cdot \sigma(\Delta p_j)} \qquad (3.38)$$

The correlation of price movement between a trade list X and a benchmark index Y can also be computed directly from the covariance matrix C as follows:

$$\rho_{xy} = \frac{w_x^t C_r w_y}{\sqrt{w_x^t C_r w_x} \sqrt{w_y^t C_r w_y}} = \frac{X'CY}{\sqrt{X'CX}\sqrt{Y'CY}} \qquad (3.39)$$

Beta

Stock beta is a measure of the stock's sensitivity to market returns. It evolved from portfolio theory based on the single factor model used in CAPM. Beta provides traders with valuable insight into the risk decomposition of the trade list. It allows us to distinguish between systematic risk (market risk) and idiosyncratic (stock specific) risk. A positive beta indicates that the stock returns moves in the same direction as the market and a negative beta indicates a stock that moves in the opposite direction of the market. A stock with beta of 1 moves in conjunction with the market, a stock with a beta between 0 and 1 move less rapidly than the market and stocks with a beta greater than 1 move more rapidly than the market. Finally, a beta of zero indicates that the stock does not have any relationship with the market whatsoever. By definition, the beta of a stock is the covariance of its price returns with the market divided by the variance of the market. That is:

$$\beta_k = \frac{Cov(r_1, r_m)}{Var(r_m)}$$

For cases where covariance and variance are expressed in \$/share the stock beta β_i is computed as follows:

$$\beta_i = \frac{cov(r_i, r_m)}{var(r_m)} = \frac{\dfrac{1}{p_i}\dfrac{1}{p_i} \cdot cov(\Delta p_i, \Delta pm)}{\dfrac{1}{p_m^2} \cdot var(\Delta pm)}$$

yielding,

$$\beta_i = \frac{p_m}{p_i} \cdot \frac{cov(\Delta p_i, \Delta p_m)}{var(\Delta p_m)} \qquad (3.40)$$

where
p_m is the current value of the market index and Δp_m is the day-to-day dollar change in the market index (this is equivalent to treating the market index as a single share of stock).

The beta of the trade list X represents the portfolio's sensitivity to market movement. It provides traders a measure market risk (movement attributable to the market) and idiosyncratic risk. This information is used to develop appropriate risk reduction trading strategies. For example, traders could hedge market risk through instruments such as index futures.

Trade list best is interpreted identically as the individual stock beta and is computed as follows:

$$\beta_x = \sum_i w_i \beta_i$$

or alternatively in matrix notation,

$$\beta_x = \frac{w_x^T C_r w_y}{w_y^T C_r w_y}$$

For cases where the covariance matrix is expressed in \$/share β_i is computed as follows:

$$\beta_x = \frac{cov(r_x, r_y)}{var(r_y)} = \frac{w_x^t C_r w_y}{w_y^t C_r w_y} = \frac{\dfrac{1}{V_x V_y} \cdot X^t C Y}{\dfrac{1}{V_y^2} \cdot Y^t C Y}$$

yielding,

$$\beta_x = \frac{V_y}{V_x} \cdot \frac{X^t C Y}{Y^t C Y} \qquad (3.41)$$

The trade list beta provides a measure of the quantity of total risk attributable to market movement and is used to compute the total dollar risk exposure to the market. For example, the single factor model estimates the change in portfolio value as follows:

$$R_x = \alpha_x + \beta_x R_m = \varepsilon$$

The dollar value change is computed by multiplying by V_x:

$$V_x R_x = V_x \alpha_x + V_x \beta_x R_m = V_x \varepsilon$$

Then its variance is computed as follows:

$$\sigma^2(V_x R_x) = \sigma^2(V_x \alpha_x) + \sigma^2(V_x \beta_x R_m) = \sigma^2(V_x \varepsilon)$$
$$= V_x^2 \beta_x^2 \sigma^2(R_m) + V_x^2 \sigma^2(\varepsilon)$$

since, $\sigma^2(V_x \alpha_x) = 0$

The quantity of risk attributable to the market is:

$$\sigma(V_x R_x | R_m - \sqrt{V_x^2 \beta_x^2 \sigma^2(R_m)}$$

Now, substituting in $\beta_x = \dfrac{cov(r_x, r_m)}{var(r_m)}$ we get,

$$\sigma(V_x R_x | R_m) = \sqrt{V_x^2 \left(\frac{cov(r_x, r_m)}{var(r_m)}\right)^2 var(r_m)} = V_x \frac{cov(r_x, r_m)}{\sqrt{var(r_m)}}$$

or, alternatively computed using C in \$/share it is:

$$\sigma(V_x R_x | R_m) = V_x \frac{cov(r_x, r_m)}{\sqrt{var(r_m)}} = V_x \frac{\dfrac{1}{V_x}\dfrac{1}{V_y} x^t C Y}{\sqrt{\dfrac{1}{V_y^2} Y^t C T}} = \frac{X^t C Y}{\sqrt{Y^t C Y}}$$

So the total dollar risk exposure to the market Y for the trade list X is:

$$RX(X, Y) = \frac{X^t C Y}{\sqrt{Y^t C Y}} \tag{3.42}$$

Risk Exposure

Risk exposure is a measure of the quantity of risk attributable to an index or some other specified benchmark. It is intended to provide insight into the potential change of the trade list given a corresponding change in the benchmark index. This measure allows traders to identify where risk is attributable so as to develop appropriate execution and hedging strategies. Similar to beta, the risk exposure of a trade list to a benchmark index provides insight regarding potential hedging opportunities. For example, suppose the risk exposure of a trade list to the technology sector is $100,000. Traders could reduce this exposure by first shorting the technology index then trading out of the position while simultaneously executing the trade list.

The quantity of dollar risk exposure of the trade list X to some benchmark index Y denoted as $RE(X,Y)$ is computed in a similar fashion as the risk exposure to the market. Mathematically it is calculated as follows:

$$RE(X|Y) = \frac{w_x^t C_r w_y}{\sqrt{w_y^t C_r w_y}} \cong V_x \cdot \frac{\dfrac{1}{V_x}\dfrac{1}{V_y} X^t CY}{\sqrt{\dfrac{1}{V_y}\dfrac{1}{V_y} Y^t CY}} = \frac{X^t CY}{\sqrt{Y^t CY}}$$

Therefore, we define total dollar risk exposure to any index Y as:

$$RE(X, Y) = \frac{X^t CY}{\sqrt{Y^t CY}} \tag{3.43}$$

Notice the similarity between this calculation and trade list beta. They are identical calculations except for the choice of the benchmark index. In order for traders to determine the risk exposure to an index, they need to first define that index. For example, to compute the risk exposure to some sector one can use a sector index such as that provided by the S&P or some other service.

Important Note:

The cumulative risk exposure to multiple indices, such as to each sector index, may result in a quantity of risk that over- or understates the total systematic risk of the trade list. This would occur if there is correlation between those chosen indices (which is often true) and/or if those indices do not account for all systematic risk (which is also often true). Unless the specified index Y was used in the derivation of stock risk decomposition we really cannot specify that the quantity of risk is totally attributable to that index. Rather, a more correct statement is that the quantity of risk is associated with the index. In Chapter 8, Timing Risk, we provide investigation into multifactor risk models.

Risk Contribution

Risk contribution (RC) is an assessment of the total quantity of risk attributable to an individual stock or group of stocks (such as sector). It is a measure of how much risk the stock or group of stocks adds to or reduces from the total. For the most part stocks are positively correlated. But they often provide risk reduction through diversification (same side, buy-buy or sell-sell) and hedging (opposite side, e.g., buy-sell). It is important to understand what stocks or groups of stocks are adding incremental risk and what stock or groups of stocks are decreasing risk.

The RC for a specified stock k in a trade list x is computed as:

$$RC_\$(k) = x^t Cx - x^{*t} Cx^* \tag{3.44}$$

where $x_{i \neq k}^* = x_i$ and $x_{i=k}^* = 0$. That is:

$$x = \begin{pmatrix} x_1 \\ \vdots \\ x_k \\ \vdots \\ x_m \end{pmatrix}, \qquad x^* = \begin{pmatrix} x_1 \\ \vdots \\ 0 \\ \vdots \\ x_m \end{pmatrix}$$

The risk contribution of a subset of stock of the trade list is computed in an identical manner where the x^* vector contains a zero for every stock in that grouping. This definition allows traders to easily compute the risk contribution to any group or subset of the trade list.

The risk contribution measure is an important statistic for traders executing a list of stock following a prescribed trading schedule. It provides insight into how and when a trader should deviate from the prescribed strategy to accelerate and complete an order. For example, suppose a trader has opportunity to complete an order that otherwise would have been executed over the entire day. If a particular stock were contributing risk to the list, e.g., $RC > 0$, then it would be in the trader's best interest to complete the order ahead of time because the result would be lower market impact cost and lower residual risk. However, if the particular stock were reducing risk of the list, e.g., $RC < 0$ then the trader should not execute the order ahead of schedule because the higher risk may result in an even higher transaction cost from potential adverse price movement. If, however, the RC is just slightly less than zero, then the trader executing the list needs to decide if the reduction in market impact from immediate execution outweighs the incremental increase in risk.

The risk contribution measure is only appropriate for a single execution. If two stocks are found to be contributing risk to the list, traders cannot assume that the execution of both names would result in overall reduced residual risk. It is quite possible that the execution of both orders will result in higher residual risk. Every time a trader executes shares it will change the risk composition of the list and risk contribution from each stock. Therefore, the risk contribution analysis will need to be updated. A more in-depth risk analysis that simultaneously evaluates multiple orders is considered in Chapter 12, Advance Trading Techniques.

Finally, the risk contribution discussed above is an important "all-or-none" measure but it does not quantify risk reduction from partial order executions. That analysis, marginal contribution to risk, is discussed next.

Marginal Contribution to Risk

The marginal contribution to risk (MCR) is a concept widely used by portfolio managers to determine the portfolio's risk sensitivity to a change in the holding of an asset. This provides managers with an indication of how the total risk of the portfolio would change if the holding of an asset changed. It assists managers to determine what orders to adjust shares so to better manage portfolio risk.

To determine the marginal contribution to risk of an asset many practitioners suggest varying the asset holdings by 1%. The MCR is thus computed as the difference in risk between the original portfolio and the revised portfolio consisting of 1% more or less shares of the asset similar to the risk contribution calculation from above. In addition to computing the marginal contribution to risk in this manner, managers can alternatively compute the marginal contribution to risk for an asset by differentiating with respect to that asset. That is:

$$MCR(x_i) = \frac{\partial}{\partial x_k} \sqrt{X^t C x}$$

Traders, however, have a different interest with respect to the marginal contribution to risk than money managers. They are genuinely concerned with marginal contribution to risk for orders that must be executed over some period of time. Traders do not have the liberty of adding or subtracting shares from the orders they are required to trade. Our discussion of marginal contribution to risk for traders, hence, will focus on how MCR can be used to better implement a trade list. Suppose that a trader is executing a trade list over the day following a prescribed schedule, but notices from time to time that it is possible to execute larger positions at favorable prices than specified by the prescribed trade schedule.

The question that needs to be answered is how will acceleration of the trade list change the risk composition of the list? In other words, will transacting in a stock more aggressively than specified cause residual risk to increase or decrease?

Similar to the risk contribution methodology described above, this analysis is only for evaluation of an individual stock. If two stocks are found to be contributing to risk one can not assume that execution of shares from both orders will result in lower residual risk. Every time a trader executes shares it will change the risk composition of the list and the marginal contribution to risk from each stock. Therefore, *MCR* needs to be updated after every execution. A more in-depth risk analysis that simultaneously evaluates multiple orders is considered in Chapter 12, Advance Trading Techniques.

Traders indeed have interest in the *MCR* for those names in the trade list. But rather than use the information to increase or decrease the portfolio holding, traders often utilize the information to develop an appropriate risk minimizing trading strategy.

An interesting aspect of *MCR* is that it provides insight into how much of an order can be traded at any point in time without increasing the residual risk of the trade list. For example, suppose a trade list is comprised of three stocks and has current risk R*. If shares are executed from the first order then the remaining shares (those not yet traded) will have a different quantity of risk. This residual risk could either be larger, smaller, or the same. Obviously, it is not in anyone's best interest to execute shares such that the residual risk will be higher than original. The *MCR* statistic is intended to provide guidelines to traders who have opportunity to execute a large block or a large number of shares of an existing order at favorable prices, but do not want to adversely affect the residual risk of the list. If *MCR* is positive for all shares in the order then the stock is contributing to the overall risk and it would be beneficial to execute as many of those shares as possible. If *MCR* is negative for all shares in the order then the stock is decreasing overall risk and it would be best not to execute any shares because it would result in higher residual risk. However, *MCR* is not static and will vary depending on the number of shares remaining in the order and its covariance with all other stocks in the list. It is quite possible for some shares in an order to be reducing risk while other shares are contributing to risk.

The risk contribution computation presented above is a special case of *MCR* where one considers the change in risk if all the shares in an order are executed. Risk contribution does not provide insight into residual risk for partial executions and solely relying on the all-or-none case could lead one to make erroneous trading decisions. The *MCR* analysis, hence, is preferred over *RC*.

Figure 3.8. Residual Risk Trajectories

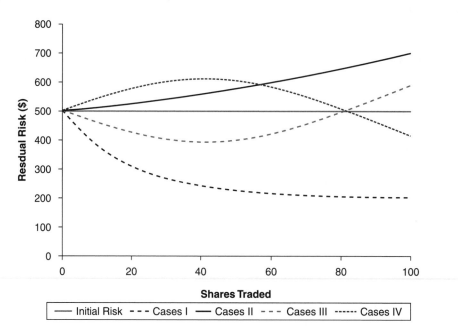

Example

A trade list is comprised of three names. The initial risk is $500 and the first order (XYZ) contains 100 shares. Figure 3.8 provides potential residual risk trajectories if shares of XYZ are executed ahead of schedule. The x-axis shows the number of shares executed and the y-axis shows resulting residual risk. There are four potential trajectories labeled case I through case IV. Case I describes a potential situation where the *MCR* is positive for all shares in the order meaning the order is contributing to the overall risk. Notice the trajectory for case I decreasing over all shares. The execution of any number of shares (0–100) will result in lower residual risk. The *RC* analysis for this case provides identical insight as the *MCR*, namely, that XYZ is contributing to risk and should be executed providing favorable prices. Case II describes a potential situation where the MCR is negative for all shares, meaning that the order is reducing risk. Notice the trajectory of residual risk for case II increasing for all shares. Therefore, the execution of any shares will damage the hedge and cause higher residual risk. The RC analysis for this case again provides identical insight as *MCR* analysis, namely, that XYZ is reducing risk and should not be executed in an accelerated manner. Case III describes a potential situation where the MCR is not constant for all shares in the order. Here, some of the shares reduce risk but other shares contribute to risk. The trajectory of residual risk in case III decreases through a minimum point at 40 shares, increases back to the original risk at 80 shares, and continues to a higher residual risk at 100 shares. This case provides significant insight into managing overall trade list risk.

For example, traders could execute up to 80 shares of the order and have resulting residual risk less than or equal to the initial risk. Or they could execute exactly 40 shares to minimize residual risk. Traders who only performed RC analysis would be incorrectly informed that the order is reducing risk and may not elect to execute any shares of the order. Clearly *MCR* presents the complete risk picture. Case IV describes a phenomenon opposite to case III where residual risk increases to maximum value at 40 shares, decreases back to the original quantity of risk at 80 shares, and continues to decrease to an even lower residual risk at 100 shares. If this case were feasible then it would imply that traders could achieve risk reduction by executing at least 80 shares of the order, but execution of less than 80 shares would result in higher residual risk. Case IV, however, cannot arise in practice. It is only possible to attain a minimum not a maximum value. As it turns out, residual risk trajectories are concave functions with a single minimum. This is further explained as follows.

Let,

$$Risk = \sqrt{X^tCX}$$

The first derivative provides insight into possible maximum or minimum. It is computed as follows:

$$\frac{\partial Risk}{\partial X} = \frac{\partial}{\partial X}\sqrt{X^tCX} = \frac{X^tC}{\sqrt{X^tCX}}$$

The zeros of the equation occur at $X^tC = 0$ since $X^tCX > 0$. Also, since X^tC is a first degree equation there will be a single zero indicating a single minimum or maximum.

The second derivative, the Hessian matrix H, provides insight into a maximum or minimum. It is computed as follows:

$$\frac{\partial^2 Risk}{\partial X^2} = H = \frac{CXX^tC + (X^tCX)C}{(X^tCX)^{3/2}}$$

Here H is a positive definite matrix because C is a symmetric positive definite matrix, X^tCX is a positive scalar, and CXX^tC is positive definite since, $y^tCXX^tCy = (X^tCy)^t(X^tCy) = \|X^tCy\|^2 > 0$ thus indicating the value above is a minimum.

(In the explanation above we have $\|X^tCy\|^2 = (X^tCy)^2 > 0$ since X and y are vectors. We presented a more general case.)

Traders use the *MCR* as a decision tool to determine the number of shares of an order to execute to minimize residual risk and the maximum number of shares that can be executed such that the residual risk will not be greater than the initial quantity of risk. Each technique is discussed below.

Minimize Risk

The total number of shares of stock **i** to execute to minimize risk is found by differentiating risk with respect to that order x_i. This is:

$$\frac{\partial Risk}{\partial X} = \frac{X^t C}{\sqrt{X^t C X}}$$

Set equal to zero and solve for X:

$$\frac{X^t C}{\sqrt{X^t C X}} = 0$$

when $X^t C = 0$ since $X^t C X > 0$. Solving for X yields:

$$X = ABX$$

where,

$$A = -inverse(diagonal(C)), \quad a_{ij} = \begin{cases} -1/c_{ii} & \text{if } i = j \\ 0 & \text{if } i \neq j \end{cases}$$

$$B = C + inverse(A), \quad b_{ij} = \begin{cases} 0 & \text{if } i = j \\ c_{ij} & \text{if } i \neq j \end{cases}$$

It is extremely important to note that the solution $X = ABX$ is only valid for execution in a single stock. The residual risk minimization does not hold for execution in multiple orders.

The number of shares in a single stock i that minimizes residual risk is computed as:

$$x_{i,\min} = e^t(i)ABX \tag{3.45}$$

where, $e(i)$ is i^{th} column of the identity matrix.

Finally, the total number of shares of stock i to trade to minimize residual risk is:

$$X_i - z_i = x_{i'\min} \rightarrow z_i = X_i - x_{i'\min}$$

But we do have a constraint around the number of shares to trade, namely,

$$0 \leq z_i \leq X_i$$

Therefore, we need to make an adjustment to z as follows:

Buy Order   Sell Order

$$z_i^* = \begin{cases} z_i & 0 \le z_i \le X_i \\ X_i & z_i > X_i \\ 0 & z_i < 0 \end{cases} \qquad z_i^* = \begin{cases} z_i & 0 \ge z_i \ge X_i \\ X_i & z_i < X_i \\ 0 & z_i > 0 \end{cases}$$

Note: this solution is only valid for a specific order. As soon as shares from the trade list are executed, the *MCR* and this quantity will change. Traders will need to continuously update this amount after each execution.

Maximize Shares

The maximum number of shares in stock i that can be executed at any given time so that the residual risk will be equal to the initial risk quantity is computed as follows.

Let,

$$X = \begin{pmatrix} x_1 \\ \vdots \\ x_i \\ \vdots \\ x_n \end{pmatrix} \quad Y = \begin{pmatrix} 0 \\ \vdots \\ y_i \\ \vdots \\ 0 \end{pmatrix} \quad X - Y = \begin{pmatrix} x_1 \\ \vdots \\ x_i \\ \vdots \\ x_n \end{pmatrix} - \begin{pmatrix} 0 \\ \vdots \\ y_i \\ \vdots \\ 0 \end{pmatrix} = \begin{pmatrix} x_1 \\ \vdots \\ x_i - y_i \\ \vdots \\ x_n \end{pmatrix}$$

where,
    X = initial trade list.
    Y = column vector for y_i in the ith position to represent the number of shares of stock i to trade.
    $X-Y$ = residual trade list.

This maximum share amount is calculated as follows:
Set the risk of the initial trade list X equal to the residual risk ($X-Y$):

$$\sqrt{X^t C X} = \sqrt{(X - Y)^t C (X - Y)}$$
$$\left(\sqrt{X^t C X}\right)^2 = \left(\sqrt{(X - Y)^t C (X - Y)}\right)^2$$
$$X^t C X = (X - Y)^t C (X - Y)$$

Set equal to zero and solve for y_i:

$$X^tCX - (X - Y)^tC(X - Y) = 0$$

$$x^tCX - (X^tCX - X^tCY - Y^tCX + Y^tCY) = 0$$

$$-X^tCY - Y^tCX + Y^tCY = 0$$

We know,

$Y^tCY = c_{ii}y_i^2$ since Y is column vector of zeros with a single entry y_i in the ith position,

and,

$X^tCY = Y^tCX$ since C is symmetric and definition of Y, so, $-X^tCY - Y^tCX = -2XC(i)y_i$ where $C(i)$ is the ith column of matrix C.

Therefore,

$$-X^tCY - Y^tCX + Y^tCY = 0$$

$$-2X^tCY + Y^tCY = 0 \qquad \text{(3.46)}$$

$$-2XC(i)y_i + c_{ii}y_i^2 = 0$$

and can be solved using the quadratic formula,

$$y_i = \frac{-b \pm \sqrt{b^2 - 4ac}}{2a} \qquad \text{(3.47)}$$

where,

$$a = c_{ii}$$
$$b = -2X^tC(i)$$
$$c = 0$$

The solutions to this

$$y_i = 0 \quad \text{and} \quad y_i = \frac{b}{a}$$

which is,

$$y_i = 0 \quad \text{and} \quad y_i = \frac{X^tC(i)}{c_{ii}} \qquad \text{(3.48)}$$

The maximum number of shares z_i of stock i that can be executed, such that the residual risk will be equal to the initial risk is:

$$z_i = X_i - y_i$$

But once again we have a constraint on the number of shares that can be traded, namely,

$$0 \leq z_i \leq X_i$$

Therefore, we need to make an adjustment to z as follows:

Buy Order   Sell Order

$$z_i^* = \begin{cases} z_i & 0 \leq z_i \leq X_i \\ X_i & z_i > X_i \\ 0 & z_i < 0 \end{cases} \qquad z_i^* = \begin{cases} z_i & 0 \geq z_i \geq X_i \\ X_i & z_i < X_i \\ 0 & z_i > 0 \end{cases}$$

Note: this solution is only valid for a specific order. As soon as shares from the trade list are executed the *MCR* and this quantity will change. Traders will need to continuously update this amount after each execution.

Example
A trader with trade list X and covariance matrix C expressed in \$/share is asked to determine the following:

i) Calculate the number of shares that need to be traded in each order to minimize residual risk.
ii) Calculate the maximum number of shares that can be traded such that the residual risk will be less than or equal to the initial risk.

$$X = \begin{pmatrix} 150 \\ -150 \\ -50 \end{pmatrix}, \quad C = \begin{pmatrix} 0.080 & 0.043 & 0.027 \\ 0.043 & 0.036 & 0.001 \\ 0.027 & 0.001 & 0.120 \end{pmatrix}, \quad \sqrt{X^t C X} = \$24.19$$

Solution:
Part i)
The number of shares of each order to trade to minimize residual risk is computed as:

$$z_i = x_i - x_{i,\min} = x_i - e^t(i)ABX$$

Solving we find:

$$Z = X - x_{\min} = \begin{pmatrix} 150 \\ -150 \\ -50 \end{pmatrix} - \begin{pmatrix} 98 \\ -178 \\ 33 \end{pmatrix} = \begin{pmatrix} 53 \\ 28 \\ -18 \end{pmatrix}$$

But since we have a restriction on z we make an adjustment following our trading rule and have:

$$Z^* = \begin{pmatrix} 53 \\ 0 \\ -18 \end{pmatrix}$$

So we can buy 53 shares of x_1 or sell 18 shares of x_3. There is no feasible number of shares of x_2 that will minimize residual risk because x_2 is providing the list with risk reduction.

Part ii)
The maximum number of shares of each order that can be traded such that the residual risk is less than or equal to the initial risk is computed as follows:

$$z_i = x_i - y_i = x_i - \frac{X^t C(i)}{c_{ii}}$$

Solving we find:

$$Z = X - y = \begin{pmatrix} 150 \\ -150 \\ -50 \end{pmatrix} - \begin{pmatrix} 53 \\ 28 \\ -18 \end{pmatrix} = \begin{pmatrix} 98 \\ -178 \\ -33 \end{pmatrix}$$

But since we have a restriction on z we make an adjustment following our trading rule and have:

$$Z^* = \begin{pmatrix} 98 \\ 0 \\ -33 \end{pmatrix}$$

So we can buy 98 shares of x_1 or sell 33 shares of x_3. There is no feasible number of shares of x_2 that will minimize residual risk because x_2 is providing the list with risk reduction.

Figure 3.9 depicts the associated residual risk with execution of various shares of each order. It shows the minimum residual risk and maximum shares corresponding to the results above and also shows the increasing residual risk that would occur if any shares were executed. Notice that for stock 2 the residual risk is always above the original risk

Figure 3.9. Marginal Contribution to Risk Example

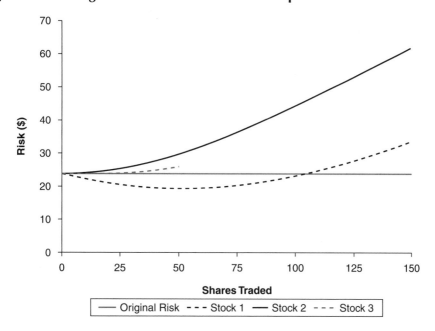

quantity, therefore, it is never in one's best interest to execute shares of stock 2. For stock 1 and stock 3, however, the residual risk trajectories show the region where residual risk would be less than original. For both these stocks the trajectories depict the minimum risk that could arise and the maximum number of shares to execute to have a lower quantity of risk.

Finally, the residual risk discussed here is the corresponding risk if execution only occurred in one of the stocks in the list. *MCR* is not intended to provide insight into the residual risk of multiple executions. It is essential that traders update these values after any and all executions from the trade list. The affect on residual risk for executions of multiple orders is a much more complicated issue and is considered in Chapter Twelve, Advanced Trading Strategies.

Tracking Error

The tracking error of the trade portfolio is a measure of how well the portfolio compares to some benchmark index. While there are many different views of tracking error, the most common industry measure is the standard deviation of the differences in returns between the trade portfolio r_x and a benchmark index r_y. That is:

$$\text{TE}\ (r_x, r_2) = \sigma(r_x - r_y)$$

The tracking error between a trade portfolio and a benchmark index is estimated using the covariance matrix C_r as follows:

$$TE(r_x, r_y) = \sqrt{(w_x - w_y)^T C(w_x - w_y)}$$

where w_x is the weights of the stocks in the trade portfolio and w_y is the weights of the stocks in the benchmark index. It is important to note that the length of the weight vector w needs to be the same. If the trade portfolio does not include a stock in the benchmark index, or if the benchmark index does not include a stock in the trade portfolio, the weight of that stock is simply zero. The tracking error provides important insight into potential hedging strategies that could be used to offset list risk during the execution of a list. If a buy list has a low tracking error with some index, for example, S&P 500, traders could short that S&P 500 at the start of trading as a hedging strategy to reduce risk.

If the covariance matrix C is expressed in $/share, the tracking error of the trade list X compared to a benchmark index Y is computed as follows:

$$TE(X, Y) = \sqrt{(w_x - w_y)^t C_r (w_x - w_y)}$$

$$\cong \sqrt{\left(\frac{1}{V_x - V_y}\right)^2 (X - Y)^t C(X - Y)}$$

$$= \frac{1}{V_x - V_y} \sqrt{(X - Y)^t C(X - Y)}$$

Tracking error is computed in total dollars by multiplying above by the current value of the trade list as follows:

$$TE_\$(X, Y) = \frac{V_x}{V_x - V_y} \sqrt{(X - Y)^t C(X - Y)} \tag{3.49}$$

The tracking error is often a misinterpreted financial statistic. Its computation provides insight into the expected deviation from the expected difference in returns, not necessarily the expected deviation in returns from the index. For example, consider the following.

$R_x(\Delta t)$ = return from portfolio over Δt
$R_y(\Delta t)$ = return from benchmark index over Δt

Suppose:

$E(R_x(\Delta t) - R_y(\Delta t)) = E(R_x(\Delta t)) - E(R_y(\Delta t)) = r^*$
$Var(R_x(\Delta t) - R_y(\Delta t)) = \Delta t (w_x - w_y)^t C(w_x - wy) = \Delta t v^*$

Then a 95% confidence interval for the expected difference is:

$$(r^* - 1.96\sqrt{\Delta t}\sqrt{v^*}, r^* + 1.96\sqrt{\Delta t}\sqrt{v^*})$$

If $r^* << 0$, the investor's portfolio will dramatically underperform the benchmark index even if the tracking error is small. The tracking error computed as expected standard deviation of returns ignores the expected difference in returns. For short-term horizons where $E(R_x) \cong E(R_y)$, the tracking error is indeed a reasonable estimate for expected difference in returns. But for longer horizons where $E(R_x) \neq E(R_y)$, traditional tracking error is a deficient measure. Of course, investors could always minimize the expected difference in returns simply by mimicking the index exactly.[4]

An alternative measure to tracking error is shortfall probability and is simply the probability that the portfolio will underperform the benchmark index. Its advantage is that it incorporates both expected difference and variance of returns. Hence, rather than minimizing tracking error managers would simply minimize shortfall probability as follows:

$$Min \quad Prob(R_x < R_y)$$

This can also be rewritten in terms of a Sharpe ratio as follows:

$$Max \quad \frac{E(R_x) - E(R_y)}{Var(R_x - R_y)} \tag{3.50}$$

Trade List Summary

The trade list summary provides the detailed statistics specified previously for every stock in the trade list for individual name analysis and assessment of potential trading difficulty. The stock specific data also serves as the necessary data for cost estimation and strategy evaluation. A complete pre-trade system should allow analysts to search and sort the data as well as display the data visually in graphical format. The more descriptive depictions are the scatter plot and distribution plots. These data also need to be summarized by grouping schemes (e.g., side, market, sector, capitalization, country) for use in risk or principal bid solicitation and broker selection.

---

[4]While this seems like an obvious solution there are often reasons why managers do not duplicate the entire index exactly. For example, often managers are prohibited from investing more than a specified quantity in any one company. Mangers may not want their holdings to be too illiquid, which would prohibit a quick exit in a company if needed. Managers may wish to invest in a limited number of companies so that they can closely track company fundamentals. Also, managers may be adhering to some investment strategy, such as an enhanced index or titled index strategy. These are only a few of the possible reasons.

Program Profile

The program profile includes total list statistics such as the total dollar value of the list, total number of shares, average share price, average order size as percentage of average daily volume, total list risk, portfolio beta, and so forth. The information section should also include groupings and categorization by side, market, capitalization, sector, and country. The inclusion of these statistics is also intended to function as a feedback loop for detecting errors prior to trading and before mishaps have a chance to occur. Any disagreement between the investment objective and trade list can be brought to the manager's attention before trading begins. Of course, this does not eliminate all mistakes, but it does greatly reduce what could be costly errors.

Cost Estimates

Pre-trade analysis systems should be capable of summarizing and compiling the necessary data in order to provide traders with costs and risk estimates for the trade list. These systems need to be structured such that the trading cost estimates can be developed for specified trading strategies and also to determine the optimal trading strategy subject to specified goals and objectives of the fund. The pre-trade analysis is the first analytical step before implementation of the trade list. After collecting and analyzing the data, traders need to perform the actual cost and risk forecasts using the pre-trade data, then select the appropriate trading strategy. The pre-trade analysis should supply traders with the necessary data to estimate trading costs and develop trading strategies.

Principal Bid Solicitation

Pre-trade analysis is intended to provide managers and traders with the essential characteristics of the trade list that allow the solicitation of principal bid transaction (also known as risk bids and blind bids). Most commonly, managers and traders solicit principal bids from broker dealers by providing characteristics of the list instead of the actual trade list itself. If mangers or traders were to provide brokers with the actual trade list before entering into the transaction with brokers, brokers could use the information to trade ahead of the fund. If brokers know the exact constitutes of the trade list, they could accumulate position in these names and in doing so push up the price of buy orders and push down the price of sell orders, thus making the actual transaction price of the stock more expensive for managers. This could occur whether they are awarded the principal bid transaction or not. To protect themselves from information leakage managers and traders commonly only provide brokers with characteristics of the trade list. Brokers then provide a principal bid estimate based on the submitted characteristics of the list rather than the list itself. The pre-trade summary needs to summarize the list in a way that can be used by managers to solicit these blind risk bids.

Broker Selection

Pre-trade analysis provides traders with the essential characteristics of the trade list that allows one to select the broker most capable of efficiently executing the list as well as the most appropriate trading venue for minimizing costs. These choices are based on the historical performances of brokers executing lists with similar characteristics. It is important to have this information on hand at the time the investment decision is finalized in order to reduce the delay cost associated with selecting the trading venue and broker dealer. This decision is achieved by each fund maintaining a database of the historical transaction costs and performances by brokers and trading venues for each list traded. Then, simply by knowing the makeup and characteristics of the list, traders can immediately select the broker who is best suited to facilitate the trade, and where the list should be traded. This assists in reducing the delay transacation cost component which is often associated with hesitation in selection of executing broker. Chapter 13, Post-Trade Analysis, provides the framework and analytical approach for evaluating broker performance as well as for measuring costs.

CHAPTER FOUR

Price Appreciation

PRICE APPRECIATION REFERS TO THE natural price movement of a stock. It specifies how prices would evolve in the market without any uncertainty, any unexpected events, and without noise. Price appreciation is also commonly referred to as price trend, mean return and sometimes, drift term.

Transaction costs are dependent on price movement, the side of the transaction, and the actual execution strategy. Assume a stock is trending up. Buyers slicing the order over multiple periods incur a higher cost because each successive trade is consummated at a higher price. Sellers slicing the order over multiple periods achieve a lower cost or savings because each successive trade is at the higher price. It is reasonable then in this case to expect buyers to trade utilizing aggressive strategies and sellers to trade via passive strategies. However, costs derived from price appreciation are but one component of transaction costs. Traders also need to consider the effects of market impact and timing risk. Overly aggressive buying strategies cause buyers to incur excessive cost due to market impact; too passive a strategy will expose sellers to excessive market risk, which may yield less favorable prices. Skilled traders can add substantial value to the implementation process by developing the trading strategy around price appreciation, market impact, and timing risk, all of which result in reduced transaction costs. This chapter focuses on the process required to estimate transaction costs due to price appreciation.

Figure 4.1 depicts price appreciation of a stock currently trading at $50/share and expected to increase 25% to $62.50/share over the next year. Here we assume a linear trend over the year. Price evolution, assuming a returns or growth model, would be slightly different. Other price evolution estimation techniques include compounded returns and exponential growth. Each technique is subsequently discussed.

Figure 4.1. Price Appreciation

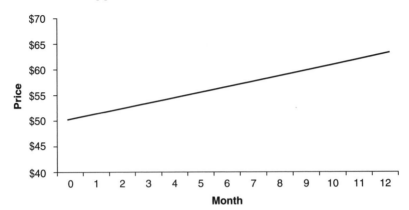

Price Appreciation Model

Estimating the price appreciation transaction cost component is a three-step process:

    I. Develop price forecast.
   II. Apply price forecast to trading horizon.
  III. Estimate costs from price forecast, side, and trading strategy.

Step I: Develop Price Forecast

Fundamental Analysis

Fundamental analysis focuses on company attributes, industry and macro-economic influences, and how in various combinations these forces affect a firm's stock price. While fundamental analysis is concerned mainly with developing long-term price forecasts, it provides a good indication of natural short-term movement when stock prices are over- or undervalued. Readers can find additional information regarding fundamental analysis and company valuation in *Valuation: Measuring and Managing the Value of Companies,* Murrin, Copeland, and Koller (2000); *Damodaran on Valuation,* Damodaran (1994); and *Managing Bank Risk,* Glantz (2002).

Technical Analysis

Technical analysis consists of developing price appreciation forecasts using only historical trading data (e.g., price and volume activity). Technical analysts do not concern themselves with the financial conditions of the company; they believe that all relevant information is already reflected in the data and that future activity can be inferred from the past. Technical analysts believe that historical trading patterns reappear in the future, and studying historical activity provides insight into future performance. Tech-

Table 4.1. Applying Price Forecast to Trading Horizon: Three Techniques

Approach	Notation	Definition	Average	Forecast $P(\Delta t = m)$
Constant	ΔP	$\Delta P = p_i - p_{i-1}$	$\overline{\Delta P} = \dfrac{1}{n}(P_t - P_0)$	$P_0 + \displaystyle\sum_{i=1}^{m} \Delta P_i = P_0 + m\overline{\Delta P}$
Percentage	r_i	$r_i = \dfrac{P_i}{P_{i-1}} - 1$	$\bar{r} = \sqrt[n]{\dfrac{P_t}{P_0}} - 1$	$P_0 \displaystyle\prod_{i=1}^{m}(1 + r_i) = P_0(1 + \bar{r})^m$
Growth	g_i	$g_i = \ln\left(\dfrac{p_i}{p_{i-1}}\right)$	$\bar{g} = \dfrac{1}{n}\ln\left(\dfrac{P_t}{P_0}\right)$	$P_0 \cdot \exp\left\{\displaystyle\sum_{i=1}^{m} g_i\right\} P_0 \exp\{m \cdot \bar{g}\}$

Note: Where N is the number of trading periods in T.

nical analysts rely heavily on bar charts, moving averages, supply-demand imbalances, and indicators such as the Relative Strength Index (RSI) and stockastics to develop expectations about the future. Technical analysis is mainly focused on uncovering short-term price trends; however, many analysts do make use of technical analysis for long-term forecasts of price trends. Readers can find additional information regarding technical analysis in *Technical Analysis from A to Z*, Achelis (1995), *Technical Analysis Explained*, Pring (2002), or *Technical Analysis of the Financial Markets: A Comprehensive Guide to Trading Methods and Applications*, Murphy (1999).

The result from either methodology is an estimated future price P_n or an expected trend. Regardless of the technique employed, accurate price appreciation estimates enhance a trader's ability to plan executions, perfect implementation strategies, and lower overall transaction costs.

Step II: Apply Price Forecast to Trading Horizon

The result of the price forecast is either an expected future price P_n or expected rate of change (trend). Regardless of the result, traders should derive targeted prices for all periods in the trading interval (i.e., apply the price forecast to all trading periods). For example, if the trading intervals are fifteen-minute periods, they need to compute the expected price in each fifteen-minute period. This is accomplished using one of the following three price evolution techniques: constant price change ΔP, percentage return r, or exponential growth rate g (see Table 4.1).

In cases where the price forecast is provided as a future price P_n or expected trend over a period larger than the trading interval (e.g., day, week, month, or year), analysts need to adjust the forecast to the appropriate time of the trading interval (e.g., fifteen-minute or half-hour interval). First, determine the number of trading intervals n over the analysts' price forecast; second, compute the average return per period; and third, compute the price forecast for each trading interval from the average return. For example, if the price forecast provided by the analyst is for a one-year period and we are trading in thirty-minute intervals, we need to determine the number of thirty-minute trading intervals in a trading year by applying unit conversion analysis. Compute average return per period (using the previous definition). Finally, estimate the expected price in each period by applying the forecast described earlier. These steps follow:

1. Unit Conversion Analysis

The first step in developing the trading interval price forecast is to determine the total number of trading periods in the price forecast. This is easily determined by applying a common process from physics called unit conversion analysis. We provide three examples depicting the process.

Example 1. An analyst's price return forecast is 25% over the next year and the trading intervals are a fifteen-minute period (26 periods per trading day). Then the number n of trading periods in the year is found as follows:

$$n = \frac{\text{trading periods}}{1 \text{ year}} = \frac{250 \text{ trading days}}{1 \text{ year}} \cdot \frac{26 \text{ trading periods}}{1 \text{ trading day}}$$

$$= 6,500 \text{ trading periods/year}$$

Example 2. An analyst's price forecast is 50bp over the next two weeks and the trading intervals are thirty-minute periods (13 intervals per trading day). Then the number n of trading periods is found as follows:

$$n = \frac{\text{trading periods}}{2 \text{ weeks}} = \frac{10 \text{ trading days}}{2 \text{ weeks}} \cdot \frac{13 \text{ trading periods}}{1 \text{ trading day}}$$

$$= 130 \text{ trading periods/2 weeks}$$

Example 3. An analyst provides a one-week price forecast. If the trading intervals are five-minute periods, then the number n of trading periods is:

$$n = \frac{\text{trading periods}}{1 \text{ week}} = \frac{5 \text{ trading days}}{1 \text{ week}} \cdot \frac{75 \text{ five-minute periods}}{1 \text{ trading day}}$$

$$= 365 \text{ five-minute periods/1 week}$$

2. Calculate the Average Return per Trading Interval

The next step in developing the price forecast over the trading horizon is to compute the average return per trading period. We determine this directly from the current stock price P_0, the targeted price at some time in the future P_t, and the number of trading periods n in the analysts forecast.

Example 4. A stock currently trading at $50 is targeted to increase to $62.50 after one year. There are 6,500 fifteen-minute trading periods over the forecasted horizon. Find the average return per period using each of the price evolution techniques presented previously. This is as follows:

$$\overline{\Delta P} = \frac{1}{n}(P_t - P_0) = \frac{1}{6500}(\$62.50 - \$50) = \$0.00192/\text{share}$$

$$\overline{r} = \sqrt[n]{\frac{P_t}{P_0}} - 1 = \sqrt[6500]{\frac{62.50}{50.00}} - 1 = 3.433 * 10^{-5} = 0.0034\%$$

$$\overline{g} = \frac{1}{n}\ln\left(\frac{P_t}{P_0}\right) = \frac{1}{6500}\ln\left(\frac{62.50}{50.00}\right) = 3.433 * 10^{-5} = 0.0034\%$$

3. Develop Price Return Forecast Over the Trading Horizon

Once the average return per trading period is estimated, we estimate expected prices in each period using the average return per period.

Example 5. Let us revisit Example 1. A stock currently trading at $50 is forecast to increase 25% over the next year to $62.50. In (1.) we determined the number of fifteen-minute trading periods in the year. In (2.) we developed the average return per period. Now we apply the forecasting technique to estimate expected price per period over a five-day trading horizon. For example, the expected price at the trading period at the end of two days calculates as follows.

The expected price in two days is equal to $n=52$ fifteen-minute trading periods, so determine the forecasted price using each technique as follows:

$$\Delta P: \quad P_t = P_0 + n * \overline{\Delta P} = 50 + 52 * \$0.00192 = \$50.10$$
$$\overline{r}: \quad P_t = P_0 \cdot (1 + \overline{r})^n = 50 \cdot (1 + 0.000034)^{52} = \$50.09$$
$$\overline{g}: \quad P_t = P_0 \cdot \exp(n \cdot g) = 50 \cdot \exp(52 * 3.4433 * 10^{-5}) = \$50.09$$

The forecast over the entire trading horizon can be determined by applying our forecasting technique to each period (see Figure 4.2). As shown in the figure there is minimal difference between the constant price change methodology and the growth rate methodology. This is always the case for short time periods such as trading horizons. Further, there is no distinguishable difference at all between the percentage change and growth rate.

When Is Each Approach Commonly Used?

The linear growth model is commonly used to price fixed income instruments. The returns model is often used to compute interest (e.g. bank accounts, mortgages, etc) and as a point of reference. The growth model is commonly used to estimate volatility and price derivative instruments such as futures and options. The most notable difference between these

Figure 4.2. Comparison of Price Evolution

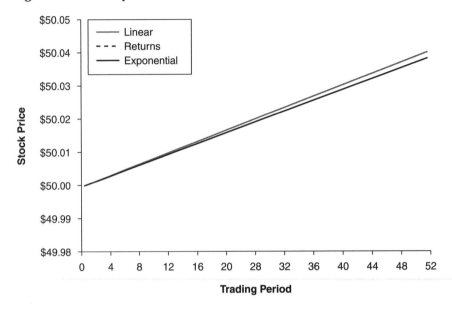

approaches deals with how they incorporate the effect of historical change and return compounding.

Comparison of Forecasting Approaches

Each of the described forecasting approaches begins and ends with identical prices but differs on how they increment prices period to period. For short-term periods, say, fifteen-minute trading intervals, the difference between forecasts will be insignificant since intervals are too short to produce much impact. Figure 4.2 depicts the price evolution from each model for stock XYZ currently trading at $50 expected to increase 10% to $55 in a year (a reasonable expectation). The figure shows that over a two-day period there is relatively little difference between estimates from each forecasting model. In fact, there is virtually zero difference between the returns and growth model. The largest difference between price evolution techniques over the two days is $0.0019 (much less than 1⁄2 cent) or 0.37bp. Finally, the effect of this difference on the cost of the strategy is much less because the strategy executions over multiple periods are usually concentrated at the period's beginning when the divergence is minimal. The total difference this impact will have on the cost of a strategy executing shares in equal amounts over the two days is approximately $0.009 or 0.18 bp, a very negligible difference indeed. This difference is further minimized for strategies executed over a day or less. Hence, for simplicity and ease of calculation we recommend using the linear price appreciation forecast model.

What Causes These Differences?

Differences between these approaches are determined by successive price increments. In the linear growth model, we assume that the price changes by the same quantity each period regardless of the current price. In percentage return and growth models we assume that the price changes by a constant percentage of the current period price. Each approach has advantages and disadvantages.

Returns Model Compared to Growth Model

An investor with $100 is deciding between opening an account between two banks. They each pay an interest rate of 10% per year but they differ on when they credit the interest to the account. Bank 1 pays interest only at the end of the year. Bank 2 pays interest every six months. If the investor deposits the funds with bank 1, the $100 dollar investment will be worth $110 after one year. If the investor deposits the funds with bank 2, the $100 investment will be worth $105 after six months and $110.25 after one year, slightly more than the value from bank 1. The reason for the difference is bank 2 pays and applies interest to the principal every six months. The interest payment in the second six months will include an interest payment on the earned interest during the first six months. Each subsequent interest payment includes a payment for previously accumulated interest. Bank 1 pays 10% interest at the end of every year. Bank 2 pays interest at a rate of 5% but applies the payment at the end of every six months (i.e., twice a year). The value of the investment at the end of each year from each bank works out as follows:

$$F_1 = 100 * (1 + 10\%) = \$110.00$$

$$F_2 = 100 * \left(1 + \frac{10\%}{2}\right)^2 = \$110.25$$

Mathematically, we see this as follows. Let r be the annual interest rate paid by the two banks. If bank 1 pays interest once a year and bank 2 pays interest twice a year (every six months), the total cumulative returns of each bank R_1 and R_2 are:

$$R_1 = (1 + r) = 1 + r$$

$$R_2 = \left(1 + \frac{r}{2}\right)^2 = \left(1 + \frac{r}{2}\right)\left(1 + \frac{r}{2}\right) = 1^2 + 2 * \frac{r}{2} + \left(\frac{r}{2}\right)^2 = 1 + r + \frac{1}{4}r^2$$

$$R_1 > R_2 \text{ since } \left(1 + r + \frac{1}{4}r^2\right) > (1 + r) \text{ when } \frac{1}{4}r^2 > 0.$$

The effect of compounding here increases the return from bank 2 by $1/4\ r^2$. The effect is even more pronounced if interest is credited monthly (12 times per year), weekly (50 times per year), or daily (365 times per year). This is shown as:

$$\text{Monthly: } P_t = P_0 * \left(1 + \frac{r}{12}\right)^{12t}$$

$$\text{Weekly: } P_t = P_0 * \left(1 + \frac{r}{52}\right)^{52t}$$

$$\text{Daily: } P_t = P_0 * \left(1 + \frac{r}{365}\right)^{365t}$$

Relationship Between the Percentage Return and Growth Rate Model

The calculation to determine the value of an investment P_0 at some point in time P_t if the investment pays interest to the account n times per year is:

$$P_t = P_0\left(1 + \frac{r}{n}\right)^{nt}$$

If we consider a scenario where the number of interest payments per year becomes increasingly larger, for example, n=100, 1000, 10000, . . ., ∞, then the equation begins to represent that of continuous compounding, that is, $n \to \infty$ and the returns model approaches that of the growth model. That is:

$$P_t = P_0 \cdot \left[\lim_{n \to \infty}\left(1 + \frac{r}{n}\right)^{nt}\right] = P_0 e^{rt}$$

There is virtually no real difference between the returns change and growth rate methodology when the time interval is a fifteen-minute or thirty-minute period, or any short-term trading horizon. Therefore, we can use the percentage change and growth equation interchangeably.

Step III: Estimate Costs From Price Forecast, Side, and Trading Strategy

After developing the price forecast over the entire trading period, we are ready to estimate the price appreciation transaction cost associated with a specified trading strategy. This is determined as follows.

Let,
$\quad p_0$ = stock price at the beginning of trading
$\quad \Delta p$ = linear price forecast
$\quad p_j$ = forecasted price in period j
$\quad X$ = order size, $X>0$ denotes buy and $X<0$ denotes sell
$\quad x_j$ = number of shares traded in period j
$\quad \mu(x)$ = transaction cost of strategy x attributable to price appreciation

The cost of the strategy is computed following the implementation shortfall methodology as follows:

$$\mu_\$(x) = \sum_{j=1}^{n} x_j p_j - X p_0$$

Since, $p_j = p_0 + j\Delta p$ and $X = {}^n\sum_{j=1} x_j$ we have,

$$\sum_{j=1}^{n} x_j p_j = x_1 p_1 + x_2 p_2 + \dots + x_n p_n$$

$$= x_1(p_0 + 1\Delta p) + x_2(p_0 + 2\Delta p) + \dots + x_n(p_0 + n\Delta p)$$

$$= x_1 p_0 + x_1 1\Delta p + x_2 p_0 + x_2 2\Delta p + \dots + x_n p_0 + x_n n\Delta p$$

$$= x_1 p_0 + x_2 p_0 + \dots + x_n p_0 + x_1 1\Delta p + x_2 2\Delta p + \dots + x_n n\Delta p$$

$$= \left(\sum_{j=1}^{n} x_j\right) p_0 + \sum_{j=1}^{n} x_j j\Delta p$$

$$= X p_0 + \sum_{j=1}^{n} x_j j\Delta p$$

Hence, the price appreciation transaction cost component is estimated as:

$$\mu_\$(x) = \sum_{j=1}^{n} x_j p_j - X p_0 = X p_0 + \sum_{j=1}^{n} x_j j\Delta p - X p_0 = \sum_{j=1}^{n} x_j j\Delta p \qquad (4.1)$$

$$\mu_\$(x) = \sum_{j=1}^{n} x_j j\Delta p$$

The cost is expressed in \$/share or basis points by dividing by the appropriate term as follows:

$$\mu_{\$/share}(x) = \frac{\sum_{j=1}^{n} x_j j\Delta p}{X} \qquad (4.2)$$

$$\mu_{bp}(x) = \frac{\sum_{j=1}^{n} x_j j\Delta p}{X p_0} \qquad (4.3)$$

Price Appreciation Cost for a Trade List

Estimating the price appreciation cost for a trading list of m-stocks is no different than trading a single name or block. The price appreciation cost

Table 4.2.   Execution Strategies and Price Forecast

	1	2	3	4	5
Shares	30,000	30,000	25,000	10,000	5,000
Prices	$20.05	$20.10	$20.15	$20.20	$20.25

component is an additive function because total dollars are additive. This calculation is as follows:

Let the subscripts *ij* represent stock *i* in period *j*. Then the price appreciation cost for a strategy x_k is:

$$\mu_\$(x_k) = \sum_{i=1}^{m} \sum_{j=1}^{n} x_{ij} j \Delta p_i \tag{4.4}$$

Example 6.   A trader is planning to execute a 100,000 shares order over five trading periods. The current stock price is $25 and the price is expected to increase $0.05/share per period. The execution strategy and price forecast are shown in Table 4.2. If trading will commence in the first period compute the associated price appreciation cost of the strategy.

The cost is calculated as follows:

$$\mu_\$(x) = \sum_{j=1}^{n} x_j j \Delta p = 30,000 \cdot 1 \cdot \$0.05 + 30,000 \cdot 2 \cdot \$0.05 + 25,000 \cdot 3 \cdot \$0.05$$

$$+10,000 \cdot 4 \cdot 0.05 + 5,000 \cdot 5 \cdot \$0.05$$

$$= \$11,500$$

Figure 4.3 illustrates the price forecast and the execution strategy for the stock graphically. The figure shows the number of shares expected to execute in each period along with the corresponding price. The dotted line in the figure indicates the average execution price for the strategy.

Example 7.   A trader plans to execute a list of three stocks over five periods (see Table 4.3). The trader expects stock 1 to increase at a rate of

Figure 4.3. Execution Strategy

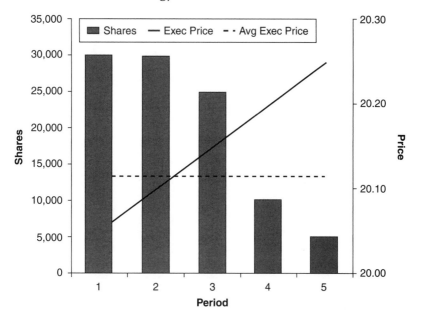

Table 4.3

Prices	Current	1	2	3	4	5
Stock 1	$10	$10.02	$10.04	$10.06	$10.08	$10.10
Stock 2	$25	$25.01	$25.02	$25.03	$25.04	$25.05
Stock 3	$50	$50.05	$50.10	$50.15	$50.20	$50.25

Strategy	Order	1	2	3	4	5
Stock 1	100,000	30,000	30,000	25,000	10,000	5,000
Stock 2	75,000	25,000	25,000	25,000	0	0
Stock 3	50,000	10,000	10,000	10,000	10,000	10,000

$0.02/share, stock 2 at $0.01/share, and stock 3 at $0.05/share. Compute the price appreciation transaction cost for this strategy in dollars.

The cost is calculated as follows:

$$\mu_\$(x_k) = \sum_{i=1}^{m} \sum_{j=1}^{n} x_{ij} j \Delta p_i = \$13,600$$

CHAPTER FIVE

Market Impact

MARKET IMPACT IS MOVEMENT IN the price of the stock caused by a particular trade or order. It is the difference between the stock's price trajectory with the order and what the price trajectory would have been had the order not been submitted to the market. Market impact is a difficult measure ex-post because it requires observations of both scenarios. Unfortunately, there is no way to set up a controlled experiment where one scenario would record the stock's price movement with the order and the other scenario would record price movement without the order. If this were possible, the market impact of an order would simply be the difference between the two scenarios. Because we cannot simultaneously measure these two occurrences, market impact is referred to as the Heisenberg Uncertainty Principle of finance (a reference to physicists' inability to simultaneously measure a particle's position and velocity at a point in time). This is depicted in figure 5.1.

Because of this limitation, market participants often state market impact as the difference between the stock price at the beginning of trading and the order's average execution price. However, this calculation misses the mark since it measures the cumulative effect of all market orders, not just a particular order. The measurement of market impact as the difference in execution price and decision price is actually the order's total trading cost. This is because it includes the cumulative market impact of all trades, the stock's natural price movement, and volatility.

Market impact always represents a cost to investors and produces a less favorable trading environment, causing investors to pay premiums to complete buy orders and provide discounts to complete sell orders. This

Figure 5.1. Market Impact

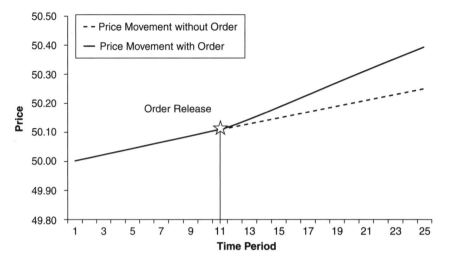

sweetener results in investors buying higher and selling lower. Market impact can be thought of as the incentive that must be provided to attract additional liquidity into the marketplace so orders can be completed in a reasonable time. Without the incentive, investors would be required to wait for additional order flow to arrive naturally. However, new liquidity may arrive at a more unfavorable price, a risky proposition. Thus, this "sweetener" can also be thought of as an "economic bribe" investors offer to persuade other market participants to transact at a time and price that they otherwise would not.

There is no precise way of determining how a stock price evolves in the market if the order had not been released. However, market impact does indeed cause a higher transaction cost. This is even true in cases where the measured trading cost (difference between execution price and strike price) indicates a realized savings to investors, that is, an execution at a more favorable price than the price at the beginning of trading.

Comparison of Market Impact and Trading Cost

Figure 5.2 illustrates the trading cost and market impact of investors purchasing stock in a rising market by depicting the stock's price trajectory with and without the order. It shows how prices deviate once the order is released to the market. Notice the trajectory of the price with the buy order is higher than the stock price trajectory without the buy order. Here, the buy order caused the stock price to increase more rapidly than it would have without the order. In this example, the stock price at the time the order was released

Figure 5.2. Market Impact Buying in a Rising Market

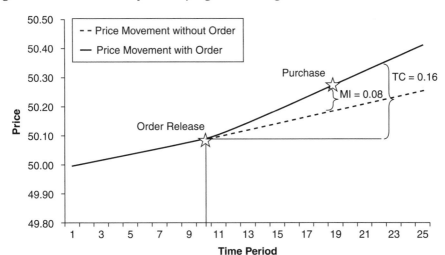

was $50.10 and the actual execution price $50.26. The trading cost of this execution, which is the difference between the execution price and the price at the time the order was released, is $0.16 ($50.26–$50.10=$0.16) or approximately 32bp. The market impact, on the other hand, is the difference in the price between the two trajectories at the time of the trade. In this case, it is $0.08 ($50.26–$50.18=$0.08) or approximately 16bp because the stock price would only have been $50.18 had the order not been submitted.

$$MI(bp) = \frac{50.26 - 50.18}{50.18} \cdot 10^4 = 16bp$$

$$TC(bp) = \frac{50.26 - 50.10}{50.10} \cdot 10^4 = 32bp$$

Figure 5.3 illustrates the trading cost and market impact for an investor buying a stock in a falling market by depicting the price trajectories of the path both with and without the order. It reveals that prices begin to deviate once the order is released to the market. Notice that the trajectory of the price with the buy order is again higher than the price trajectory without the order even though both trajectories slope downwards. The consequence of the buy order prevented the stock price from falling as rapidly as it would without the order. But the effect of the buy order caused the price to be higher than if the order was not entered into the market. In this example, the price of the stock at the time the order was released was $49.80 and the actual execution price $49.70. Therefore, the trading cost of this execution is a savings of $0.10 ($49.70–$49.80=$–0.10). But the market

Figure 5.3. Market Impact Buying in a Falling Market

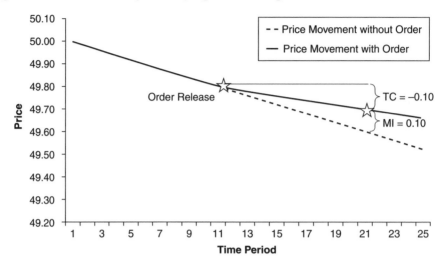

impact cost, on the other hand, the difference in the two price trajectories, is $+0.10 ($49.70–$49.60=$0.10).

$$MI(bp) = \frac{49.70 - 49.60}{49.60} \cdot 10^4 = 20bp$$

$$TC(bp) = \frac{49.70 - 49.80}{49.80} \cdot 10^4 = 20bp$$

The same result, albeit in the opposite direction, occurs with sell orders: Selling pressure will push the stock price lower without the order causing investors to sell at less favorable prices. As we have described in these examples, market impact always has a negative effect on implementation regardless of price or market movement.

What Causes Market Impact?

Market impact cost stems from two primary reasons: liquidity demand and information leakage. The liquidity demand of the order causes an imbalance in the supply-demand equilibrium price and requires investors to pay a premium to attract additional liquidity to execute the order. Information leakage communicates to the market information regarding the investment and trading intentions of investors making the market prices more expensive.

Market impact is caused by:
  ▲ Supply-demand imbalance (liquidity needs)
  ▲ Information leakage

Figure 5.4. Supply–Demand Equilibrium

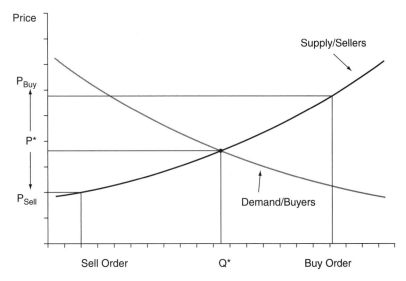

Supply-Demand Imbalance

To the extent that the efficient market hypothesis holds true (or at least close to true), markets continuously adjust prices to ensure that buying demand equals selling demand. Thus, if markets are in an equilibrium state, any additional order causes an imbalance in the supply-demand equilibrium of the stock. As investors seek to buy shares, they are required to raise their price to attract additional sellers into the market. As they seek to sell shares, they are required to lower their price to attract additional buyers into the market. Buy and sell orders are associated with an increase/decrease in price; both cases produce higher costs to investors. This cost is dependent upon the size of the order or imbalance; the price elasticity of the stock; and the side of the order, as it is not guaranteed that a buy order will have the same costs as sell orders for the same number of shares. The market impact cost associated with an imbalance is described economically using the traditional supply-demand curve (see Figure 5.4). This graph shows how prices react to changing supply and demand for a good or service. Thus, every time investors enter an order they either demand shares from or supply shares to the market. Nevertheless, investors' trading intentions are actually liquidity demanders. That is, investors either demand stock in exchange for cash or demand cash in exchange for stock. In either scenario, they are demanding counterparties to enter the market to take the opposite side of their transaction. Therefore, they must pay a premium to attract the opposite side.

Liquidity Demander

The market impact cost for a liquidity demander can be observed using a variation of the supply-demand equilibrium curve (see Figure 5.5). Here, we

Figure 5.5. Liqidity Demand

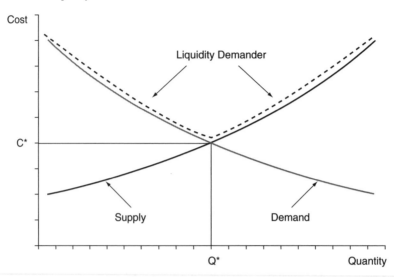

show the cost associated with any order (buying or selling) as the upper envelope in the diagram. As investors require additional stock, they increase the price to attract additional sellers. As investors wish to sell more shares, they lower their price to attract additional buyers. In either scenario, investors incur a cost.

Order Book

Market impact cost can also be explained from the immediacy needs of investors. Very often investors have orders that are larger than the quantity of shares available at the best market quote. Thus, to achieve immediate execution it is often necessary to "eat into" the limit order book making each successive transaction more expensive. For example, suppose an investor with a 4,000 share buy order requires immediate execution in a stock with the limit order book shown in Figure 5.6. Here the best bid and ask are $49.90 and $50.10 respectively. However, there are only 500 shares at the best quotes. Immediate execution of the entire order thus requires the investor to transact at the next higher prices. That is, purchase of 500 shares at $50.10, 1,000 shares at $50.20, 500 shares at $50.30, 1,800 shares at $50.40, and the final 1,200 shares at $50.50. The average execution price of this transaction is $50.305 resulting in a market impact cost of $0.305 ($50.305–$50=$0.305). Investors seeking immediacy often find it useful to analyze the execution using the cumulative limit order book Figure 5.7. This chart depicts the cost (y-axis) one would incur by executing the number of shares on the x-axis. Since market price is defined to be the midpoint of the bid-ask spread, the cost of shares executed on the best bid or ask is always equal to one-half of the spread. The cumulative limit order book is a good estimate of the cost of immediacy as long as the order is less than

Figure 5.6. Order Book

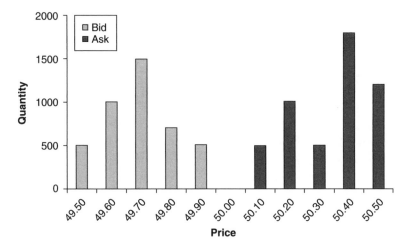

Figure 5.7. Cumulative Order Book

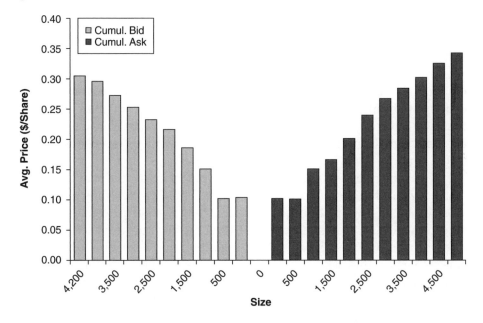

the cumulative amount of shares listed. However, in many situations the size of the order is even larger than the total quantity of shares entered in the limit order book, thus requiring investors to pay an even higher premium if they require immediate execution of their order.

Information Leakage

Every time an order is released to market, it conveys information regarding the investment and trading intention of investors resulting in a more costly execution. The investment information leakage of orders pertains to the quantity and quality of information communicated to the market regarding investors' current and future expectations of the stock price. The belief is that investors are making their buy/sell decisions on proprietary derived information that is not readily available to the market. This typically signals that the stock is under- or overvalued. However, as soon as the market learns this information and its incorrect valuation of the stock it quickly adjusts its price to more fairly reflect the true market value. The better able investors are at disguising the true investment intention, the lower the market impact cost

However, investors do not usually base investment decisions on proprietary information or a belief of a market mispricing. These liquidity investors, for example, indexers, are likely to be required to hold specified quantities of certain stocks. These investors do not convey investment information to the market. However, markets have a difficult time deciphering between liquidity traders and informed traders. Thus, all orders are perceived at least in part as information-driven investment decisions subsequently causing the market to adjust its prices, which makes the transaction more expensive.

Information leakage regarding the trading intentions of investors also causes a higher trading cost. Astute participants who learn or infer the names of the stocks in the trade list can take advantage of the investment research by mimicking the fund's buying and/or selling behavior and achieve a free-rider on the research efforts. They can buy/sell the undervalued/overvalued security without expending any investment resource of their own. This creates an even more excessive buying or selling pressure in the stock causing the prices to move away quicker, which often negates the value of uncovering the superior investment opportunity.

Investor orders also communicate information to the market regarding the size and urgency needs of investors. Thus, participants who would normally be willing to transact at the current market prices may require managers to pay a higher premium to complete the transaction if they believe investors are required to implement the decision. Additionally, market participants who may not have otherwise been interested in the stock may quickly accumulate a position in the stock with intentions to flip the shares at a later point in time to the fund at a higher cost.[1]

Figure 5.8 illustrates the market's reaction to a buy order. Once the market believes that it has undervalued a stock, it quickly adjusts its price to make the stock more expensive to buy, thus making the stock more

---

1. Transacting in this fashion is referred to as front-running an order and is a highly speculative practice. For example, if a participant believes a fund is planning to buy a large quantity of stock the participant may purchase shares in the stock before the fund has completed its order with the intention of selling the shares into the market at a later point in time hoping the price will move higher due to the market impact of the imbalance. A similar but opposite situation would occur if the participant believes that the fund has a large sell position.

Figure 5.8. Information Leakage Buy Order

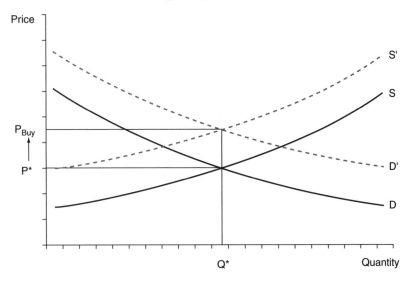

Figure 5.9. Information Leakage Sell Order

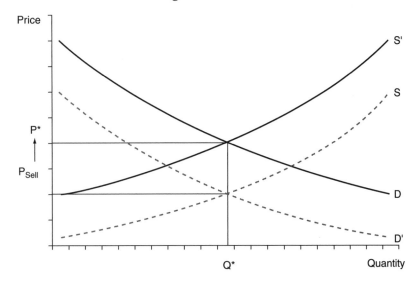

fairly valued. Figure 5.9 illustrates this phenomenon for a sell order. Once the market believes that it has overvalued a stock, it lowers its price. In effect, the market buys the stock from investors at a lower price.

Total Market Impact Cost

The total market impact cost of an order can be rationalized as a temporary cost due to the liquidity demand causing an imbalance in the market

Figure 5.10.   Total Market Impact Cost Liquidity Demander

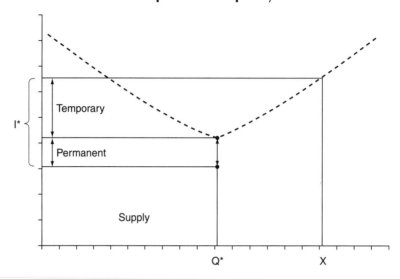

supply-demand equilibrium plus a permanent cost due to the market's belief of the true market price. Figure 5.10 is an illustration of the total market impact cost I* due to an order of X shares. Notice that I* consists of two components: the permanent impact cost resulting from the market's reevaluation of the true stock price and the temporary market impact cost resulting from the liquidity demand and imbalance caused in the supply-demand equilibrium. Investors will always incur a market impact cost due to liquidity demands and information leakage.

Common Misconceptions Surrounding Market Impact and Trading Costs

Some industry professionals refer to market impact as the difference between the average execution price of an order and the price of the stock at the beginning of trading. This is not entirely correct. As we discussed earlier, this notion only holds in an environment with distinctly no natural price appreciation, no market movement, and without any other orders released to the market. What some market professionals refer to as market impact is actually a trading cost. It is naïve to view prices and quotes as static, particularly if an order has not been released to the market. There are numerous factors that affect price: appreciation, volatility, cumulative impact of other investors, news, information, and so on.

Another incorrect notion is that market impact is equal to the difference between an order's average transaction price and some benchmark price such as the open, close, VWAP, average of the open, high, low and close, and so on. This is an incorrect market impact statistic. These investors are attempting to derive a measure of trading performance; they are interested in determining how well their trader or broker implemented the investment decision. It is simply incorrect to measure the trading cost as the difference between the execution price of the order and some benchmark price. In Chapter 13, Post Trade Analysis, we discuss techniques to distinguish between trading cost and trading performance.

Market Impact: A Mathematical Description

Market impact is the phenomenon that causes a stock's price trajectory to deviate from its naturally intended price path. Market impact is considered somewhat of an amorphous concept because it cannot be measured or observed in exactness. This concept can be explained in mathematical terms as follows:

> Let $g(x)$ be the price evolution of the stock without the order
> Let $f(x)$ be the price evolution of the stock with the order

Then market impact can be explained as the disturbance κ in stock price that causes $f(x)$ to deviate from $g(x)$ at the time that the order was released to the market.[2] That is:

$$\kappa(t) = f(t) - g(t)$$

What Causes This Displacement?

Each time an order is released it conveys information. In the majority of cases, this information only pertains to the immediacy and liquidity demands of investors, causing an imbalance in supply and demand. However, other times the information results in a changed belief of a stock's intrinsic value. If information conveyed to the market pertains only to the immediacy and liquidity demands of investors, the price disturbance will be short lived. Nevertheless, when information pertains to a change in the future value of the stock or economy, then this disturbance will persist for a prolonged period, possibly indefinitely. These two types of price disturbance are referred to as temporary and permanent market impact. As the names imply, temporary market impact is the short-lived disturbance in the price trajectory of the security, and permanent market impact is a very prolonged or permanent disturbance in the price trajectory of the stock.

---

2. The notation of κ to represent market impact was suggested by Agustin Leon (1999). It is based on the notation used in engineering and physics to describe the displacement of a system, which is the exact phenomena we are observing with market impact.

Temporary Market Impact

Temporary market impact occurs whenever an order is released to the market but does not provide fundamental news or information that alters the market's long-term outlook or current valuation. Market impact is always temporary unless the order provides information or reason for a price adjustment (e.g., changing future price targets). Immediacy requirements and liquidity demands cause a temporary market impact effect. In these instances, trades cause temporary increases in price for buy orders and temporary decreases in price for sell orders subsequently followed by a price reversion back to the initial price trajectory. The question remaining deals with the extent (time) the price disturbance will last. This is difficult to determine at the micro-level and will vary depending on the market's belief regarding size of investor orders.

The most common description of temporary market impact is that of the market impact bubble (see Figure 5.11). Here an investor's order triggers a price increase causing the investor to buy at a higher price—then immediately followed by a price decline after execution. The investor purchased the stock at the highest price, on top of the bubble.

Mathematically, temporary market impact is explained as a short-lived disturbance in price at the time the order was released to the market followed by a reversion back to the original intended trajectory. The time for full convergence lasts for a period of time t. The exact period is most affected by the information leakage of the order that allows the market to infer expectations about the size of the order and the trading demands of investors.

Figure 5.11. Market Impact Bubble

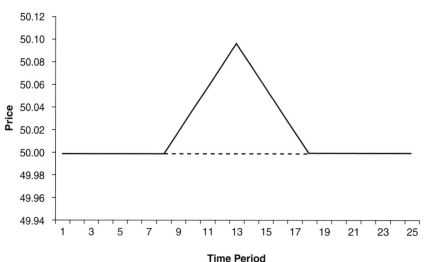

Thus, for buy orders the price trajectory with the order $f(x)$ will be greater than the price trajectory without the order $g(x)$ for a period of time t followed by a convergence of the two price trajectories:

$$f(x) = \begin{cases} = g(x) & \text{for } x < s \\ > g(x) & s \le x \le t \\ = g(x) & x > t \end{cases}$$

Figure 5.12 depicts the effect of temporary market impact. This example illustrates how a buy order can cause the price trajectory to deviate from its normal path to a higher state for a temporary period of time. Notice the trajectory reverts to its normal course, but the time associated with the deviation is unknown (at best extremely difficult to measure). The time it takes for the trajectory to return to its original intended path has been described as the half-life or half-trade of market impact (Almgren & Chriss 1997). Defined as the period required for one-half of the market impact to dissipate, it is entirely dependent upon the information content of the trade and varies manager to manager, fund to fund, and under different market conditions.

For example, a passive manager executing large orders over the course of days effects a longer lasting temporary market impact than an aggressive manager preferring immediacy and who trades aggressively over a short period. This occurs even if these investors execute the exact same order in the exact same fashion; the market is likely to expect the passive manager may desire stock not yet released to the market. Therefore, potential sellers are less willing to transact at current market prices with hopes that the passive manager will transact at even higher prices. Much of the information conveyed to the market results from the name of the

Figure 5.12. Temporary Market Impact

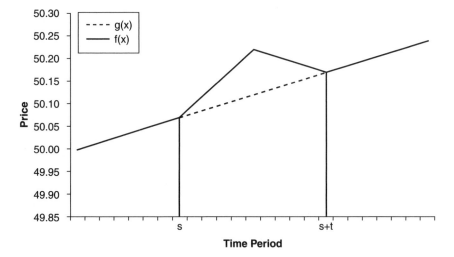

investor. Anonymous trading practices greatly reduce temporary market impact cost.

Permanent Market Impact

Permanent market impact is the change in price caused by an order that leads the market to believe that future prices will be different than originally expected or there is a change in the stock's intrinsic value. This in turn brings about a quick price adjustment causing a jump or drop in price. It occurs when an order contains information that alters the market's belief of a firm's long-term growth potential. This signals that the stock is incorrectly priced in the market and an arbitrage opportunity exists. Thus, participants quickly adjust their prices to the new perceived fair value. This naturally affects the price forecast and results in a new price appreciation path.

A manager begins accumulating or selling off a position in a stock. Assume this manager has repeatedly anticipated results realizing huge gains. When the market eyes this particular manager buying or selling stock, the market reassesses its valuation. Other participants who ordinarily would not be interested in the stock transact on the same side as our manager expecting to realize some of the large gains. Investors who otherwise would have transacted at the current market prices quickly realize that market prices do not properly reflect "intrinsic" value and demand higher selling prices or lower buying prices. This causes the price trajectory to move on a different path resulting in a permanent shift in the natural price appreciation of the stock. In other words, a disturbance in the price trajectory that never reverts back to the normal trend—a permanent market impact effect.

Permanent market impact may also occur if the relative performance of the stock and/or its attractiveness as an investment vehicle compared to other alternative investment opportunities, for example, commodities or bonds, is changed. Thus, it is possible for investors to cause permanent market impact in a stock without even transacting. For example, suppose a well-known investor, Mr. Big, begins shifting assets from stock to bonds. Judging from past experience Mr. Big always seems to have a jump on the rest of the market. This implies that the future risk-reward profile for bonds versus stocks has improved making stocks less attractive without any change in company fundamentals. Information conveyed to the market from Mr. Big's action caused permanent market impact. This could also arise if Mr. Big typically invested in company A over company B and achieved stellar returns. But suddenly Mr. Big accumulates stock in company B over company A, signaling that B is a better investment than A, or that A and B are incorrectly valued in the market. The market quickly adjusts itself if it believes its prices are incorrect.

Figure 5.13. Permanent Market Impact

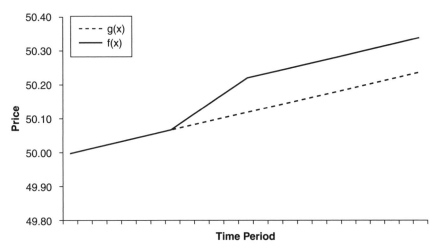

Mathematically, permanent market impact is defined as a disturbance in the price of the stock such that the price trajectory with the order $f(x)$ will always be greater than the intended trajectory without the order $g(x)$ after the time of the order release t. There will not be any mean reversion back to the original natural trend. That is:

$$f(x)>g(x) \text{ for all } x>t$$

Figure 5.13 provides an illustration of the effect of permanent market impact on the price trajectory of a security. Notice how the trajectory deviates from its original intended course after release of the order to the market. The trajectory then continues on a different path where it is expected to end up at the revised future price point. The trajectory shown in this graphic becomes parallel to the original path. However, this is not always the case. The new trajectory can vary from the original one; for example, it may increase at a greater rate. Permanent market impact effect will not allow the path of $f(x)$ to converge back to $g(x)$. They will always be different.

Temporary Disguised as Permanent

Temporary market impact occurs much more frequently than permanent market impact, and to a much greater magnitude. Further, the cost associated with a temporary market impact effect is much greater than the cost associated with a permanent market impact effect. Quite often, temporary market impact appears to investors as a permanent market impact effect.

Figure 5.14.   Long-lived Temporary Market Impact Effect

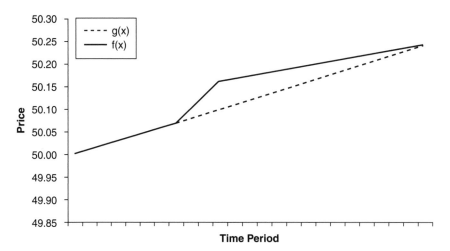

This occurs whenever the information conveyed to the market does not change the market's assessment of company fundamentals or current market valuation of the stock but does convey that there is a large order that will be executed over a long period. In these instances, market participants know there is an investor implementing an investment decision over a longer time horizon thus causing an imbalance in the buying or selling pressure and that it will persist over a long period of time. Thus, liquidity suppliers adjust their prices upwards for buys and downwards for sells because they know the investor is required to implement the investment decision. Liquidity suppliers hold the prices artificially high for buy orders and artificially low for sell orders until the investor's order is fully implemented. The effect of the price trajectory for a long-lived temporary market impact is depicted in Figure 5.14. We see a sharp change in price followed by a new price trajectory. The stock does not revert to its original path until a sufficient length of time has passed.

Market Impact versus Total Price Change

When we discuss price impact, two price issues apply: market impact and total price movement. We distinguish these terms as follows. *Market impact* is the difference between the average execution price of the order and the equilibrium price of the stock without the order. In economic terms, we think of market impact κ as the average cost of the order. *Price movement*, on the other hand, is the total difference in the market price of the stock and the equilibrium price of the stock without the order. In economic terms, the total price movement P_t can be thought of as the marginal price of the next

Figure 5.15. Comparison of Average Price to Total Price Change

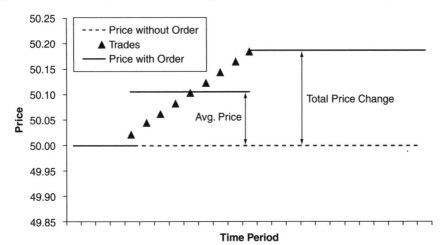

share traded in the market. This point is illustrated in Figure 5.15. The figure shows a price trajectory along with a series of transactions. Here the average execution price is less than the marginal price at the end of trading (total price change). Depending upon liquidity demands (of investors) it is possible for the marginal price to be more than, equal to, or less than the average price of an order. However, in the majority of cases the marginal price will be higher than the average price for buys and lower than the average price for sells.

The average market impact cost is important as it enables investors to gain an understanding of the total cost consequence of orders and helps to develop effective trading strategies. The marginal price impact is an important realization as well. The marginal price helps investors evaluate the expected cost of the next shares traded in the market. For example, a manager is typically interested in determining the average cost of an order and the volume of shares that are purchased or sold within a specified price range. While the average market impact is important in informing a manager how much the order will cost, the marginal price impact provides information pertaining to the number of shares that can be purchased within a specified price. Often, traders and managers work together to determine the optimal quantity of shares that can be transacted within a price range, serving as a means of reducing the opportunity cost of orders. For example, a manager can reduce the order size so that all shares can be executed better than the specified price or increase the order size so more shares are executed. It is essential to distinguish between average and marginal price impact to develop an implementation strategy that meets fund objectives—that is, a best execution strategy.

The marginal price at time t is the expected price of the next share transacted. This may not be fair representation of the true market price because the marginal price will consist of permanent and temporary market impact, as well as the natural price movement. Temporary market impact cost refers to the cost of liquidity and it will dissipate. Permanent market impact refers to the shift in the perceived fair value and will persist. Permanent market impact together with price appreciation are important concepts when we estimate opportunity cost.

Similarities Between Investor Market Impact and Dealer Pricing Schemes

To gain insight into the market impact function let us examine its closely related cousin—the dealer function. Dealers are in business to earn a trading profit through the matching of buy and sell orders—that is, buying at the lower price and selling at the higher price. This process requires dealers to accumulate inventory of stock, either long or short, while waiting for offsetting orders to arrive. This holding period subjects dealers to potential adverse price movement (i.e., risk) waiting for those orders to arrive. Thus, they specify their spreads to protect themselves from potential adverse price movement. The more risky the stock the higher the potential for adverse price movement, thus, the higher the spread cost.

Luckily for investors, dealers do not have complete control over prices; they are set by market forces (e.g., competitive process through multiple dealers, through interaction with investor limit orders, as well as systematic market movement). If dealers charge excessive spreads, investors refrain from transacting through them, but if spreads are too low, losses may occur. Therefore, it is essential for dealers to maintain spreads to balance the trade-off between profitability and total price risk. As it turns out, the factors that attribute most to dealer pricing practices play similar roles in investor market impact cost. Knowledge learned on the dealer side provides important insight into development of market impact models.

The factors most relevant to dealers in determining the appropriate spread include current inventory levels, price volatility, the expected arrival rate of orders, and information. For investors, the corresponding factors are order size, price volatility, trading style, and dissemination of information. The associated cost of information leakage is not limited to investors; it also exists for dealers. For example, if a dealer transacts with a party who knows more about the short-term price movement of the stock, they will incur a loss. Moreover, if not a loss, they will definitely experience a decrease or lower profit level. Whenever dealers believe they are transacting with a more-informed trader, they factor in a premium for

Table 5-1.   Dealer Spreads Versus Investor Market Impact

Factor	Dealer Spreads	Investor Market Impact
Inventory Level/Order Size	Positive ↑	Positive ↑
Price Volatility	Positive ↑	Positive ↑
Arrival Rate/Trading Style	Negative ↓	Positive ↑
Information Content	Positive ↑	Positive ↑

loss protection. In addition, the more informed they believe investors, the more they will charge. Dealers want to protect themselves from being disadvantaged by engaging in a transaction with informed traders. Similarly, if dealers perceive a large order that has not yet been released to the market, they are likely to increase their spreads to protect against adverse price movement. Furthermore, depending on their belief of the urgency of the investor to execute the order they will adjust their quotes to take best advantage of the situation. The similarities between dealer spreads and market impact cost are summarized in Table 5.1. Readers interested in learning more about the dealer function are referred to O'Hara (1995) or Schualtz (1991).

In Chapter 8, The Holy Grail of Market Impact, we introduce an approach to estimate market impact.

CHAPTER SIX

Timing Risk

TIMING RISK REPRESENTS UNCERTAINTY SURROUNDING the forecasted trading cost estimate for a specified trading strategy. It consists of price volatility and fluctuations in market volume.[1] First, during implementation of a trade list, price generally moves due to market swings, changing economic outlook, news announcements, information, paradigm shift, random noise, and so on. As a result, the prevailing price is higher or lower than expected. This is referred to as the price volatility or price risk of the order. Second, uncertainty surrounds market volumes and intraday trading patterns. Market activity is often higher or lower than anticipated. When investors transact with higher levels of market volume their orders generally cause a lesser degree of imbalance, hence less market impact. When investors transact with lower levels of market volume their orders generally cause a higher degree of imbalance hence a lower amount of market impact. The uncertainty in transaction cost due to unknown market volumes is referred to as the liquidity risk of the order. Finally, unanticipated buying and selling pressure from other market participants also affects transaction costs. However, to the extent that this price movement is captured in the price volatility expression it does not need to be incorporated as its own component.

1. In actuality, the complete timing risk term consists of price volatility, liquidity risk (i.e., uncertainties in market volumes), and estimation error surrounding the market impact parameter term. However, the incorporation of the estimation error of the market impact parameters into the timing risk expression (to be introduced in Ch. 8) is beyond the scope of this introductory book.

We define:

> Timing risk is the associated uncertainty in trading cost estimates due to price volatility and liquidity risk. Price volatility affects the price appreciation estimate and liquidity risk affects the market impact estimate.

Many industry professionals associate a transaction's timing risk solely with price risk. However, this is not the full story. Transaction cost analysis requires a "total uncertainty" focus surrounding trading cost estimates, not solely a security's potential price fluctuations. It is naïve to discount the effect of market conditions. In the short term, an execution's total timing risk of a trade schedule $\Re(x_k)$ will be greater than the price volatility over the trading period $\sigma(x_k)$ making the transaction cost more uncertain than that associated with price movement. That is:

$$\Re(x_k) > \sigma(x_k)$$

The inclusion of liquidity risk with price volatility introduces an increased layer of complexity into the computation process. For example, consider the expected trading cost equation developed in Chapter 8:

$$\phi_\$(x) = \sum_j \left(x_j j \Delta p + \frac{0.95 x_j^2 I}{X(x_j + 0.5 v_j)} \right) + 0.05 I$$

where,

I_i = instantaneous market impact cost for stock i in period j.
Δp_i = expected per period price trend for stock i
X_i = order size
x_{ij} = shares of stock i to trade in period j
v_{ij} = expected volume for stock i in period j

and,

$x_{ij} > 0$ indicates a buy order
$x_{ij} < 0$ indicates a sell order

In this formulation of the transaction cost estimate there is uncertainty surrounding the exact values of Δp_i, v_{ij}, and I_i. Thus, the uncertainty needs to incorporate the standard error of all associated variables.

Computing Timing Risk

The uncertainty of the trading cost estimate is computed as the standard deviation of the trading cost equation $\phi(x_k)$ and is calculated as follows:

$$\Re(\phi) = \sqrt{E\big[(\phi - E[\phi])^2\big]}$$

A simplified procedure for estimating the uncertainty of the trading cost estimate is to assume that volume and price movement is independent. However, this assumption is an oversimplification of reality. First, it is true that there is a negligible degree of correlation between price change and market volume, that is:

$$\rho(\Delta p, v) \cong 0$$

for,

Δp = close-to-close price change. $\Delta p > 0$ indicates an increase in price and $\Delta p < 0$ indicates a decrease in price
v = market volume on the day

But the absolute value of price change and market volume is indeed correlated. That is:

$$\rho(|\Delta p|, v) > 0$$

or alternatively written as:

$$\rho(\Delta p^2, v^2) > 0$$

True independence of random variables requires zero correlation of all moments, that is,

$$\rho(\Delta p^\kappa, v^\kappa) > 0$$

for all κ. Or more simply put,

$$f(\Delta p, v) = g(\Delta p) \cdot h(v)$$

where,

$f(\Delta p, v)$ is joint pdf of price change and volume
$g(\Delta p)$ is pdf of price change
$h(v)$ is pdf of volume

This means that while high volume days are associated with high price movement and low volume days are associated with low price movement, we cannot make any assessment of the direction of price movement on the amount of volume. That is, if the day is a high volume day, it is likely that there will be a large price movement but the presence of high volume does not give any indication of the direction of price movement. Our simplification allows us to compute the risk of each expression separately then combine to obtain the timing risk of the strategy. This is as follows:

$$\Re(\phi) = \sqrt{\underbrace{\sigma^2(\mu(x_k))}_{Price\ Volatility} + \underbrace{\sigma^2(\kappa(x_k))}_{Liquidity\ Risk}} \tag{6.1}$$

In this chapter we provide a thorough investigation into the derivation of volatility and the covariance matrix C as well as provide some insight into calculation of the liquidity risk expression.

Price Volatility

Price Volatility of Single Stock

The computation of the price risk associated with a specified trading strategy is equivalent to computing the risk of a one-stock position that changes from one period to the next, regardless if the position consists of a single stock or trade list. If r is the number of shares held in the position and σ^2 is the variance of the stock expressed in \$/share, the total dollar risk $\sigma(x)$ of the position held over n-periods is computed as follows:

$$\sigma^2(n - periods) = \underbrace{r^2\sigma^2 + r^2\sigma^2 + \ldots + r^2\sigma^2}_{n-times} = \sum_{j=1}^{n} r^2\sigma^2 = nr^2\sigma^2$$

Hence,

$$\sigma(r) = \sqrt{n} \cdot r\sigma$$

Taking n to be time periods we see that volatility scales with time. Now suppose the number of shares r_j in the portfolio changes from one period to the next due to additional cash investments and/or redemptions. If r_j represents the number of shares held in the portfolio in period j, the total dollar risk of the portfolio held over the n-periods is computed as follows:

$$\sigma^2(r) = r_1^2\sigma^2 + r_2^2\sigma^2 + \ldots + r_n^2\sigma^2 = \sum_{j=1}^{n} r_j^2\sigma^2 \tag{6.2}$$

and the risk is,

$$\sigma(r) = \sqrt{\sum_{j=1}^{n} r_j^2 \sigma^2}$$

Price Risk of a Strategy for a Single Stock

The total dollar risk associated with a specified trade schedule x is computed according to Equation 6.2 by representing the trade schedule as a changing position over time. Each position r_j in period j is computed as the number of unexecuted shares at the beginning of the period and x_j represents the number of shares traded in period j. This is as follows:

$$r_j = \sum_{k=j}^{n} x_k$$

Thus, if σ^2 is the per period variance expressed in $/share, the price risk of the strategy x is computed in terms of the residuals following Equation 6.2 as follows:

$$\sigma^2(x) = r_1^2 \sigma^2 + r_2^2 \sigma^2 + \Lambda + r_n^2 \sigma^2 = \sum_{j=1}^{n} r_j^2 \sigma^2$$

$$\sigma(x) = \sqrt{\sum_{j=1}^{n} r_j^2 \sigma^2}$$

Example 1. A trader with a specified trading strategy x for an order $X = 10,000$ executes 5,000 shares in the first period, 2,500 shares in the second period, and 2,500 shares in the third period. If the per period stock volatility is $\sigma = \$0.05/$share, compute the price risk of the trading strategy.

From the specified trading strategy we have:

$$x^t = (5,000 \ 2,500 \ 2,500)$$
$$r^t = (10,000 \ 5,000 \ 2,500)$$

Therefore, the risk of the strategy works out to:

$$\sigma^2(x) = 10,000^2 \cdot 0.05^2 + 5,000^2 \cdot 0.05^2 + 2,500^2 \cdot 0.05^2 = \$328,125$$

$$\sigma(x) = \sqrt{\$328,125} = \$572$$

Price Risk of a Trade List

The computation approach described previously can extend to a portfolio of stock. For example, if r represents a vector of stock positions where r_i is the number of shares held in the ith stock and C is the per-period covariance matrix expressed in \$/share, the total dollar risk of the portfolio $\sigma_p(r)$ is:

$$\sigma_p(r) = \sqrt{r^T C r}$$

The risk of this portfolio held over n periods is:

$$\sigma_p^2(r) = \underbrace{r^T C r + r^T C r + \ldots r^T C r}_{n-times} = \sum_{j=1}^{n} r^T C r = n \cdot r^T C r$$

$$\sigma_p(r) = \sqrt{n \cdot r^T C r}$$

Now suppose that the number of shares held in each stock changes from period to period. Let r_k represent the column vector such that r_{ik} represents the number of shares of stock i in period k. That is:

$$r_k = \begin{pmatrix} r_{1k} \\ r_{2k} \\ \vdots \\ r_{mk} \end{pmatrix}$$

Then the total dollar variance of the changing portfolio $\sigma_p(r)$ over n periods is:

$$\sigma_p^2(r) = r_1^T C r_1 + r_2^T C r_2 + \cdots + r_n^T C r_n = \sum_{j=1}^{n} r_j^T C r_j$$

Price Risk of a Trade Strategy

The associated price risk of a trade schedule for a list of stock is derived similarly to the risk of a changing portfolio. Suppose that a trader is implementing an investment decision following a specified trade strategy. Let x_k be a column vector where x_{ik} represents the number of shares of stock i to trade in period k, that is,

$$x_k = \begin{pmatrix} x_{1k} \\ x_{2k} \\ \vdots \\ x_{mk} \end{pmatrix}$$

Then the price risk of the strategy is computed in terms of the residual shares in the trade list.

Let, r_k be the column vector of residual shares where r_{ik} denotes the number of unexecuted shares of stock i in period j and

$$r_{ik} = \sum_{j=k}^{n} x_{ij}$$

Then, the total dollar risk $\sigma(x_k)$ associated with the specified trading strategy x_k is found as follows:

$$\sigma^2(x_k) = r_1^T Cr_1 + r_2^T Cr_2 + \cdots + r_n^T Cr_n = \sum_{j=1}^{n} r_j^T Cr_j$$

$$\sigma(x_k) = \sqrt{\sum_{j=1}^{n} r_j^T Cr_j}$$

We now denote the risk of a trade schedule x_k as:

$$\Re(x_k) = \sqrt{r_j^t Cr_j} \qquad (6.3)$$

Example 2. A manager has instructed his trader to execute order X where $X^t = (10,000, 5,000, -15,000)$, where the specified trading strategy x_k and corresponding covariance matrix C are defined as follows:

$$x_k = \begin{pmatrix} 5,000 & 2,500 & 2,500 \\ 5,000 & 0 & 0 \\ -10,000 & -5,000 & -0 \end{pmatrix}$$

$$C = \begin{pmatrix} .00250 & .00075 & .00120 \\ .00075 & .00090 & .00054 \\ .00120 & .00054 & .00360 \end{pmatrix}$$

First, compute the matrix of residual shares R:

$$R = \begin{pmatrix} 10000 & 5000 & 2500 \\ 5000 & 0 & 0 \\ -1000 & -5000 & 0 \end{pmatrix}$$

Second, apply Equation 6.2 to compute the risk of the trading strategy as follows:

$$\sigma^2(x_k) = \sum_{i=1}^{n} r_j^T Cr_j = \$824,625$$

$$\sigma(x_k) = \sqrt{\$824,625} = \$908$$

Timing Risk Reduction

The timing risk for a trade list (portfolio, program, or basket) achieves risk reduction in much the same way as investment portfolios. That is, the risk of the list is less than the sum of the risk of each name. For a two-stock portfolio p where r_i represents the number of shares in the ith order and σ_i represents the price volatility in \$/share, the risk of the list is shown as follows:

$$\sigma_p = \sqrt{r_1^2\sigma_1^2 + r_2^2\sigma_2^2 + 2r_1r_2\rho_{12}\sigma_1\sigma_2} \le r_1\sigma_1 + r_2\sigma_2$$

since, $\rho_{ij} = -1 \le \rho_{ij} \le 1$

In a more general case, we can show that total volatility of a trade list that consists of all buys or sells is less than the weighted sum of each risk as follows:

$$\sigma_p^2 + \sqrt{r^t Cr} \le r^t \sigma$$

where,

$$r = \begin{pmatrix} r_1 \\ r_2 \\ \vdots \\ r_n \end{pmatrix}, \sigma = \begin{pmatrix} \sigma_1 \\ \sigma_2 \\ \vdots \\ \sigma_n \end{pmatrix}, C = \begin{pmatrix} \sigma_1^2 & \sigma_{12} & \sigma_{1m} \\ \sigma_{21} & \sigma_2^2 & \sigma_{2m} \\ \vdots & \vdots & \cdots & \vdots \\ \sigma_{n1} & \sigma_{n2} & \sigma_n^2 \end{pmatrix}$$

The risk of a trade list consisting of buy and sell orders is less than the risk of an identical list consisting of all buys or all sells. This can be shown as follows:

$$\sigma_p^2 = \sqrt{r^t Cr} < \sqrt{|r^t||C||r|}$$

since,

$$\sum_i \sum_j sign(r_i) \cdot sign(r_j) \cdot r_i r_j \cdot 2\rho_{ij}\sigma_i\sigma_i < \sum_i \sum_j |r_i| \cdot |r_j| \cdot 2\rho_{ij}\sigma_i\sigma_i$$

Observations Regarding Risk of a Strategy

Following Equation 6.2 it is apparent that associated risk of a trading strategy that executes a list over a specified period is less than the risk of that list scaled over the entire period. That is, $\Re(x_k) < \sqrt{n} \cdot X^T CX$ where X represents the column vector of total shares in the list.

Figure 6.1. Timing Risk

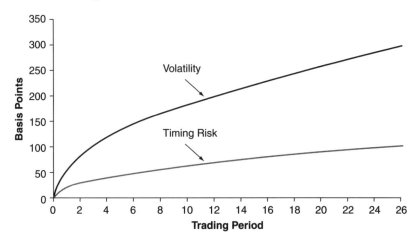

If a trader were to execute an order of x shares in a single stock over n-periods by trading at a constant rate α the corresponding risk of the strategy is approximated as follows:

$$\Re(x_k) \cong \sqrt{1/3} \cdot \sqrt{n \cdot x^T C x} \qquad (6.4)$$

A constant trading rate refers to an execution strategy where equal shares are executed in each period or the quantity of shares executed is equal to the same percentage of period volume.

Figure 6.1 illustrates the difference between stock volatility and timing risk for a constant trade rate. Timing risk is always less than the price volatility at the end of trading because timing risk is determined using a shrinking portfolio.

Calculating Liquidity Risk for a Trading Strategy

Liquidity risk is risk associated with unknown volume profiles of the stocks. When we develop a trading strategy, we anticipate expected market volume. Nevertheless, as market conditions change, our actual market impact cost will be different than anticipated. For example, we incur a higher market impact cost with less volume (e.g., our strategy becomes more aggressive) and vise versa (e.g., our strategy becomes more passive). This occurs even in cases where our price forecast and market impact relationship coincides. Therefore, to completely account for total quantity of risk surrounding our price forecast we need to assess this liquidity risk.

Let us consider the following market impact expression:

$$\kappa(x) = \frac{I}{X} \sum_j \frac{x_j^2}{(x_j + 0.5v_j)} \tag{6.5}$$

For simplicity, we assume that successive volumes are independent from one period to the next, and ignore the estimation error of I, that is

$$\rho(v_j, v_{j-1}) = 0$$
$$\sigma^2(I) = 0$$

Then liquidity risk $\sigma(\kappa(x))$ is:

$$\sigma^2(\kappa(x)) = \sigma^2\left(\frac{I}{X} \sum_j \frac{x_j^2}{(x_j + 0.5 \cdot v_j)} \right) = \left(\frac{I}{X} \right)^2 \sigma^2\left(\sum_j \frac{x_j^2}{(x_j + 0.5 \cdot v_j)} \right)$$

$$= \left(\frac{I}{X} \right)^2 \sum_j \sigma^2\left(\frac{x_j^2}{(x_j + 0.5 \cdot v_j)} \right)$$

since the only random variable is v_j. This is solved through use of the following theorem.

Theorem:[2]

Let v be a random variable with and. $E(v) = \mu$ and $\sigma^2(v) = \sigma^2$. If $Y=H(v)$ then,

$$E(Y) \cong H(\mu) + \frac{H''(\mu)}{2} \sigma^2$$
$$\sigma^2(Y) \cong [H'(\mu)]^2 \sigma^2$$

If the expected value and variance of each period j is $E(v_j) = v_j$ and $\sigma^2(v_j) = \sigma^2_{vj}$ respectively, we compute liquidity risk as follows:
Let,

$$H(v) = \frac{x^2}{(x + 0.5 \cdot v)}$$

Then,

$$H'(v) = \frac{-x^2}{2(x + 0.5 \cdot v)^2}$$

---

2. The theorem is based on the assumption that the function is at least twice differentiable. The proof uses a Taylor series expansion and assumes the remainder term to be zero for simplification. For an outline of the proof see Meyer (1970).

By application of theorem 1 we have the following:

$$\sigma^2(Y) = \frac{x^4 \sigma^2(v)}{4(x + 0.5v)^4}$$

Therefore, the liquidity risk of the execution schedule is:

$$\sigma^2(\kappa(x)) = \left(\frac{I}{X}\right)^2 \sum_j \sigma^2\left(\frac{x_j^2}{(x_j + 0.5 \cdot v_j)}\right) = \left(\frac{I}{X}\right)^2 \sum_j \frac{x_j^4 \sigma^2(v_j)}{4(x_j + 0.5 \cdot v_j)^4}$$

with $\sigma(\kappa(x)) = \sqrt{\sigma^2(\kappa(x))}$

The liquidity risk for a trade list is determined following above, with the following assumptions:[3]

   i. $\rho(v_{ij}, v_{kj}) = 0$
   ii. $\rho(v_{ij}, v_{ij-1}) = 0$

Here we make an assumption of independence based on zero correlation of excess volumes (volume quantities above/below the mean in each trading interval) across stocks and across periods for the same stocks. Our concern is with the correlation of volumes in each trading interval. Thus, if x_k represents the trade schedule, then the liquidity risk of x_k calculates as follows (assuming independence):

Liquidity Risk

$$\sigma^2(\kappa(x)) = \sum_i \left(\frac{I_i}{X_i}\right)^2 \sum_j \frac{x_{ij}^4 \sigma^2(v_{ij})}{4(x_{ij} + 0.5 \cdot v_{ij})^4} \tag{6.6}$$

Timing Risk of Trade Schedule

The total timing risk of a trade list is computed by assuming independence of price and volume. Observations suggest that high volume days are associated with large price movement and low volume days with small price movement. However, the observation is between total volume and the magnitude of price movement. There is no statistically significant evidence showing any relationship between volume quantities and directional price change. For example, high volume days are equally associated

---

3. It has been observed that there is correlation in volumes across stocks and also across periods. However, there is little evidence finding correlation of excess volume quantities (above/below expected) across stocks or serial correlation of excess volumes across periods.

with large positive and large negative price changes. Similarly, low volume days are equally associated with small positive and small negative price changes. We assume independence between volume and price. The total timing risk of the trade schedule is:

$$\Re(x_k) = \sqrt{\sum_j r_j^T C r_j + \sum_i \sum_j \left(\frac{I_i}{X_i}\right)^2 \frac{x_{ij}^4 \sigma^2(v_{ij})}{4(x_{ij} + 0.5 \cdot v_{ij})^4}} \qquad (6.7)$$

Estimating Volatility

The forecast of any estimate (volatility or covariance) requires that the period of the data set be consistent with the period over the decision. Money managers derive volatility using weekly or monthly data since most (investment) decisions call for holding periods of at least this long in time (although it is not true for active equity traders or those involved with buying and selling derivative instruments). Traders are mainly concerned with the immediate term—minutes, hours, or days. Therefore, we measure trading volatility using daily data; narrow intervals offer a more realistic representation of price movement over the trading horizon.

Volatility estimates include historical moving averages (HMA), exponential weighted moving average models (EWMA), and the autoregressive and generalized autoregressive conditioned heteroscasdity models (ARCH and GARCH). We consider each of these techniques next.

Definition

Let us examine stock volatility based on the following equation:

$$r_i = \bar{r} + \varepsilon_i$$

That is, the return of the stock in period j is equal to its expected return plus random noise. We estimate the variance σ^2 as:

$$\hat{\sigma}_i^2 = E[(r_i - \bar{r})^2] = \frac{1}{(n-1)} \sum_{i=1}^{n} (r_i - \bar{r})^2$$

where,

r_i denotes the ith previous change, and r_i is defined as:

$$r_i = \ln\left(\frac{p_i}{p_{i-1}}\right)$$

Note: In these calculations it is also possible to define $r_i = (P_i/P_{i-1} - 1)$ without the loss of accuracy since the estimates are almost identical for small changes, that is,

$$0.20 \le \ln((p_i/p_{i-1}) \cong (p_i/p_{i-1} - 1) \le 0.20$$

and in the vast majority of cases daily returns are within ±20% unless of course there is unexpected news or information regarding the company.

In order for our volatility formula to satisfy estimation requirements, it needs to satisfy the following two conditions:

    i. ε_i is independent and identically distributed random variable
    ii. $\varepsilon_i \sim N(0, \sigma^2)$

The first condition states that successive price changes are independent of one another, hence, $\rho(\varepsilon_i, \varepsilon_{i-1}) = 0$. The second condition states that the expected error is normally distributed with zero mean and constant variance. More advanced estimation techniques allow us to relax the normality requirement, however, they are not considered here. For more advanced techniques see Dodd (1998) or Cambell, Lo, and MacKinley (1997).

Observations on Historical Time Periods

To determine if actual data satisfy these two conditions we examine successive price increments and test for independence and stability of variance.

If price movement is independent, then standard deviation (volatility) will scale with the time period $\sqrt{\Delta t}$. That is,

$$\sigma\left(\sum_{\Delta t} r_i\right) = \sqrt{\Delta t} \cdot \sigma$$

To test this we computed the volatility of four stock indices, the DJIA, S&P 500, S&P 400, and S&P 600, using daily, weekly, monthly, and annual price change data for the period 1950 through 2001. Then we annualized the estimates by scaling by the appropriate factor. That is:

$$\sigma_{Annual} = \sqrt{250}\sigma_{daily}$$

$$\sigma_{Annual} = \sqrt{52}\sigma_{weekly}$$

$$\sigma_{Annual} = \sqrt{12}\sigma_{monthly}$$

In every instance, the annualized data were the highest using daily data. The S&P 400 and S&P 600 indices showed a subsequent decrease in annualized volatility moving from daily to weekly to monthly to annual (see

Figure 6.2.   Annualized Volatility

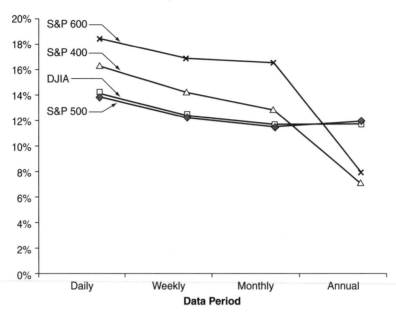

Figure 6.2). The S&P 500 and DJIA also showed higher annualized estimates using daily data but the other time periods did seem to scale correctly. Thus, evidence that volatility does not scale with the square root of time and suggests that successive price increments may not be independent.

To test for stability (stationarity) in price returns we investigated daily price returns for the S&P 500 from 1950–2001 (see Figure 6.3). We performed this analysis to test the stability of volatility to ensure stationarity. The independence property implies that the price change in one period has no effect on the price change in the next period. The stationary property implies that the standard deviation is constant from one period to the next. However, empirical evidence using S&P 500 price returns does not find this to be true. Notice the periods of volatility clustering. High excess returns tend to be followed by high excess returns. The opposite holds for low excess returns.

As a final test, we computed the serial correlation of excess returns. If the data were independent we would find the correlation of successive increments to be zero. This analysis was performed for lags of one day through twenty days (see Figure 6.4). The serial correlation for one- and two-day lags is statistically different from zero offering evidence that excess returns may not necessarily be independent. We also computed the serial correlation for the excess returns squared. If the data were stationary, we should again find serial correlation approximated zero. Again, this was not the case. For a large number of lags we found the serial correlation to

Figure 6.3. S&P 500 Daily Returns (1950–2001)

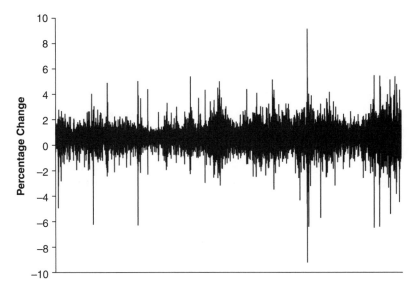

Figure 6.4. S&P 500 Daily Returns (1950–2001)

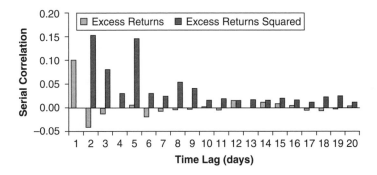

be statistically different from zero. This provides further evidence that large excessive returns are followed by large excessive returns in either direction. Again, the reverse holds true for small excess returns. Hence, the data are not stationary.

These analyses provide strong evidence suggesting that the price returns may not satisfy the conditions of independence and stationarity.

Volatility Forecasting Techniques

Many practitioners and authors suggest the use of actual returns as opposed to excess returns in developing volatility models. The reason behind using r_i in place of e_i is due to those models that are revised using only the previous day's price change (e.g., GARCH). In these cases, it is difficult to determine the mean trend on the day, thus presenting difficulty in determining the actual excess return. A simplifying assumption here is that the expected trend on the day was zero; therefore, $r_i = e_i$ and the two are identical. For our needs, a volatility model based on actual returns is more intuitive than using excess returns in cases where there is no anticipation regarding price trend on the day because our primary concern here is potential movement from the current price. Another argument supporting the usage of $r_i = e_i$ is that for small enough time periods Δt over continuous trading there is no expected natural price movement, that is $\bar{r} = 0$, thus, $r_i = e_i$. However, it is up to analysts to determine the more appropriate measure. Proceeding forward, we use r_i for illustration purposes, but readers can substitute e_i if felt appropriate.

1. Historical Moving Average

The historical moving average (HMA) is a volatility estimate dependent on the previous n-observations. Each successive day produces a new forecasted value. HMA applies equal weights to all data points. The unbiased estimate of variance $\hat{\sigma}^2$ is:

$$\hat{\sigma}_t^2 = \frac{1}{n-1} \sum_{i=1}^{n} r_i^2 \tag{6.8}$$

Advantages

- ▲ Very easy to calculate
- ▲ Provides fairly accurate estimates
- ▲ Should be used as the benchmark to compare all alternative models

Disadvantages

- ▲ Assumes all data are independent normally distributed variables
- ▲ Assumes the data are stationary and volatility is constant (i.e., unchanging over time).
- ▲ Does not detect shifts in structure
- ▲ Large movements persist throughout sample period with weights equal to most recent observations

2. Exponential Weighted Moving Average (EWMA)

The exponential weighted moving average (EWMA) volatility estimate is based on a moving average technique similar to the HMA, but it does not place equal weight to all data:

$$\sigma_t^2 = w_1 r_1^2 + w_2 r_2^2 + \ldots w_n r_n^2$$

Weights are applied following an exponential smoothing technique so that they decrease geometrically in time. The weights are determined using an exponential smoothing parameter $0 < \lambda < 1$ so that the weights applied to any historical observation j are:

$$w_j = \frac{(1 - \lambda)\lambda^{j-1}}{\sum_{i=1}^{n} (1 - \lambda)\lambda^{i-1}}$$

In the HMA calculation the weights applied to each jth data point are constant, $w_j = 1/(n-1)$. The EWMA places more emphasis on the most recent data and less emphasis on older data. The belief is that the more recent data points provide greater explanatory power than the older data points, thus, better detecting structural shifts in volatility and accounts for volatility clustering. The EWMA has some very interesting properties. If we allow the historical period to grow increasing large (e.g., $n \rightarrow \infty$) the weight applied to the observation in any period j simplifies to:

$$w_j = (1 - \lambda)\, \lambda^{j-1}$$

since, $\lim_{n \to \infty} \sum_{i=1}^{n} (1 - \lambda)\lambda^{i-1} = 1$. Then, the EWMA can be written as:

$$\hat{\sigma}_t^2 = (1 - \lambda)\sum_{i=1}^{\infty} \lambda^{i-1} r_i^2$$

With a little algebra this can be shown to reduce to:

$$\hat{\sigma}_t^2 = (1 - \lambda)r_{t-1}^2 + \lambda\sigma_{t-1}^2 \qquad \text{(6.9)}$$

The most appealing aspect of the EWMA is that subsequent forecasts only depend upon the previous forecasted value σ_1^2 and the previous return r_1^2. We do not continuously need to update our forecasts using streams of historical data.

Estimating the smoothing parameter λ. The smoothing parameter λ used in the computation of the EWMA is found through mimizing square errors as follows:

$$\underset{\lambda}{Min} \sum_{i=2}^{n} \left(r_i^2 - \hat{\sigma}_i^2\right)^2 = \sum_{i=2}^{n} \left(r_i^2 - \left((1 - \lambda)r_{i-1}^2 + \lambda\hat{\sigma}_{i-1}^2\right)\right)^2$$

After solving for λ it is not necessary to continuously update its value. Only the forecast needs to be updated.

Advantages

- ▲ Fairly easy to calculate
- ▲ Does not require numerous data
- ▲ Allows volatility to vary from one period to the next
- ▲ Can explain volatility clustering

Disadvantages

- ▲ Does not provide quick recovery from shocks or jumps
- ▲ Relies on a single parameter that may not provide accurate results
- ▲ Does not account for asymmetry in data

3. Autoregressive Conditional Heteroscedasticity

The autoregressive conditional heteroscedasticity model is a non-stochastic process used to forecast volatility. It is autoregressive in the sense that its forecast incorporates previous observations; that is, it predicts future volatility based on past observations, and is conditional heteroscedasticity in that volatility is not forced to be constant, it allows variance to be time varying. These models work well when (1) returns are serially correlated, (2) returns exhibit leptokurtosis (fat tails and peaked means), and (3) volatility clustering exists. That is, large and small excess returns tend to repeat.

The two most common autoregressive conditional heteroscedasticity models are the ARCH(p) model introduced by Engle in 1982 and the GARCH(p,q) model introduced by Bollerslev in 1986.

The ARCH(p) model captures the conditional heteroscedasticity of price returns using excess returns over the previous p-periods as follows:

$$\sigma_t^2 = \omega + \alpha_1 r_1^2 + \alpha_2 r_2^2 + \ldots + \alpha_p r_p^2$$
$$\omega > 0, \; \alpha_1, \alpha_2, \ldots, \alpha_p \geq 0$$

The GARCH(p,q) model is a generalized form of the ARCH(p) model. In addition to forecasting volatility based on the previous p observations of excess returns it also incorporates the previous q forecasts of volatility. Its formulation is as follows:

$$\sigma_t^2 = \omega + \alpha_1 r_1^2 + \ldots + \alpha_p r_p^2 + b_1 \sigma_{t-1}^2 + \ldots + b_q \sigma_{t-q}^2$$
$$\omega > 0, \; \alpha_1, \ldots, \alpha_p, b_1, \ldots, b_q \geq 0$$

The simplest of the GARCH family of models is the GARCH(1,1) model defined as follows:

$$\sigma_t^2 = \omega + \alpha r_1^2 + b \sigma_{t-1}^2 \tag{6.10}$$

with $\omega > 0, \; \alpha, b \geq 0$

In this formulation, all one needs to forecast volatility is the previous day's excess return and the previous day's volatility forecast (along with constant). It has been found that even in this simplified form of GARCH(1,1) the results have been very favorable.

Estimating ARCH and GARCH Parameters. The parameters of the ARCH and GARCH models are determined through maximum likelihood estimation (MLE). For example, if $r_1, r_2, . . ., r_n$ are the returns over some period of time and we assume that each r_i is normally distributed with mean zero and standard deviation σ, then the likelihood of observing those exact returns is:

$$L(\sigma^2|r_1, r_2, \ldots r_n) = \prod_{i=1}^{n} f(r_n)$$

where each r_i has pdf:

$$f(r) = \frac{1}{\sqrt{2\pi\sigma}} e^{\left(\frac{r^2}{2\sigma}\right)}$$

The exact values of the parameters ω, α, and β are found by maximizing L in the previous equation. But this is also equivalent to maximizing ln(L) or equivalently by minimizing –ln(L). This log-likelihood transformation of L can be simplified as follows:

$$Min: -\ln(L) = \frac{n}{2}\ln(2\pi) + n\ln(\sigma) - \frac{1}{2\sigma^2}\sum_{i=1}^{n} r_i^2$$

Advantages
- ▲ Models data stationary and jumps in volatility
- ▲ Handles volatility clustering
- ▲ Nests the EWMA and HMA models, that is, provides an estimate equal to the HMA and EWMA; when those are the appropriate models.

Disadvantages
- ▲ Parameters difficult to compute
- ▲ ARCH(p) model requires many data points for a forecast
- ▲ Does not account for asymmetry (skewness) in the data

Comparison Between GARCH/EWMA/HMA

There is also a strong relationship between the GARCH, EWMA, and HMA models. For instance, in the GARCH(1,1) model, $\omega=0$ and $\alpha=1-\beta$, the

GARCH reduces to the EWMA. Thus, if the EWMA is the more appropriate model and one set out to compute the parameters of the GARCH, the resulting parameters will indicate an EWMA. Additionally, if a HMA is the more appropriate model and one set out to solve a GARCH model, the resulting parameters will indicate a HMA. Unfortunately, the opposite is not true. Solving a HMA or the parameter of the EWMA will never suggest a GARCH structure. Henceforth, our recommended approach is to use the GARCH estimation technique.

Forecasting Covariance

Portfolio risk consists of two parts: the variance of stock price returns and the covariance of price movement between stocks. Therefore, risk forecasts require estimates of both variance and covariance.

The return R_p of a portfolio of m stocks is the weighted average of price returns as follows:

$$R_p = \sum_i w_i r_i$$

where w_i is the weight of the ith stock in the portfolio. Portfolio risk, however, is not a weighted average of individual volatility due to the co-movement of prices across stocks. The variance of an m-stock portfolio is determined as follows:[4]

$$\sigma_p^2 = E(R_p - E(R_p))^2 = E(R_p - \overline{R_p})^2$$

$$= \sum_{i=1}^{m} w_i^2 \sigma_i^2 + \sum_{i=1}^{m} \sum_{j=1}^{m} w_i w_j \sigma_{ij} (i \neq j) = \sum_{i=1}^{m} \sum_{j=1}^{m} w_i w_j \sigma_{ij}$$

where σ_{ij} is the covariance of price movement of i and j with $\sigma_{ij} = \sigma_i^2$ for $i = j$.
In matrix notation portfolio risk can be written as:

$$\sigma_p^2 = \sqrt{w^t C w}$$

where w is the vector of weights in the portfolio and C is the variance-covariance matrix. That is:

$$C = \begin{pmatrix} \sigma_1^2 & \sigma_{1,2} & \sigma_{1,3} & \cdots & \sigma_{1,m} \\ \sigma_{2,1} & \sigma_2^2 & \sigma_{2,3} & \cdots & \sigma_{2,m} \\ \vdots & & & & \\ \sigma_{m,1} & \sigma_{m,2} & \sigma_{m,3} & \cdots & \sigma_m^2 \end{pmatrix}$$

---

4 Elton and Gruber (1995) provide a detailed explanation of the derivation of portfolio risk.

Here the diagonal entries of the matrix are the stock variances and the off-diagonal are the covariances. The matrix is symmetric meaning $\sigma_{ij} = \sigma_{ji}$ of price movement. In total, for an m-stock portfolio there are $(m^2 + m)/2$ unique entries (parameters) to estimate.

How Many Data are Required to Significantly Estimate Parameters?

The solution of the covariance matrix requires a sufficient number of data points in order to ensure accuracy. As every elementary algebra student is quite aware, there need to be at least as many data points as there are independent variables in order to solve a system of equations. For example, consider a deterministic system of n-equations and m-unknowns. In order to determine a solution for each unknown we need to have $n \geq m$. If $n < m$ then the set of equations is underdetermined meaning no unique solution exists. The solution of each entry in the covariance matrix is further amplified because we are not solving for a deterministic set of equations. We are seeking to estimate the value of each parameter rather than solve for its exact value. And as any elementary statistics student will attest, there should to be at least 20 data points to have statistically meaningful results.

Consider the covariance matrix C with $(m^2 + m)/2$ unique parameters. Thus, there needs to be at least $20*(m^2 + m)/2$ data points. So if N is the number of historical observations, we need $N \geq (20*(m^2 + m)/2$ in order to solve for each parameter using historical data. In our case, we are interested in daily price changes. Therefore, for each day we have one data point for every stock and m data points in total. Over a t-day period there are $m*t$ data observations. The number of days required to accurately estimate C for m stocks is:

$$mt \geq 20 \cdot (m^2 + m)/2$$
$$t \geq 10(m + 1)$$

If a portfolio consists of only two stocks, we are required to forecast two variance terms and one covariance term. This is not too difficult an exercise and only requires 30 days of data. If a portfolio consists of 15 stocks, we are required to forecast 15 variances and 105 covariance terms, 120 parameters in total. This requires 160 days of data. This is more than one-half a year of daily observations for only 15 stocks. Now consider a rebalance of a portfolio that consists of 500 stocks. This covariance matrix contains 125,250 parameters and requires more than 13 years of data. Finally, consider a covariance matrix C for a universe of U.S. stocks (say 8,000). This requires about 220 years of daily observations! Even if we have this quantity of data, it is not reasonable to expect the relationship to remain constant over such a long period. Companies change their scope of business; there are growth and economic cycles, mergers and takeovers, and so on. Structures do change, even over short periods such as years or perhaps even months.

Figure 6.5.   Number of Unique Parameters in C

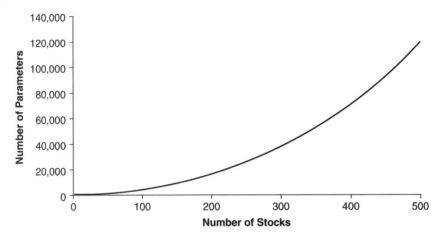

Figure 6.6.   Number of Days of Data

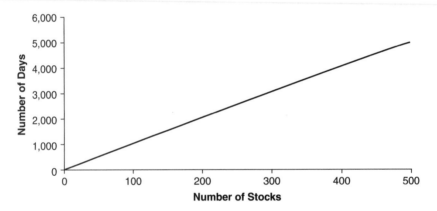

Figure 6.5 illustrates how the number of unique entries in the covariance matrix increases with the number of stocks in the portfolio. Figure 6.6 is an illustration that depicts the number of days of data to obtain a statistically accurate covariance matrix.

Mathematical Explanation Using the Rank

Mathematically we can discuss the data requirements for the covariance matrix in terms of the rank of the matrix C. Recall that the rank of a matrix is the number of linearly independent columns or rows in that matrix. Additionally, the number of linearly columns in a matrix is always equal to the number of linearly independent rows. Suppose that A is an $n{\times}n$ matrix with column vectors a_k, as follows:

$$A = (a_1 \, a_2 \, . \, . \, . \, a_n)$$

If A has full rank, Rank$(A) = n$, then A is non-singular and can be inverted (i.e., A^{-1} exists). But if Rank$(A) < n$ then A is a singular matrix. That is A^{-1} does not exist and there is no unique solution to $Ax = b$. This additionally implies that at least one column of the matrix a_k can be expressed as a linear combination of the other columns. That is:

$$a_k = \sum_{i=1}^{n} b_i a_i \text{ for } i \neq k$$

Suppose that A is an $n \times m$ matrix. Since the number of linearly independent columns is always equal to the number of linearly independent rows the rank of A cannot be greater than the minimum number of columns or rows. That is, maximum Rank(A) is min(n,m). For example, if A is a 3×5 matrix the maximum rank for the matrix is min$(5,3) = 3$.

Some basic properties regarding the rank of matrix A follow:

1. Rank$(A) \leq$ min(m,n)
2. Rank$(A) =$ Rank(A^T)
3. Rank$(A^T A) =$ Rank(A)
4. If $C = AB$, then Rank$(C) \leq$ min(Rank(A), Rank(B))
5. If A is an $m \times n$ matrix with rank r and $Pm \times m$ and $Qn \times n$ are non-singular matrices then, Rank$(A) =$ Rank$(PA) =$ Rank$(QA) =$ Rank(PAQ)

Recall our covariance matrix C. This matrix derives from the set of historical observations of stock prices. Let A represent the matrix of historical prices, A is a $t \times n$ matrix where t is the number of observation periods and n is the number of stocks. Since random price fluctuations occur in the market it is safe to assume that stock price returns are independent of one another and the rank(A)=min(t,n). If this assumption were not true, then we could accurately determine the price movement in one stock based on a linear combination of the movement of some set of stocks. That is, there would be perfect correlation. It can be shown that the covariance matrix C is related to $A^T A$ (shown next). Indeed, prices are a manifestation of random shocks related through the covariance matrix in the following way:

$$A^T = \sqrt{C}\Sigma$$

where Σ is a matrix of random perturbations, that is, Σ can be written as

$$\Sigma = \begin{bmatrix} \varepsilon_{11} & \varepsilon_{12} & \cdots & \varepsilon_{1n} \\ \varepsilon_{21} & \varepsilon_{22} & \cdots & \varepsilon_{2n} \\ \vdots & \vdots & \ddots & \vdots \\ \varepsilon_{t1} & \varepsilon_{t2} & \cdots & \varepsilon_{tn} \end{bmatrix}$$

with the ε_{ij}'s sampled from i.i.d. standard normal variables.

We also use the notation $\sqrt{C}$ to denote any matrix such that $C = \sqrt{C}\sqrt{C}$ (this can be obtained through a Cholesky factorization).

But the asymptotic properties of sampled i.i.d. normal variables, we have that, almost surely,

$$\frac{1}{n}\Sigma^T\Sigma \to I$$

where I denotes the $n \times n$ identity matrix. Another way of writing this is:

$$\frac{1}{n}\Sigma^T\Sigma = I + B_n,$$

where $B_n \to 0$ in the limit
Therefore,

$$A^TA = \sqrt{C}\Sigma\Sigma^T\sqrt{C} = n\sqrt{C}(I + B_n)\sqrt{C} = n\left(C + \sqrt{C}B_n\sqrt{C}\right)$$

$$= C\left(nI + nC^{-1}\sqrt{C}B_n\sqrt{C}\right) = CQ^{-1}$$

where $Q = (nI + nC^{-1}\sqrt{C}B_n\sqrt{C})^{-1}$, which is non-singular for large n (since $C^{-1}\sqrt{C}B_n\sqrt{C} \to 0$).

That is, for some non-singular matrix Q, the covariance matrix C can be derived in terms of A and Q as follows:

$$C = A^TAQ$$

By application of the properties stated here we can determine the rank of C as follows:

$$\begin{aligned}
Rank(C) &= \min(Rank(A^T A), Rank(Q)) \\
&= \min(Rank(A), Rank(Q)) \\
&= \min(\min(t, n), n) \\
&= \min(t, n)
\end{aligned}$$

Therefore, when we have ample observation periods, $t \geq n$, C is a non-singular matrix because C has full rank n. However, if $t \leq n$ then C has reduced rank $= t$. In this case, C is a singular matrix, that is:

1. Its inverse does not exist.
2. We can find at least one column c_k that can be expressed as a linear combination of a set of the other columns.

This brings to light problems for managers and traders. First, it creates false positive correlation structures. This means that because not all the columns are linearly independent we can express the covariance vector of a stock as a linear combination of a set of other stocks. This suggests we would find a perfect hedge between stocks. We would incorrectly claim that the price returns of some specified stock could be represented in terms of other stocks. That is the stock is perfectly correlated with some set of stocks implying the opportunity for a perfect hedge (which we know is not true). However, if we rely on the calculated covariance matrix C to assess the risk elements of the list, this is exactly what we would get. This would lead to improper and incorrect risk management techniques as well as incorrect trading strategy optimization. Furthermore, many times managers perform quantitative exercises in their stock selection process that are dependent on the underlying risk matrix C and its inverse to determine an optimal portfolio mix. If the inverse does not exist, quantitative solutions cannot be employed.

Small Portfolios

Is it possible to estimate each of the parameters for a small portfolio in cases when we do have enough observations? Unfortunately, the only way we can ascertain an accurate covariance measure is if we simultaneously estimate the covariance in price movement of all stocks. This requires us to estimate the covariance of returns across all stocks in the universe even if our list or portfolio only includes a few names. There is no way we can isolate and accurately estimate only the pairwise movement in prices for those stocks in the portfolio. Clearly, something needs to be done! Are there procedures that accurately estimate parameters of our covariance matrix? Fortunately, there are, but consider again our covariance matrix. Here, our covariance values are stated in terms of (stock) volatility and the correlation coefficient between them as follows:

$$\sigma_{ij} = \rho_{ij}\sigma_i\sigma_j$$

Since we have developed a procedure for estimating variances, we turn our focus to developing a sound methodology for estimating correlation between variables.

Risk Models

There is simply not enough historical data to accurately assess the correlation structure between all pairs of stocks. Fortunately, we gain insight into the correlation structure employing risk models. Here we evaluate three procedures for estimating the correlation between stocks: sector correlation model, single factor model, and various multifactor models.

Risk Components

Risk modeling offers insight into stock return behavior and risk, and a stock or list's decomposition by separating risk into systematic and idiosyncratic risk. That is:

$$Risk = Systematic\ Risk + Idiosyncratic\ Risk$$

External factors denote systematic risk, known also as market or undiversifiable risk. Idiosyncratic risk is the associated risk of a stock or list not explained by the model. This risk genus is independent of the market because it is stock specific. We think of idiosyncratic risk as unsystematic or diversifiable risk. This risk is diversifiable because idiosyncratic returns across stocks are independent. Thus, adding stocks with diverse macroeconomic sensitivities to a portfolio lowers idiosyncratic risk.

The decomposition of risk into systematic and idiosyncratic risk provides the foundation to estimate the covariance of price movement between any two stock groups without the data limitations encountered previously. We accomplish this by measuring how stock prices change in relationship to a specified factor. Decomposition is essential when we forecast correlation portfolio risk.

Sector Correlation Model

The basic principal of the sector correlation model is that for the most part stocks tend to move in conjunction with one another. In its simplest form, the sector correlation model is a matrix P of correlations across all pairs of stocks computed over some historical period (Elton and Gruber 1995). Stocks are designated based on their sector and we compute the average correlation across all stocks in each sector and the average correlation across stocks in different sectors. This model provides an estimate of correlation that will be the same for all stocks in a sector but will differ from one sector to another. If P represents the historical sample correlation matrix from stock returns, the average correlation $\overline{\rho_{LM}}$ between sector L and M is as follows:

$$\overline{\rho_{LM}} = \frac{1}{k} \cdot \underbrace{\sum_i \sum_j \rho_{ij}}_{i \in L, j \in M}$$

where ρ_{ij} is the historical correlation between stock i and j and k is the number of intersections between sector L and M. An attractive appeal of the sector correlation model is that it is straightforward and does not require superfluous historical observations. Further, as with the sample volatility

Table 6.1. Average Sector Correlation Models

January 2000–December 2001

	Cons Discr	Cons Staple	Energy	Financials	Health Care	Industrials	Info Tech	Materials	Telecom Svc	Utilities
Cons Discr	0.26	0.11	0.07	0.23	0.11	0.22	0.18	0.22	0.16	0.08
Cons Staple	0.11	0.26	0.07	0.17	0.14	0.12	–0.03	0.16	0.05	0.15
Energy	0.07	0.07	0.57	0.08	0.09	0.10	0.02	0.13	0.02	0.19
Financials	0.23	0.17	0.08	0.42	0.16	0.22	0.16	0.22	0.17	0.14
Health Care	0.11	0.14	0.09	0.16	0.20	0.13	0.07	0.12	0.07	0.10
Industrials	0.22	0.12	0.10	0.22	0.13	0.23	0.18	0.23	0.15	0.10
Info Tech	0.18	–0.03	0.02	0.16	0.07	0.18	0.39	0.10	0.19	0.00
Materials	0.22	0.16	0.13	0.22	0.12	0.23	0.10	0.36	0.12	0.11
Telecom Svc	0.16	0.05	0.02	0.17	0.07	0.15	0.19	0.12	0.29	0.04
Utilities	0.08	0.15	0.19	0.14	0.10	0.10	0.00	0.11	0.04	0.40

estimate (HMA), it can serve as the base case model to judge other more sophisticated approaches. This approach is reasonable providing a relatively small number of stocks in the sector do not dominate price movement for all names. Table 6.1 reveals the results of our sector correlation model using daily returns for those stocks that comprise the S&P 500 over the period January 2000–December 2001 (two years).

Single Factor Model

The single factor model is actually a risk-return model based on the underlying assumption that a single factor plus stock specific idiosyncratic risk explains stock returns. The single factor model uses the market returns as the model factor.[5] It was the predecessor to the formulation of the CAPM model by Sharpe.[6]

In matrix notation the single factor model follows:

$$y = Xb + e$$

5. The most common proxy for the market is the S&P 500 index, although some managers use the Wilshire 5000 index because they believe it is a better representation of the entire market.
6. The difference between the single factor model and the CAPM is very subtle. The single factor model is intended to provide insight into the risk decomposition of a stock or a list and is based on the assumption that residual returns across stocks are independent of one another. CAPM is a model of expected returns and does not require residential returns to be independent across stocks.

where,

$$
y = \begin{bmatrix} y_1 \\ y_2 \\ \vdots \\ y_n \end{bmatrix}, \quad X = \begin{bmatrix} x_0 & x_1 \end{bmatrix} = \begin{bmatrix} 1 & R_1 \\ 1 & R_2 \\ \vdots & \vdots \\ 1 & R_n \end{bmatrix}, \quad b = \begin{bmatrix} b_0 \\ b_1 \end{bmatrix}, \quad e = \begin{bmatrix} e_1 \\ e_2 \\ \vdots \\ e_n \end{bmatrix}
$$

y = column vector of stock returns
x_k = column vector of factor k
x_0 = column vector of ones
x_1 = column vector of market returns
R_j = market return in period j
e = column vector of stock residual returns
b_0 = stock return independent of the market
b_1 = stock return sensitivity to market returns

For stock i in period j the single factor model requires:

1. e_{ij} i.i.d. $\sim N(0, \sigma^2_{ei})$ for all stocks i
2. $E(x_k, e) = 0$
3. $E(e_{i,j}\, e_{i,j-1}) = 0$
4. $E(e_{ij} e_{kj}) = 0$

The parameters of the model $b^T = [b_0, b_1]$ for each stock i are solved via ordinary least squares regression technique. In matrix notation the solution is:

$$
b_i = \begin{bmatrix} \alpha_i \\ \beta_i \end{bmatrix} = (X^T X)^{-1} X^T y_i
$$

with,

$$
\sigma^2(b_i) = \left(\frac{1}{n-2} e_i^T e_i \right) \cdot (X^T X)^{-1}
$$

providing that $(X^T X)^{-1}$ is non-singular.

For our purposes it is necessary to gain an understanding into the systematic and idiosyncratic risk to make assessments regarding the covariance and correlation across pairs of stocks. These calculations follow Eltor and Craber and are as follows (see Elton and Gruber (1995) for full derivation):

Risk Decomposition

$$
\sigma^2(y_i) = E(y_{ij} - E(y_{ij}))^2 = \underbrace{\beta^2 \sigma^2_m}_{\text{Systematic}} + \underbrace{\sigma^2_{ei}}_{\text{Idiosyncratic}} \tag{6.11}
$$

The risk decomposition for a stock can also be written as:

$$\sigma^2(y_i) = \beta_i^2 \sigma_m^2 + \sigma_{ei}^2 = \left(\frac{Cov(y_i, r_m)}{\sigma_m^2}\right)^2 \sigma_m^2 + \sigma_{ei}^2 = \frac{[Cov(y_i, r_m)]^2}{\sigma_m^2} + \sigma_{ei}^2$$

so,

$$\sigma(y_i) = \frac{Cov(y_i, r_m)}{\sigma_m} + \sigma_{ei}$$

since market returns are independent of residuals.

Portfolio Risk Decomposition

$$\sigma_p^2 = \sum_{i=1}^{n} w_i^2 \sigma_i^2 + \sum_{i=1}^{n} \sum_{\substack{j=1 \\ i \neq j}}^{n} w_i w_j \sigma_{ij}$$

$$= \sum_{i=1}^{n} \sum_{j=1}^{n} w_i w_j B_i B_j \sigma_m^2 + \sum_{i=1}^{n} w B_i^2 \sigma_{ei}^2$$

or in matrix notation as:

$$\sigma_p^2 = w^t C w = w^t(B^T \sigma_m^2 B + \Lambda)w = w^t B^T \sigma_m^2 B w + w^t \Lambda w \qquad \textbf{(6.12)}$$

$$= (Bw)^t \sigma_m^2 Bw + w^t \Lambda w$$

where Λ is the d iagonal matrix of idiosyncratic variance.

Covariance Between Two Stocks

$$\sigma_{ij} = E[(y_i - E(y_i))(y_k - E(y_k))] = B_i B_k \sigma_m^2$$

Historical Covariance Matrix C

$$C = B^T \sigma_m^2 B + \Lambda \qquad \textbf{(6.13)}$$

where $B = [B_1 B \ldots B_n]$, $\sigma_m^2 B = \begin{bmatrix} \sigma_m^2 B_1 \\ \sigma_m^2 B_2 \\ \vdots \\ \sigma_m^2 B_n \end{bmatrix}$, and $\Lambda = \begin{bmatrix} \sigma_{e1}^2 & 0 & \cdots & 0 \\ 0 & \sigma_{e2}^2 & 0 & 0 \\ \vdots & 0 & \ddots & \vdots \\ 0 & 0 & \cdots & \sigma_{en}^2 \end{bmatrix}$

Correlation Between Two stocks

$$\rho_{ik} = \frac{\sigma_{ik}}{\sigma_i \sigma_k} = \frac{B_i B_k \sigma_m^2}{\sigma_i \sigma_k} \tag{6.14}$$

Multifactor Model

The multifactor model is a risk-return model based on the underlying assumption that a set of factors plus stock specific idiosyncratic risk explains (stock) returns. Additionally, we can select multifactor sets that explain a larger percentage of returns, further reducing regression error and improving our systematic risk analysis. Arbitrage Pricing Theory (APT) is an example of a multifactor model.

The multifactor model follows:

$$y = Xb + e$$

where,

$$y = \begin{bmatrix} y_1 \\ y_2 \\ \vdots \\ y_n \end{bmatrix}, \quad b = \begin{bmatrix} b_0 \\ b_1 \\ \vdots \\ b_m \end{bmatrix}, \quad e = \begin{bmatrix} e_1 \\ e_2 \\ \vdots \\ e_n \end{bmatrix}$$

$$X = [x_0 \ x_1 \ \cdots \ x_m] = \begin{bmatrix} 1 & x_{11} & \cdots & x_{m1} \\ 1 & x_{12} & \cdots & x_{m2} \\ \vdots & \vdots & \ddots & \vdots \\ 1 & x_{1n} & \cdots & x_{mn} \end{bmatrix}$$

y = column vector of stock returns
x_i = column vector of factor k
e = column vector of residual returns
b_k = stock return sensitivity to factor k

Model Enhancements

Quite often in multifactor analysis the selection of the factors is constructed to have mean 0 and variance 1 through a normalization process as follows:

$$x_{kl}^* = \frac{x_{kl} - E(x_k)}{\sigma(x_k)}$$

Each factor x_k is constructed so that each is orthogonal for example, independent of one another. That is:

$$Cov(x_k, x_l) = E(x_k - \overline{x_k})(x_l - \overline{x_l}) = E(x_k k_l) = 0 \text{ for all } k \text{ and } l$$

With these relationships in place, the covariance matrix of factor returns Ω reduces to the identity matrix.

$$\Omega = \begin{bmatrix} E(x_1 x_1) & E(x_1 x_2) & \cdots & E(x_1 x_n) \\ E(x_2 x_1) & E(x_2 x_2) & \cdots & E(x_2 x_n) \\ \vdots & \vdots & & \vdots \\ E(x_n x_1) & E(x_n x_2) & \cdots & E(x_n x_n) \end{bmatrix} = \begin{bmatrix} 1 & 0 & \cdots & 0 \\ 0 & 1 & \cdots & 0 \\ \vdots & \vdots & \cdots & \vdots \\ 0 & 0 & \cdots & 1 \end{bmatrix} = I$$

since $E(x_i x_i) = 1$ and $E(x_k x_l) = 0$, for $k \neq l$.

For the multifactor model and stock i in period j we have:

1. e_{ij} i.i.d. $\sim N(0, \sigma^2_{ei})$ for all stocks i
2. $E(x_{ik}, e) = 0$
3. $E(x_{ik}, x_{il}) = 0$
4. $E(e_{i,j} e_{i,j-1}) = 0$
5. $E(e_{ij} e_{kj}) = 0$

The parameters are then solved via ordinary least squares regression. In matrix notation the solution is:

$$b_i = \begin{bmatrix} b_{i0} \\ b_{i1} \\ \vdots \\ b_{ik} \end{bmatrix} = (X^T X)^{-1} X^T y_i$$

with

$$\sigma^2(b_i) = \left(\frac{1}{n-k} e_i^T e_i \right) \cdot (X^T X)^{-1}$$

providing that $(X^T X)^{-1}$ is non-singular.
The sensitivity of stock i to factor k is found as:

$$b_{ik} = \frac{Cov(y_i, x_k)}{\sigma^2(x_k)} \tag{6.15}$$

Risk Decomposition:

$$\sigma^2(y_i) = b_i^t \Omega b_i + \sigma_{ei}^2 = b_i^t b_i + \sigma_{ei}^2 \tag{6.16}$$
$$= b_1^2 + b_2^2 + \ldots + b_k^2 + \sigma_{ei}^2$$
$$= Cov(y_i, x_1) + Cov(y_i, x_2) + \ldots + Cov(y_i, x_k) + Cov(e_i, e_i)$$

since,

$$b_{ik} = \frac{Cov(x_i, x_k)}{\sigma_k^2}$$

Trade List Risk Decomposition

$$\sigma_p^2 = w^t B^T \Omega B w + w^t \Lambda w$$
$$= w^t B^T I B w + w^t \Lambda w \tag{6.17}$$
$$= w^t B^T B w + w^t \Lambda w$$

Stock Covariance:

$$\sigma_{ik} = b_i^t \Omega b_k = b_i^t b_k \tag{6.18}$$

Covariance Matrix

$$C = B^T \Omega_B + \Lambda = B^T I B + \Lambda$$
$$= B^T B + \Lambda$$

Correlation Between Two Stocks

$$\rho_{ik} = \frac{b_i^t \Omega b_k}{\sigma_i \sigma_k} = \frac{b_i^t I b_k}{\sigma_i \sigma_k} = \frac{b_i^t b_k}{\sigma_i \sigma_k} \tag{6.19}$$

The appealing aspect to these operations is that they allow analysts and traders to rapidly compute covariance and correlation without the requirements of having access to the actual factors used in the model.

Important Note: Many practitioners formulate their risk models as an excess return model and factor out the risk-free rate of return R_f to gain an understanding of the return premium for a given level of risk (e.g., CAPM and APT). For our purposes of determining the correlation structure across stocks, the result is the same if we specify the model with or without the risk-free rate asset. For example, consider the single factor model formulated as an excess returns model where $R_{f,t}$ is the risk-free rate of return in period t. That is,

$$Y_{i,t} - R_{f,t} = \alpha_i + \beta_i(R_{m,t} - R_{f,t}) + e_{i,t}$$

In this example, the expected return is different than that stated in our model without the risk-free return but the risk is the same. That is:

$$E(Y_{i,t} - R_{f,t}) = E(Y_{i,t}) - R_{f,t}$$
$$\sigma^2_i(Y_i - R_f) = \sigma^2_i(Y_i)$$

since R_f is a constant and independent of the movement of the portfolio.

Types of Multifactor Models

Multi-Index Models

The index-based multifactor model is an extension of the single factor model. We capture the covariance and correlation of residual price movement across stocks within the same sector or industry. As mentioned earlier, there is sufficient empirical evidence to suggest that the market index does not completely explain all systematic returns. Empirical findings reveal correlation between residual returns across stocks in the same industry. Hence, it seems appropriate to incorporate sector or industry index returns to explain at least some of the residual price movement. We accomplish this by adding stock specific sector index into the single factor model.

The multi-index model has the general form:

$$y = Xb + e$$

with,

$$X = [x_0 \ x_1 \ . \ . \ . \ x_k]$$

where,

x_0 = column vector of ones
x_1 = column vector of market returns
r_k = column vector kth sector returns for $k > 1$
x_k = dummy variable column

$$x_k = \begin{cases} r_k & \text{if } \in \text{ sector } k \\ 0 & \text{otherwise} \end{cases}$$

Macroeconomic Models

A macroeconomic multifactor model attempts to explain stock returns and risk through a set of macroeconomic variables that are common to all stocks (e.g., inflation, industrial production). This approach suggests potential explanatory variables of stock returns and risk (they are incorporated and highly scrutinized in many pricing models). For example, in the most basic of all stock pricing models, the growth dividend model, assumptions center on expected growth rate, interest rates, and inflation. Thus changes to any variable influence security prices. The appeal of macroeconomic data lies in the intuitiveness of the data. All macroeconomic variables are readily measurable and have real economic meaning. For example, if there is a measured decrease in industrial production, and an increase in unemployment and inflation, it is likely that the economy as a whole has begun to slow down. These models do provide good insight into future growth of the economy and expected returns of stock. Stocks are expected to increase less rapidly in a slowing economy and more rapidly in an increasing economy. However, these models are often quite sensitive to specified macroeconomic variables and thus any measurement error could easily produce inaccurate results. Further, a significant amount of data comes from government sources along with the inevitable time lag; the data may be suspect. Therefore, while these models offer some insight into the likely direction of the economy, they do not sufficiently capture the most accurate correlation structure of price movement across stocks—vital information to help us develop our short-term covariance matrix. Finally, macroeconomic models may not do a good job capturing the covariance of price movement across stocks in "new economies" or a "shifting structure." For example, many practitioners have been using macroeconomic variables to model returns of technology and "e-commerce" companies identical to those used to model strong industrials and blue chips of earlier years.

Ross, Roll, and Chen[7] identified the following four macroeconomic factors to have significant explanatory power:

1. Unanticipated changes in inflation
2. Unanticipated changes in industrial production
3. Unanticipated changes in the yield between high-grade and low-grade corporate bonds
4. Unanticipated changes in the yield between long-term government bonds and t-bills (slope of the term structure)

Other macroeconomic factors that have been incorporated into these models include changes in interest rates, growth rates, GDP, capital investment, unemployment, oil prices, housing starts, exchange rates, and so on. The parameters are typically determined via regression analysis using monthly data over a five-year period, for example, 60 observations.

Cross-Sectional Models

Cross-sectional multifactor models determine the relationship between stock return and risk and a set of variables specific to each company rather

7. Chen, N., Roll, R., and Ross, S., "Economic Forces and the Stock Market," *Journal of Business,* July 1986.

Table 6.2. A Listing of Cross-Sectional Variables

Fundamental Variables *"Cross-Sectional"*	*Technical Variables* *"Market Driven"*
Market	Liquidity
Market Capitalization	Turnover
Price/Earning	Relative Strength Index
Book/Price	Volatility
Debt/Equity	Momentum
Leverage	
Revenue/Price	
Dividend Yield	
Interest Rate Sensitivity	

than through factors common across all stocks. Cross-sectional models specify factors based on fundamental and technical data. The fundamental data consist of the company characteristics and the technical data (also called market driven) consist of observations of trading activity for the stock in the market. Because of the reliance on fundamental data, many authors use the term *fundamental model* instead of cross-sectional model. The rationale behind the cross-sectional model is similar to the rationale behind the macroeconomic model. That is, since managers and decision makers incorporate fundamental and technical analysis into their stock selection process it is only reasonable that these factors provide insight into risk and return of those stocks. French and Fama[8] reported that the three factors of market, size, and book/value have considerable explanatory power. However, the exact measure of these variables remains a topic of much discussion. We offer a listing of cross-sectional variables in Table 6.2. While many may find it intuitive to incorporate cross-sectional data into multifactor models because it is based on the analytical techniques performed by many for pricing and selecting stocks, these models have several limitations and shortcomings. First, data requirements are cumbersome requiring analysts to develop models using company specific data (each firm requires its own set of factors). Second, it is often difficult to find a consistent set of robust factors across stocks that provide strong explanatory power. Ross and Roll had difficulty determining a set of factors that provided more explanatory power than the macroeconomic models without introducing excessive multicollinearity into the data. The parameters are typically determined via regression analysis using company specific monthly data over a five-year period, for example, 60 observations.

8. Fama, E., French, K., "The Cross Section of Variation in Expected Stock Returns," *Journal of Finance*, June 1992.

Statistical Models

The statistical factor model is the multifactor modeling approach that most closely resembles the original APT work of Ross and Roll (1976). The factors used in this model to explain return and risk are "implicit" factors. That is, they are not known or readily observed in the marketplace; instead, they are derived from the actual returns of the stock. The statistical multifactor model differs from the previously mentioned models in that they estimate both the factors (x_k's) and the sensitivity loadings (b_{ik}'s). This model does not make any prior assumptions regarding the explainers of return or risk, or force any preconceived structure into the model. These models are data driven. That is, they let the actual stock returns dictate the set of factors, thus providing better correlation and covariance estimates.

These statistical models derive the set of factors through mathematical algorithms such as factor analysis, principal component analysis, and/or singular value decomposition. The statistical model determines the set of factors $x_1, x_2, \ldots, x_k$ such that each factor is independent of one another with mean zero and variance one. Statistical models are similar to the multi-index and macroeconomic models in that there is a common set of factors that are applied across all stocks. The factor loadings (b_{ik}'s) are determined via regression analysis with the sample historical measured covariance matrix as the starting point.

Misconceptions of the Statistical Model

Factors Do Not Have Real Economic Interpretation. The literature suggests that statistical models are the least intuitive of all the multifactor models because they do not provide insight into actual drivers of return. Managers find explicit models appealing (index, macroeconomic, and cross-sectional) because factors deal with real economic variables or company information. Having factors associated with real variables makes it easy to conjecture how stock prices will move in relation to unanticipated changes in interest rates, bond prices, and so on. However, the same is not true with statistical factor models. The majority of statistical models do a better job determining a stock's (or portfolio's) "true" risk decomposition, providing better correlation and covariance estimates.

Models Exhibit Slow Reaction to the Changing Environment. Some propose that statistical models suffer from a slow reaction to structural changes. This statement is correct if the historical period carries sufficiently into long periods, years, for example. However, time horizons used in statistical models are often short, with only a few months of data. Furthermore, to the extent that statistical models are used mainly for determining the correlation structure across stocks, it is less likely a company will encounter an abrupt change in price return movement in conjunction with other securities. Correlation structures across stocks exhibit a much greater amount of persistence than stock volatility paradigms.

Unable to Identify Risk Exposures. Some maintain that, because statistical models infer actual factors and do not exhibit any real economic significance, they do not offer insight into risk exposures of real economic variables or indexes. Nevertheless, the same holds for all models. The only complete means of determining risk exposures and risk attribution is for managers to include the specified variable in the actual model. Thus, macroeconomic models do not directly provide insight into risk exposure to fundamental variables and vice versa. Further, neither model provides direct insight into risk exposures by sector or industry. However, risk exposures can be computed to any specified variable for any family of models.

Trading Covariance Matrix C

Now that we have established approaches to estimate price volatility and measure the correlation structure across all pairs of stocks, we are ready to construct the trading correlation matrix. This matrix C is a hybrid model that incorporates the volatility estimate and the correlation structure. The preferred approach for constructing the trading covariance matrix is estimating volatility using the GARCH(1,1) approach because it is the most general of the models discussed and the statistical factor model based for determining the correlation structure across stocks. How do we construct the trading covariance matrix?

Suppose that the correlation structure across the universe of stocks is *R:*

$$R = \begin{bmatrix} 1 & p_{12} & \cdots & p_{1n} \\ p_{21} & 1 & & \vdots \\ \vdots & & \ddots & \\ p_{n1} & \cdots & & 1 \end{bmatrix}$$

where, $p_{i,k}$ is the correlation between *i* and *k* calculated as follows:

$$\rho_{ik} = \begin{cases} 1 & \text{for } i = k \\ \dfrac{b_i^t b_k}{\sigma_i \sigma_k} & \text{for } i \neq k \end{cases}$$

with, σ_i historical stock volatility.

Then, the covariance matrix in \$/share is computed as follows:

$$C = P \, SRSP$$

where P is a diagonal matrix of current prices, and S is a diagonal matrix of forecasted volatility, that is,

$$
P = \begin{bmatrix} p_1 & 0 & \cdots & 0 \\ 0 & p_2 & & \vdots \\ \vdots & & \ddots & 0 \\ 0 & \cdots & 0 & p_n \end{bmatrix}
\qquad
S = \begin{bmatrix} \hat{\sigma}_1 & 0 & \cdots & 0 \\ 0 & \hat{\sigma}_2 & & \vdots \\ \vdots & & \ddots & 0 \\ 0 & \cdots & 0 & \hat{\sigma}_n \end{bmatrix}
$$

In this chapter we have only discussed techniques based on linear models using historical data. Readers interested in exploring alternative models are referred to Cambell, Lo, and MacKinlay (1996), Peters (1994), and Hamilton (1994) for non-linear techniques or Vinod (1982) for estimation techniques based on maximum entropy methods. Readers interested in estimation using implied stock volatility and other models can visit the web sites of Advanced Portfolio Technologies, Barra, Northfield Information Services, or Quantal International.

CHAPTER SEVEN

Opportunity Cost

OPPORTUNITY COST REPRESENTS THE FORGONE profit of not being able to fully implement an investment decision. Opportunity cost exists because insufficient market liquidity prevents completion of the order or the price moves outside a specified range. Opportunity cost combines the price change over the trading horizon and number of unexecuted (residual) shares R. It is measured following the implementation shortfall methodology and can also be decomposed into an investment and trading-related cost component as follows:

$$\phi(R) = \underbrace{(X - \sum x_j)}_{\text{Unexecuted Shares}}\underbrace{(P_n - P_d)}_{\text{Price Change}} = \underbrace{(X - \sum x_j)(P_0 - P_d)}_{\substack{\text{Investment Related}\\\text{Opportunity Cost}}} + \underbrace{(X - \sum x_j)(P_n - P_0)}_{\substack{\text{Trading Related}\\\text{Opportunity Cost}}} \quad \text{(7.1)}$$

with,
P_d = stock price at time of investment decision
P_0 = stock price at commencement of trading
P_n = stock price end of trading

Investment-related opportunity cost is a component of delay cost and results when managers hesitate to give an order to traders and/or traders hesitate in releasing the order to the market. Proper transaction cost management via minimal delay can easily eliminate this component. However, opportunity cost and delay cost resulting from close to open price jumps is unavoidable. It is a consequence of noncontinuous trading. The trading-related opportunity cost refers to the actual cost of not being able to implement a trading decision. We derive trading-related opportunity cost (OC) by incorporating price change over a trading horizon as follows:

$$OC(R) = \left(X - \sum x_j\right) \cdot \left(P_n - P_0\right) \qquad (7.2)$$

Opportunity cost either specifies a cost or saving—but more typically a cost—when the end of trading price is less favorable than the opening price. In other words, when the price of buys is higher at the end of the trading horizon and the price of sells is lower at the end of the trading horizon. First, as we know every execution conveys information to the market resulting in permanent and temporary market impact. Permanent market impact cost persists in all subsequent periods after the trade. This causes buy prices to be higher and sell prices to be lower. Secondly, to the extent that managers buy stocks increasing in price and sell stocks decreasing in price the price at the end of trading will also be less favorable.[1] Finally, we know that opportunity cost exists in part because of adverse price movement and the resistance of investors to transact at less favorable prices. Therefore, if the price of a buy order becomes too high or a sell order too low, investors may cancel remaining shares. This produces unexecuted shares, less favorable prices, and opportunity cost. Investors rarely cancel orders because the price becomes too attractive. Thus, cancellation bias causes opportunity cost to be more cost than saving.

Transaction cost management (TCM) is key to minimizing trading-related opportunity cost. We use cost estimation techniques to determine the likelihood of executing orders within a specified price range and under a set of market conditions. Pre-trade analysis alerts managers to insufficient liquidity conditions and corresponding difficulty implementing an order. Transaction cost estimation helps us predict trading cost and risk—whether the order executes within a specified price range. Having this information before trading allows traders and managers to communicate effectively, the order can be revised if not executed completely, and invested in the next attractive opportunity. Further, with TCM we know the feasibility of increasing order size and executing our position within *a* specified price range. Finally, by monitoring real-time market conditions (and the progress of trading) we can anticipate unfavorable trading conditions.

1. A better explanation here is that managers typically buy stocks that have increased in price and sell stocks that have decreased in price. However, Plexus has found evidence suggesting that prices continue to move adversely even after the investment decision through the time trading commences. That is, buy orders have increased in price and sell orders have decreased in price. This represents the delay cost component (Wagner 2001).

Example 1. A trader receives an order to buy 100,000 shares of ABC but can only execute 80,000 shares by the end of the day. If the manager's decision price was $P_d = \$20$, the trader begins trading at $P_0 = \$20.50$ and the closing price is $P_n = \$21.50$, compute the opportunity cost of the order. Opportunity cost is decomposed into its investment and trading related components as follows:

$OC(Investment) = (100,000 - 80,000)(\$20.50 - \$20.00) = 20,000 \cdot \$0.50 = \$10,000$
$OC(Trading) = (100,000 - 80,000)(\$21.50 - \$20.50) = 20,000 \cdot \$1.00 = \$20,000$
$Total\ OC = \$10,000 + \$20,000 = \$30,000$

Example 2. A manager discovers two undervalued stocks. The first, ABC, trades at $25 anticipated to increase 8% to $27. The second XYZ trades at $50 anticipated to increase 7% to $53. The manager decides to invest $1,000,000 purchasing 40,000 shares of ABC and 0 shares of XYZ. However, before trading the trader analyzes the list, determines a 70% likelihood of executing the order at better than $27, and alerts the manager. The manager revises the order to 20,000 shares of ABC and 10,000 shares of XYZ, resulting in greater than 95% likelihood of executing each order within the price range. This illustrates how exchanging a high return stock with a lower return stock but higher probability of execution could actually result in higher portfolio returns.

Estimating Opportunity Cost

Opportunity cost is a function of price movement over the trading period and the number of unexecuted shares:

$$E[OC] = (E[P_n] - P_0)\left(X - \sum_{j=1}^{n} x_j \right) \tag{7.3}$$

The random variable in the equation is $\Delta P = E(P_n) - P_0$ and a function of price appreciation and permanent market impact. Temporary market impact is not incorporated into the estimation of opportunity cost because it represents payment for liquidity and will quickly dissipate. Temporary market impact does not persist in the long-term and does not reflect a stock's true intrinsic value. Therefore, opportunity cost is estimated based on expected price appreciation, expected permanent market impact cost and specified trade schedule.

A thorough discussion of the estimation process of permanent market is provided in Chapter 8, The Holy Grail of Market Impact. For discussion purposes let us define the total market impact of an order in dollars to be I where 95% is temporary (i.e., will dissipate) and 5% is permanent (will persist). Hence, expressing these quantities in dollars per share we have:

$$Temporary\ MI(\$/share) = \frac{0.95I}{X}$$

$$Permanent\ MI(\$/share) = \frac{0.05I}{X}$$

Now we estimate the expected prevailing price at time t_n in terms of price appreciation and market impact as follows:

$$E[P_n] = P_0 + n\Delta p + \frac{0.05I}{X}$$

where $n\,\Delta\,p$ represents the natural price appreciation at time n and the last expression is the permanent price inpact. Thus, the expected trading related opportunity cost in a future period t is estimated as follows:

$$E[OC(t)] = \left(\left(P_0 + t\Delta p + \frac{0.05I}{X}\right) - P_0\right)\left(X - \sum_{j=1}^{t} x_j\right)$$

$$= \left(t\Delta p + \frac{0.05I}{X}\right)\left(X - \sum_{j=1}^{t} x_j\right)$$

where $(x - \sum_{j=1}^{t} x_j)$ is the number of residual shares in period t. Thus, we have,

$$E[OC(t)] = \left(t\Delta p + \frac{0.05I}{X}\right)\left(X - \sum_{j=1}^{t} x_j\right) \tag{7.4}$$

Depending upon the price forecast and trading schedule the opportunity cost of a schedule has different shapes. The shape might depict a concave function with time where maximum opportunity cost exists, or a decreasing function, for example, no expected price appreciation cost or negative expected price appreciation cost.

Let us evaluate the shape of our price appreciation cost. *For Example,* let the trading strategy x be defined by a trading rate α such that the number of shares traded in any period j is:

$$x_j = \alpha X$$

and the number of shares executed in total by the end of j is $j\alpha X$ and the number of residual shares are $X - j\alpha X$. Then the expected opportunity cost of the schedule over the trading horizon solves as:

$$E[OC(t, \alpha)] = \left(t\Delta p + \frac{0.05I}{X} \right)(X - t\alpha X)$$

The first derivative with respect to time is:

$$\frac{\partial E[OC(t, \alpha)]}{\partial t} = \Delta pX - 2t\Delta p\alpha X - .05\alpha I$$

This function attains either a maximum or minimum at $\partial/\partial t = 0$. Solving for t in this equation we get:

$$t = \frac{\Delta pX - .05\alpha I}{2\Delta p\alpha X}$$

for $\Delta p \neq 0$.

For $\Delta p = 0$ the opportunity cost of the schedule will be a continuously decreasing function since it would only be dependent upon the permanent market impact cost. The global maximum or minimum cost is determined from the second derivative with respect to time. This is:

$$\frac{\partial^2 E[OC(t, \alpha)]}{\partial t^2} = -2\Delta pX\alpha$$

A maximum will occur if $\Delta px > 0$ since $\alpha > 0$ and $\partial^2/\partial t^2 < 0$. It is important to note here that a maximum will always result in presence of adverse price movement. A minimum value will occur if $\Delta px < 0$ since $\alpha > 0$ and $\partial^2/\partial t^2 > 0$. A minimum opportunity cost value will only result in presence of favorable price movement.

Figure 7.1 depicts potential opportunity cost shapes for three scenarios: positive price appreciation, no price appreciation, and negative price appreciation. In each case we assume a permanent impact of $0.12/share exerted into the market immediately. Many have proposed applying permanent impact in proportion to the number of shares traded so that total permanent impact will be $0.12/share. Analysts are encouraged to consider both possibilities. Notice the shape of each scenario in the figure. For $\Delta p = 0.05$/period the shape is concave, increasing to a maximum point then falling to zero. The scenario with zero price trend shows the opportunity cost function is a strictly decreasing function. For $\Delta p = -0.05$/period the

Figure 7.1. Potential Opportunity Cost Scenarios

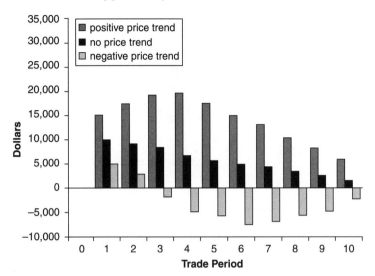

shape is a convex function, decreasing to a minimum then increasing to zero. This scenario may at first appear counterintuitive, but given the price trend and trade schedule it is indeed an accurate representation. Analysts can refer to these potential scenarios to gain insight into opportunity cost evolution of their order for any trading period given the trade schedule and expected price trend.

Example 3.   A trader receives an order to buy 100,000 shares of ABC currently trading at $25 by executing 10,000 shares each period. If period-to-period price appreciation is $\Delta P = \$0.01/$share and permanent market impact is $0.05/share, compute the opportunity cost of the schedule over the ten trading periods. We show this in Table 7.1.

Figure 7.2 illustrates evolution of the opportunity cost of a trade schedule for Example 3. It shows the number of residual shares at the end of each period along with expected price in each period due to price appreciation and permanent market impact. The opportunity cost at each trade interval is the product of the expected price and residual shares.

Trading Cost of Residuals

We should not regard measured price change over a period as synonymous with costs associated with completing the remaining shares. Further, observed price change is not associated with the cost of immediate execution

Table 7.1.   Illustration of Opportunity Cost Trajectory

	0	1	2	3	4	5	6	7	8	9	10
Trade Schedule											
Shares Traded		10,000	10,000	10,000	10,000	10,000	10,000	10,000	10,000	10,000	10,000
Residual Shares	100,000	90,000	80,000	70,000	60,000	50,000	40,000	30,000	20,000	10,000	0
Price Information											
Price Appreciation		0.05	0.10	0.15	0.20	0.25	0.30	0.35	0.40	0.45	0.50
Permanent MI		0.05	0.05	0.05	0.05	0.05	0.05	0.05	0.05	0.05	0.05
E[Price]	25.00	25.10	25.15	25.20	25.25	25.30	25.35	25.40	25.45	25.50	25.55
Opportunity Cost											
OC($)		$9,000	$12,000	$14,000	$15,000	$15,000	$14,000	$12,000	$9,000	$5,000	$0
OC($/share)		$0.09	$0.12	$0.14	$0.15	$0.15	$0.14	$0.12	$0.09	$0.05	$0.00
OC (bp)		36	48	56	60	60	56	48	36	20	0

Figure 7.2.   Opportunity Cost of Trade Schedule

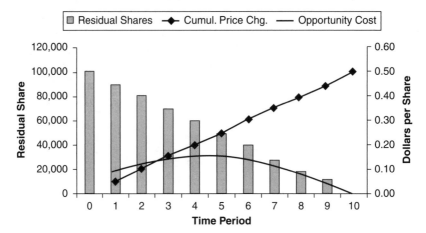

of residual shares. Observed price change is an ex-post measure and has no explanatory power in estimating the trading cost of residual shares.

The cost of immediate execution of residual shares is equivalent to computing the instantaneous cost of those shares. However, in this case we are concerned only with temporary market impact because price appreciation and the order's permanent market impact are embedded in the stock price. Our concern is cost measured as differences between the price at opening (of trading) and average execution price. We incorporate these two costs as follows:

Let,
$X - \Sigma x_j$ = residual shares at time j
$I(X)$ = instantaneous market impact cost of order X

Then the immediacy cost for execution for the residual shares $K(R_j)$ can be shown according to our cost allocation scheme as follows:

$$\hat{E}\big[K(R_j)\big] = \underbrace{(X - \sum x_j)}_{\text{Shares to Trade}} \cdot \left(\underbrace{(P_j - P_0)}_{\text{Actual Price Change}} + \underbrace{0.95I}_{\text{Temp MI}} \cdot \underbrace{\frac{(X - \sum x_j)}{X}}_{\text{Cost Allocation}} \cdot \underbrace{\frac{1}{(X - \sum x_j)}}_{\text{Cost Participation}} \right)$$

This reduces to:

$$E\big[K(R_j)\big] = (X - \sum x_j) \cdot \left((P_j - P_0) + \cdot \frac{0.95I}{X} \right) \qquad \textbf{(7.5)}$$

The expected average price for execution of the residuals is:

$$\overline{P(R_j)} = P_j + \frac{0.95I}{X}$$

The actual price change is the estimated cost due to price appreciation and permanent market impact. Some argue that quantity underestimates permanent market impact cost because it is unlikely that a trader's investment strategy would be completely absorbed in the market before the execution is complete. However, since the next trade is for the residual shares, the permanent market impact cost of that decision is not absorbed by the market until after the residual shares are completed. Thus, that cost component does not affect investors. The temporary market impact cost is high because of the large liquidity demand on the stock. The temporary cost per share remains the same, but there are no participation savings because in an instantaneous execution there are no other market participants involved in the transaction. This is:

$$\frac{1}{x + 0.5v} = \frac{1}{x} \rightarrow \frac{1}{R_j} = \frac{1}{X - \sum x_j}$$

Recall the immediacy execution is synomonous with investors bearing all temporary market impact costs, i.e., $\sqrt{} = 0$.

Relationship Between Opportunity Cost and Timing Risk

Another misconception surrounding transaction cost analysis is the belief that opportunity cost is the list's associated price volatility. The misconception arises because of failure to properly differentiate between historical measures and forecast estimates. Since opportunity cost is often positive (indicating a cost) rather than negative (indicating a savings), participants confuse a positive opportunity cost with price volatility.

Let us evaluate this in two ways. First, let us compare expected price change to potential price change (price volatility). Recall that expected price change is due to price appreciation and permanent market impact. These formulas are:

$$E[P(t)] = t\Delta p + 0.05 \cdot I/X$$
$$\sigma(t) = \sqrt{t} \cdot \sigma$$

These equations show that the similarity between expected and potential price changes are increasing functions with time (assuming $\Delta p > 0$). The expected price change is a linear function and the price volatility is a square root function. Second, let us evaluate the relationship between opportunity cost and the residual risk of a trade schedule. By residual risk we mean the potential total dollar change from the starting price P_0. These formulas are:

$$OC(x_k, t) = \left(X - \sum_{j=1}^{t} x_j \right) (t\Delta p + 0.05 \cdot I/X) \qquad (7.6)$$

$$\Re(x_k, t) = \sqrt{\left(X - \sum_{j=1}^{t} x_j \right)^2 \sigma^2 \cdot \sqrt{t}} \qquad (7.7)$$

Example 4. Consider the following. A stock trades at $25. Daily volatility is 300bp, which is equivalent to approximately $0.21/share per half-hour trading interval. The expected price appreciation is $0.05/period and permanent market impact of the order is $0.05/share. A 100,000-share order trades equally over 25 periods (almost two full days), for example, 4,000 shares in each period. Compare price volatility with expected price change, and the opportunity cost with the residual risk of the trade strategy. We represent this graphically in Figure 7.3 and Figure 7.4.

Figure 7.3 illustrates the relationship between expected price change and price volatility. Notice the similarities between the two trajectories; for example, both increase over time. However, since price change is linear and price volatility the square root, we find in early periods price volatility dominates (is greater) but for later periods the expected price change dominates. Figure 7.4 depicts the relationship between a trade schedule's opportunity cost and residual risk. The figure shows the similarity between both trajectories. They are at zero since no price change occurs before trading opens. The trajectory increases to a maximum value, decreasing to zero at the conclusion of trading. We see that the timing risk trajectory dominates in early periods, then converges close to the opportunity cost trajectory.

As shown in this example, the opportunity cost and residual risk of a trade list are similar but do vary. Managers and traders should understand the formulation of each measure in order to add value and achieve best execution for investors. If confusion persists it will inescapably lead to improper implementation decisions.

Figure 7.3. Comparison Between Expected Change and Price Volatility

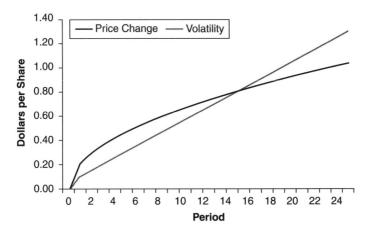

Figure 7.4. Comparison Between Residual Opportunity Cost and Residual Timing Risk

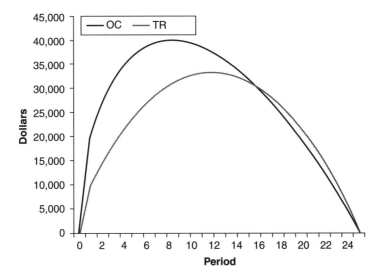

CHAPTER EIGHT

The Holy Grail
of Market Impact

RECENTLY THERE HAS BEEN A trend towards developing market impact estimation models. Some of the more notable work by researchers is attributable to Almgren and Chriss (1997, 2000, 2002), Bertsimas and Lo (1998),
Gringold and Kahn (1999), Ferstenberg (2000), Kissell and Malamut (2000,
2002), Cox (2001), and Wagner (1993). Some of the more noteable work by
companies is attributable to Instinet, ITG, Plexus Group, and Barra.

In this chapter, we focus on the development of a market impact estimation model. Our approach is twofold: first to develop a structured estimation model, and second, to apply that model to a specified trading strategy.
To accomplish this goal we rely on the findings of those mentioned above.

The measurement of market impact has proven to be extremely elusive due to our inability to simultaneosuly measure how stock price would
evolve in the market both with and without the order or trade (e.g., the
Heisenberg Uncertainty Principle of Market Impact). Thus, the quest for
an appropriate estimation model is often referred to as the "Holy Grail" of
transaction cost modeling. But while market impact remains an ambigu-
ous concept, there is a common theme regarding the factors that contribute
to market impact. First, market impact is positively related to the size of
the order and the imbalance it causes in supply-demand equilibrium. The
larger the order the higher the imbalance and the higher the cost. Second,
market impact is related to volatility. Stocks with higher volatility exhibit
greater price elasticity and a higher trading cost. Third, market impact is
related to trading intensity—the more aggressive the strategy the higher
the cost and the more passive the strategy the lower the cost. Finally,

market impact cost is dependent upon the prevailing market conditions over the trading horizon. The higher the liquidity the lower the cost and the lower the liquidity the higher the cost. Hence, market impact can be specified as follows:

$$K = f \text{ (Imbalance, Volatility, Trading Style, Market Conditions)}$$

Random Walk with Market Impact

The development of a market impact estimation model begins with investigation of the random walk model. Let P_0 be the current stock price and ΔP_j be the expected price change of the jth trade. Then the expected price of each subsequent trade is estimated as follows:

$$P_1 = P_0 + \Delta P_1 + \varepsilon_1$$
$$P_2 = P_1 + \Delta P_2 + \varepsilon_2 = P_0 + \Delta P_1 + \Delta P_2 + \varepsilon_2 + \varepsilon_2$$
$$\vdots$$
$$P_j = P_0 + \sum \Delta P_i + \sum \varepsilon_i$$

where, ε_i is i.i.d. $\sim N(0,\sigma^2)$. But this representation of price evolution is overly simplified because it does not incorporate the buying and selling pressure of each trade, namely, temporary impact due to liquidity requirements and permanent impact caused by information leakage. To incorporate these effects let $k(x)$ represent the temporary impact and $f(x)$ represent the permanent impact resulting from x shares transacted. Further, let the sign of these functions be dependent on the side of the transaction x. If $x > 0$, then the transaction was a buy and $k(x) > 0$, $f(x) > 0$. If $x < 0$ then the transaction was a sell and $k(x) < 0$, $f(x) < 0$. Buy orders increase price and sell orders decrease price. Now, if x_j denotes the number of shares executed in the jth trade the random walk model can be rewritten as follows:

$$P_1 = P_0 + \Delta P_1 + k(x_1) + f(x_1) + \varepsilon_1$$
$$P_2 = P_1 + \Delta P_2 + k(x_2) + f(x_2) + \varepsilon_2 - k(x_1)(1-e^{-c})$$

here, e^{-c} represents exponential rate of decay of temporary impact and $(1-e^{-c})$ represents the percentage of temporary impact that has dissipated from the last trade (Bertsimas and Lo, 1998). This has also been referred to as the half-life of temporary impact (Almgren and Chriss, 1997). Now, substituting for P_1 we estimate P_2 as follows:

$$P_2 = P_0 + \sum_{i=1}^{2} \Delta P_i + \sum_{i=1}^{2} k(x_i)e^{-(2-i)c} + \sum_{i=1}^{2} f(x_i) + \sum_{i=1}^{2} \varepsilon_i$$

and P_3 as follows:

$$P_3 = P_0 + \sum_{i=1}^{3} \Delta P_i + \sum_{i=1}^{3} k(x_i)e^{-(3-i)c} + \sum_{i=1}^{3} f(x_i) + \sum_{i=1}^{3} \varepsilon_i$$

Continuing in this manner we derive the general formulation of the random walk with market impact and estimate the price of the jth trade to be:

$$P_j = P_0 + \sum_{i=1}^{j} \Delta P_i + \sum_{i=1}^{j} k(x_i)e^{-(j-i)c} + \sum_{i=1}^{j} f(x_i) + \sum_{i=1}^{j} \varepsilon_i \qquad (8.1)$$

Unfortunately, this is quite a complex estimation model because it requires analysts to know exactly (or at least approximately) the temporary and permanent impact cost functions and rate of dissipation of temporary market impact cost, i.e., the constant c in e^c. Additionally, there still remains some uncertainty if the exponential decay function is in fact the correct means to model dissipation of temporary impact. Nevertheless, this formulation provides a theoretical basis and foundation for estimating future trade prices and market impact cost.

Simplified Formulation

Investigation of equation 8.1 reveals three distinct expressions: ΔP, which represents price appreciation, $k(x)$ and $f(x)$, which represent market impact, and ε_i, which represents volatility. Henceforth, our focus will be on the market impact expressions of this equation. That is:

$$MI(x_j) = \sum_{i=1}^{j} k(x_i)e^{-(j-i)c} + \sum_{i=1}^{j} f(x_i) \qquad (8.2)$$

In light of the stated difficulties surrounding the estimation of the above parameters we simpify the formulation through the following set of assumptions:

A1) Market Impact is the Same for Buys and Sells.
- ▲ Let market impact cost be the same for buy and sell orders. This states that a buy order will have the same temporary and permanent effect as a sell order for the same number of shares. Mathematically, this is written as $k(-x) = -k(x)$ and $f(-x) = -f(x)$. While there has been some evidence suggesting that sells are more costly than buys, thus seeming to invalidate this assumption, we can adjust our estimates via a correction mechanism in the final market impact expression.

A2) Market Impact is Proportional to the Size of the Trade.
▲ Let the temporary and permanent market impact functions be proportional to the size of the trade, that is, let $k(x)$ and $f(x)$ be linear functions. Therefore, $k(x) = xk$ and $f(x) = xf$. It is important to note here that the linearity assumption is used throughout finance, most noteably in CAPM and APT. Furthermore, many non-linear functions can be fairly well approximated via linear simplifications.

A3) Temporary Market Impact Does Not Persist Beyond the Current Period.
▲ As specified in earlier chapters, temporary impact is primarily due to the liquidity demands and immediacy needs of investors. In cases where markets are fairly resilient, orders are replenished at a fast enough rate such that compounding of temporary impact will not arise. Thus, temporary impact will be short-lived. In cases where a buy order follows a sell order, or vice versa, the liquidity demands of the previous trade will have little impact on market prices for orders on the opposite side of that trade. Sell limit orders are not affected by buy transactions and buy limit orders are not affected by sell transactions. Therefore, if the exponential rate of decay c in 8.2 is large enough, e.g., $c>>0$, we have $e^{-(j-i)c} = 0$ for $j \neq i$ and $e^{-(j-i)c} = 1$ for $j=i$. Thus, temporary impact is only incurred by that specific transaction.

A4) Only Liquidity Demanders Incur Temporary Market Impact Cost.
▲ We have previously provided a definition for liquidity demanders and liquidity suppliers. Namely, liquidity demanders are required to implement an investment decision and in doing so contribute to the supply-demand imbalance. Liquidity demanders transact at market prices. Liquidity suppliers, on the other hand, only transact if prices are deemed favorable. Thus, it is appropriate to specify that only liquidity demanders pay tempoary impact.

A5) Information from Offsetting Orders Cancel.
▲ The information content from offsetting orders cancels one another. Since all trades convey some quantity of investment information to the market, there is a continous reassessment of the stock's current intrinsic value. Buy orders push the price up and sell orders push the price down. But since we assume information content is proportional to the size of the trade A2) and equal for buy and sell trades A1), the net information content over any period will be proportional to the net buy-sell imbalance over that period. Thus, permanent impact is a function of the buy-sell imbalance. Permanent impact is due to the net effect of all market participants, not solely due to liquidity demanders.

A6) All Participants Pay Permanent Impact Cost.
▲ Following A5) we can state that all market participants incur permanent impact cost. However, since this cost is a function of the side of the imbalance, participants on the same side as the imbalance transact at less favorable prices and all participants on the opposite side of the imbalance transact at more favorable prices. Restated, we have the liquidity demander incurring a cost and the liquidity supplier realizing a savings. This again is consistent with our definition of these two transactors.

Following assumptions A1) – A3) we simplify the total market impact cost of the jth trade in dollars to be:

$$MI(x_j) = \sum_{i=1}^{j} k(x_i)e^{-(j-i)c} + \sum_{i=1}^{j} f(x_i) = x_j k + \sum_{i=1}^{j} x_i f$$

Following A4) we compute the total market impact cost in dollars exerted into the market after *n*-trades to be:

$$MI_n = \sum_{j=1}^{n} x_j k + \sum_{j=1}^{n} \sum_{i=1}^{n} x_i f$$

But this still requires estimates of k and f. To alleviate this difficulty we restate market impact in terms of the liquidity demander formulation from Chapter 5. That is:

$$MI_n = \sum_{j=1}^{n} x_j k + \sum_{j=1}^{n} \sum_{i=1}^{j} x_i f = \alpha I + (1 - \alpha)I$$

where α represents the percentage of temporary impact and $1 - \alpha$ represents the percentage of permanent impact. I represents the total market impact cost expressed in dollars and is of course dependent upon the size of the imbalance and volatility of the stock.

By A4), only liquidity demanders pay temporary impact, and by A5) – A6), permanent impact is a function of the net imbalance. Therefore, we can compute an average temporary and permanent cost expressed in $/share as follows:

$$\bar{k} = \frac{\sum\limits_{j \in side} x_j k}{\sum\limits_{j \in side} x_j} = \frac{\alpha I}{V_{side}}, \; \bar{f} = \frac{\sum\limits_{j=1}^{n} \sum\limits_{j=1}^{j} x_i f}{\sum\limits_{j=1}^{n} x_j} = \frac{(1 - \alpha)I}{Q}$$

where I is the total impact cost, V_{side} is the traded volume from liquidity demanders (i.e., on the same side as the imbalance, $j \in side$), and Q is the net imbalance.

Subsequently, the market impact cost equation expressed in \$/share is:

$$MI_{\$/share} = \frac{\alpha I}{V_{side}} + \frac{(1-\alpha)I}{Q} \qquad \text{(8.3)}$$

Impact cost of an order X

We compute the market impact cost for an order of X shares as follows:

$$MI_{\$}(X) = X \cdot \left(\frac{\alpha I}{V_{side}} + \frac{(1-\alpha)I}{Q} \right) \qquad \text{(8.4)}$$

It is easy to see that in 8.4 if the order is equal in size to the imbalance and if the order accounts for all liquidity demand, that is, $X=Q=V_{side}$, the total impact cost incurred by the investor's order is I. The largest difference between the random walk model (8.2) and the simplified model (8.4) is that the formulation in 8.2 is a bottom up approach. We start at the trade level and work up towards a cost for the order. The formulation in 8.4 is a top down approach. We start with the total cost amount and work our way down to a cost for the order.

Impact cost of a strategy x_k

Traders are often interested in understanding the cost associated with a specified trading strategy x_k. This is useful for those seeking to develop an appropriate slicing strategy and are interested in analyzing the cost repercussions of trading too aggressively or too passively. Following 8.1 we find that the percentage of temporary impact in any trading period k is equal to the percentage of the imbalance in that period. This is found as follows:

$$MI_{\$}(k) = \frac{\sum\limits_{j \in k} x_j k}{\sum\limits_{j=1}^{n} x_j k} = \frac{\sum\limits_{j \in k} x_j}{\sum\limits_{j=1}^{n} x_j} = \frac{q_k}{Q}$$

where q_k is the net imbalance in period k.

Total temporary impact cost can then be allocated to each trading period based on the percentage of imbalance in each period. Since we apply an average permanent impact cost across all trades it is not necessary to allocate total permanent impact cost across periods. This makes things much simpler. The market impact cost of an associated trading strategy x_k is computed as follows:

$$MI(x_k) = \sum_{k=1}^{n} x_k \left(\frac{q_k}{Q} \cdot \frac{\alpha I}{V_{side}} + \frac{(1-\alpha)I}{Q} \right)$$
(8.5)

Estimating Model Parameters

In this section we investigate techniques to estimate the parameters of our market impact model. Let us begin by rewritting 8.4 over an entire trading day and with $X = Q$ as follows:

$$MI_\$(X = Q) = Q \cdot \left(\frac{\alpha I}{V_{side}} + \frac{(1-\alpha)I}{Q} \right) = \frac{\alpha IQ}{V_{side}} + (1-\alpha)I$$
(8.6)

Since I is a function of imbalance and volatility, and if $\eta = V_{side}/Q$ the above reduces to:

$$MI_\$(Q) = I(Q, \sigma) \cdot (\alpha \eta^{-1} + (1-\alpha)) = I(Q, \sigma) \cdot d(\eta)$$

Notice that the proposed market impact formulation is now represented as a product of two functions. To increase the number of data observations for use in estimation of the parameters we normalize imbalance and cost. We present an aggregated market impact model. Investors seeking finer precision should consider a stock specific model and could eliminate volatility from the cost equation. Imbalance is stated as a percentage of average daily volume and cost in stated is basis points. Thus we have,

$$MI_{bp} = I_{bp}(Z, \sigma) \cdot d(\eta)$$

The instantaneous market impact function needs to be specified by the analyst. The dissipation function $d(\eta)$ has already been specified by the simplified random walk equation 8.1. We investigate three possible structures for the instantaneous market impact function below. They are:

$$\text{Linear Model:} \quad I_{bp} = a_1 Z + a_2 \sigma + a_3$$
$$\text{Non-linear Model:} \quad I_{bp} = a_1 Z^{a_2} + a_3 \sigma + a_4$$
$$\text{Power Function:} \quad I_{bp} = a_1 Z^{a_2} \sigma^{a_3}$$

The first is the classical linear regression model and the most common of all regression models. The second is a non-linear model. Variations of this model are common in economics and the physical sciences. The third model is the classical power function and has the same formulation as the Cobb-Douglas production function found in economic literature. It is also a very common formulation in the sciences. Estimation of market impact now reduces to the estimation of parameters a_i's in the above formulations and of α in $d(\eta)$.

Readers are encouraged to experiment with alternative non-linear formulations. Variations of these structured models have been proposed by Cox (2000), Feistenberg (2000), Almgren and Chriss (1997, 2000), Barra (1997), Kaufman (1999), and Plexus.

Data Sampling Procedure

Unlike ordinary regression analysis where the exogenous variables are specified, our needs require us to compute the model factors. An appropriate technique for each of the variables is discussed next.

Market Imbalance

The calculation of the true market imbalance over any horizon requires knowledge of the investment intention for every trade/order executed in the market. Unfortunately, this level of detail is not readily available and the investment intentions of participants is rarely released publicly. To work around this difficulty we apply a technique proposed by Lee and Ready (1991) to infer the trading intentions of investors. This allows us to derive corresponding imbalances as the difference between buy-initiated volume and sell-initiated volume.

Lee and Ready Tick Algorithm

The Lee and Ready tick algorithm consists of designating trades as either buy or sell initiated. The methodology involves matching the trade price to the market quote at time of execution. If the transaction price is higher than the midpoint of the quote the trade is designated as a buy-initiated trade. If the transaction price is lower than the midpoint of the quote the trade is designated as a sell-initiated trade. If the trade occurs exactly at the midpoint of the quote the transaction is designated as buy or sell initiated based on the previous tick change. The assumption is that buyers push up the price and sellers push down the price.

The actual mapping of market transactions to the prevailing market quote at time of execution is still a difficult process. Actual market execution data and prevailing market quotes are not reported together. Thus, analysts need to determine the prevailing quote at the time of the execution by matching trade and quote data. But this is often still a difficult process because there could be a time lag between the time a trade executes and when it is reported.

The Lee and Ready algorithm can be modified so that it relies only on trade data as opposed to both trade and quote information. This approach consists of labeling all executions that occur on an up tick + or zero up tick 0+ as a buy-initiated transaction and any execution that occur on a down tick–or zero down tick 0– as a sell-initiated transaction. A zero up tick refers to a transaction at the same price as the previous trade where the last price change was up. A zero down tick refers to a transaction at the same price as the previous trade where the last price change was down. In other words, a tick is designated as a buy-initiated trade if the previous change was up and as a sell-initiated trade if the previous change was down. The up tick–down tick rule here serves as a proxy for buy-initiated and sell-initiated transactions suggested by Lee and Ready.

Market imbalance is then simply computed as the difference between buy-initiated and sell-initiated volume. The calculation can easily be expressed in terms of signed volumes where $sign(v_i) = v_i$ if the trade was designated as a buy-initiated trade and $sign(v_i) = -v_i$ if the trade was designated as a sell-initiated trade. Mathematically, imbalance is computed as follows:

$$Q = \sum_{i=1}^{n} sign(v_i)$$

Values of $Q > 0$ indicates a buy imbalance of Q shares and $Q < 0$ indicates a sell imbalance of Q shares. The imbalance Z expressed as a percentage of average daily trading volume is:

$$Z = \frac{|Q|}{ADV} \cdot 100$$

where ADV is simply the average daily traded in the stock over the previous 30 days. The use of the absolute value sign is required because we are not distinguishing between buy and sell orders in our model.

The modified tick rule does have its shortcomings. There are times when this methodology may cause us to incorrectly designate a buy-initiated trade as sell initiated or a sell-initiated trade as buy initiated. This can occur if there is a dramatic change in the market quote from one transaction to another. For example, suppose the prevailing market quote is $25.00–$25.10 and the trade occurred at $25.10. Assume a jump in the market quote to $25.20–$25.30. If the next trade is a sell at the bid price of $25.20 our up tick-down tick rule would incorrectly designate this transaction as a buy because $25.20 is higher than the previous trade of $25.10. The good news is, for more liquid stocks, jumps do not occur that frequently. And even in those rare instances, there is still a 50% chance that we will designate initiation correctly. Overall, we have found this approach to work fairly well in practice.

Liquidity Demand Volume

The liquidity demander volume, alternatively referred to as volume on the same side of the imbalance or more simply as V_{side}, is also computed using the buy-sell designation following the modified Lee and Ready tick algorithm. In terms of signed volume, this calculation is as follows:

$$V_{side} = \sum_{i \in Q} sign(v_i)$$

where $i \in Q$ indicates that the traded volume was on the same sign as the imbalance Q.

Price Volatility

The price volatility factor is computed following the traditional statistical definition as the standard deviation of price returns. This measure is used as a means to determine the price sensitivity of the stock to buying and selling pressure. The most typical measure of price change is the close-to-close change in price, but many suggest that using the open-to-close or the vwap-to-vwap price change is a more appropriate measure of price sensitivity because it better focuses on the intraday trading activity. For purposes of determining the price elasticity of demand (price sensitivity) we suggest a simple close-to-close measure of the volatility of logarithmic price change for the previous thirty trading days.

$$\sigma = \sqrt{\frac{1}{n-1} \sum_{i=1}^{30} (g_i - \bar{g})^2}$$

where, $g_i = ln(P_i/P_{i-1})$. Analysts could alternatively measure the stock volatility as the standard deviation of price returns $r_i = P_i/P_{i-1}-1$ since there is relatively little difference between the values for reasonable changes (e.g., less than 20%). This is: $ln(p_t/p_{t-1}) \cong p_t/p_{t-1}-1$ for $-20\% \leq (p_t/p_{t-1}-1) \leq 20\%$

Trading Style

To develop a "good" structured model it is necessary to quantify a qualitative trading style measure. We express this variable in terms of a participation number η. It is a measure of trading style that represents the number of equal size orders executed in the market over the same trading period as the investor's order. The lower the participation number the shorter the trading time horizon and the more aggressive the strategy. The larger the participation number the longer the trading time horizon and the more passive the strategy. The participation number is calculated as follows:

$$\eta = V_{side} / |Q|$$

The absolute value sign is required to ensure that the participation number will be positive.

Trading Cost

The computed market imbalance Q corresponds to an average execution price P_Q defined as the volume weighted average price for those shares on the same side as the imbalance. For example, the average execution price corresponding to a positive imbalance is the volume weighted average price for those shares designated as buy-initiated trades and the average execution price corresponding to a negative imbalance is the volume weighted average price for those shares designated as sell-initiated trades. This follows from assumption A4 where we specify that liquidity demanders cause temporary impact cost. The calculation for P_Q is computed as follows:

$$P_Q = \left\{ \frac{\sum_i V_i P_i}{\sum_i V_i} \text{ for } i \in Q \right.$$

The associated trading cost is computed according to the following trading cost equation:

$$\varphi_Q(\$) = \Sigma x_j p_j - XP = XP_Q - XP = X(P_Q - XP)$$

The cost of the imbalance expressed in total dollars, $/share, and basis points is as follows:

$$\varphi_Q(\$) = Q(P_Q - P_0)$$
$$\varphi_Q(\$/share) = sign(Q)(P_q - P_0)$$
$$\varphi_Q(bp) = sign(Q) \cdot \left(\frac{P_Q}{P_0} - 1 \right) \cdot 10^4 \, bp$$

where P_0 designates the starting price.

The computation of average execution price shown here typically finds positive imbalances to be associated with (1) average prices higher than the price at the beginning of trading and (2) negative imbalances to be associated with average prices lower than the price at the beginning of trading, thus resulting in a trading cost. However, there are times when positive imbalances are associated with average prices less than the starting price P_0, and negative imbalances are associated with average prices greater than the starting price P_0, indicating a savings. While this is usually a rare event it could occur for several reasons. First, it could be the result of price appreciation, volatility, or noise. Second, it could be due to an incorrect designation of buy- or sell-initiated trades. Third, it could be due to the sequence of order arrivals in the market. Fourth, it could be due to the correlation of stock price movement to general market movements. The first three concerns are alleviated through the incorporation of a sufficiently large enough data set. The fourth concern is addressed by adjusting for market movement (discussed next).

Adjustment for Market Movement

The calculation of the average execution price and trading cost associated with the imbalance presented above does not adjust for market movement. It assumes all price movement is the result of buying and selling pressure. However, to the extent that prices are correlated with the market (at least to some extent) it is necessary to make appropriate adjustment for market movement. We discuss two techniques.

First, one can add a market movement term to the specified model, say r_m, where r_m is the change in some general market index similar to how it is incorporated in CAPM. For the linear formulation above this would take new form:

$$I = a_1 Z + a_2 \sigma + a_3 \eta + a_4 r_m + a_5$$

where, a_1, a_2, a_3, and a_4 are the sensitivities to the associated factors and a_5 is a constant. In this formulation, the coefficient a_4 takes on the same meaning as beta β in CAPM. This relationship, in fact, has been studied by Chordia, Roll, and Subrahmanyan (2001), and Aiyagari (1993). This formulation, however, does not ensure that the correlation across all variables is zero. Empirical evidence shows that there is often a degree of correlation between imbalance and market movement (Barra, 1997). Thus leading to a multicollinearity problem and potentially incorrect conclusions from a poorly specified model. For a thorough discussion of multicollinearity see Greene (1993), Oujarti (1988).

A second technique is one that filters out the effect of market movement via a boot-strap approach. Here, data points are selected at random such that the average market movement r_m of the sample is zero or at least reasonably close to zero. In this case the model formulation does not need to incorporate a market movement variable. For a thorough explanation of this process see Sall and Lehman (1996), Chapter 12 and Chapter 13. More indepth methods on data reduction techniques for non-linear regression models can be found in Dudeuicz and Mishra (1988), Chapter 8. Finally, Glantz (2000) presents alternative approaches for data reduction and grouping through data mining and filtering techniques.

Robust Estimation Adjustment

A concern of any regression analysis is with what ultimately is going to be forecasted, how accurate are the results, and how well does the model behave. In our case, we are interested in a model that will produce equally accurate estimates over all reasonable possibilties of size, volatility, and participation. Our goal is to develop a model that fits all data equally well. Unfortunately, the approach described above will be biased towards those observations that arise most often, not necessarily those observations that may be of the most concern. For example, one may find that the model estimates market impact reasonably well for small imbalances and average volatility but does a poor job at estimating market impact for large imbalances or for stocks with higher or lower volatility. Luckily, this can be addressed via a simple weighting scheme. The approach is as follows. First, group the data into category bins based on imbalance, volatility, and market movement. For example group all data points with an imbalance of 5% ADV, volatility of 300bp/day, and participation number of $\eta=5$ into the same category. Second, weight each observation in the category by w_i where:

$$w_i = \frac{\text{total number of sample observations}}{\text{number of observations in the category}}$$

Third, peform non-linear regression analysis incorporating the above weighting scheme similar to how one makes an adjustment for heteroscadisticity in ordinary least squares.

Best-Fit Estimation Models

Since the structure of the market impact model is the product of two functions $I(Z,\sigma)$ and $d(\eta)$ the parameters need to be estimated via more advanced regression techniques than traditional OLS. The more common non-linear approaches are non-linear least squares (NLS), maximum likelihood estimators (MLS), non-linear instrumental variable estimators (NIV), and generalized method of moments (GMM). For further information on these procedures, see Greene (2000), Mittelhammer, Judge, and Miller (2000), or Kennedy (1998).

The results of our non-linear regression estimates shown below are based on numerous analyses, e.g., various samples of sizes, volatility, participation rate, and mixed data samples. Our preferred result for each model is is shown below:

$$\textbf{Linear:} \quad I_{bp}(Z,\sigma) = (8Z + 0.30\sigma + 90) \tag{8.7}$$

$$\textbf{Non-linear:} \quad I_{bp}(Z,\sigma) = (35Z^{0.65} + 0.30\sigma + 15) \tag{8.8}$$

$$\textbf{Power Function:} \quad I_{bp}(Z,\sigma) = (25Z^{0.38}\sigma^{0.28}) \tag{8.9}$$

$$\textbf{Dissipation Function:} \quad d(\eta) = (0.95\eta^{-1} + 0.05) \tag{8.10}$$

Each of these models yields fairly consistent results across size and volatility. However, the non-linear and power function models had smaller regression errors thus implying that the true relationship between cost and size is non-linear. The parameters of these models are also consistent with our expectations—namely, a positive relationship with size and volatility and a negative relationship with participation number.

Important Note:

We determined the above relationship using a limited data set over a small time horizon. We recommend anyone developing a market impact model incorporate a sufficiently large enough data set and evaluate the robustness of the model over various time periods. Furthermore, we have chosen to present the results without any discussion of regression errors or statistical significance of factors. Suffice it to say that all variables were significant. Since we performed non-linear regression a thorough investigation of the results is quite involved. Analysts seeking to develop their own models need to comprehensively investigate all variables and perform proper sensitivity analysis.

Dissecting the Market Impact Model

Instantaneous Impact Cost *I**

The instantaneous market impact cost represents the theoretical cost associated with immediate execution of the entire order to the market. It can be regarded as the premium required to attract the necessary liquidity (counterparties) to complete the order, while still providing participants with protection against potentially transacting with informed investors (information content) and incurring a loss from adverse selection. Our estimates for instantaneous cost are in basis points rather than dollars. To convert back to dollars, multiply the basis point cost by the initial value of the position. That is:

$$I_{\$} = I_{bp} \cdot 10^{-4} \cdot Q \cdot P_0$$

The total market impact model cost can be dissected into two parts: temporary and permanent. These two components play an instrumental role in evaluating the cost of a trading strategy (discussed next). This can be expressed as follows:

$$\hat{k}_{\$} = I_{\$} \cdot (0.95\eta^{-1} + 0.05) = \underbrace{0.95I_{\$} \cdot \eta^{-1}}_{\text{Temporary Impact}} + \underbrace{0.05I_{\$}}_{\text{Permanent Impact}}$$

Temporary Impact

The temporary market impact associated with an order is that part of market impact cost due to liquidity requirements and immediacy needs of investors. It is also the quantitiy of impact cost that can be completely avoided. Our analysis of impact cost brought forth an interesting discovery. We found that in almost all regressions the actual value of the temporary impact parameter was approximately $\alpha = 95\%$. Furthermore, this value appeared to be time invariant and independent of size. The estimate of the temporary parameter was approximately $\alpha = 95\%$ of total for large and small orders. This confirms intuition that temporary impact cost comprises by far the larger percentage of impact cost.

As one participates with an increasing quantity of market volume, the participation number of the execution becomes increasingly larger and the temporary market impact cost becomes increasingly smaller. It can be shown mathematically that temporary cost will tend to zero as participation number increases. That is:

$$\lim_{\eta \to \infty} 0.95I_{\$}\eta^{-1} = 0$$

The participation number representation here also provides some interesting insight into impact cost. The inverse of the participation number is a measure of the percentage of temporary impact cost incurred. Thus, the temporary impact savings (avoided temporary cost) is simply:

$$TempSavings_{\$} = 1 - \eta^{-1} \cdot I$$

Permanent Impact

The permanent market impact cost component is the quantitiy of impact that is not avoidable regardless of the trading strategy or prevailing market conditions. It represents the structural shift in the price trajectory of the stock. Information leakage of the order causes the market to change its valuation of the stock usually resulting in a jump or dip in its market price. Overall, this amount is a relatively small percentage of the pure cost component. Our analyses estimate this percentage to be 5% of total. What this means is that on average, every order conveys information to the market that results in a change in stock price of 5% of total instantaneous cost. It can easily be seen that the permanent impact cost resulting from information leakage to the market is independent of trading style because it does not include the participation number expression in its derivation. It also follows the conventional wisdom of the market, namely, that the larger the order the higher the information content of the order, and the more likely that the market price of the stock is incorrectly valued. While we determine the permanent impact effect to be a constant of 5%, it should not be confused as a constant quantity over all orders. Since the instantaneous cost does vary with size and volatility, the permanent market impact of an order will also vary with size and volatility.

Forecasting Market Impact

In this section we investigate techniques for forecasting market impact cost for a specified order and trading strategy. The actual forecast of market impact requires coincident estimates of average daily trading volume, market volumes in each period, and incremental imbalance from all other market participants. Our forecasting equations of an order and srategy are extensions of equation (8.5) respectively, as follows:

$$K(X) = I(0.95\eta^{-1} + 0.05) \qquad \text{(8.11)}$$

$$K(x_k) = \sum x_k \frac{0.95 I q_k}{Q \cdot v_{k,side}} + \frac{0.05 I}{Q} \qquad \text{(8.12)}$$

Notice that the forecasting equation requires estimated values for imbalance Q, liquidity demander volume by period $v_{k,side}$, and instantaneous cost I. We discuss forecasting techniques for two cases: 1) the imbalance is equal to the size of the order, and 2) there is incremental imbalance due to other market participants.

Imbalance Equal to Size of Order

First let us consider the homogeneous case where the order size is equal to market imbalance. Here the assumption is that $Q = X$ and each $x_k = q_k$. This is a very common assumption because it is often difficult to ascertain the buying and selling demand from other participants before trading begins. Now let us turn our attention to the estimate of instantaneous cost I and liquidity demander volume by period.

Instantaneous Cost

Instantaneous market impact cost is forecasted following one's preferred estimation equation (8.7–8.9). The general form is:

$$I_\$ = f(Z, \sigma) \cdot 10^{-4} \cdot P_0 \cdot Q$$

where,

$$Z = |X| / ADV \cdot 100$$

Liquidity Demander Volume

Liquidity demander volume by period is estimated as follows. First, computed the expected volume on the day $V(t)$ as follows:

$$V(t) = ADV \cdot DOW(t)$$

where, $DOW(t)$ is the day of week adjustment factor (chapter 3) to account for the weekly volume effect. Second, compute the percentage of volume in each trading period by applying the stocks volume profile (chapter 3) as follows:

$$v_k = V(t) \cdot u_k = ADV \cdot DOW(t) \cdot u_k$$

Since expectations are that the total imbalance will be equal in size to the investor's order, v_k will consist of an equal amount of buy-initiated and sell-initiated volume. Therefore, the liquidity demander volume will be equal to the imbalance in each period x_k plus ½ of the market volume. That is:

$$v_{k,side} = x_k + 0.5v_k$$

Substituting these values into (8.5) we compute the market impact for an order X implemented over n-trading periods following strategy x_k as follows:

$$\hat{K}_\$(x_k) = \sum_{k=1}^{n} x_k \left(\frac{0.95Ix_k}{X \cdot (x_k + 0.5v_k)} + \frac{0.05I}{X} \right) \qquad (8.13)$$

Market impact cost expressed in dollars is a cumulative function. Therefore, we compute the market impact cost for a list of m-stocks traded over n-periods as the sum of costs for all orders as follows:

$$\hat{K}_\$(x_k) = \sum_{i=1}^{m} \sum_{k=1}^{n} |x_{ik}| \cdot \left(\frac{0.95I_i|x_{ik}|}{|X_i| \cdot (|x_{ik}| + 0.5v_{ik})} + \frac{0.05I_i}{|X_i|} \right) \qquad (8.14)$$

The additional subscript i is used to indicate that the variable corresponds to stock i. For example, I_i refers to the instantaneous market impact cost of the order for stock i, X_i refers to the total number of shares to trade in stock i, x_{ik} refers to the number of shares of stock i to execute in period k, etc. Also, it is important to include the absolute value sign to distinguish between buy and sell orders in the trade list.

Estimating Market Impact Cost in the Presence of Incremental Imbalance

There are often times when investors have realistic expectations regarding buying and selling pressure from other market participants. Sometimes this is based purely on intuition, but in general these expectations are motivated by quantitative and/or qualitative analysis combined with a little touch of art (and reliable rumors and whispers are always helpful). These expectations can arise from information and/or the usual buying and selling habits of traders. It may also occur when investors solicit cost estimates from an agency or principal bid broker where they provide the broker with the actual order list or the characteristics of the list (e.g., blind bid). But expectations pertaining to incremental imbalance will also occur during times of index reconstitution. Investors often infer incremental imbalance in specific stocks based on the changing weightings of those stocks in the index and the quantity of investment dollars tied to those indexes.

Our discussions of market impact up through this point focused on the impact cost associated with an imbalance equal to the size of the order X (e.g., the net imbalance of all other market participants is zero). But in situations where the net imbalance of other investors Y is not zero, our estimates need to reflect this information. Thus, we need to make appropriate adjustments to Z and V_{side}. These calculations are discussed next.

Instantaneous Cost

Instantaneous market impact cost is again forecasted following one's preferred technique (8.7–8.9). But here we need to compute the instantaneous cost for the net market imbalance $X+Y$. The general form is:

$$I_\$ = f(Z,\sigma) \cdot 10^{-4} \cdot P_0 \cdot |X + Y|$$

where,

$$Z = |X + Y|/ADV \cdot 100$$

It is important to distinguish here that X or $Y > 0$ indicates a buy order and X or $Y < 0$ indicates a sell order.

Liquidity Demander Volume

Liquidity demander volume in presence of incremental imbalance is computed in a similar fashion as above, but incorporates the expected period imbalance from all market participants. Notice that this requires investors to have expectations regarding total incremental imbalance on the day Y and also incremental imbalance in every trading period y_k. When this is known, the liquidity demander volume in each period is simply:

$$v_{k,side} = |x_k + y_k| + 0.5v_k$$

The absolute value function is extremely important here because the investor's order and incremental imbalance can and often is on opposite sides. The investor may have a buy order while the incremental imbalance reflects selling pressure, and vice versa.

Incremental Sign Adjustment

Since we are dealing with incremental market imbalance it is quite possible for investors to incur a savings rather than a cost. This will occur whenever the incremental imbalance Y is larger in magnitude and on the opposite side of the investor's order. To address this potential savings, we define a cost function as follows:

$$sign(k) = sign(X) \cdot sign(X + Y)$$

This ensures that the calculation will provide the investor with the correct sign for market impact cost. Subsequently, the market impact forecasting equation in presence of incremental imbalance is:

$$\hat{K}_{\$}(x_k) = sign(k) \cdot \sum_{k=1}^{n} x_k \left(\frac{0.95I|x_k + y_k|}{|X + Y| \cdot (|x_k + y_k| + 0.5v_k)} + \frac{0.05I}{|X + Y|} \right) \quad (8.15)$$

For a list of m-stocks market impact forecasting equation is:

$$\hat{K}_{\$}(x_k) = \sum_{i=1}^{m} \sum_{k=1}^{n} sign(k_i) \cdot |x_{ik}| \cdot \left(\frac{0.95I_i|x_{ik} + y_{ik}|}{|X_i + Y_i| \cdot (|x_{ik} + y_{ik}| + 0.5v_{ik})} + \frac{0.05I_i}{|X_i + (Y)_i|} \right) \quad (8.16)$$

It is important to note that this formulation is only appropriate in cases where the imbalance in each period does not change signs, that is, $sign(q_1)=sign(q_2)= \ . \ . \ . \ =sign(q_n)$. Otherwise, the assumption that offsetting orders negate the effect of one another is violated. When the sign of net imbalance differs over the trading periods, analysts will need to incorporate two cases to account for positive and negative imbalance.

Minimizing Market Impact

Many times investors are solely interested in minimizing market impact cost. This strategy is determined by taking the first derivative of the market impact equation, setting equal to zero, and solving for each of the decision variables x_k. The resulting market impact minimizing strategy when the order is equal in size to the imbalance is:

$$x_k = X \cdot \frac{v_k}{V} \qquad (8.17)$$

Notice that in this case the market impact cost minimizing strategy is a VWAP strategy. In the presence of incremental imbalance the market impact minimizing strategy is:

$$x_k = (X + Y)\frac{v_k}{V} - y_k \qquad (8.18)$$

Notice that in this case the market impact cost minimizing strategy is not a VWAP strategy, however, it does represent a VWAP strategy for the combined imbalance.

Future Prices

Before presenting a methodology for estimating stock price in any given period it is necessary to distinguish between intrinsic value S and prevailing price P. The intrinsic value of the stock is simply its worth or consensus value. The intrinsic value of the stock will change due to natural price appreciation and permanent market impact. Permanent market impact here can be thought of as the revaluation of the stock due to information leakage of investor orders. The prevailing price, however, is the price that the stock will transact at in the market. This price includes price appreciation, permanent and temporary market impact. Recall that temporary market impact is the price sweetener offered by liquidity demanders to attract additional buyers or sellers into the market. This amount reflects the general market consensus regarding the stock's worth plus the price of liquidity. We discuss estimation procedures for each case where there is no incremental imbalance, e.g., $Y=0$.

Intrinsic Price

The expected intrinsic stock value S_k in period k is a function of cumulative price appreciation over t (chapter 4) and permanent impact cost only. It is computed as follows:

$$S_k = P_0 + k\Delta p + \frac{0.05I}{|X|} \qquad (8.19)$$

Prevailing Price

The expected prevailing stock price P_k in period k is a function of cumulative price appreciation over the period, permanent market impact cost, and the quantitiy of temporary impact cost allocated in the period. This is computed as follows:

$$P_k = P_0 + k\Delta p + \frac{0.95I|x_k|}{|X|} + \frac{0.05I}{|X|} \tag{8.20}$$

The above equations are extremely useful for managers evaluating the likelihood of executing a trade at a price better than some specified price. Furthermore, they are especially useful in developing micro-pricing strategies consisting of a mix of market and limit orders, and are useful in rule based trading algorithms.

Important Considerations

The methodology criteria used in this chapter are based on the assumption that stock price movement is solely attributed to market impact: we do not assume any price appreciation over the trading horizon, thus, price appreciation is not incorporated into the cost calculations. Also excluded from the calculations is trading risk. This is not a realistic expectation and is only excluded to focus on the calculation of market impact cost. Investors need to incorporate all cost components when developing trading strategies to achieve their implementation objectives, omission of any of the cost components will likely result in a suboptimal strategy and reduced portfolio returns.

Managing total trading costs is not as simple as slicing an order and trading passively via a market impact cost minimization strategy because associated with a passive strategy is an increase in timing risk. Market impact cost and timing risk are opposite phenomena (trader's dilemma). As one component increases the other component decreases. Hence, a strategy that reduces one cost component will increase the other cost component. A passive trading strategy will lower market impact but increase timing risk, and an aggressive strategy will lower timing risk but increase market impact. A trader needs to manage the trade-off between market impact and timing risk. Price appreciation, on the other hand, is not directly related to either market impact or timing risk. The cost due to price appreciation is based on the trend of the stock and the side of an order. For example, suppose the price of the stock is increasing throughout the day. Then a passive strategy causes a buy order to incur a higher cost because investors would be buying at higher prices. A sell order has an opposite effect and causes investors to incur a lower cost because they would be selling some of the order at higher prices. An aggressive strategy, on the other hand, accelerates all trading and causes a buy order to obtain better prices and a sell order to obtain worse prices. For the most part, money managers buy stocks that are increasing in value and sell stocks that are decreasing in value. So a passive strategy typically causes a fund to incur higher costs due to adverse price movement, while an aggressive strategy typically causes a fund to incur a lower amount of costs. Truly skilled traders evaluate and incorporate all of these cost components into their trading strategy and manage the trade-off between total cost and risk. Since price trends are pretty negligible over a short period of time, traders can focus on the trade-off between market impact and timing risk. Only planning in this manner will achieve best execution. Developmen of such as strategy is the topic of chapter nine.

Examples

General Assumptions

The following sets of examples are provided to help readers better understand the market impact estimation process and to reinforce the material in this chapter. Each subsequent example is based on a fictitious stock ABC with current market price of $50, daily volatility of 300bp/day, and average daily traded volume of 1,000,000 shares. All examples assume that the market imbalance is due to the investor's order unless otherwise specified. For simplicity, these examples do not assume any price appreciation over the trading horizon.

Example 1.   A manager has a buy order for 100,000 shares. Compute the expected instantaneous market impact cost in dollars using each of the three estimation models provided above (8.7–8.9).

Solution:
   First, compute the imbalance as a percentage of ADV:
   $Z = 100,000 / 1,000,000 \cdot 100 = 10$

   Second, estimate instantaneous impact cost:
   $I_\$ = (8 \cdot 10 + 0.3 \cdot 300 + 90) \cdot 10^{-4} \cdot \$50 \cdot 100,000 = \$130,670$ Million
   $I_\$ = (35 \cdot 10^{0.65} + 0.3 \cdot 300 + 15) \cdot 10^{-4} \cdot \$50 \cdot 100,000 = \$148,083$ Million
   $I_\$ = (25 \cdot 10^{0.38} \cdot 300^{0.28}) \cdot 10^{-4} \cdot \$50 \cdot 100,000 = \$130,000$ Million

Example 2.   A manager has a buy order for 100,000 shares. The corresponding instantaneous cost is $I = \$150,000$. The manager chooses to execute the order over an entire day but understands that costs estimates will vary from day to day because of weekly volume patterns. If the DOW adjustment for Monday and Thursday is 0.90 and 1.05, respectively, compute the expected market impact cost in dollars for these days.

Solution:

We compute impact cost as follows:

V_{mon} = 0.90 · 1,000,000 = 900,000
η_{mon} = (100,000 + 0.5 · 900,000)/100,000 = 5.5
K_{mno} = \$150,000 · (0.95 · 5.5^{-1} + 0.05) = \$33,409

V_{thu} = 1.05 · 1,000,000 = 1,050,000
η_{thu} = (100,000 + 0.5 · 1,050,000)/100,000 = 6.25
K_{thu} = \$150,000 · (0.95 · 6.25^{-1} + 0.05) = \$30,300

Notice the expected cost is higher for Monday than Thursday because there is less volume on Monday. There are fewer participants and less liquidity, thus, a higher temporary market impact cost.

Example 3. A manager has a buy order for X = 100,000 shares and chooses to execute the order with a participation number of η = 6. In this example the manager believes that there will be an additional imbalance of Y = 100,000 shares on the same side as the order executed over the same trading horizon. Determine the manager's market impact cost using the power function (8.9) to estimate instantaneous cost.

Solution:

Z = |100,000 + 100,000|/1,000.000 · 100 = 20
I = (25 · 20$^{0.38}$ · 300$^{0.28}$) · \$50 · 200,000 = \$385,412
$sign(\kappa) = sign(X) \cdot sign(X + Y) = + \cdot + = +$
K = +\$385,412 · (0.95 · 6.0^{-1} + 0.05) = +\$80,294

Example 4. A manager has a buy order for X = 100,000 shares and believes that there will be an incremental market imbalance of Y = –50,000 shares. The manager believes that the incremental imbalance will be executed over the same period as the manager's order. If the manager executes the order with a participation number of η = 6, compute the manager's market impact cost using the non-linear instantaneous cost model (8.8).

Solution:

Z = |100,000 + –50,000|/1,000.000 · 100 = 5
I = (35 · 5$^{0.65}$ + 0.30 · 300 +15) · \$50 · 50,000 = \$51,158
$sign(\kappa) = sign(X) \cdot sign(X + Y) = + \cdot + = +$
K = +\$51,158 · (0.95 · 6.0^{-1} + 0.05) = +\$10,657

Example 5. A manager has a buy order for X = 100,000 shares and believes that there will be an incremental market imbalance due to other market participants of Y = –250,000 shares. The manager believes that the incremental imbalance will be executed in the market over the same period as the manager's order. If the manager executes the order with a participation number of $\eta = 5$, compute the manager's market impact cost using the linear instantaneous cost model (8.7).

Solution:

$$Z = |100,000 + -250,000| / 1,000.000 \cdot 100 = 15$$
$$I = (8 \cdot 15 + 0.30 \cdot 300 + 90) \cdot \$50 \cdot 150,000 = \$225,000$$
$$sign(\kappa) = sign(X) \cdot sign(X + Y) = + \cdot - = -$$
$$K = -\$225,000 \cdot (0.95 \cdot 6.0^{-1} + 0.05) = -\$46,875$$

Notice in this example that the manager incurs a savings (negative cost) because there was a greater magnitude of imbalance on the opposite side of the order.

Example 6. A manager has a buy order for X=100,000. If the instantaneous cost of the order is \$150,000, compute the expected market impact cost for the strategy and market conditions shown in Table 8.1.

Solution:

$$K = \frac{\$150,000}{100,000} \sum_{j=1}^{5} \left(\frac{0.95x_k^2}{x_k + 0.5v_k} + 0.05 \right) = \$33,005$$

Example 7. A manager has a buy order for X=100,000 shares and believes there will be an incremental market imbalance of Y=100,000. If the instantaneous cost of the order is \$350,000, compute the expected market impact cost for the strategy and market conditions shown in Table 8.2.

Solution:

$$K = \frac{\$350,000}{200,000} \sum_{j=1}^{5} \left(\frac{x_k \cdot 0.95(x_k + y_k)}{(x_k + y_k) + 0.5v_k} + 0.05 \right) = \$121,140$$

Example 8. A manager has a buy order for X=100,000 shares and believes there will be an incremental market imbalance of Y = −250,000. If the instantaneous cost of the order is \$250,000, compute the expected market impact cost for the strategy and market conditions shown in Table 8.3.

Solution:

$$K = -\frac{\$250,000}{100,000} \sum_{j=1}^{5} \frac{x_k \cdot 0.95(x_k + y_k)}{(x_k + y_k) + 0.5v_k} + 0.05 = -\$116,780$$

Table 8.1.

	1	2	3	4	5
Shares:	20,000	20,000	20,000	20,000	20,000
E(Mkt Volume):	250,000	200,000	100,000	200,000	250,000

Table 8.2.

	1	2	3	4	5
Trade Strategy					
Shares:	20,000	20,000	20,000	20,000	20,000
Incr. Imbalance:	35,000	30,000	20,000	10,000	5,000
Net Imbalance:	55,000	50,000	40,000	30,000	25,000
E(Mkt Volume):	250,000	200,000	100,000	200,000	250,000

Table 8.3.

	1	2	3	4	5
Trade Strategy					
Shares:	20,000	20,000	20,000	20,000	20,000
Incr. Imbalance:	−60,000	−50,000	−30,000	−50,000	−60,000
Net Imbalance:	−40,000	−30,000	−10,000	−30,000	−40,000
E[Mkt Volume]	250,000	200,000	100,000	200,000	250,000

Here the manager incurred a savings because there was a larger imbalance on the opposite side of the manager's order. It is also important to note that the calculation procedure only works because the net imbalance in each period does not change signs.

Example 9. In presence of incremental imbalance the volume follow strategy is not necessarily the strategy of minimum market impact cost. Using data provided in Table 8.2, determine the trading strategy that will result in the minimal market impact.

Solution:
The cost minimizing strategy is found by equating the period imbalances in proportion to market volume according to 8.17 as follows. The minimum cost trading strategy x for the manager is found to be:
$$x = (15,000 \ 10,000 \ 0 \ 30,000 \ 45,000)^t$$

Example 10. A manager has a buy order for $X = 100,000$ shares. The manager has deemed the stock is a value to buy at $50.15 or less. Does the prescribed strategy shown in Table 8.3 cause the manager to pay a price higher than $50.15?

Solution:

This solution requires the computation of the prevailing price in each period because the manager is interested in the expected transaction price of the stock. Prevailing price in each period is computed according to 8.20 and is:

$P_t(k)$ = ($50.08 $50.09 $50.15 $50.09 $50.08)^t

Since the expected transaction price is less than or equal to $50.15 in each period the strategy does not cause the manager to incur a price higher than what is deemed a value. It is an acceptable strategy for the manager.

CHAPTER NINE

Optimal Trading Strategies

UP THROUGH THIS POINT WE have provided a thorough investigation and detailed analysis of transaction costs. We have also provided estimation and forecasting techniques for the variable trading related transaction cost components of price appreciation, market impact, and timing risk, as well as opportunity cost. In this chapter we provide a framework to simultaneously evaluate these trading-related cost components and risk. We provide an optimization technique to determine optimal trading strategies and propose an approach to derive Almgren and Chriss' Efficient Trading Frontier. We compute cost profiles for agency execution strategies and contrast these strategies to principal bid transactions. We introduce the capital trade line—and the idea of a mixed strategy that incorporates an agency execution with a principal bid to develop an execution strategy with an improved cost profile. Finally, we build on previous work and demonstrate how investors—analysts, traders, or managers—can use these techniques to estimate costs and risks, and most importantly to develop best execution strategies.

Notations Used

a_{ij} denotes a stock i in period j
n total number of trading periods
m total number of stocks in the list
X_i order size
Z_i size of order expressed as percentage of ADV
x_{ij} shares of i to execute in period j
ADV_i average daily volume
V_i expected daily volume

v_{ij}	expected period volume
P_i	market price at beginning of trading (midpoint of bid-ask spread)
p_{ij}	prevailing period stock price
Δp_i	expected period price change in \$/share
r_{ij}	residual shares (unexecuted shares)
C	variance-covariance matrix in \$/share (scaled to the trading period)
I_i	instantaneous market impact cost \$/share
α_i	trading rate
σ_i	daily stock volatility
μ	price appreciation cost
κ	market impact cost
φ_i	measured trading cost
ϕ_i	expected cost
$\Re_i$	estimated timing risk
θ_i	cost profile (ϕ, $\Re$)

Trading Decisions

Before managers select an appropriate execution strategy, they need to consider issues dealing with implementation. Fund managers and traders need to work together to determine the most appropriate strategy given fund objectives and market conditions. One invalid inference propagating across trading floors is centered on the notion that implementation strategy is deduced from the fund's investment style. For example, brokers, on more than a few occasions, recommend that momentum investors execute a list with aggressive strategies while index fund trading should be passive because these strategies match investment style. This rationale is flawed because many times momentum investors will lose all potential profits to increased market impact cost from the aggressive strategy and indexers will subject their investors to an inappropriate quantity of risk by trading too passively. These are many times when momentum investors are best served with a passive execution strategy and an index fund is best served with an aggressive strategy.

Some primary implementation concerns to traders are the following:

- ▲ What are the associated costs?
- ▲ What is the corresponding timing risk?
- ▲ What is the appropriate execution strategy for the fund?
- ▲ How are alternative strategies evaluated?
- ▲ Is the selected strategy optimal?
- ▲ Will the selected strategy achieve best execution?
- ▲ Can we perform better?
- ▲ Is an agency execution or principal bid most appropriate?

Trading Costs

Trade costs are important attributes of implementation. While the question of implementation seems straightforward, it is not. Querying a trade cost is equivalent to asking the travel time from A to B without knowing transportation means, available funds, or constraints such as lowest cost, quickest route, or most scenic route. One needs to know a fund's objectives *and* have a sound command of trading cost execution.

A trading cost:

- ▲ Represents the difference between execution price and the stock price at the beginning of trading
- ▲ Cannot be predicted as a single cost estimate
- ▲ Is a distribution consisting of an expected cost and risk parameter
- ▲ Is dependent upon the selected trading strategy

Goal of Implementation

A common misconception of implementation is, "Always get the best prices in the market." While execution at the best prices is a worthy objective, it is unrealistic to expect round-the-clock implementation at the most favorable prices. A further misconception is the notion that the goal of trading is to minimize expected trading cost ϕ because pure cost minimization ignores timing risk and could in fact lead to an even higher trading cost. It is possible for a low cost passive strategy to cause investors to incur highest costs. For example, consider associated costs that arise by passively buying stocks in a rapidly rising market or passively selling stocks in a rapidly falling market.

In presence of this uncertainty, we can specify the goal of implementation to be preservation of asset value in the presence of risk. There are three potential means of achieving this: (1) minimize costs subject to a specified level of risk, (2) balancing the trade off between cost and risk, and (3) maximize the probability of price improvement, that is, maximize the likelihood of executing better than some specified cost.

These goals quantify as:

I. Minimize Cost in Presence of Risk

$$\text{Min } \phi(x_k)$$
$$\text{s.t. } \Re(x_k) \le \Re^*$$

where $\Re^*$ is the maximum risk exposure

II. Balance Tradeoff Between Cost and Risk

$$\text{Min } \phi(x_k) + \lambda \cdot \Re(x_k)$$

where λ is the level of risk a version and represents the marginal rate of substitution between cost and risk.

III. Maximize Probability of Price Improvement

$$\text{Max } \text{Prob}(\phi(x_k) \leq L^*)$$

where L^* is the largest acceptable cost. This value can be thought of as an average limit order price for the list. That is, execute the list better than L, and $\Re^*$, λ and L^* are specified by investors.

The selection of appropriate execution strategy, of course, is dependent upon expected market conditions as well as the goals and objectives of the fund. This is a recurring theme throughout the remainder of the book.

Measuring Trading Cost

The most appropriate means of measuring trading costs follows from the implementation shortfall methodology. This is:

$$\varphi_\$(x_k) = \sum \sum x_{ij} p_{ij} - X_i P_i \qquad (9.1)$$

In this representation, X_i, $x_{ij} > 0$ for buy orders and X_i, $x_{ij} < 0$ for sell orders. The total cost can be expressed in total dollars \$, \$/share or in bp by dividing by the appropriate denominator. From this definition it can be seen that $\varphi > 0$ indicates a cost and $\varphi < 0$ indicates a savings.

Trade Schedule

After managers decide on the desired orders, the implementation is usually left to the trader. Most often, these order sizes are more than the market can readily absorb without adverse price impact due to liquidity demands and information leakage. Therefore, as a means of minimizing unfavorable price movement traders often attempt to disguise the true size of the order by slicing the order into smaller pieces and executing over a period of time rather than all at once. The market can usually absorb these smaller slices resulting in reduced market impact cost. We label the prescribed order slicing strategy *trading schedule* or *trading strategy*. The reference to trading schedule specifies the total number of shares executed in each period. The reference to trading strategy specifies whether the per-

Figure 9.1.   Trade Strategy

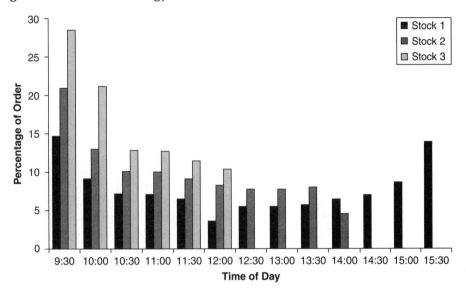

centage is associated with the total order or the number of shares executed in each period. For example, the trading strategy x_k is represented as:

$$x_k = \begin{pmatrix} x_{1k} \\ x_{2k} \\ \vdots \\ x_{km} \end{pmatrix}$$

where x_{jk} denotes the number of shares of stock j that are to be traded in period k. Figure 9.1 illustrates a potential trading strategy for an order consisting of three stocks. Notice that each stock is executed over a different period and each bar represents the percentage of the total order to be executed in the particular period.

Estimating Trading Costs

To estimate the trading cost of a particular strategy we only need to apply those equations derived for price appreciation, market impact, and timing risk. The equations that represent these costs in dollars are as follows:

Price Appreciation

$$\mu_\$(x_k) = \sum_i \sum_j x_{ij} \Delta p_i j$$

Market Impact

$$\kappa_{\$}(x_k) = \sum_i \sum_j \frac{0.95 I_i x_{ij}^2}{|X_i|(|x_{ij}| + 0.5v_{ij})} + \frac{.05 I_i x_{ij}}{|X_i|}$$

Trading Cost

The total expected trading cost ϕ associated with a trading strategy x_k is then written as:

$$\phi(x_k) = \sum_i \sum_j \underbrace{x_{ij} \Delta p_i j}_{Price\ Appreciation} + \underbrace{\frac{0.95 I_i x_{ij}^2}{|X_i|(|x_{ij}| + 0.5v_{ij})} + \frac{0.05 I_i x_{ij}}{|X_i|}}_{Market\ Im\ pact} \qquad (9.2)$$

where, ϕ represents the expected trading cost of the list.

Timing Risk

The associated risk of the strategy derives according to the following equation:

$$\Re(x_k) = \sqrt{\sum_j r_j^T C r_j} \qquad (9.3)$$

where r_j is a column vector of residual shares in period j as follows:

$$r_j = \begin{pmatrix} r_{1j} \\ r_{2j} \\ \vdots \\ r_{nj} \end{pmatrix}$$

and $r_{ij} = \sum_{k=j}^{n} x_{ik}$. Here we only refer to the timing risk of the strategy as the price risk. The incorporation of liquidity risk into our timing risk term and the trading strategy evaluation is beyond the scope of this introductory text.

Example 1. A manager asks a trader to examine the associated trading costs for an order of 100,000 shares of ABC with current market price of $50/share and daily volatility 300bp. If the associated instantaneous market impact cost is $I = \$125,000$ and the expected market volumes over the trading period are shown in Table 9.1, compute the associated cost

Table 9.1. Expected Market Volumes over the Trading Period

Market Conditions	1	2	3	4
Total Volume	200,000	150,000	100,000	50,000
Buy Volume	100,000	75,000	50,000	25,000
Sell Volume	100,000	75,000	50,000	25,000
Trade Strategy				
VWAP	20,000	15,000	10,000	5,000
Opening	40,000	30,000	20,000	10,000
Closing	0	0	0	0
Market Conditions	5	6	7	8
Total Volume	50,000	100,000	150,000	200,000
Buy Volume	25,000	50,000	75,000	100,000
Buy Volume	25,000	50,000	75,000	100,000
Trade Strategy				
VWAP	5,000	10,000	15,000	20,000
Opening	0	0	0	0
Closing	10,000	20,000	30,000	40,000

and timing risk for a VWAP, opening (α = 20%), and closing (α = 20%) strategy.

Mathematically, these trading strategies can be defined as:

$$VWAP: \qquad x_{VWAP,j} = X \cdot \frac{v_j}{V}$$

$$Opening(\alpha): \qquad x_{opening,j} = \min\left(\alpha \cdot v_j, X - \sum_{k=1}^{i-1} x_k \right)$$

$$Closing(\alpha): \qquad x_{closing,n-j+1} = \min\left(\alpha \cdot v_j, X - \sum_{k=1}^{j-1} x_{n-j+1} \right)$$

Solution.   Since the expected price appreciation of ABC over the trading horizon is zero (e.g., $E(\Delta p_j) = 0$), the expected trading cost is due entirely to market impact. These calculations are as follows:

$$\phi(x_k) = \sum_j \frac{0.95 I x_j^2}{|X|(|x_j| + 0.5 v_j)} + \frac{.05 I x_j}{|X|}$$

$$\Re(x_k) = \sqrt{\sum_j x_j^2 \sigma^2}$$

Table 9.2.   Cost and Risk Estimates for Each Strategy

Strategy	Total Dollars ($)		Dollars/Share ($/share)		Basis Points (bp)	
	Cost	Risk	Cost	Risk	Cost	Risk
VWAP	$26,042	$74,750	$0.26	$0.75	52	149
Opening	$40,179	$52,321	$0.40	$0.52	80	105
Closing	$40,179	$110,057	$0.40	$1.10	80	220

Table 9.2 depicts cost and risk estimates for each strategy. Of the three strategies defined previously the VWAP strategy yields the lowest expected cost—52bp compared to 80bp for both the opening and closing. However, the VWAP strategy does not offer the lowest risk. The opening strategy with risk of 105bp is the lowest risk strategy then, followed by VWAP at 149, and closing strategy at 220bp. The opening strategy delivers lowest risk because it minimizes the trade list's market exposure and completes trading in the least time, by midday. The VWAP and closing strategies deliver higher risks because they expose the trade list to potential adverse price movement over the entire trading day. In this example, opening and closing strategies impart identical (expected) trading cost because three conditions hold: (1) there is no expected price movement over the trading horizon; (2) market volumes are symmetric over the trading day, that is, $v_j = v_{n-j+1}$; and (3) opening and closing strategies are based on the same trading rate (20%). If any of these conditions are not true then the cost estimates for the opening and closing strategies will be different.

Cost Profile

The associated cost and risk estimate of a strategy x_k is termed the cost profile of the strategy. It contains the parameters used to described the cost distribution and is expressed as:

$$\theta_k = (\phi(x_k), \Re(x_k)) \tag{9.4}$$

Statistical Distributions

The use of statistical distributions to describe trading cost estimates is relatively new to traders and other professionals analyzing transaction cost. Statistical distribution graphs, for example, probability density functions (pdfs) and cumulative density functions (cdfs), are highly useful tools for depicting the complete trading cost scenario associated with a strategy. The trading cost distribution graph allows us to illustrate the complete set of potential costs by depicting the expected cost of the strategy, the potential dispersion about the mean, and areas of high concentration of probability. It serves to alert investors to potential high costs that may arise due to adverse price movement as well as potential savings that may occur from favorable price movement. These distribution graphs are essential for comparing alternative agency trading strategies. The cumulative trading cost distribution allows us to compute the likelihood of incurring an execution cost φ better than or worse than some specified cost L and assists in the development of the price improvement strategies. Furthermore, similar to investment analysis, the cdf plays an extremely important role and allows us to compare an agency execution to a principal bid transaction and perform in-depth risk analysis (e.g., VaR and shortfall analysis). Most importantly, statistical distributions provide the foundation to develop optimal trading strategies, construct the efficient trading frontier, derive the capital trade line, and ultimately determine the execution strategy that best preserves asset value given the goals and objectives of the fund. That is, the true best execution strategy.

Our empirical data found the distribution of trading costs to be approximately normal. We encounter evidence of leptokurtosis—distributions with fat-tails and peaked means but not nearly to the extent found for stock returns. Nevertheless, the normal distribution offers valuable insight to a potential execution decision's impact. The trading cost distribution derives from the equation of the normal curve. Fat-tails and peaked means in our data are similar to that uncovered for daily price returns but not nearly to the same extent. As with traditional risk management, we employ the usage of the normal distribution for evaluating and comparing strategies with negligible loss of accuracy. This provides us with the necessary detail to derive trading cost distributions and perform risk analysis.

The cumulative cost distribution applies to traditional value-at-risk (VaR) analysis. This is similar to probability shortfall analysis, but rather than provide the probability of executing worse than some specified value it provides the cost value L associated with that probability level α. The value L computes as the inverse of $F(L)$ evaluated at the specified probability level $F^{-1}(\alpha)$. The more common VaR probability levels are 95% and 99%. These calculations for expressing VaR in basis points and in total dollars following our trading cost notation are as follows.[1]

Trading Cost Distribution

$$f(\varphi) = \frac{1}{\sqrt{2\Pi\Re^2}} e^{-\frac{(\varphi-\phi)^2}{2\Re^2}}$$

(9.5)

Cumulative Trading Cost Distribution

$$F(\varphi) = P(\varphi \leq L) = \int_{-\infty}^{L} \frac{1}{\sqrt{2\Pi\Re^2}} e^{-\frac{(\varphi-\phi)^2}{2\Re^2}} d\varphi$$

(9.6)

---

1. The formula holds for any monetary unit.

Figure 9.2. Trading Cost Distribution (Cost = 30, Risk = 50)

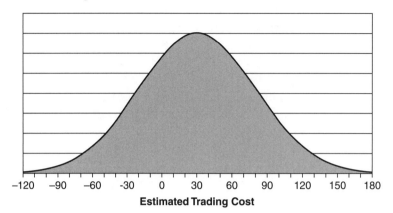

Estimated Trading Cost

Shortfall Probability

$$P(\varphi \geq L) = \int_{L}^{\infty} \frac{1}{\sqrt{2\Pi\Re^2}}\, e^{-\frac{(\varphi-\phi)^2}{2\Re^2}}\, d\varphi = 1 - F(L) \qquad (9.7)$$

Value-at-Risk

$$F^{-1}_{bp}(\alpha) = Z_{\alpha} \cdot \Re + \phi \qquad (9.8)$$

$$F^{-1}_{\$}(\alpha) = \left(Z_{\alpha} \cdot \Re + \phi\right) \cdot 10^{-4} \cdot \sum x_i p_i \qquad (9.10)$$

where Z_{α} is the number of standard units associated with α on the standard normal curve.

Figure 9.2 is a depiction of a trading strategy with $\theta = $ (30bp, 50bp). This illustration shows the complete set of potential trading costs that could arise due to adverse or favorable price movement. This depiction provides insight into the likelihood that the actual cost will fall within a specified range. For example, the probability that actual cost will fall within one standard deviation of the expected cost [–20, 80] is approximately 67% and within two standard deviations [–70, 130] is approximately 95%.

Figure 9.3 is an illustration of a cumulative trading cost distribution for a strategy with $\theta = $ (30bp, 50bp). Statistically speaking, the cumulative cost distribution provides investors with probabilistic estimates that the actual trading cost will be less than or equal to a specified cost. For example, one can use the curve to estimate that the likelihood of incurring a cost less than 55bp is approximately 70% and less

Figure 9.3. Cumulative Cost Distribution (Cost = 30, Risk = 50)

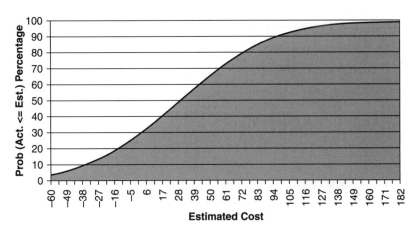

than 95bp is approximately 90%. This curve is also highly effective in analyzing alternative execution strategies and comparing agency to principal bids. It should not be surprising that the likelihood of executing at a cost less than 30bp is 50% since 30bp is the expected cost (mean) of the distribution.

Comparison of Strategies

Let us revisit the trading cost estimates from Example 1. These cost profiles are as follows:

$$\theta_{opening} = (80 \text{ bp}, 105 \text{ bp})$$
$$\theta_{closing} = (80 \text{ bp}, 220 \text{ bp})$$
$$\theta_{VWAP} = (52 \text{ bp}, 149 \text{ bp})$$

The VWAP strategy has the lowest expected cost of 52bp, and both the opening and closing strategies have expected costs of 80bp. The closing strategy, however, has a much higher timing risk (more than double), 220bp compared to 105bp. The closing strategy exposes the trade list to a greater quantity of timing risk than the opening but does not provide any reduction in cost. The opening strategy, conversely, minimizes risk exposure with no increase in cost. Why then would investors interested in preserving asset value and achieving best execution select the closing strategy over the opening strategy? In this example, the closing strategy is inferior to the opening because it creates additional risk but the same cost. The opening strategy stochastically dominates the closing strategy. But how can we be certain that the opening strategy is the best choice? Is there an alternative strategy with less risk at the same cost, lower cost for the same risk, or lower cost and less risk? One would believe, and rightly, that it is irrational to choose an implementation strategy with identical expected cost *and* higher risk than an alternative strategy. Further, it is irrational to select a strategy with the same risk *and* higher cost than an alternative strategy. The answer: Develop an optimal trading strategy.

Optimal Trading Strategies

Investors interested in exercising proper transaction cost management will certainly seek execution via an optimal strategy—that is, a strategy that has the lowest cost for the associated level of risk and the least risk for the corresponding cost. Only this type of optimal strategy that will preserve asset value and achieve best execution.

Traders Dilemma

Market impact cost and timing risk are conflicting terms. Market impact cost is a decreasing function with time and volume while timing risk is an increasing function with time and volume. Trading too aggressively will cause investors to incur high market impact cost and low timing risk. But trading too passively will cause investors to incur high timing risk and low market impact cost. Investors cannot reduce one component without adversely affecting the other. To determine an appropriate optimal strategy, traders need to simultaneously balance these cost components subject to some acceptable level of risk aversion. While this may seem like a trivial process, it is complicated and requires usage of a mathematical optimization algorithm.

    Financial modeling employs optimization techniques in stock selection and portfolio construction. The earliest origin of financial optimization is the mean-variance optimization introduced by Harry Markowotiz (1952), which determines the portfolio with the highest expected return for a specified level of risk or the portfolio with least risk for an expected return. More recently, Bertsimas and Lo (1996), Almgren and Chriss (1997), and Kissell and Malamut (2000) apply optimization to minimize price impact under uncertainty. Bertsimas and Lo provide a way to minimize impact-based information, while Almgren and Chriss expand on the idea of trade schedule optimization and introduce a mean-variance optimization framework to solve the traders dilemma. Their approach includes a risk-aversion parameter to specify investors' level of risk tolerance; the goal is to determine the trade schedule that optimally balances the two conflicting terms (impact cost and timing risk) based on investors' appetite of risk. While techniques presented here build on Almgren and Chriss work, *we employ a mean-risk optimization process,* rather than utilize a mean variance and introduce alternative decision making criteria.

The advantage of minimizing with the risk term over variance is that risk is a more intuitive measure for the potential price movement for investors. However, risk introduces numerous complexities into the optimization. For example, the risk term introduces a square root function in the objective function. Further, optimization algorithms become much slower when constraints and the objective function include terms that are not quadratic or linear. In Chapter 12, Advanced Trading Techniques, we provide a complete examination of our optimization formulation and techniques for improving the computation time to that of minutes as is required by traders.

Optimization Formulation

The formulation of our trading cost optimization can be explained as follows. An investor seeking to minimize cost within some specified level of risk $\Re^*$ is as follows:

$$Min \ \phi(x_k)$$
$$s.t., \ \Re(x_k) \le \Re^*$$

Alternative investors seeking to minimize risk within some specified level of cost ϕ^* is as follows:

$$Min \ \Re(x_k)$$
$$s.t. \ \phi(x_k) \le \phi^*$$

However, this formulation introduces somewhat of a problem to investors. It is difficult to predetermine the preferred level of cost ϕ^* or $\Re^*$ beforehand. To address this difficulty we follow Almgren and Chriss and formulate an objective function that contains both cost and risk where investors specify their preferred level of risk aversion as follows:

$$Min_{x_k} \sum_{i=1}^{m} \sum_{j=1}^{n} \phi(x_k) + \lambda \cdot \Re(x_k) \tag{9.10}$$

The parameter λ specifies the investor's preferred level of risk aversion and the trade-off between cost and risk. For example, a risk aversion level of $\lambda = 1$ indicates investors equally concerned with cost and risk. A risk aversion level of $\lambda \ge 1$ indicates investors more concerned with risk than cost thus preferring an aggressive strategy to a passive one. A risk aversion level of $\lambda \le 1$ indicates investors more concerned with cost than risk thus preferring a passive strategy to an aggressive strategy. In economic terms λ represents the marginal rate of substitution between cost and risk. The complete formulation of this objective function is:

$$\underset{x_k}{Min}\underbrace{\underbrace{\sum_{i=1}^{m}\sum_{j=1}^{n}\underbrace{j\cdot x_{ij}\Delta p_i}_{\text{Price Appreciation}} + \underbrace{\sum_{i=1}^{m}\sum_{j=1}^{n}\underbrace{\frac{0.95I_i x_{ij}^2}{|X_i|(|x_{ij}| + 0.5v_{ij})}}_{\text{Temporary}} + \underbrace{\frac{0.05I_i |x_{ij}|}{|X_i|}}_{\text{Permanent}}}_{\text{Market Impact}}}_{\text{Trading Cost}} + \lambda\cdot\underbrace{\sqrt{\sum_{j=1}^{n}r_j^T Cr_j}}_{\text{Timing Risk}}$$

(9.11)

Graphical Illustration of Optimization

An illustration of the optimization procedure for the objective of balancing the tradeoff between cost and risk is shown in Figure 9.4 for a risk aversion level of $\lambda = 1$. The objective function calculates the total cost by summing price appreciation and market impact plus one unit of timing risk ($\lambda = 1$). If a different value is specified for risk aversion lambda, the objective adds that quantity of risk to the cost. The total cost curve of the objective function is a convex function and attains a minimum value at $t = 3$. Therefore, the lowest cost strategy for the specified level of risk aversion is one that executes the list over three units of time (these units can be defined as minutes, hours, days, etc.). The output from the optimization includes the trading schedule λ_k (i.e., the number of shares of each stock to trade in each period as shown in Figure 9.1) and estimates for each of the cost components (i.e., the cost profile θ corresponding to the trade schedule x_k).

Figure 9.4. Trading Strategy Optimization

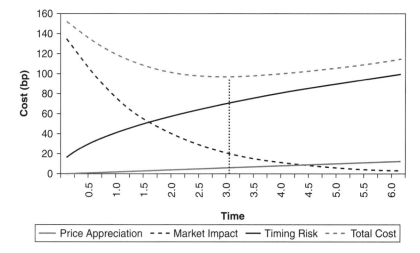

Real-World Constraints

The previous formulated optimization problem is shown as an unconstrained problem. Unfortunately, in the real world managers often require implementation within some set of guidelines. For example, in an unconstrained problem the optimal solution may state to execute 50% of the order in the first period and 50% in the second period. However, the manager may feel that this strategy would be too aggressive and would like to reduce participation in periods. In light of such real-world trading constraints we re-formulate our optimization as follows:

Balance Tradeoff between Cost and Risk

$$\underset{x_k}{Min} \sum_i \sum_j jx_{ij}\Delta p_i + \frac{0.95 I_i x_{ij}^2}{|X_i|(|x_{ij}| + 0.5v_{ij})} + \frac{0.05 I_i x_{ij}}{|X_i|} + \lambda \cdot \sqrt{\sum_j r_j^T C r_j}$$

s.t.

i) $\quad \sum_j x_{ij} = X_i$

ii) $\quad |r_{ij}| \leq |r_{ij-1}|$

iii) $\quad \dfrac{|x_{ij}|}{|x_{ij}| + v_{ij}} \leq \alpha$

iv) $\quad -D_{min} \leq \sum_{i=1}^{m}\sum_{j=1}^{k} x_{ij}\left(P_i + j\Delta p_i + \dfrac{0.95 I_i x_{ij}}{|X_i|(|x_{ij}| + 0.5v_{ij})} + \dfrac{0.05 I_i}{|X_i|} \right) \leq D_{max}$

Explanation of Constraints

i. Completion

The completion constraint is included to ensure that the optimization routine will provide a strategy that executes all shares in the order over the specified trading horizon n.

ii. Shrinking Portfolio

The shrinking portfolio constraint ensures that the portfolio is continuously decreasing in shares. This constraint prevents the optimization algorithm from acquiring a larger position (making the position either longer or shorter than the original) then offsetting the increased position at an accelerated rate over the remainder of the day as a means to hedge risk. For example, if a trader has an order to purchase 100,000 shares of ABC, the optimization algorithm will not provide a strategy that first sells 25,000 shares then buys 125,000 shares so that the net position at the end of the horizon is 100,000 shares. For most funds, this does not entail a reasonable trading strategy even if it is in the best way to manage costs. This is because a trading halt on the stock or insufficient liquidity could cause the manage to be stuck with an unfavorable position. For those funds that would consider such a trading strategy, the objective function would need to be rewritten to account for the market impact cost due to the liquidity demands of the opposite position. That is, the market impact cost associated with the sell and buy orders. Our market impact function is purely one-sided (for buys or sells).

iii. Participation Rate

The participation rate constraint is included to place an upper bound on the maximum quantity of shares that can be traded in any given period. Quite often traders limit their trading to be no more than some specified percentage of each period's volume, for example, do not participate with more than 25% of the volume in each period.

iv. Cash Balancing

The cash balancing constraint is typically included in the implementation of a trade list that consists of buy and sell orders to ensure that the net cash position in any period is within some specified dollar amount D*. Cash balancing constraints are more commonly specified as a means to minimize risk and preserve a buy-sell hedge. While this constraint is no longer needed to manage risk it may still be required to ensure that managers do not provide brokers with incremental funds due to a potential trading halt. For example, if a trading strategy calls for a portfolio rebalancing to execute buys more aggressively than sells, buys will be completed at an earlier time than sells. If there is a trading halt and the buys are fully completed but the sells are not, the trader is required to pay the broker for those shares that were bought and will not have the incremental cash from the sells. The incorporation of the cash balancing trading constraints serve as a safety net so that even if there is a trading halt the fund will have ample funds on hand to make payment to the broker if required.

Trading Frontier

The trading frontier is the collection of strategies that contain the lowest cost for the specified quantity of risk. The strategies are determined by solving the optimization algorithm for all values of lambda ($-\infty \leq \lambda \leq \infty$). It is important to note that a strategy with the lowest cost for a specified quantity of risk does not necessarily imply that it is the lowest cost strategy for that level of risk.

Figure 9.5. Trading Frontier

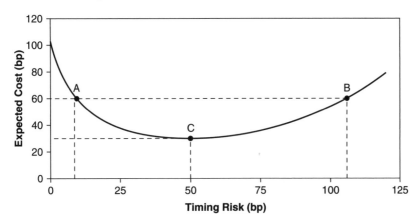

We depict a trading frontier in Figure 9.5. Here the cost curve is a convex function. It is decreasing function over the range $0 \le \Re \le 50$bp and then increasing over the range $\Re \ge 50$bp. The minimum cost occurs at $\Re = 50$bp. In the presence of price trend a passive strategy will cause investors to incur incremental price appreciation cost. In some instances, the passiveness of a strategy may cause the incremental price appreciation cost to dominate the market impact cost reduction, thus resulting in an increase of trading cost. This point is illustrated in Figure 9.5. Points A and B are strategies with cost profiles $\theta_A = (60,10)$ and $\theta_B = (60,105)$ respectively. While they each contain the least cost for the specified risk, only A is a true optimal strategy because it contains the least risk for the cost value. Here, it is easy to see that only points that lie on the trading frontier to the left of strategy C are optimal strategies because only they contain the least quantity of risk for the corresponding level of cost and the least cost for the corresponding quantity of risk. Points to the right of point C contain the least risk for the specified cost but do not contain the least cost for the quantity of risk. Strategy C with cost profile $\theta_c = (30,50)$ is the minimum cost of the frontier.

Each of the points on the trading frontier corresponds to a unique level of risk aversion (e.g., value of λ). Strategy C (minimum cost strategy) is associated with $\lambda = 0$. Points on the curve to the left of C (e.g., A) are associated with $\lambda > 0$ and points on the curve to the right of C (e.g., B) are associated with $\lambda < 0$. To understand this, let us recall the optimization equation:

$$\textit{Min: } \phi + \lambda \cdot \Re isk$$

It is easy to see that the minimum cost will occur at $\lambda = 0$ since risk is excluded from the optimization equation. For values of $\lambda > 0$, we obtain points with higher costs and lower risk than at the minimum point C. For values of $\lambda < 0$ the optimization equation is reduced to:

$$Min: \phi + (-\lambda) \cdot \Re isk = \phi - \lambda \cdot \Re isk$$

This optimization is minimized at the value where the quantity of risk is maximized (since risk is always positive). Therefore, the optimization will be dominated by risk if trading is spread over as long a period as possible. But this strategy may also be associated with a strategy where price appreciation cost begins to dominate market impact cost. This would occur if price appreciation cost is increasing over time (i.e., buying stocks that are rising and selling stocks that are falling) and causes total trading cost to decrease. Then increase again. Hence, it is obvious that investors would only want to implement a trade with a positive level of risk aversion $\lambda > 0$.

Efficient Trading Frontier

The efficient trading frontier (ETF) is the set of all true optimal trading strategies—that is, the set of strategies that contain the lowest cost for the specified level of risk and the least risk for a specified level of cost. The ETF includes those strategies associated with a risk aversion of $\lambda \geq 0$. The ETF shows investors how expected cost varies with risk and how the trading strategy affects the cost strategy. An aggressive strategy incurs higher costs but lower risk while a passive strategy incurs lower cost but higher risk. The only way traders can incur a lower trading cost is through a strategy with a higher quantity of risk, and the only way traders can reduce risk is through a strategy with a higher cost. The ETF presents investors that very trade-off. The ETF is used to depict the cost profile of various optimal implementation strategies. Finally, the ETF serves as the basis to determine the best execution trading strategy given the goals and objectives of the fund.

Robert Almgren and Neil Chriss (1997) introduced the ETF to the financial community in their paper titled "Optimal Liquidation Strategies". The naming of the efficient trading frontier follows the nomenclature used by Markowitz to designate the set of all optimal investment portfolios. Henceforth, we identify Markowitz's efficient frontier as the *efficient investment frontier* (EIF) and Almgren and Chriss' efficient frontier as the *efficient trading frontier* (ETF) as a means to distinguish between investment and trading decision making.

Managers or traders selecting an implementation strategy that does not fall on the ETF are not making rational trading decisions because alternative strategies can always be found with less risk for the same cost, lower cost at the same level of risk, or both lower cost and risk. For example, in Figure 9.7 notice that strategy D does not fall on the ETF. Thus, it is not rational because we can find an alternative strategy with lower risk

Figure 9.6. Efficient Trading Frontier

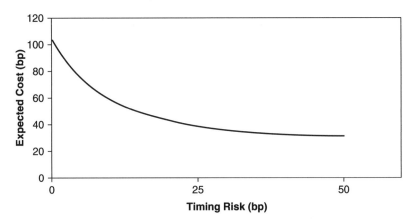

Figure 9.7. Efficient Trading Frontier

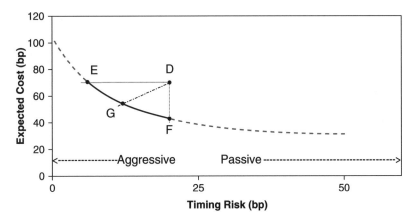

and the same cost (E), lower cost and the same risk (F), or lower cost and lower risk (G). In fact, in this example, every point between E and F is associated with an improved cost profile over D and increased benefits to investors. Rational traders would never select a strategy such as D. In economic terms we state: Strategy D is stochastically dominated by all strategies on the ETF between points E and F. That is, strategy D has a higher likelihood of incurring any cost than strategies on the ETF between E and F. We represent this mathematically as:

$$F(\varphi(X)) \geq F(\varphi(D))$$

for X being any strategy between E and F. For example, strategy G stochastically dominates strategy D because it has lower cost and less risk. Henceforth, a strategy that does not lie on the ETF is considered an irrational trading decision and is dominated by at least one optimal strategy.

Approximation of Efficient Trading Frontier

The complete construction of the ETF requires one optimization per every possible value of $\lambda \geq 0$. The solving of the optimization with the incorporation of real-world constraints for a single strategy can be extremely time consuming especially for large trade lists or a long trading horizon and may not provide an answer for traders in an appropriate amount of time. Traders rarely have the luxury of time to spend on implementation analysis. They usually receive a list just before the market opens or in some cases during the trading day. Therefore, the derivation of the ETF for all values of $\lambda \geq 0$ is not a realistic option.

We can approximate the true ETF quickly and accurately by fitting an exponential decay curve to a select set of points (9.12). The parameters of this equation require the cost profiles from three optimal strategies. Consider the three strategies x_l, x_r, and x_λ. Strategy x_l is the left endpoint of the ETF. It intersects the y-axis at I^* and has zero risk; its cost profile is $\theta_l = (I^*, 0)$. The right endpoint of ETF is the strategy of minimum cost. This occurs at a level of risk aversion of $\lambda = 0$ and is found by minimizing the objective function with respect to cost only. The solution of the cost profile of this strategy, $\theta_r = [\phi(\lambda = 0), \Re(\lambda = 0)] = (\phi_r, \Re_r)$, is a much simpler optimization since it does not depend upon the risk term. The third point is the cost profile for any optimal strategy with $\lambda = \lambda' > 0$. For best results, we recommend a value of λ equal to or close to 1 (e.g., $\lambda' = 1$). The result of this optimization will provide a cost profile $\theta_\lambda = (\phi_\lambda, \Re_\lambda)$.

$$\phi = a_1 \, e^{-\frac{\Re}{a_2}} + a_3 \tag{9.12}$$

Then, the parameters of the approximated ETF are computed as follows:

$$a_1 = \phi_l - \phi_r$$

$$a_2 = \frac{-1}{\Re_\lambda} \cdot \ln\left[\frac{\phi_\lambda - \phi_r}{\phi_l - \phi_r}\right]$$

$$a_3 = \phi_r$$

This technique provides a rapid construction of a very accurate ETF curve. This allows investors to quickly assess the trade-off between cost and risk and select their preferred strategy. However, this approximate curve does not provide the corresponding trading strategy x^* at the desired level of cost ϕ^* or timing risk $\Re^*$. Therefore, after deciding upon the implementation strategy traders need to perform an additional optimization at their specified level of risk aversion (λ^*).

Description of ETF parameters

As it turns out the parameters of the ETF have some very interesting meanings:

- a_1 denotes the total quantity of cost that can be eliminated. This is the quantity of cost savings achievable through a passive trading strategy. This parameter is equal to $a_1 = I - a_3$. In the absence of price appreciation, we have $a_1 = 0.95I$ which is the total quantity of temporary market impact.
- a_2 is the trading rate parameter. It is an indication of how quickly the temporary impact cost dissipates due to the natural diversification and hedging of the list. A more diversified or hedged list has a higher trading rate parameter than one not as well diversified or hedged. The higher this parameter the more passive one can trade without incurring unnecessary risk, thus achieving large cost reduction. This parameter is always a function of the diversification of the risk of the trade list.
- a_3 denotes the minimum cost of the trade list. This is the total unavoidable cost, which consists of permanent market impact cost and the price appreciation cost. In absence of price appreciation, we have $a_3 = 0.05I$.

Figure 9.8 is an illustration of the comparison of an approximated ETF to the actual data points. The equation of this curve is:

$$\phi = 190e^{-0.05\Re} + 10$$

Figure 9.8. Efficient Trading Frontier

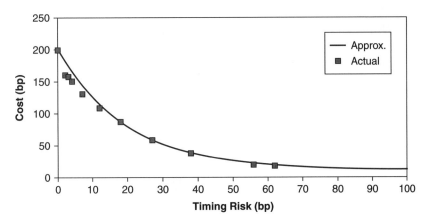

Notice how well the approximated curve fits the data points. Some points are slightly off for those low risk or aggressive trading strategies. However, these slight errors are due to optimizing over trading intervals of specified size, for example, thirty minutes. If one decreases the length of time in each trading interval, these points would move closer to the ETF.

Relationship Between Lambda λ and Cost Components ϕ and $\Re$

In a similar fashion where we derived the cost curve ϕ as a function of risk $\Re$ from the approximated ETF, we can determine the level of risk aversion λ^* corresponding to a specified cost ϕ^*. The relationship between cost and risk aversion is approximated as follows:

$$\phi = I - (I - \phi_r)e^{-\beta\lambda}$$

where,

$$\beta = -\frac{1}{\lambda'}\ln\left(\frac{I - \phi_\lambda}{I - \phi_r}\right)$$

The value of lambda λ^* at the desired level of cost ϕ^* is:

$$\lambda^* = -\frac{1}{\beta}\ln\left(\frac{\phi^* - I}{\phi_r - I}\right) \tag{9.13}$$

Figure 9.9 is a depiction of our risk aversion factor lambda as a function of cost. Notice the non-linear relationship.

Figure 9.10 is a depiction of cost as a function of lambda. Notice how the cost function approaches I^* as lambda increases in size. This figure shows that there is relatively no difference between cost for $\lambda \geq 12$. Furthermore, because of the high quantity of temporary market impact cost it is very unlikely that investors will choose to execute via a strategy with $\lambda \geq 3$.

Relationship Between Lambda λ and Risk $\Re$

As shown in figure 9.11 and following the same process, we determine the relationship between lambda λ and risk $\Re$ to be:

$$\Re = \Re_r e^{-\gamma\lambda}$$

where,

$$\gamma = -\frac{1}{\lambda'}\ln\left(\frac{\Re_\lambda}{\Re_r}\right)$$

Figure 9.9.   Lambda as a Function of Cost

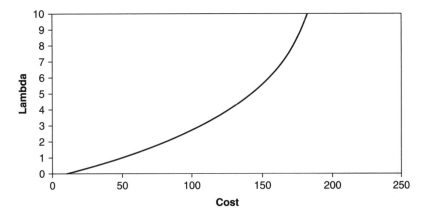

Figure 9.10.   Cost as a Function of Lambda

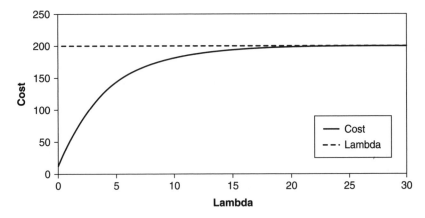

Figure 9.11.   Cost as a Function of Risk

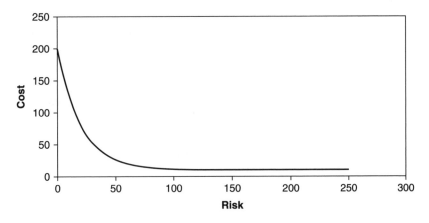

The value of lambda λ^* at the desired level of risk $\mathfrak{R}^*$ is:

$$\lambda^* = -\frac{1}{\gamma} \ln\left(\frac{\mathfrak{R}^*}{\mathfrak{R}_r}\right)$$ (9.14)

Price Improvement

A price improvement strategy is a strategy that maximizes the likelihood of incurring a cost less than some specified value B. Since each strategy on the ETF has a corresponding cost profile, there will be an associated probability level that the actual cost will be better than the specified cost. The trader's goal for price improvement is to determine the strategy x_k that maximizes the following:

$$Max_{x_k} \; P(\phi \leq B) = Max_{x_k} \; L = \int_{-\infty}^{B} \frac{1}{\sqrt{2\Pi\mathfrak{R}_k^2}} e^{-\frac{(\phi-\phi_k)^2}{2\mathfrak{R}_k^2}} d\phi$$ (9.15)

Example 2.   A trader has three available optimal strategies to implement a trade list. If the manager instructs the trader to implement the list better than 100bp, which strategy should the trader select if the cost profile of each strategy is: $\theta_A = (79,20)$, $\theta_B = (43,34)$, and $\theta_C = (13,83)$?

Solution.   Following 9.15 the trader determines the associated probability of price improvement for each strategy to be $p_A = 85\%$, $p_B = 95\%$, and $p_C = 85\%$. Thus, the price improvement strategy is strategy B and provides the highest opportunity to achieving price improvement over a cost of 100bp. This is computed as follows:

Graphical Representation

We can illustrate price improvement strategies graphically. Since each strategy x_k on the ETF contains a cost profile $\theta_k = (\phi_k, \mathfrak{R}_k)$ it will have an associated probability of incurring a cost less than some specified cost B. While each strategy on the ETF has a unique cost profile it is not true that a unique probability exists for all strategies. It is quite possible for two strategies with different profiles to have the same price improvement probability. However, there is only one strategy that maximizes the likelihood of price improvement.

We can compute the price improvement probability of any cost B directly from the equation of the ETF. Suppose that the equation of the ETF is defined by the following equation:

$$\phi_{ETF} = 190e^{-0.05\mathfrak{R}} + 10$$

Figure 9.12. Efficient Trading Frontier

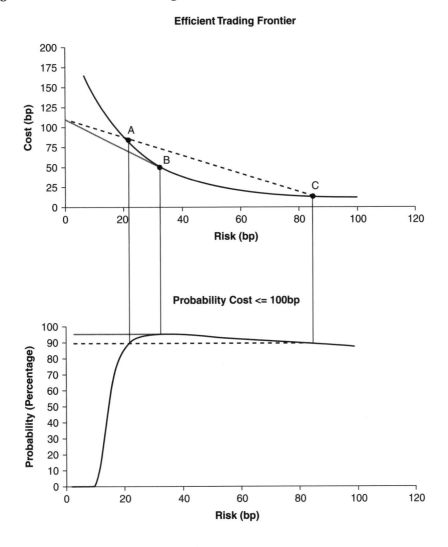

Figure 9.12 is a depiction of this ETF and the corresponding price improvement probabilities for B = 100bp for each of the three strategies in Example 2. The top graph is the ETF and the bottom graph represents corresponding price improvement probability values. We have highlighted the three strategies and have drawn a line to the corresponding probability level in the bottom graph. Each of the strategies is mapped to a corresponding probability level. Further, the graph of these probability levels contains a unique maximum point.

There are two interesting aspects from this illustration:

1. All strategies on the line passing from the specified cost on the *y*-axis through the ETF will have identical probabilities of price

improvement. In Figure 9.12 the line from 100bp on the y-axis inter-
secting the ETF at strategy A and C has the same probability (85%)
of executing better than 100bp.

2. The strategy that maximizes the probability of executing better than a
specified cost is found by drawing a line from the cost on the y-axis
tangent to the ETF. Notice in Figure 9.12 that this is true. The line drawn
from 100bp on the y-axis tangent to the ETF intersects at point B is the
strategy with maximum probability.

Tangent Line Proof

Theorem: The strategy x_k that maximizes the probability of price
improvement over B is defined as the point of tangency of the line passing
through the point (0,B) on the cost axis and the efficient trading frontier.

Proof: This proof was first derived by Roberto Malamut in 1999.

Step I: Show that the maximizing strategy x_k should lie on the ETF.

Let, x_k be a strategy that lies on the ETF. Then,

$$P(\varphi(x_k) \le B) = P\left(\frac{\varphi(x_k) - \phi(x_k)}{\Re(x_k)} \le \frac{B - \phi(x_k)}{\Re(x_k)} \right) = \psi\left(\frac{B - \phi(x_k)}{\Re(x_k)} \right)$$

where ψ is the standard cumulative normal function. Now if x_k' represents
a strategy that does not lie on the ETF it either has an expected cost or timing risk higher than that of strategy x_k which lies on the ETF. Hence,

$\psi\left(\frac{B - \phi(x_k)}{\Re(x_k)} \right) \ge \psi\left(\frac{B - \phi(x_k')}{\Re(x_k')} \right)$ and implies that the probability maximizing

strategy must lie on the ETF. Figure 9.13 shows the optimal strategy x_k
lying on the ETF and the non-optimal strategy x_k' lying above the ETF.
Notice the x_k' is irrational because an alternative strategy can be found
with less cost and same risk, less risk and same cost, or both less cost and
less risk.

Step II: Show that the strategies with the same probability of beating the cost B lie on a line that passes through the point (0,B).

Since ψ is an increasing function, the strategy that maximizes

$\psi\left(\frac{B - \phi(x_k)}{\Re(x_k)} \right)$ is the same as the strategy that maximizes. $\frac{B - \phi(x_k)}{\Re(x_k)}$.

If $\gamma = \dfrac{B - \phi(x_k)}{\Re(x_k)}$, then $B = \phi(x_k) + \gamma \cdot \Re(x_k)$. This implies that the point ($\phi(k_x)$,

Figure 9.13.   Efficient Trading Frontier

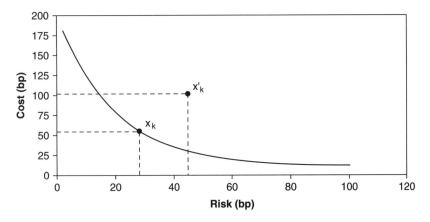

Figure 9.14.   Efficient Trading Frontier

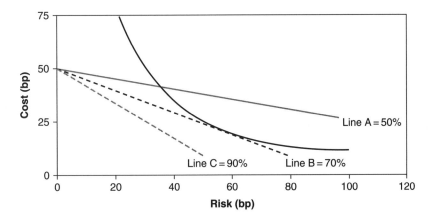

$\Re(x_k)$) on the ETF satisfies the line equation in x and y, namely, $B = x + \gamma \cdot y$. Therefore, γ is the signed changed value of the slope of the line connecting the points and $(0, B)$ and $(\phi(x_k), \Re(x_k))$. Consequently, our problem is transformed to the following: Determine the strategy x_k on the ETF that maximizes $-\gamma$ for the slope γ of the line connecting the points $(0, B)$ and $(\phi(x_k), \Re(x_k))$. This is the strategy that corresponds to the tangent point of the line passing through $(0, B)$ and tangent to the ETF.

Figure 9.14 depicts three lines each consisting of points with the identical probability of executing better than $B = 50$. Points on line A represent strategies that have a 50% chance of executing better than $B = 50$. However, as shown previously, each of these strategies can improve. Line B consists of those strategies that have a 70% chance of executing better than 50bp. And unlike those points on point A, there exists an optimal strategy on line B that cannot be improved upon. Line C consists of those strategies that theoretically have a 90% chance of executing better 50bp. However, none of these points corresponds to a real strategy, hence the cost profile is unattainable. Therefore, the strategy that maximizes the probability of executing better than 50 is strategy x_k shown on line B. It corresponds to the strategy found at the point of tangency between the ETF and the line drawn from (0,50) on the y-axis tangent to the ETF

Mathematical Derivation

The exact point of tangency can also be determined mathematically as follows:

Let, the point of tangency between the line ϕ_L passing through point B on the y-axis and the ETF ϕ_{ETF} be the point $(\Re_t, \phi_t)$.

Then the equation of this line is:

$$\phi_L = \frac{\phi_t - B}{R_t} \cdot \Re + B$$

and the equation of the ETF is:

$$\phi_{ETF} = a_1 e^{-a_2 \Re} + a_3$$

At the point of tangency, we know that the estimated cost from both equations is the same and the slopes of each equation evaluated at $\Re = \Re_t$ are equal. Therefore, the exact value of the point of tangency is found when the following two conditions are met:

i. $\phi_L(R_t) = \phi_{ETF}(R_t) \quad \Rightarrow \quad \dfrac{\phi_t - B}{R_t} \cdot R_t + B = d_1 e^{-a_2 R_t} + a_3$

ii. $\left. \dfrac{d\phi_L}{d\Re} \right|_{\Re = R_t} = \left. \dfrac{d\phi_{ETF}}{d\Re} \right|_{\Re = R_t} \quad \Rightarrow \quad \dfrac{\phi_t - B}{R_t} = -a_1 a_2 e^{-a_2 R_t}$

Solving in terms of ϕ_t for each we get:

i. $\phi_t = a_1 e^{-a_2 R_t} \cdot a_3$
ii. $\phi_t = -R_t a_1 a_2 e^{-a_2 R_t} + B$

Setting i = ii and solving for B we get:

$$R_t = \frac{B - a_3}{a_1 a_2} e^{a_2 R_t} - \frac{1}{a_2}$$

This equation is not solvable analytically because it has form $R_t = k_1 e^{k_2 R_t} + k_3$; however, it can be solved via an approximation or convergence algorithm solution.

Almgren and Chriss (2002) propose an alternative approach for determining a specific execution strategy based on a variation of the Sharpe ratio. While the approach was initially presented as a means for principal brokers to determine an appropriate implementation strategy to execute a list that won with a bid B, it can also be used to provide insight to investors seeking price improvement for an investment decision. This technique is as follows:

Let,
B   = the principal bid amount (revenue)
$\phi(x_k)$ = cost of the implementation strategy
$\Re(x_k)$ = risk of the implementation strategy

Thus, the expected gain (profit) using the specified implementation x_k is $\pi(x_k) = B - \phi(x_k)$. In presence of risk an appropriate implementation decision is to maximize the ratio of expected profit to risk as follows:

$$Max: \frac{\pi}{\Re(x_k)} = \frac{B - \phi(x_k)}{\Re(x_k)}$$

Using the formula for our ETF, we have:

$$Max: \frac{B - \phi}{\Re} = \frac{B - (d_1 e^{-a_2 \Re} + a_3)}{\Re}$$

and its maximum value occurs at:

$$\frac{\partial}{\partial \Re} \frac{B - (a_1 e^{-a_2 \Re} + a_3)}{\Re} = 0$$

and solving for $\Re$ we find:

$$R = \frac{B - a_3}{a_1 a_2} e^{a_2 R_t} - \frac{1}{a_2}$$

Thus our price improvement strategy is identical to the strategy that maximizes ratio of expected gain to risk. That is:

$$Max: \underbrace{\frac{B - (a_1 e^{-a_2 \Re} + a_3)}{\Re}}_{\text{Sharpe Ratio}} = \underbrace{Max: \int_{x_k}^{B} \frac{1}{\sqrt{2\Pi \Re_k^2}} e^{-\frac{(\phi - \phi_k)^2}{2\Re_k^2}} d\phi}_{\text{Price Improvement}}$$

This can be easily seen if one draws a line from the cost value B tangent to the ETF then horizontal back to the *y*-axis. The angle *t* made by these lines

Figure 9.15.   Maximizing Sharpe Ratio

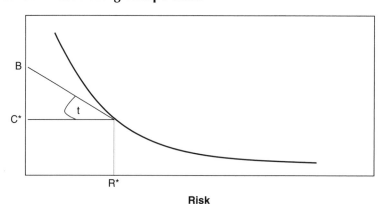

is the ratio of expected gain to risk. However, this angle also has another meaning. It also happens to be the standardized z-score associated with the probability of executing more favorably than the cost B. Thus, maximizing the gain to risk ratio is identical to our price improvement strategy. This is depicted graphically in Figure 9.15. We prefer the nomenclature price improvement over the Sharpe ratio because it fits in better with the terminology used regarding best execution and it avoids any confusion with its meaning on the investment side.

Relationship Between ETF and Lambda

There is a corresponding relationship between the ETF and lambda. That is, the risk aversion level λ associated with a specified level of risk is equal to the negative value of the slope of the ETF evaluated at that quantity of risk. Thus, for any level of risk the associated value of lambda required to obtain the optimal strategy is found by differentiating ETF and evaluating at the preferred level of risk. That is:

$$\lambda^* = -\frac{\partial}{\partial \Re}\, \phi = -\frac{\partial}{\partial \Re}\left(a_1 e^{-a_2 R} + a_3\right) = -\left(-a_1 a_2 e^{-a_2 R}\right)$$

which reduces to:

$$\lambda^* = a_1 a_2 e^{-a_2 R^*} \tag{9.16}$$

since $a_1, a_2, e > 0$.

This allows analysts to first derive the ETF to determine their preferred execution strategy (either cost minimization in the presence of risk or price improvement) then optimize with a value of $\lambda = \lambda^*$ to determine the actual optimal trading strategy. This would not be possible, or at least as easy, if it were not for the quick and efficient derivation of ETF.

Capital Trade Line

Markowitz (1952) provided the financial industry with the proper analytical framework for evaluating return and risk (e.g., mean-variance optimization). Sharpe (1964) expanded this work and showed how the inclusion of a risk-free asset (such as a bond, note, or bill) with the market portfolio could improve the risk-reward trade-off of the preferred pure equity portfolio. This contribution, Capital Market Line (CML), has proven to be equally as important to financial theory as Markowitz's EIF and combined the two form the underlying foundation of modern portfolio theory.

More recently, Almgren and Chriss (1997) have applied Markowitz's mean-variance optimization to solve the trader dilemma. In similar fashion, one can derive an improved cost profile by the introduction of a risk-free transaction such as a principal bid transaction[2] into an implementation decision. This provides traders with an improved set of cost profiles that is achievable through pure agency execution alone. Thus by allocating between principal bid and agency one can achieve an improved cost profile (e.g., lower cost, less risk, or both). This enhanced set of points is coined the Capital Trade Line (CTL) in honor of Sharpe.

We construct the CTL by drawing a line from the principal bid tangent to the ETF. The point of tangency of the CTL and ETF is the strategy with *x-y* coordinates $(\mathfrak{R}_t, \phi_t)$ and represents the strategy that maximizes the likelihood of executing more favorably than the principal bid. Henceforth denoted as the bid improvement strategy.

The equation of the CTL is as follows:

$$CTL: \phi = \frac{-B + \mathfrak{R}_t}{\phi_t} \mathfrak{R} + B \tag{9.17}$$

Figure 9.16 depicts the CTL with a risk-free transaction of 60bp. Notice how the CTL intersects the *y*-axis at the value of the risk-free transaction and is tangent to the ETF at point *x*. The point of intersection is *bid improvement strategy* and follows from the identification of the market portfolio in investment theory. The lower frontier of this curve represents the improved set of cost profiles derived for a mixed strategy consisting of an allocation between principal and agency. This could amount to a

---

2. In actuality, a principal bid is not necessarily a risk-free transaction. In those instances where the pricing of the bid occurs at some future point the investor bears all market risk. The only time a principal bid is a true risk-free transaction is in those instances where the bid is priced at the exact time the agreement is reached.

Figure 9.16. Capital Trade Line

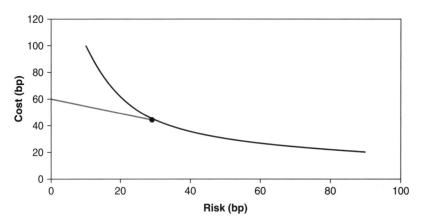

considerable improvement in cost and risk over a pure agency strategy, especially for those investors with a higher quantity of risk aversion.

The CTL provides traders with the analytical framework to evaluate and develop a mixed strategy consisting of an optimal agency strategy at the point of tangency and a principal bid transaction.[3] Before the introduction of the CTL, investors had at their disposal decision tools to evaluate pure strategies, that is, either entirely agency or principal implementation. Investors can now use the capital trade line to improve trading cost estimates by careful allocation between agency and a principal using the CTL as a guideline.

Mixed Trading Strategies

A mixed trading strategy is one that allocates the trade list between a principal bid and an agency execution. If the ETF has form $\phi_{ETF} = 190e^{-0.05\Re} + 10$ and the lowest cost principal bid is 100bp, demonstrate when it is appropriate for investors to allocate between principal and agency to obtain an improved cost profile over their preferred pure agency or pure principal choice.

Case One

Figure 9.17 depicts the ETF and CTL for an investor with a preferred agency execution y with cost profile $\theta_y = (125, 10)$. On the surface, it may appear that the principal bid is the more attractive of the two strategies because it contains lower cost (100bp compared to 125bp) and zero risk (0bp com-

---

3. The idea of a mixed strategy is not entirely new. We have been proponents of mixed execution strategies for some time now; however, we have been met with powerful objections from those parties providing only pure execution options (e.g., agency-only or principal-only). More recently, many firms have begun offering mixed strategies services. Our contribution here is not in the introduction of mixed strategies but in the approach to evaluate and develop mixed strategies.

Figure 9.17. Case One

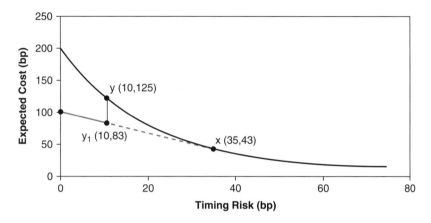

Figure 9.18. Case Two

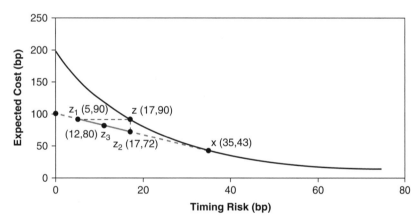

pared to 10bp). However, this trader could allocate the trade list between the principal bid and the optimal agency strategy x to arrive at strategy y_1. The associated cost profile of y_1 is $\theta_{y1} = (83, 10)$. The mixed strategy contains a lower cost than the pure principal and agency strategies and is at the trader's level of risk comfort. Furthermore, the trader could allocate the list between principal and strategy x to arrive at any strategy to the left of strategy y_1 resulting in a lower cost than the principal bid and less risk exposure than their specified level of risk comfort. Hence, any mixed strategy on the CTL with risk $\Re^* < 10$bp provides an improvement over the preferred pure agency strategy.

Case Two

Figure 9.18 is a depiction of the cost scenario for an investor with preferred pure agency strategy to be strategy z with cost profile $\theta_z = (90, 17)$. This strategy provides a decrease in cost of 10bp over the principal but does

Figure 9.19. Case Three

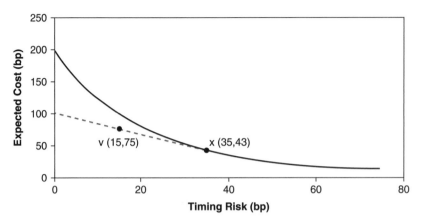

incur 17bp of risk. Careful allocation of the trade list between principal and strategy x allows the investor to find an improved strategy over the pure agency in cost and risk. First, the trader could develop a mixed strategy z_1 with cost profile $\theta_{z1} = (90, 5)$ resulting in the same expected cost but lower risk. Second, the trader could develop a strategy z_2 with cost profile $\theta_{z2} = (72, 17)$ resulting in the same risk but reduced cost. Finally, the trader could develop a strategy such as z_3 with cost profile of $\theta_{z3} = (80, 12)$ resulting in reduced cost and risk.

Case Three

Figure 9.19 is a depiction of an investor with preferred strategy x with cost profile of $\theta_x = (43,35)$. In this case, traders cannot allocate between principal and agency to generate a lower cost strategy because all strategies on the CTL will contain a higher cost than the point of intersection. The trader, however, can incorporate the principal transaction into the implementation to reduce the risk of the strategy. One such strategy is that labeled v with corresponding cost profile $\theta_v = (15,75)$. Here, the incorporation of the principal bid with the trader's preferred strategy provides a reduction in risk of 1bp for an increase in cost of 1.6bp. The slope of the CTL defines the trade-off between costs provided by a mixed strategy.

Case Four

Figure 9.20 is a depiction of a cost profile for a risk neutral investor. This strategy falls in the chart as w and has cost profile $\theta_w = (20, 70)$. Here, the incorporation of the principal bid will not improve the trader's pure agency cost profile because the CTL is only defined between the y-axis and the point of tangency on the ETF. Hence, the trader is best off with a pure agency strategy.

Figure 9.20. Case Four

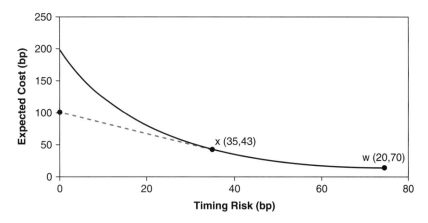

Table 9.3.

Risk Exposure R*	Risk Aversion Level	Execution Strategy
$R^* = 0$	$\lambda^* = \infty$	Pure Principal
$0 < R^* < R_t$	$\lambda_t < \lambda^* < \infty$	Mixed
$R^* \geq R_t$	$\lambda^* \geq \lambda_t$	Pure Agency

Generalization on Mixed Strategies

Any investor more risk averse than the quantity of risk at the point of tangency of the CTL and ETF can improve the cost profile of a pure agency strategy by the incorporation of the principal bid. An investor less risk averse than the point of tangency of the CTL and ETF cannot improve the cost profile of their pure agency strategy by incorporation of the principal bid and is thus best served by the pure agency strategy. If a trader is completely risk averse (e.g., risk comfort level of zero), then they are best served by a pure principal transaction. Table 9.3 summarizes these points.

In general, investors could improve the cost profile of their preferred pure agency strategy by the incorporation of a principal bid and the development of a mixed trading strategy when the following relationship holds true:

$$\phi_{CTL}(\Re^*) \leq \phi_{ETF}(\Re^*) \rightarrow \frac{-B + \Re_t}{\phi_t}\Re^* + B \leq a_1 e^{-a_2 \Re^*} + a_3$$

where, ϕ_t, $\Re_t$ represent the estimated cost and risk at the point of tangency and $\Re^*$ represents the investor's preferred level of risk aversion. Another way to determine if a principal bid transaction should be combined with an agency execution is to compare the investor's preferred level of risk aversion $\Re^*$ to the risk level at the point of tangency $\Re_t$. If $\Re^* < \Re_t$ then a mixed strategy should be employed to improve the cost profile.

Example 3. An investor decides to utilize a mixed strategy for the implementation of an investment decision rather than the preferred pure agency only strategy by allocating α to the principal broker and $(1 - \alpha)$ to the agency execution. If the cost of the principal bid is B and the optimal strategy at the point of tangency has cost profile $\theta_x = (\phi, \Re)$, the cost profile of the mixed strategy calculates as follows:

$$\theta_{mixed} = (\phi_{mixed}, \Re_{mixed})$$

$$\phi_{mixed} = \alpha B + (1 - \alpha)\phi_x$$

$$\Re_{mixed} = \sqrt{\alpha \Re_B^2 + (1 - \alpha)^2 \Re_x^2 + \alpha(1 - \alpha)\rho_{x,B} \Re_B \Re_x} = (1 - \alpha)\Re_x$$

since $\rho_{x,B} = 0$ and $\Re_B = 0$

CHAPTER TEN

Principal Bid Transactions

THE MATHEMATICAL FRAMEWORK AND QUANTITATIVE techniques previously presented in this book were primarily intended for analyzing and developing optimal agency trading strategies. In this chapter we concentrate our discussion on the principal bid process.

In a principal bid transaction investors receive immediate and complete execution of the trade list at a set price in exchange for a commission charge known as the bid premium. The transaction price of a principal bid is typically taken as the midpoint of the bid-ask spread at an agreed upon point in time (e.g., the close). In the principal bid transaction investors do not pay direct cost due to price appreciation and market impact and all timing risk is transfered to executing brokers. A principal bid is synonymous with a capital commitment, risk bid and also blind bid. It is called a capital commitment because the transaction requires principal brokers to commit the necessary funds (capital) and securities to facilitate the transaction at an agreed upon price at a specified time. Broker-dealers provide investors with stock from their inventory for stocks purchased and provide investors with cash for stocks sold. When brokers enter into a principal bid transaction agreement, they acquire the investor's position and all associated risks. Brokers acquire the uncertainty surrounding the exact execution price and the price risk of the position. A principal broker earns a profit by executing better than the bid premium. But in an environment with severe adverse price movement the broker could suffer a large loss. The principal bid is intended to protect the broker from incurring losses similar to an insurance policy.

While it has been said over and over again that market impact is an amorphous concept, the same is true for the principal bid process. However, the principal bid process remains elusive because it is in the principal broker's best interest to keep their decision-making process secretive so that it is difficult to critique. Recall, market impact is a difficult concept because it is an unobservable phenomena not a hidden measurement process. Also, in the industry there has been very little "fair" publication regarding the principal bid. The work that has presented a fair representation is Almgren and Chriss (2003), Kissell (1998, 2000, 2001), Chriss (2001), Grinold and Kahn (2000), Barra (1997), Domowitz (2002), and Mandavan (1999, 2001). The goal of this chapter is to introduce a degree of transparency to the principal bid process and introduce a framework to analyze and compare principal bid transactions to agency executions. In Chapter 13, Post Trade Analysis, we propose a post trade performance for the principal bid.

Recall an agency transaction is an execution whereby investors (trader or broker on behalf of investors) trade the list in the market over a time and accept market prices. The execution price is unknown in advance. Investors incur costs due to market impact and price appreciation, and bear timing risk (price and liquidity risk). If prices move unfavorably, investors will incur a higher cost and vice versa if prices move favorably. An agency execution does not guarantee that investors will complete the trade list. If prices move too adversely or if insufficient liquidity, investors may not be willing to execute at the higher cost and orders will remain unfilled. In return for their service and access to the trading venue agency brokers charge investors a fee in terms of a commission and often the stock spread. Those brokers that only provide access to the trading venue, such as ECNs, will only charge the commission since they do not typically buy and sell from their inventory of stock, they only match buyers and sellers.

In a principal bid transaction, brokers charge a bid premium—the principal bid—usually much higher than the associated commission and spread cost associated with executing the list via agency transaction. The higher fee compensates principal brokers for trading the position, the cost of price appreciation and market impact, and compensation for inheriting price and liquidity risk. Table 10.1 compares principal bid transactions and agency executions.

There are several conflicting opinions in the industry regarding a principal bid transaction, most of which are propagated by sell-side firms to make the principal bid seem either more or less attractive. For example, agency brokers attempt to make the principal bid appear as a much more costly option so investors will be dissuaded by high costs and select the agency transaction. Principal brokers attempt to make the principal bid appear as the more attractive option by touting the principal bid as a "risk-free" transaction with guaranteed completion and at a specified price thus providing execution cost certainty. Further, they argue that investors should not be concerned about adverse price movement or opportunity cost because timing risk is completely transfered to brokers and the list is executed in full.

Table 10.1. The Spread between Principal and Agency

Investor Cost Implications	Agency Execution	Principal Bid Transaction
Trading Costs		
Commission	Yes	No
Price Appreciation	Yes	No
Market Impact	Yes	No
Timing Risk	Yes	No
Opportunity Cost	Yes	No
Premium Fee	No	Yes
Known Price	No	Yes
Guaranteed Completion	No	Yes
Trading Cost Forecast	Distribution of Costs	Single Value Estimate

With all these conflicting opinions, investors indeed need a framework to compare the two alternatives to determine the most appropriate option for the fund and specific trade list. Finally, although rarely mentioned there are times when investors benefit from a mixed strategy: part principal, part agency (Chapter 9, Optimal Trading Strategies).

The Principal Bid Is Not Necessarily a "Risk-Free" Execution

Typically, the execution price of the principal bid is set at some future point in time such as the close of the day. Here, investors incur price risk from the time the contract is signed through the close of the day. Thus, investors will incur less favorable transaction prices if adverse price movements prevails. For example, a money manager may decide to purchase 150,000 shares of XYZ at $50 via principal transaction agreed at 1 P.M. set at the stock's closing price plus a $0.25/share bid premium. However, the exact transaction price is still unknown; the price will fluctuate during the day and the close will be higher or lower. The potential adverse price movement constitutes risk to the manager. The transaction is only risk free if the agreement specifies a transaction price of $50 (current price) plus the $0.25/share premium. Figure 10.1 illustrates the potential price movement for $50 stock with a daily volatility of 350bp. Notice associated price risk approximates $1.20/share.[1] The price range for this execution is $48.80 to $51.20, a considerable range for a three-hour window.

---

1. The volatility calculation is scaled over the remaining three-hour period.

Figure 10.1.   Potential Price Movement XYZ

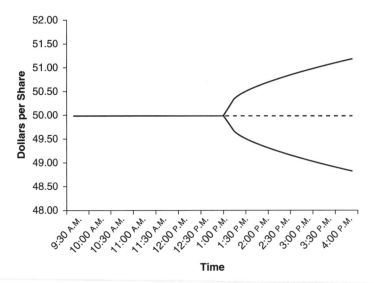

The only time a principal bid does not cause investors to incur price risk is when bid pricing is at the exact point investors contact brokers, when the solicitation is made after the market closes using the closing price on the day or when the exact stock price is specified in the contract. Nevertheless, the associated principal bid is typically much higher for agreements made using known transaction prices such as when agreements are made after the close using the closing price.

The Total Cost of a Principal Bid May Be More Than the Premium

Actual trading cost can also be higher than the bid premium because of information leakage similar to an agency execution. During the principal bid process investors solicit bids from numerous brokers. These brokers become privileged to either the exact names of the stocks in the list or more commonly to the list characteristics, which they can quite often infer based on historical investment practices of the investor.[2] Brokers can use this information to accumulate positions in those names from the time of the solicitation through the close of the day (e.g., the time at which the bid is priced) causing adverse price movement from market impact. The result is an overall higher trading cost because the market impact associated with accumulating the position is incorporated into the closing price. Thus,

2. Investors typically solicit blind-bids where they provide only the list characteristics rather than the actual names in the list as a means of protecting against information leakage and price run-up.

Figure 10.2.   Price Run-Up XYZ

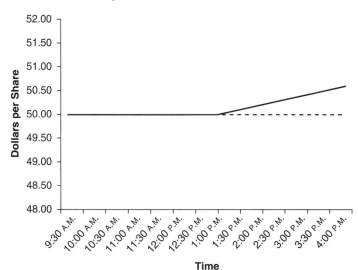

investors incur market impact cost twice: in the price of the bid premium specified by brokers and in the closing price of the stock.

The true cost of the principal bid to the investor for a buy order is:

$$\text{cost} = (P_{Close} - P_t) + bid$$

where P_{Close} is the closing price, P_t is the actual price at the time of solicitation of the bid (not the time of the agreement), and bid is the principal bid charged by the broker.

It is in investors' best interest to minimize this total quantity. For example, enter into a principal bid after the market closes or at prices set by the market at the time agreements are entered.

Figure 10.2 depicts an example where an investor enters into a principal bid agreement at 1 P.M. to purchase 150,000 shares of XYZ. The stock is currently trading at $50, and the bid premium is $0.25. The principal broker begins to accumulate a position in XYZ to offset the investor's order at the market close. The buying pressure exerted by the broker pushes the price of the stock up from $50 to $50.60/share. The investor's cost is much higher than the principal bid. The total cost is Cost = ($50.60 – $50.00) + $0.25 = $0.85/share

To minimize information leakage, traders solicit principal bids from a small number of broker-dealers (e.g., 2–3) and provide only list characteristics. Investors can protect against cost run-ups by soliciting bids during market hours but not entering into contracts until after the close to keep brokers from knowing if they won business so they do not aggressively acquire positions. But even in this case investors are still subjected to price

Figure 10.3. Price Risk and Potential Run-Up

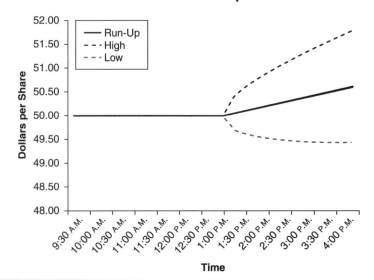

volatility and potential run-up. First there is the natural price volatility of the stock that could cause the future price (close) to be higher or lower, making the transaction either more or less expensive. Second, there is the potential that the brokers who were solicited for the bid will gamble hoping they will be selected and begin to accumulate an offsetting position. This results in a more expensive closing price for the stock. Figure 10.3 illustrates this, depicting a one standard deviation price range to be $49.40 to $51.80 with an expected cost of $50.60 for a principal bid on a stock with a current market price of $50/share.

Principal Brokers Price the Bid from Their Perspective

Brokers' cost to offset a list is not identical to investors' because brokers often have trading options available that are not readily accessible to investors due to pricing issues or fund mandates such as engaging in risk management using derivatives. Thus, when pricing bids, brokers estimate execution cost and risk incorporating the trade list, their internal inventory position, expected customer order flow, and available hedging and risk management vehicles. Brokers estimate trading cost from the list characteristics—buy/sell ratios, average liquidity, sectors breakdown, and so on. When brokers do not or cannot infer names and quantities in the list they still can derive accurate cost estimates for the entire list. Thus, list characteristics provide sufficient information for pricing needs while protecting investors from price run-ups. Brokers will never price the bid any less than this cost regardless of the circumstances.

Figure 10.4. Broker Pricing Schemes

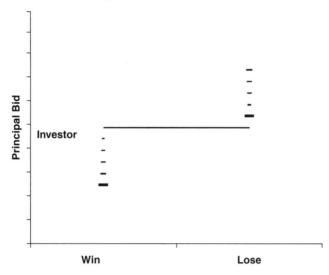

In a principal bid brokers have an advantage over investors. First brokers know the trade's expected cost from the perspective of investors, that is, without any incremental customer order flow or risk reductions options. Second, since brokers know which investors are soliciting the bid they usually incorporate favors owed to them such as dinners or other enticements. Brokers then set the bid to be the price they believe investors are willing to pay as long as it is higher than their incremental cost to offset the position and provides a fair compensation for the acquired risk.

Additionally, brokers price bids to win or lose (see Figure 10.4). To win, they price as close to investors' maximum price level while still being the lowest cost bid. In some cases, a broker may not want to win the bid because it may be costly to execute or may increase risk exposure beyond the maximum level imposed by the company. They set out to be the lowest bid just above what investors are willing to accept or to position them as the next most attractive alternative.

Principal Bids Can Be Lower Than the Least Cost Agency Alternative

It is quite possible for a principal bid to be lower than the investors the least cost agency alternative. Since broker-dealers price the list incorporating their own inventory with the trade list and make use of hedging and risk reduction tools, the result may be a lower cost execution. The composite of these may provide natural crossing opportunities (buy orders offset by sell orders and vice versa) and reduced total risk enabling the total inventory to be offset more passively than the trade list resulting in a lower cost. Investors determine the ETF for the trade list based on their internal constraints and

Figure 10.5. Efficient Trading Frontier

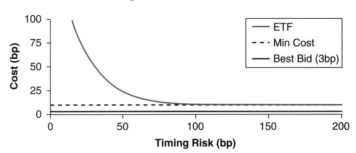

In a principal bid transaction the broker-dealer will either price the bid competitively to win the list at the highest possible price or lose the list at the lowest possible price. Thus, the amount of the bid does very little to signal the true trading cost for the list or provide insight into expected market conditions. There is very little price discovery information available to the investor via the principal bid transaction.

trading mandates. Further, they do not offset orders from other investors.

Figure 10.5 shows how investors can use the ETF to compare the bid to agency alternatives. Here the bid is better than the least cost of all agency alternatives, hence the best execution option.

Principal Broker-Dealer Perspective

Current Broker Pricing Schemes

The principal bid process begins with investors contacting brokers and providing them list characteristics—not the exact names, quantities, and side so to minimize information leakage. This is a blind-bid solicitation. Brokers develop the bid price based upon a list's liquidity and risk characteristics along with their existing inventory position, future order flow expectations, and risk reduction tools.

Some broker-dealers price the trade list based on the incremental cost contribution it brings to their overall inventory position. The more sophisticated brokers, however, do not price this way. They price the bid to stay competitive. Typically, their pricing scheme has two objectives—win the business and acquire trade lists or lose the business but be the next most attractive choice. Brokers desire to air the bid when they feel it is a profiting opportunity to win the bid brokers want to price the bid competitively, just slightly better than the next most attractive bid. Broker may not desire to win the bid because it would be too costly to trade; they may have no disposable revenue to apportion to the list; or the acquisition of the trade list would expose them to a higher level of risk than allowable. Rather than provide investors with the "real" principal bid for the list, brokers will offer a "fake" low bid, low enough to be competitive but high enough to lose. The following set of examples show how a principal bid could vary from broker to broker and not provide any insight into the expected trading costs of the list of expected market conditions.

Example 1. An investor solicits a principal bid from a broker with a balanced inventory of stock (i.e., minimal risk exposure and neither too long or too short any position) for a sell list with list characteristics consistent with an S&P 500 portfolio. Since the broker's position is balanced, acquisition (of the list) results in a long position that will need to be traded. Further, since the trade list characteristics are consistent with an S&P 500 portfolio the broker has a large array of risk management tools (e.g., futures, options, exchange traded funds) and is likely to provide a bid premium based on the true cost of the trade list—a fair bid premium.

Example 2. An investor solicits a principal bid for a sell list with list characteristics consistent with an S&P 500 portfolio from a broker who is short a similar inventory position. Thus, winning the bid would cause the broker to acquire a position they are currently short, which balances their inventory and decrease their risk exposure. Here the broker would provide an aggressive bid to ensure winning the list. In this case it may even be less than the least cost agency alternative. In cases where investors hold exact positions, they could price the bid at zero cost or pay investors to win the business so that they could lock in a profit.

Example 3. An investor solicits a principal bid for a sell list with list characteristics consistent with an S&P 500 portfolio from a broker who is currently long a similar position. Thus, winning the position would increase the brokers inventory and corresponding risk exposure. If the potential risk exposure is outside the firm-specified constraint, or estimated cost too high they would not be willing to accept the list. But rather than price the bid at the high level and lose the possibility of being called upon at a future date they would price the bid so that it is just above what they believe the investor would be willing to pay or what they feel will be the winning bid from a different broker.

Example 4. A broker has a balanced inventory of stock. Investor A has a buy list for S&P 500 stocks and Investor B has an identically sized sell list for S&P 500 stocks. Suppose that Investor A solicits a bid from a broker-dealer for the buy list by midday and agrees to a bid of $0.25/share from the broker.[3] Later in the day Investor B solicits a principal bid from the same broker for the offsetting position. Since the broker wants to lock in a

---

3. The bid amount of $0.25/share is used here only for illustrative purposes. The exact bid amount is highly dependent upon the number of shares, liquidity, risk, trade value, and so on, and may differ greatly from broker to broker and from day to day.

profit and reduce risk they bid for B very aggressively at $0.05/share to ensure winning the business.

In this example, both investors have identical trade lists (albeit different sides) but are charged different amounts. Investor A pays higher for being the first to enter into the agreement while B is rewarded for being late to the market with a complementary position. Neither of these investors are charged fairly for incremental cost and risk their list brings to the broker. However, the broker earns a profit of $0.30/share, which is unfair to investors. While we are not suggesting a zero priced bid for both investors we are noting that they are being incorrectly charged.

Example 5.   Suppose the same situation as Example 4 but investor B also has a buy list. Investor A would agree to a bid of 0.25/share, but Investor B would receive a much higher principal bid from brokers (e.g., bid >> $0.25/share). Here A is rewarded for being the first to enter the agreement and B is being punished for being late with an identical list. If Investor B agrees to accept the much higher bid, brokers should have ample chance to earn a profit. However, if Investor B does not agree to accept the bid at the high price, brokers still gain a great deal of information. Brokers know that there is very likely a second buyer in the market and needs to execute the position at an accelerated rate to protect themselves from adverse price movement. In either case, both investors again are not provided with a bid that reflects the true cost for their list in light of current market conditions.

Example 6.   An investor solicits a principal bid for an illiquid trade list from three brokers. Each of the brokers estimates an extremely high price for the bid and decides that they really do not want to win the list because either it increases their level of risk exposure beyond the firm-specified limit or the money can be better used elsewhere. But rather than provide the investor with the extremely high-priced bid and risk losing future business, the brokers offer the investor a "fake" bid just slightly higher than what they believe the investor is willing to pay. Suppose that each broker calculates his or her "true" or "fair" bid amount for the list to be 130, 140, and 150bp. If the brokers believe that the investor is only willing to pay up to 50bp for a principal transaction, they would each price the bid higher than but close to 50bp. If the three fake bids are 55, 60, and 65bp, none of the principal brokers will win the business. The investor is not going to select the principal bid transaction because it is higher than their maximum level. The investor is likely to feel good about these brokers because their bids were not too much out of the ballpark. The brokers will then stay on the investor's preferred list for future solicitations (which was the only goal of the brokers in this case).

Example 7.   Use the same scenario as in Example 6 but the brokers miscalculate the investor's maximum bid amount. Thus, the investor accepts the lowest bid of 55bp. Here the broker is stuck with a list with expected cost closer to 130–150bp; it is much higher than what they received for compensation and they are very likely to realize a loss. This is an example of a broker's mispricing strategy causing the brokerage house to incur a loss.

Blind Bid

We have mentioned that the best way to protect from information leakage and accompanying price run-up from brokers investors should never provide brokers with the exact trade list. Instead, they provide trade list statistics. This includes liquidity and risk summaries such as percentage of ADV, volatility and risk, and breakdowns by side (buy/sell), market (listed/Nasdaq), sector, and information pertaining to tracking error. However, investors still need to be careful. Even in cases where brokers are only privileged to the list characteristics they may still do a very good job at deciphering what stocks, quantities, and side comprise the trade list simply from the name and past trading patterns of investors. Investors surrender a good deal of information to the principal broker just from their name. When brokers identify the party, they derive the bid by taking into account the past investment practices and transaction behavior of that investor. For example, consider an investor known to track the S&P 500 index. If this investor receives an inflow of cash and solicits a bid from the principal broker, brokers will know exactly what investors wish to buy just by the name and observed practices. Of course, this is not the case with every fund or manager, but the more informed brokers can gain valuable insight into what investors are looking to buy/sell from the name and list statistics. The good news for brokers is that it is possible to develop cost and risk estimates using trade summaries that are just as accurate as can be developed from the trade list.

Broker-Dealer Execution Strategies

Let us assume the broker has won a trade list for a principal bid amount denoted B. Once brokers have acquired a trade list they add the position to their existing inventory of stock. Their usual goal is to keep this level balanced such as reducing the position to zero or to some specified level to accommodate future transactions (the specified level is usually a long position). Regardless of the preference, brokers will be left with a quantity of shares that need to be traded. They will need to sell those shares that are long and buy those shares that are short.

Let us denote the broker's inventory position as X:

$$X = \begin{pmatrix} X_1 \\ X_2 \\ \vdots \\ X_i \\ \vdots \\ X_n \end{pmatrix}$$

where X_i is the number of shares to execute in stock i, $X_i > 0$ represents a buy order—they are currently short the position, $X_i < 0$ represents a sell order they are currently long the position, and $X_i = 0$ is a balanced position where no transaction needs to take place.

Broker Execution Objective

After the principal broker enters into an agreement with the investor they acquire a discounted trade list. That is, a trade list worth more in the market than they paid. The difference between the two values is exactly the principal bid B. For example an investor who executed a buy list via principal bid transaction B actually paid the broker B greater than the current market value of the list. An investor who executed a sell list via principal bid transaction B actually sold to the broker B less than the current market value. An investor with a list consisting of buys and sells bought shares at an amount B more than and sold shares at an amount B less than the current market value. Thus, the principal broker has a list worth B more than which they transacted. The principal bid transaction does not specify a bid amount for each position. The quantity B is typically stated in \$/share or in bp for the entire list.

Very often principal brokers will enter principal bid agreements with several investors causing the broker to have an aggregated inventory position X where the broker paid less than the cultured current market value of those positions. Let the difference between the transacted value and current market value be B. The broker's profit from these transactions will be difference between their revenue B and trading cost ϕ. Therefore, the principal broker is faced with the same type of problem encountered by an investor during an agency execution, namely, to minimize trading costs.

Principal brokers are very astute market participants and understand that cost minimization comes at an increase in risk. Thus the problem of earning a profit reduces again to controlling the tradeoff between cost and risk during implementation by following an appropriately developed optimal trading strategy. This process is described next.

Let us begin by evaluating the profit profile of the trade.

Expected Profit:

$$E(\pi) = E(B - \phi) = E(B) - E(\phi)$$
$$= B - E(\phi)$$

Risk:

$$\Re(\pi) = \sqrt{\sigma^2(B - \phi)} = \sqrt{\sigma^2(B) - \sigma^2(\phi)} = \sqrt{0 - \sigma^2(\phi)}$$
$$= \sqrt{\sigma^2(\phi)}$$
$$= \Re(\phi)$$

However, both the cost and risk of the execution is dependent upon the specified implementation strategy x_k. The distribution of expected profit can then be described in terms of the expected cost and risk of the specified execution strategy as follows:

Profit Profile:

$$\pi\,(x_k) = (B - \phi(x_k), \Re(x_k)) \qquad\qquad (10.1)$$

Example
Let the ETF and the bid amount be defined as:

$$\phi_{ETF} = 190e^{-.05\Re} + 10$$
$$B = 80$$

Then the expected profit for each strategy is estimated as:

$$E[\pi] = 80 - (190e^{.05\Re} + 10) = 70 - 190e^{-.05\Re}$$

The relationship between profit and trading cost is illustrated in Figure 10.6. Notice the relationship between cost and profit where profit increases as costs decrease. If brokers execute the position with an inappropriate aggressive strategy they will incur too high a cost thus a loss. If brokers execute the position with too passive a strategy, they will incur lower costs on average, and higher profit margins; however, the associated risk of the strategy exposes the fund to a large quantity of risk which may also cause the broker incur a loss if adverse price movement persists. After engaging in a principal bid transaction brokers need to manage the tradeoff between cost and risk remains in the same fashion as investors. Further, they need to do so such that risk is within firm specified levels and costs are low enough to ensure they will earn a profit on the transaction, otherwise, they will not stay in business long.

Figure 10.6.   Efficient Trading Frontier

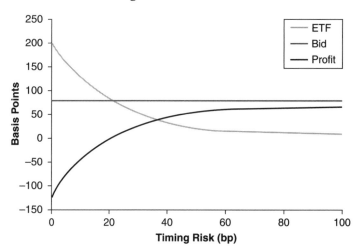

Recall that investors can base their implementation decision based on three reasonable criteria: 1) Cost Minimization Subject to Risk, 2) Balance the tradeoff between cost and risk, and 3) Price Improvement. Principal brokers also have three reasonable criteria that incorporate the need to earn a profit. They are:

▲ Maximize Profit subject to risk
▲ Balance the tradeoff between profit and risk
▲ Bid Improvement

I. Maximize Profit Subject to Risk

The strategy that maximizes broker profit subject to risk can be computed using our cost equation from the Chapter 9. For a principal bid of B broker dealer profit is estimated as:

$$\pi = B - \phi$$

Mathematically we can determine the profit maximizing strategy by differentiating with respect to the strategy as follows:

$$\pi = B - \phi$$

$$\frac{\partial}{\partial x_k} \pi = \frac{\partial}{\partial x_k} (B - \phi)$$

$$\frac{\partial \pi}{\partial x_k} = -\frac{\partial \phi}{\partial x_k}$$

Thus indicating that profit maximization is identical to cost minimization.

$$\text{Max} \quad B - \phi\,(x_k) = \text{Min} \quad \phi\,(x_k)$$

But, brokers cannot simply maximize profit or minimize cost without consideration of risk. Profit maximization formulation is:

$$\begin{aligned} \text{Max} \quad & B - \phi\,(x_k) \\ \text{s.t.} \quad & \Re\,(x_k) \le \Re^* \end{aligned} \qquad (10.2)$$

where $\Re^*$ is the maximum level of risk exposure specified by the firm. Alternatively, this can be written as:

$$\begin{aligned} \text{Min} \quad & \phi\,(x_k) \\ \text{s.t.} \quad & \Re\,(x_k) \le \Re^* \end{aligned} \qquad (10.3)$$

It is important to note that the resulting strategy will not ensure an expected profit. This would occur if the broker provided too low of bid. In this situation the broker needs to . . . increase the level of risk exposure or simply accept the strong likelihood of incurring a loss.

Brokers are typically more inclined to select the cost minimization rationale because they are usually supplied with maximum risk exposure limits. Brokers can use these limits to develop the appropriate execution strategy. The strategy can also be determined by drawing a vertical line from the quantity of allowable risk exposure $\Re^*$ to the efficient trading frontier. The point of intersection defines the strategy that minimizes cost for that level of risk We find the associated cost by drawing a horizontal line to the x-axis.

II. Balance tradeoff between Profit and Risk

Brokers can also elect to develop their implementation strategy following the risk aversion formulation. Typically, however, this rationale is more appropriate for investors who are more comfortable with the concept of risk comfort specified in terms of a utility function where lambda is the marginal rate of substitution between cost and risk. Mathematically, this is as follows:

$$\text{Max} \quad B - \phi\,(x_k) - \lambda\Re\,(x_k) \qquad (10.4)$$

where λ is the tradeoff between profit and risk. That is,

$$\lambda = \frac{\partial \pi}{\partial \Re}$$

Since B is fixed this strategy can be developed following the same formulation as for investors as follows:

$$\text{Min} \quad \phi(x_k) + \lambda \cdot \Re(x_k) \tag{10.5}$$

where λ indicates the tradeoff between cost and risk. That is:

$$\lambda = -\frac{\partial \phi}{\partial \Re}$$

Here, brokers need to ensure that the risk aversion strategy ensures an expected profit. If it turns out that $B - \phi^*(x_k) < 0$ brokers need to re-evaluate their decision or accept the strong possibility of a loss. Finally, brokers also need to ensure that the corresponding risk of the selected strategy is within the constraint of the firm.

III. Bid Improvement

Another strategy often more appropriate for principal brokers seeking to balance an acquired inventory level is one that maximizes the likelihood of earning a profit. This strategy is identical to the investors price improvement strategy. It minimizes the chance that brokers will suffer gamblers ruin and maximizes the likelihood brokers will persevere in a highly competitive environment.

For a principal bid B any cost less than B results in a profit. Profit maximization is achieved by minimizing the likelihood of incurring a cost greater than B. Mathematically, this is written as:

$$Max: \Pr ob(\phi < B) = \int_{-\infty}^{B} \psi\big(\phi(x_k), \Re(x_k)\big)$$

where ψ denotes the expression for the normal distribution with $\mu = \phi(x_k)$ and $\sigma = \Re(x_k)$. This strategy can also be found using the ETF. We draw a line from the principal bid B on the y-axis tangent to the efficient trading frontier. The point of tangency specifies the profit maximizing strategy for brokers. This is the strategy that provides the highest probability of broker profit. That is, $P(\pi > 0)$ is maximized

Important Note: Recall that our price improvement derivation is identical to the approach presented by Almgren and Chriss that calls for one to maximize the ratio of expected gain to risk, that is,

$$Max \, \frac{B - \phi(x_k)}{\Re(x_k)} \tag{10.6}$$

Almgren and Chriss suggest this approach as a means to offset the position in situations when the broker is required to balance the current position. However, as they point out, in situations where brokers continuously acquire order flow via principal bid or other arrangement the execution strategy needs to be structured so that the principal bid Sharpe ratio is maximized over all expected future events. Depending upon future order flows, the bid improvement strategy may be in the best interest of the broker in the short term but not over a long-term horizon. We wholeheartedly agree. Brokers need to be conscious of future happenings much more than investors who may have no immediate need for additional trading.

Broker Pricing Strategies

An appropriate broker pricing strategy is one that provides brokers with the best opportunity of achieving their goals. Let us assume for a moment that the goal of brokers is to maximize the likelihood of achieving a profit. Thus, the goal of brokers in deriving a bid price is to determine the bid so that they have the greatest opportunity of achieving a profit while still being competitive enough to win the business. This objective is not to price the bid as high as possible but to price the bid to win while still providing the greatest opportunity of earning future gains. In many situations one may prefer not to win a principal bid, not because the expected profit margin is not high enough or not because the probability of profiting is not high enough but possibly because the acquired position would tie up funds and keep brokers from competing for future business in the short term. The goal for brokers in pricing bids is to be competitive and to maximize profits over the long term. It should not suffice to simply seek to maximize profits in the short term.

Figure 10.7 illustrates three potential broker strategies for a principal bid of 60bp. Strategy A is the least costly: cost = 10bp and risk = 100. It has the lowest expected cost but does not provide the best opportunity for achieving a profit. Strategy C has risk exposure of 80bp and associated cost of 13bp, providing significantly less risk than strategy A for a slightly higher cost (13bp compared to 10bp). Strategy B shows the strategy with the highest potential for profit. It has cost 24bp but risk of only 52bp.

Investor Pricing Schemes

Our discussion regarding the principal bid thus far has only considered the principal bid from the perspective of the broker dealer. In this section we present a framework for investors to evaluate the price of the bid. This technique is focused on uncovering the economic fair value "FV" for immediate execution of the trade list. This concept then extends to the economic fair value for a principal bid. Before we move any further ahead it

Figure 10.7.   Efficient Trading Frontier

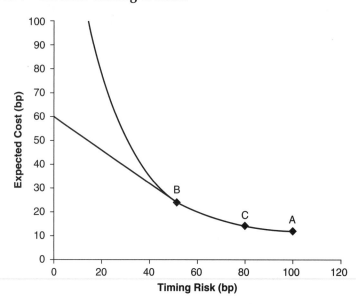

is worth noting that the FV concept has received criticism. However, those participants who have criticized the approach happen to be those sell-side brokers who have a vested interest in keeping the principal bid process as non-transparent as possible. These brokers seem to be very unwilling to provide investors with any means of evaluating their bids. On the same note, those participants who do not have a vested interest in keeping the principal bid process hidden have embraced the concept of the FV. These participants include: practitioners, academics, and many institutional investors. Regardless of the belief surrounding our FV, it is necessary for investors to have an unbiased means of evaluating a principal bid. Imagine how difficult it would be for investors to transact in futures and options if there was no process to evaluate their fair price. Or worse, imagine a scenario where there was no price discovery mechanism and investors simply took the word of brokers on worth of the stock. Hence, leave it up to our readers to draw their own conclusion regarding the FV approach.

To examine the economic fair value for a trade list let us begin by investigating the corresponding process. For investors to achieve immediate execution of the trade list they need to transfer the list to an executing broker. This broker is then responsible for executing the trade list. During the process this broker performs work in trading those stocks in the list, incurs cost from price appreciation and market impact, and is exposed to potential adverse price movement over the period of execution, i.e., timing risk. In other words, the executing broker is exposed to the same costs and risks as investors executing the list via an agency execution. Thus the executing broker needs to be compensated for these costs and risk as well as for the work performed to trade the list. The total payment to this executing broker is the cost of immediate execution to the investor. But as we show below, investors can still dictate the terms and conditions of the agreement.[4]

Our approach varies from the one we suggest earlier for the agency execution. In an agency execution, investors retain risk. Recall that cost is estimated as a random variable with mean ϕ and risk $\Re$ and dependent on execution strategy x_k. Now we are interested in developing that *fair single point estimate* for execution of the trade list.

Consider this scenario. An investor "pays" a third party (the executing broker) to execute the list. The executing party "works the list" by seeking counterparties, locating liquidity, and negotiating prices. Thus fair value should include compensation for this work, which is equivalent to the agency broker commission (i.e., agency brokers are paid for the work they do). Second, during the execution of the list the executing broker incurs price appreciation market impact and cost. If a stock trends through the day, the executing party pays market prices reflecting that trend. The executing party exerts buying and selling pressure that incurs a market impact cost. Again, this makes the price of buys higher and sells lower. In this case, price appreciation and market impact costs are out-of-pocket expenses incurred by the executing party during their role. Hence, as with any entity or subcontractor (individual or corporate) full reimbursement of out-of-pocket expenses is due. Therefore, the FV needs to reflect all expected costs from price appreciation and market impact. Finally, during the execution of the list the executing broker incurs timing risk. This consists of the potential adverse price movement of the stock (systematic and idiosyncratic risk) as well as the uncertainty associated with market volumes and intraday trading patterns (i.e., liquidity risk). Hence, the executing party should be compensated for risk. Thus, we can state the economic fair value (FV) of the trade list as:

$$ FV = \underbrace{c}_{\text{Compensation}} + \underbrace{(\mu + \kappa)}_{\text{Expense Reimbursement}} + \underbrace{f(\Re)}_{\text{Risk Premium}} $$

where c constitutes the commission charge, μ and κ are the price appreciation and market impact respectively, and $f(\Re)$ is the risk-reward required for acquiring the quantity of risk. For example, $f(\Re)=r\cdot\Re$.

Fair Value of a Trade Schedule

We have learned in previous chapters that the agency trading costs are dependent upon the actual trading schedule x_k. This must also be consid-

---

4. The question should be asked as, "What is the fair price to entice a party (broker-dealer or other) to accept the trade list and execute in the market following instructions from the investor where they would incur all cost and risk?

ered in the fair value calculation. It is easy to see that every trade schedule has a corresponding *FV*. It is calculated as follows:

$$FV(x_k) = c + \mu(x_k) + \kappa(x_k) + r \cdot \Re(x_k) \qquad (10.7)$$

This can be written in terms of the cost profile $\theta = (\phi, \Re)$ of the strategy x_k as follows:

$$FV(x_k) = c + \underbrace{\phi(x_k)}_{Expected\ Cost} + \underbrace{r * \Re(x_k)}_{Risk\ Premium} \qquad (10.8)$$

In a perfectly competitive environment consumers are willing to pay up to the value they believe the good or service is worth. The same holds for investors and capital markets. Investors are indifferent if the executing broker completes the order quickly or very slowly. Either speed constitutes the same service to the investor—an executed trade list.

Therefore, from the investor's perspective, the FV for the trade list X should be the lowest FV over all optimal trade schedules. This value, FV*, is found in a similar way to how investors determine price improvement strategies. Here we incorporate the ETF and evaluate the associated FV of all strategies to determine the one with the lowest value. This is expressed as:

$$FV^* = \min\{FV(x_k)\} \text{for all strategies } k$$

Since in the principal bid process investors in effect hire a middle person to execute the trade list (for a price), investors can dictate terms and conditions of that contract. Investors should require broker-dealers or the executing party to execute the trade list in the manner they specify. The strategy selected by investors x_k will be one with minimum FV. To determine the minimum FV investors need to evaluate the ETF (another reason to undertake a thorough agency cost analysis). Unfortunately, this is not always done. The minimum of all fair values, FV*, is what we deem to be the economic fair value for a principal bid.

Market participants, namely sell-side brokers, have stated that investors should be willing to pay up to I for a principal bid since I is the agency cost for immediate execution. Thus they state that any bid less than I is a justified bid. While this may seem reasonable, it is far from true. In perfect capital markets with perfect and complete competition, sellers become forced to reduce their prices so that they cover their expenses and earn a reasonable return on their investment. Our FV methodology follows this scheme and ensures that executing brokers are compensated fairly for their work, their expenses, and earn a fair market return on their investment (in our case risk).

Our FV calculation process will hold true if:

- ▲ In perfect capital markets
- ▲ competition amongst brokers
- ▲ Pricing transparency (e.g. price discovery mechanisms)

Figure 10.8.   Fair Value as Function of Risk

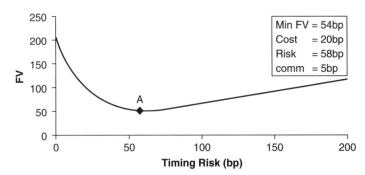

Fortunately, the first two are underlying assumptions of capital markets. The missing ingredient, however, is that investors do not have access to a transparent principal bid pricing scheme. We offer our FV* methodology as that pricing scheme for investors to use to evaluate the price of a principal bid.

Graphical Representation

The minimal FV can be shown graphically (see figure 10.8). Suppose the ETF for a trade list is derived according to the techniques shown in chapter 9 and its equation is:

$$\phi = 190e^{-0.05\,\Re} + 10$$

Now suppose that it has been agreed that fair competition for the work involved in executing the list is 5 bp and the fair risk premium is 0.5 bp per unit of risk[5], i.e., one unit of return for two units of risk. A 5bp commission rate is the equivalent of 1.5 cents per share on a $30 stock. A risk premium of 0.5bp corresponds to a 10% return for stock with volatility of 20%, close to historical averages.

The equation of the ETF provides us with a relationship between cost and risk. Thus by changing the corresponding level of cost or risk in the FV equation we attain different FVs. Figure 10.8 graphs the FV as a function of timing risk. The resulting graph is a convex function that has a minimum value. For our selected values of c and r we obtain a minimum FV of 54bp for strategy A. The corresponding cost profile of strategy A is $\theta_A=(20, 58)$. Every other optimal strategy results in a FV calculation higher than 54bp. In this example, investors should never pay an

---

5. Our selection of a commission rate of 5bp and a risk premium of 0.5bp is only for illustrative purposes. While these values are reasonable and in line with market charges, we do suggest that investors make their own decisions regarding these amounts—that is, choose higher or lower values. Regardless of the value, however, the amounts do need to be intuitive and consistent with market practices.

executing party more than 54bp to execute the list on their behalf.[6] Any amount higher than 54bp implies that the executing party is overcharging investors for the service they provide, not executing as efficiently as they could, or charging more than the market rate for risk. In any case, investors should avoid entering into an agreement with any executing party who charges more than the minimum FV of the list. Investors need to take contol and dictate the terms and conditions of these executions.

Mathematical Derivation

The minimum FV for a trade list can also be determined using differentiation techniques. First, we know that the ETF is defined by the following equation:

$$\phi = a_1 e^{-a2\Re} + a_3$$

Therefore the FV can be rewritten as follows:

$$
\begin{aligned}
FV(x_k) &= c + \phi(x_k) + r^* \Re(x_k) \\
&= c + a_1 e^{-a_2 \Re(x_k)} + a_3 + r^* \Re(x_k)
\end{aligned}
$$
(10.9)

where we replace $\phi(x_k)$ with the ETF relationship. The minimum value occurs at the point where the first derivative with respect to $\Re$ is equal to zero. This is calculated as follows:

$$
\begin{aligned}
\frac{\partial}{d\Re} FV &= \frac{d}{d\Re} c + a_1 e^{-a_2 \Re} + a_3 + r^* \Re \\
&= -a_1 a_2 e^{-a_2 \Re} + r^*
\end{aligned}
$$
(10.10)

Setting equal to zero and solving for $\Re$ we get:

$$
-a_1 a_2 e^{-a_2 \Re} + r^* = 0
$$

$$
\Re^* = \frac{1}{-a_2} \ln\left(\frac{r}{a_1 a_2}\right)
$$
(10.11)

Which is a minimum since the second derivative with respect to $\Re$ is positive. That is:

$$
\frac{\partial^2}{d\Re^2} FV = a_1 a_2^2 e^{-a_2 \Re} > 0
$$

---

6. As always, our values are specific for the ETF defined earlier and used only for illustartion purposes. In actuality, every trade list will have its own ETF and thus its own FV calculation.

since $a_1, a_2, e^{-a_2 \Re} > 0$

The FV of a trade list can be calculated directly once we determine the coefficients a_1, a_2, and a_3 defining the ETF and decide upon the appropriate commission rate c and risk premium for the list r^*.

The FV equation can then be written in terms of $\Re^*$ that minimizes the value. This is as follows:

$$FV = c + (a_1 e^{-a_2 \Re} + a_3) + r^* \Re^*$$

$$= c + a_1 \exp\left\{-a_2 \cdot \frac{1}{-a_2} \cdot \ln\left(\frac{r^*}{a_1 a_2}\right)\right\} + a_3 + r^* \cdot \frac{-1}{a_2} \cdot \ln\left(\frac{r}{a_1 a_2}\right)$$

$$= c + \frac{r^*}{a_2} + a_3 - \frac{r^*}{a_2} \cdot \ln\left(\frac{r}{a_1 a_2}\right)$$

$$= (c + a_3) + \frac{r^*}{a_2}\left[1 - \ln\left(\frac{r}{a_1 a_2}\right)\right]$$

The economic FV for a principal bid in terms of the parameters that describe the efficient trading frontier along the commission fee and risk-premium. The economic fair value "FV" for a principal bid is calculated as follows:

$$FV_{bp}^*(X) = (c + a_3) + \frac{r^*}{a_2}\left[1 - \ln\left(\frac{r^*}{a_1 a_2}\right)\right] \tag{10.12}$$

We determined the FV for the trade list to be 54bp using the graphical representation technique. Following the equation from Equation 10.12 yields the exact same answer. That is:

$$FV_{bp}^*(X) = (c + a_3) + \frac{r^*}{a_2}\left[1 - \ln\left(\frac{r^*}{a_1 a_2}\right)\right]$$

$$= (5 + 10) + \frac{0.5}{0.05}\left[1 - \ln\left(\frac{0.5}{190 \cdot 0.05}\right)\right]$$

$$= 15 + 10 \cdot [1 - -2.944]$$

$$= 15 + 10 \cdot [3.944]$$

$$= 15 + 39.44$$

$$= 54.44bp$$

Except for some slight rounding the results are exact. The total dollar amount for the bid can then be determined by simply multiplying the FV in basis points by the trade value of the list:

$$FV_\$^* = (\Sigma x_i p_i) \cdot \left((c + a_3) + \frac{r^*}{a_2} \left[1 - \ln\left(\frac{r^*}{a_1 a_2} \right) \right] \right) \qquad (10.13)$$

This amount can be converted to \$/share simply by dividing by the number of shares. That is:

$$FV_{\$/share}^* = \frac{(\Sigma x_i p_i) \cdot \left((c + a_3) + \frac{r^*}{a_2} \left[1 - \ln\left(\frac{r^*}{a_1 a_2} \right) \right] \right)}{\Sigma x_i} \qquad (10.14)$$

The importance here is that we have found an analytical solution for the economic fair value for a principal bid that is dependent upon the set of optimal trading strategies (ETF) and pricing assumptions (c and r). This further confirms the need for investors to always perform an agency cost analysis for any trade list, even in cases where it has been predetermined (for whatever reason) that the preference for implementation is a principal bid transaction.

Will the Fair Value Strategy Always Be an Optimal Strategy?

The FV strategy x_k will always correspond to an optimal strategy lying on the ETF. This is explained as follows. Consider strategy B in Figure 10.9. This strategy is not optimal since it lies above the ETF. Strategies B_1, B_2, and B_3, are optimal and lie in the "improvement region." Recall, this improvement region is the collection of alternative strategies with either less risk (same cost), less cost (same risk), or lower cost and risk. Therefore, at least one of the associated FVs, for B_1, B_2, or B_3 will be less than the FV for B. Hence we state that B is stochastically dominated by at least one of the strategies B_1, B_2, or B_3.

If r^* is the risk premium for a unit of risk, then:

$FV(B) = \phi(B) + r^* \, \Re(B)$
$FV(B_1) = \phi(B_1) + r^* \, \Re(B_1) < FV(B)$ since $\phi(B_1) < \phi(B)$ and $\Re(B_1) = \Re(B)$
$FV(B_2) = \phi(B_2) + r^* \, \Re(B_2) < FV(B)$ since $\Re(B_2) < \Re(B)$ and $\phi(B_2) = \phi(B)$
$FV(B_3) = \phi(B_3) + r^* \, \Re(B_3) < FV(B)$ since $\Re(B_3) < \Re(B)$ and $\phi(B_3) < \phi(B)$

Are Pricing Bids at the FV Reasonable for the Broker-Dealer?

Even though the fair value for a principal bid is derived from the viewpoint of investors it is still a fair price for brokers and properly compensates them for their role. *It finally places the agency and principal analysis on a level playing*

Figure 10.9.   Efficient Trading Frontier/Set of Economic Fair Values

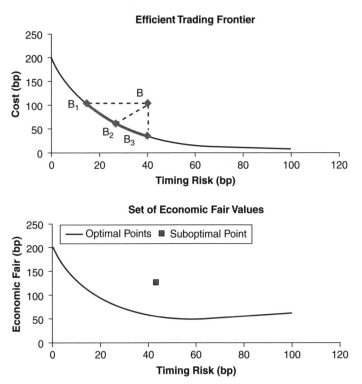

field and provides the framework for analysis. Here, broker-dealers are fairly compensated for their services provided (work performed in trading the list), out-of-pocket expenses (trading costs), plus a risk-premium (fair return on investment). Regardless of the strategy specified by investors brokers do indeed receive fair and complete compensation.

Let us evaluate a simple case with no out-of-pocket expenses. Broker-dealers should receive payment for work performed and a return on risk incurred. As long as the payment for work is correct and risk compensation is fair, brokers will be satisfied. Now consider the case with out-of-pocket expenses. Broker-dealers receive payment for trading the list. The payment structure should be identical to the commission charged by an agency broker (the quantity of work is identical). Second, the FV payment to brokers includes compensation for incurring cost associated with price appreciation and market impact. Third, the FV includes a fair return on acquired risk. Broker-dealers should be indifferent if they execute on behalf of investors aggressively or passively as long as the premium paid for taking risk is fair.

Principal Bid Process

The following example illustrates a five-step approach for solication of principal bids.

Example 8.   A money manager decides to invest $100 million across large, medium, and small cap stocks. The manager asks an analyst to evaluate if a principal bid is a viable alternative to an agency execution. The manager's goal for implementation is to preserve asset value and achieve best execution. Describe the process to solicit and evaluate principal bid transactions.

1. Agency Cost Analysis

The first step in the principal bid process is the agency cost evaluation following the framework described in previous chapters. This analysis will serve as the base case for comparing to principal bids. In some cases, agency execution is the most appropriate implementation strategy; other times it is the principal bid transaction. The analyst needs to evaluate both options to determine the most appropriate one. Suppose the analyst finds the set of all optimal agency strategies (ETF) defined by the equation:

$$\phi = 190e^{-.05\Re} + 10$$

2. Choose Broker-Dealers for Solicitation

The second step in the principal bid process consists of choosing brokers to include in the solicitation process. Funds do not solicit bids from every principal broker because they worry about information leakage and adverse price movement. Analysts will select two or three brokers for solicitation—typically brokers who provided fair and accurate principal bid prices in the recent past. For example, if an investor recently solicited bids and received reasonable ones from brokers A, B, and C, but not from D and E, they will likely utilize A, B, and C to handle the next trade list.

This selection of broker based on most competitive bid alone is not necessarily in the best interest for the fund because, as we have pointed out, the principal bid premium may not be the only cost investors incur. At times brokers infer enough information about the trade list to cause adverse price movement. What appears to be reasonable bids might have the most negative effect on the fund. The process whereby investors solicit bids from broker-dealers who have provided competitive bids may cause the most honest ones—those who provide true estimates and do not run up the price—to be excluded from the process. It is important investors be able to infer fair and accurate bids from these "fake" bids.

In a principal bid process, smart investors measure cost estimates provided by broker-dealers thoroughly both in agency and principal bid transactions. A sound approach for measuring performance of a principal bid consists of a statistical test to determine price run-up. This is discussed in Chapter 13, Post-Trade Analysis.

3. Actual Solicitation of the Bid Premium

The third step is the actual solicitation of the bid. Investors contact selected brokers and provide them with characteristics of the trade list, not the trade list itself; they keep as much information about their list hidden to avoid potential front running. For example, they may solicit a "blind" bid to keep brokers from seeing the actual names, quantities, and side of the position. Brokers' preference is to receive the exact list so that they can provide a better premium. However, by not having complete access to the actual trade list for derivation of the bid premium brokers indeed incur additional risk. Therefore, as protection against the extra risk they factor in a safety margin payment into the price of the bid. In this process, the contract between investor and broker is usually a verbal agreement or confirmation.

Investors solicit the bid from brokers usually via phone call stating their intentions and list characteristics. Brokers then require investors to provide them with the exact list characteristics in some electronic file format. This information includes size and liquidity characteristics, stock volatility and risk, and spreads. It also includes the composition of the list including buy/sell quantities, market capitalization, sector breakdowns, and the tracking error of the stock to various indices. Brokers then analyze the list characteristics to get an idea of what the acquired position would cost them to execute in the market and add this amount to the safety margin and profit level to arrive at the bid. In some cases brokers provide investors with a principal bid almost immediately and other times get back to investors a little later. Overall, the turnaround time is quick.

The principal bid premium provided to investors is most typically in $/share or basis points (bp), although there are times when brokers provide a bid amount as a total dollar ($) value.

4. Analysis of Alternatives

The fourth step is analysis of the principal bids and comparison of the best bid to the set of optimal agency strategies. Assume investors receive three principal bids of 40bp, 60bp, and 80bp.[7] On the surface, it appears the lowest bid is the best: 40bp. However, we know that a principal broker can run the stock price up (or down) into the close, triggering a higher price than bid price. This could cause the lowest principal bid to incur the highest trading cost. Indeed, investors should have excluded these brokers in step 2. If it is believed that the solicited brokers do not run-up the price on the investor then the only principal bid to evaluate is $B^* = 40bp$. We denote the lowest principal bid as B^* and evaluate this bid determining how it compares to the economic fair value of the list and the chances of a more profitable execution utilizing an agency execution. These analysis steps are as follows:

How does B^* compare to the fair value FV?

We first determine if the principal bid is fair. Recall, the pricing scheme employed to determine the economic fair value for a principal bid (relationship between cost and risk, the prevailing risk-premium, and fair

7. In actuality, the principal bid premiums from competing brokers are typically much closer to one another. We exaggerate this example with three bids of 40bp, 60bp, and 80bp for illustrative purposes.

commission rate in offsetting the position). We can apply Equation 10.12 to determine the fair value for the list:

$$FV^* (X) = (c + a_3) + \frac{r^*}{a_2}\left[1 - \ln\left(\frac{r^*}{a_1 a_2}\right)\right]$$

From step 2 we determine the values of the coefficients to be: $a_1 = 190$, $a_2 = 0.05$, and $a_3 = 10$; also, assuming a fair commission rate of 5bp and a fair risk premium of 0.5bp we determine the economic fair value for this trade list to be:

$$FV^* = (5 + 10) + \frac{0.5}{0.05}\left[1 - \ln\left(\frac{0.5}{190 \cdot 0.05}\right)\right] = 54\text{bp}$$

The principal bid of 40bp is a reasonable bid for the list because it is less than the amount investors should be willing to accept, for example, 40bp < 54bp. However, the other two bids of 60bp and 80bp should not be accepted for execution of this list because they are both greater than the FV. It should be a cardinal rule that investors are never to accept a principal bid greater than the FV of the list.

Is B* better than the minimal cost strategy?

After determining if the bid is less than the FV we check to see if there are any optimal agency strategies with lower expected cost than B*. This can be determined easily from the ETF. We have found that the cost-risk relationship becomes asymptotic at the value of a_3. This value is also the minimal cost of the trade list and is found by optimizing the trade-off between cost and risk with a level of risk aversion $\lambda = 0$. The associated strategy found from this optimization will have expected cost $\phi = a_3$. Even without considering the exact risk of the strategy we know that there is a 50% chance that the actual cost will be higher and a 50% chance that it will be lower—very valuable information for evaluating a principal bid. If the principal bid is less than the value of a_3 better than the principal transaction there is less than a 50% chance that the actual agency cost will be less than B*. Therefore, when the condition B*<a_3 holds, investors benefit by selecting the principal bid over any of the agency strategies. In these situations, there is not ample chance that the agency cost will be better than B*. This point is illustrated in Figure 10.10. Notice the total area to the left of B* is less than 50% (a fact since the total area to the left of a_3 is 50%). Any investor, thus, selecting an agency execution over the principal bid in this situation has selected a gambling game with odds against investors. Suppose the probability of executing at a cost less than B* is only 40%. Investors choose between paying B* now or pay more than B* 60% of the time. Rational investors would not throw dice when odds are unfavorable and expected payoff fails to justify risk.

Figure 10.10. Trading Cost Distribution

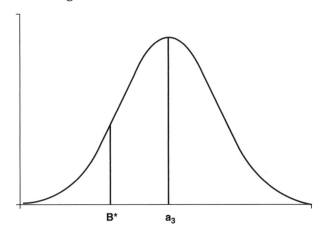

Figure 10.11. Principal Bid Improvement Strategy

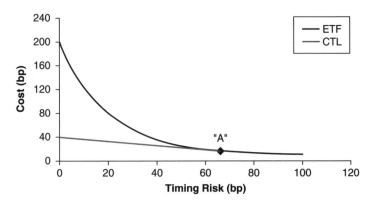

How does the bid compare to the price improvement strategies?

Once it is determined that the B* is better than the FV and higher than a_3 ($a_3 \leq$ B* $\leq$ FV) investors need to determine the bid improvement strategy, corresponding cost profile and associated probability level of price improvement. This is found (see Figure 10.11) by drawing a line from the value of B* = 40bp on the *y*-axis tangent to the ETF (determined in step 1). This is identical to the methodology we use to compute the CTL from a cost level of 40. The point of tangency in this figure is denoted as strategy *A* and is the bid-improvement strategy. This is the optimal agency strategy that provides the highest likelihood of executing better than 40bp. Using the information from the ETF we calculate the cost profile of this strategy to be θ_A=(17,66), that is, expected cost of 17bp and timing risk of 66bp.

We then determine the probability that strategy A will execute better than the bid of 40bp. This is derived using the cumulative trading cost formula and the cost profile θ_A. The associated probability levels of strategy A

Figure 10.12.   Probability Agency Cost < Principal Bid

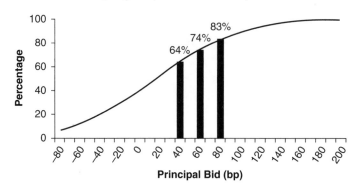

is 64%, meaning that in 64% of cases investors benefit by an agency trans-action rather than the principal bid. This can also be expressed as a gam-bling type problem where investors have a 64% chance of doing better with the agency and only a 36% chance of doing worse than the principal bid. As an aside, strategy A has a 74% likelihood of executing better than the sec-ond most attractive bid of 60bp and an 83% likelihood of executing better than the highest bid of 80bp. This is depicted in Figure 10.12.

For investors to select between the principal transaction and agency execution where the agency execution is expected to incur a lower cost than the bid 64% of the time they need to consider their trading frequency over the year along with acceptable levels of risk exposure. If investors trade often enough they would be better off with agency over principal because they have ample opportunities for gains to offset losses. In a situ-ation where only one rebalance occurs over the year—for example, Russell 2000 indexer, manager transition—investors may be better off with the principal bid since they do not have ample opportunity for any potential losses to be offset by gains.

Let us consider the cost profile of strategy A, $\theta_A = (17,66)$ for an investor who trades monthly. Assuming the average cost and risk for each execution remains unchanged then the risk of all executions decreases by a factor of $\sqrt{12}$ since each successive trade is independent of the previous (Law of Large Numbers). Thus the cost profile reduces to $\theta_A = (17,66/\sqrt{12}) = (17,19)$ and has a dramatic effect on the price improvement strategy over the year. The probability that investors will incur a cost less than 40bp in total over the year (12 executions, 1 per month) is 89%, a substantial increase from 64%. A summary of this annualized "price improvement" probability level for various trading frequencies is shown in Table 10.2. The probabilities are determined using the cumulative cost distributions with $\phi = \phi_A$ and $\Re = \Re_A/\sqrt{n}$.

The quantity of risk reduction associated with the frequency of trad-ing activity is shown graphically in Figure 10.13. The figure shows how quickly risk decreases with trading frequency. Risk reduces to 50% of its

Table 10.2. Annualized "Price improvement" Probability Level Summary for Various Trading Frequencies

Frequency of Trade	Number of Trades	Adjustment Factor	Prob of Price Improvement (Prob Cost < 40bp)
Daily	250	15.81	99.99%
Weekly	52	7.21	99.40%
Bi-Weekly	26	5.10	96.22%
Monthly	12	3.46	88.63%
Quarterly	4	2.00	75.71%
Annual	1	1.00	63.63%

Figure 10.13. Trading Risk Reduction

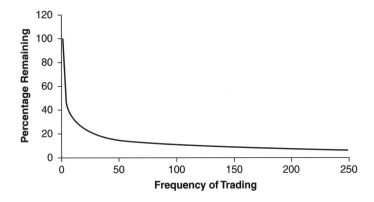

original level with only 4 executions per year (quarterly). This amount falls to 30% of its original level with 12 executions (monthly) and 20% of its original level with 24 (bi-weekly) executions. Finally, investors who trade daily will only incur 5% average risk of the quantity of each execution.[8]

Rules of Thumb

To assist in the selection of a principal bid transaction or agency execution strategy we provide a summary in Table 10.3. When B* is higher than the FV, investors should elect to trade via an agency execution. In these situations, brokers are either charging a price higher than the list or failing to offset the position in the best possible way. In either case, brokers are hurting investors. When B* is lower than parameter a_3 from the ETF equation (the lowest cost) investors should select the principal bid because there is less than 50% chance that the agency strategy will incur a lower cost than B*. Rational investors should not elect to trade where odds are unfavorable.

8. We make the assumption that the risk expressed in basis points will be the same for each trade. In reality, this quantity will change from trade to trade but Figure 10.13 still provides a good estimate of the reduction in risk from the average quantity of each execution.

Table 10.3.   Summary Table

Criteria	Trading Option
$B^* > FV$	Agency
$a_3 \leq B^* \leq FV$	Principal or Agency (need further analysis)
$B^* < a_3$	Principal

There are times when $B^* < a_3$ because brokers possess off-setting inventory, are able to anticipate order flow, or can hedge risk associated with the trade list. Finally, if B^* is less than FV but higher than a_3, investors should incorporate their level of risk aversion and trading frequency to determine the most appropriate strategy. Often investors can benefit by utilizing a mixed strategy consisting of both principal and agency strategies as discussed in Chapter 9.

Case Example,
The selection of agency execution or principal bid transaction depends as much on the utility function of the investor as it does the price of the bid. An analogy to the trading decision described earlier is one where a gambler is presented with the following game:

A person earning $250,000 annually ($1,000/day and 250 days/year) is presented with an opportunity to play a game with 60% chance of winning and 40% chance of losing. If the person plays the game and wins, then their annual salary will be doubled to $500,000. But if the person loses, then their annual salary will be zero. The odds of this game are in favor of the gambler, but most people would pass over this game even with the favorable odds because of the large loss potential. That is, the risk of losing and having to work one entire year without pay is too large.

Another possibility is where the person gets to play the same game with the same odds of winning but only bets their daily salary. Thus, they would receive $2,000 for the day if they win and zero if they lose. Since in this example the person would have ample opportunity for any losses to be offset by gains, the gambler would likely play.

5.   Transfer of the Trade List to the Broker

The fifth and final step of the principal bid process calls for investors to transfer the trade list to the executing broker. In the case where investors select the principal bid over the agency, transaction investors would provide brokers with the actual trade list (symbol, side, and shares). Brokers then transfer the exact number of shares of each buy order and the total dollar amount for all sell orders valued at the stock price of the agreed upon point in time (usually the close). Investors are then required to pay brokers the bid premium.

In addition to the transfer of shares and dollars between broker and investor, the principal broker evaluates the trade list and confirms that characteristics of the actual trade list are identical to those presented during the principal bid solicitation process. There are times when investors will try to submit to the broker a more volatile or less liquid list than described in the original list characteristics (investors can be just as sneaky and brokers need to beware). If this occurs, brokers will not take kindly to investors and will likely request an additional payment and/or may refuse to honor the agreement or do future business with investors.

In the case where investors select an agency execution over the principal bid transaction, investors transfer the exact trade list to the selected broker for agency execution. Additionally, if investors choose to execute the list themselves they will simply begin implementation at the appropriate time.

Market Efficiency and Economies of Scale

Broker-dealer pricing and execution schemes can provide a considerable amount of cost reduction for investors by aggregating order flow into a single inventory position rather than managing each investor list individually. Brokers can then pass the realized savings along to investors in the form of a lower principal bid. The associated cost savings of an aggregation order book is the result of an "economies of scale" effect. Brokers' internal inventory usually consists of numerous investor trade lists; many times these competing orders will offset or match resulting in a smaller rather than a larger broker position. The net result to brokers is a lower implementation cost from natural crosses and lower timing risk from diversification and hedging. For example, through aggregation of order flow brokers may receive two orders from different investors. One order may be to sell x shares of ABC and the other may be to buy y shares of ABC. The result of the transaction is a broker position $x-y$, which is less in magnitude than the maximum of x and y. Brokers can (and usually do) pass along some of the savings to investors in the form of a lower priced principal bid. Other times brokers' aggregated position will comprise less timing risk because of a diversification or hedging effect. This allows the executing broker to offset the acquired position at a slower rate (more passive strategy) resulting in a lower expected cost for the same quantity of risk. The overall effect is an ETF with a larger trading risk parameter (a_2) and consequently a lower fair value calculation. For example, we know that in general $x^T Cx < \sum x\sigma$ for all portfolios since $\rho_{ij} < 1$. Thus, a well-diversified or well-hedged trade portfolio will correspond to an ETF with a higher trading risk parameter a_2 than the nondiversified, portfolio that is, a_2 *(nondiversified)* $< a_2$ *(diversified)* $< a_2$ *(hedged)*. This results in a lower FV for the aggregated diversified list, that is *FV (nondiversified)* $>$ *FV (diversified)* $>$ *FV (hedged)* since a_2 is in the denominator of the FV formula. The more diversified or hedged the list becomes the higher the trading risk parameter and the lower the fair value of the list.

Cost Savings

The cost savings corresponding to the economies of scale effect is defined as the difference between the cumulative FV cost that would be assessed to each investor individually based on their own trade list less the FV cost of the aggregated trade list. In economic terms this definition is the societal benefit or market savings and is a measure of how much better all participants become by joining into a group. For example, if all investors paid the FV cost of their individual trade list to a broker, there would be a large cost paid in total. Let this amount be x. Now if all these investors got together and formed a group, the FV cost for the aggregated position would be lower because of natural matches and a more diversified and hedged portfolio. Let this amount be y. The savings earned by the group as a whole z would simply be $y–x$. This societal benefit is the advantage that a group acquires by working together for the group's best interest instead of each investor working alone toward their own best interest. In terms of the FV we calculate this savings as:

$$Societal\ Benefit = \left(\sum_i FV_\$(i) \right) - FV_\$(U) \qquad (10.15)$$

where $FV_\$(i)$ is the FV cost for investor i and $FV_\$(U)$ is the FV cost for the aggregated trade list; U denotes the universe of all investors and the corresponding trade list is the union of all investors list. In a subsequent section we provide a methodology that fairly allocates the societal benefit to each investor based upon their overall contribution to the group.

Example 9. There are two investors seeking to execute shares in ABC. Investor I has a sell order for 100,000 shares and Investor II has a buy order for 80,000 shares. If each party acts alone and solicits a principal bid from different brokers, they are likely to receive a high bid since the list comprises one-sided large block orders with no natural risk reduction. If these investors solicit bids from the same broker, there would be a considerable amount in cost savings. The aggregated trade list then would only consist of 20,000 shares rather than the 100,000 or 80,000 shares from one investor.

The societal benefit of the aggregated trade list is determined from the FV of each list. If ABC is \$30/share, has ADV of 1 million shares, and daily volatility of 300bp, we can compute the FV costs using the parameters of each ETF (using $r=1/2$ and $c=5$). These results are shown in Table 10.4.[9] The societal benefit is calculated as follows:

Societal Benefit = (\$50,118 + 36,803) − \$5,635 = \$86,912 − \$5,636 = \$81,285

9. The goal in this example is to explain the societal benefit associated with an aggregated trade list; we are not seeking to describe calculation process to determine the parameters of the ETF or calculate the FV. For a thorough explanation of those calculations please refer to the appropriate section of the text.

Table 10.4. Societal Benefit of the Aggregated Trade List: Example 9

Investor	Shares	ETF			FV	
		a_1	a_2	a_3	Bp	Dollars ($)
I	+100,000	222	.0072	12	167	$50,118
II	−80,000	205	.0079	11	153	$36,803
U	+20,000	140	.01486	7	94	$5,635

Table 10.5. Societal Benefit of the Aggregated Trade List: Example 10

Investor	Value	ETF			FV	
		a_1	a_2	a_3	Bp	Dollars ($)
I	$10 M	250	.05	12	59	$59,000
II	$10 M	250	.05	12	59	$59,000
U_1	$20 M	250	.08	12	46	$92,000
U_2	$20 M	250	.20	12	31	$62,000
U_3	$10 M	100	.20	5	22	$22,000

The aggregated cost for the combined trade lists is considerably lower than either investor could achieve on their own; thus, brokers implementing the transaction can charge a lower price and pass along the cost savings to each investor in the form of a much reduced principal bid.

An aggregated trade list can also realize a reduction in total trading cost and fair value from a more diversified and/or hedged trade list because brokers can offset the position at a more passive rate. This risk reduction is a consequence of stocks being positively but not perfectly correlated with one another (i.e., $0 < \rho_{ij} < 1$). And in the situations where the trade list comprises both buy and sell orders, it is the equivalent of a long-short portfolio with greatly hedged risk since positions are negatively correlated due to the side of the position (i.e., $-1 < \rho_{ij} < 1$).

Example 10. Two investors are each investing $10 million dollars in equity portfolios with the exact same characteristics (size, volatility, correlations, etc.). Each portfolio consists of ten stocks and is a mixture of large, mid, and small cap names, but neither is investing in the exact same stock. If each investor solicits a principal bid based solely on the characteristics of their trade list, the FV calculation should be somewhat reasonable because each list realizes some cost savings from diversification. However, if the two investors combine their trade list, they will achieve a greater quantity of diversification and a lower FV. Hence, it is in their best interest to seek to join.

The parameters describing the ETF of each investor are depicted in Table 10.5. These parameters (a_1, a_2, and a_3) are the same because of the identical list characteristics. The aggregated list does not include any of the same names so there is no corresponding increase or decrease in order sizes. Thus, there is not any reduction in cost parameters (instantaneous or minimum). This appears in the table whereby the aggregated list U_1 has the same instantaneous cost in basis points of total ($a_1 = 250$) and minimum cost ($a_3 = 12$) parameters as each individual investor. However, the increase in diversification for the aggregated list has a higher trading risk parameter ($a_2 = 0.08$ compared to $a_2 = 0.05$). The result is a lower FV calculation for the aggregated list and the societal benefit calculates as follows.[10]

$$Societal \; Benefit = (\$59,000 + 59,000) - \$92,000 = \$26,000$$

Example 11. Consider the same situation as Example 10 except that Investor II's trade list is a cash redemption. Since we do not assume any difference in the cost of buying or selling stocks, the parameters describing the ETF and the FV for Investor II do not change. However, the aggregated trade list U_2 realizes an even greater reduction in risk because of the hedging effect brought on from the buy and sell orders. This is shown in Table 10.5 where the aggregated trade list has a much higher trading risk parameter a_2 than each investor ($a_2 = 0.20$ compared to $a_2 = 0.05$). It is also higher than the aggregated list U_1 ($a_2 = 0.20$ compared to $a_2 = 0.08$). The result is a FV that is much lower for investors acting together than they would receive acting alone. The societal benefit for this example is:

$$Societal \; Benefit = (\$59,000 + 59,000) - \$62,000 = \$56,000$$

Example 12. The best possible scenario for investors is for the aggregated trade list to have cost and risk reduction.[11] The cost reduction results from matching or offsetting orders and the risk reduction results from diversification and hedging. Consider Example 11 where one investor has a buy list and the other investor has a sell list. However, this time there is some matching of orders. The aggregated trade list U_3 has lower cost parameters (a_1 and a_3) and a higher trading risk parameter (a_2). The resulting cost savings are more reflected in the dollar cost rather than bp because the aggregated trade list is for a lower value than the sum of investors' trade lists since there are some matching orders. Suppose that the aggregated trade list has an unexecuted value of $10 million dollars and ETF parameters shown in Table 10.5, then societal benefit of this scenario is:

$$Societal \; Benefit = (\$59,000 + 59,000) - \$22,000 = \$96,000$$

---

10. Readers verifying our calculations may find some differences due to rounding errors.
11. It is not reasonable to expect investor trade lists to be perfect complements of one another or provide perfect matches.

Example 13. Let us reconsider Example 9 but here both investors have buy orders, Investor I for 100,000 shares and Investor II for 80,000. The fair value calculations for their trade lists are $50,118 and $36,803 respectively. But in this case the investors do not realize a cost savings by aggregating their trade list because the aggregated position results in a more costly larger block trade for 180,000 shares and an increased risk exposure. The cost parameters of the aggregated position are much higher than for either investor ($a_1 = 281$ and $a_3 = 15$) and the trading risk parameter is much lower ($a_2 = 0.005$). The FV for the aggregated position is $116,050 and the societal benefit results in an incremental cost of $29,129.

$$Societal\ Benefit = (\$50,118 + 36,803) - \$116,050 = -\$29,129$$

A broker who acquires both trade lists would not be able to pass along any natural savings to investors in the form of a reduced principal bid. However, a conscientious broker seeks to incorporate a customized risk reduction vehicle so that the resulting aggregated cost would be less than the sum of the individual positions.

When the aggregated trade list yields a larger position and there is no corresponding risk reduction, the result will be a list with a higher FV. In these cases, the result is not unique to the principal bid transaction. The result is an indication that there is additional buying or selling pressure in the market resulting in a higher market impact cost borne by all market participants. Investors seeking to execute their individual trade list in the market using an agency execution will also incur a higher execution cost than anticipated for the specific trade list. To accurately assess the true market impact cost for an agency as well as principal transaction, investors need to incorporate the aggregated market imbalance in the stock, not just the market imbalance caused by their order. This point is illustrated in Figure 10.14 where the FV dollar is plotted as a function of order size (%ADV) for a stock with daily volatility of 350bp. The figure shows the FV curve to be a convex function in the form:

$$FV_\$(s,\sigma = 350) \cong 1200 \cdot s^{1.6}$$

Figure 10.14. FV as a Function of Size

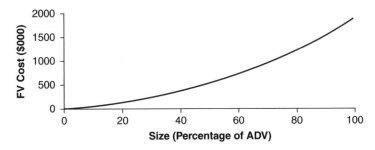

where s is the size of the order as a percentage of ADV (e.g., 5=5%). This causes the costs to increase at an accelerated rate, that is, the cost of the whole is greater than the parts. The power of s shows that the FV is not additive. This relationship shows that the FV of an aggregated trade list of several investors with some natural matching of orders may still not result in economies of scale cost reduction if some position become larger. The cost of the aggregated trade list may still be higher than the sum of each investor's trade list. To ensure a lower cost aggregated trade list there typically needs to be some corresponding decrease in risk. Fortunately, in the majority of cases the aggregated trade list will be less than the sum of the individual trade lists.

Trading Risk Parameter

There is a considerable amount of cost savings achievable from diversification and/or hedging. There is a direct relationship between this quantity and the trading risk parameter a_2. Recall that the trading risk parameter is an indication of the quantity of list diversification. The larger the parameter the more the diversification. Additionally, the larger the risk parameter, the lower the FV calculation. Thus, a market participant can use the trading risk parameter of a trade list to determine how many risk hedging vehicles to incorporate into an execution in order to bring the costs down to an acceptable level.

Our research has found an approximation to the quantity of cost change as a function of the trading risk parameter. This relationship is illustrated in Figure 10.15. This graph shows the reduction in FV cost associated with various trading rate parameters. We compute the FV cost for a trade list for a range of trading risk parameters from $a_2 = 0.005$ to $a_2 = 0.5$. We then normalize the FV cost at each trading risk parameter by dividing by the FV associated with a trading risk parameter of $a_2 = 0.005$. The graph shows that one can achieve a reduction in FV cost of approx-

Figure 10.15.   Relationship between FV and Trading Risk Parameter

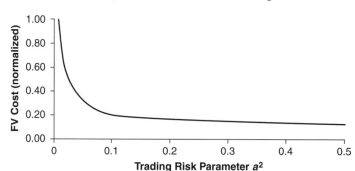

imately 80% of $a_2 = 0.005$ by incorporating risk reduction vehicles into the execution that increases the trading risk parameter to $a_2 = 0.5$, that is, $(0.2-1.0)/1.0 = -80\%$.

If one incorporates risk reduction vehicles into the execution of a trade list, the trading risk parameter changes from a_2 to a_2' the FV cost would change as follows:

$$FV \text{ } Cost \text{ } Change = \frac{FV(a_2') - FV(a_2)}{FV(a_2)}$$

This approximation holds true for trade lists with different parameters describing the ETF. Nevertheless, it is still only an approximation. It is provided here so investors (managers, traders, and brokers) can grasp the cost consequence of a trading decision without the cost calculations. A market participant could easily refer to this chart and quickly evaluate the effect of their decision on the execution in real time.

Example 14. A block trader needs to quickly evaluate the cost consequence of introducing a risk reduction vehicle into their position execution. If the current FV cost in dollars for the position is $50,000 and the trading risk parameter for the current position is $a_2 = 0.10$, should a risk reduction vehicle that increases a_2 to $a_2 = 0.15$ be incorporated into the implementation?

By referring to the graph in Figure 10.15 we read the normalized FV costs for each value of the trading rate parameter and compute the FV cost change as follows:

$$FV \text{ } Cost \text{ } Change = \frac{32 - 38}{38} = -16\%$$

Therefore, if the risk reduction vehicle augments the implementation of the position at a cost less than 16% of the current FV cost or less than $8,000 ($50,000*0.16 = $8,000), the instrument should be incorporated. It is extremely important here that we note this is only an approximation for investors who need to make an immediate decision. If the instrument can be added at a cost much less than $8,000, it should be added or if it is much higher than $8,000, it should not be included. In situations where the cost of the instrument is close to $8,000, investors need to compute a more precise figure before making the decision. In those cases investors can use the techniques shown previously; they are more accurate but do require time for the analysis.

Our final point concerning the relationship between FV cost and the trading risk parameter can be shown from the FV equation. As a_2 becomes increasing large the FV cost will approach the commission charge plus the

permanent market impact cost of the aggregated list. In any type of implementation, agency, or principal, this is the minimum execution cost anyone
could expect. That is:

$$\lim_{a_2 \to \infty} = (c + a_3) + \frac{r}{a_2}\left[1 - \ln\left(\frac{r}{a_1 \cdot a_2}\right)\right] = c + a_3$$

Economies of Scale and the Blind Bid

In the context of a blind bid brokers cannot perfectly assess the cost reduction associated with an aggregated trade list resulting from quantity of
natural matches in the trade list or even the potential increase in position
size. Therefore, brokers need to incorporate an added safety margin to
safeguard against a potentially increased position and more costly execution. Nevertheless, the additional premium should not be too high as this
will work to brokers' advantage more often than it will work against them.
It should only be high enough to compensate for the incremental risk of
incurring a loss.

Cost Savings Allocation Scheme

Now that we have discussed the corresponding cost savings and societal
benefit resulting from an aggregated trade list and the economies of scale
advantage the next question is naturally how the cost savings should be
shared across investors. This is an important point because it is unlikely
that each party will be responsible for the same amount of cost reduction
and a policy that evenly distributes benefit to all investors would be inappropriate. To resolve this issue we apply an application of "game theory"
to determine an equilibrium allocation of benefits based on the marginal
contribution of each participant to the group as a whole. However, we only
show the applied methodology. Those readers interested in a thorough
discussion of that work should consult Myerson (1991) or Owen (1982).

Consider two investors who get together to trade their lists. One
investor holds a buy list and the other a sell list. There are no natural
matches. Since the aggregated trade list is hedged, the aggregated trade
list could be executed at a lower total cost utilizing a passive strategy and
sharing the benefit than if each list was traded individually. Assume the
list is executed this manner and that there is an upward trend in the market. The investor with the sell list is better off; the investor owning the buy
list is worse off. Trading at a more passive rate causes the buyer to incur a
higher cost and the seller to incur a lower cost and possibly even a savings.
However, how exactly should the total cost savings be shared among the
investors?

Table 10.6. ETF and FV Cost for Each Investor and the Aggregated Trade List U

	Trade Value	FV(bp)	FV($)
A	$5 Million	50bp	$25,000
B	$5 Million	50bp	$25,000
U	$10 Million	40bp	$40,000

Our suggested approach involves the services of a middle person to handle the transactions. The suggested societal benefit allocation process (cost savings sharing scheme) is described through the following set of examples.

Example 15. Two investors solicit principal bids from a broker-dealer through a blind-bid process. The trade list summary indicates that one investor is investing in large cap stocks while the other is investing in small cap stocks, so there is not much likelihood that the competing order will increase any of the individual positions. From this information brokers can determine the ETF and FV cost for each investor and the aggregated trade list U. These results show a societal benefit of $10,000 (see Table 10.6).

But how should the net savings be allocated to each investor? In this case it seems rational and fair to allocate the savings across both investors equally. Both investors have trade lists that are the size list and have the same costs. Also, their contribution is the same. Each investor needs the other in order to achieve the savings. Therefore, each investor will receive a $5,000 reduction in their trade cost and the new FV principal bid is:

$$FV = \frac{\$25,000 - \$5,000}{\$5,000,000} = 40bp$$

Each investor receives a reduction of 10bp in their FV principal bid.

Cost Allocation Process

In Example 15, the allocation of the total societal benefit is straightforward since each investor's trade list has the same FV cost and each investor is equally important in the aggregated transaction. That is A would not achieve any savings without B and B would not achieve any savings without A. But the allocation process is not as direct in situations with more than two investors, when the individual FV costs for each list is different, and when the contribution of each investor is not as transparent as in the prior case. In these instances we need to evaluate how each investor contributes to the cost savings of each of the possible subsets of investors.

Our allocation methodology follows directly from that game theory where the question at hand is how to allocate or distribute costs, revenues, or even voting rights. The process is one that determines the bargaining power or contribution that an individual brings to a group or that one group brings to another group. The process determines an equilibrium allocation process such that no participant would be better off by joining another group or subgroup without someone else becoming worse off.

In the two-person case earlier the only potential grouping of investors is A, B, and AB. The allocation process thus is simple and only requires two comparisons. That is, we need to determine the cost savings (1) that A brings to AB and (2) that B brings to AB. If A and B do not join together, each investor would bear a cost of $25,000 and the societal cost would be $50,000. However, by A and B forming a group the societal cost decreases to $40,000, thus the societal benefit is $10,000. Next, we compute the cost savings attributable to each investor by calculating the cost savings each brings to every group. Here the value that A brings to the group AB is $10,000 and the value that B brings to the group AB is $10,000 (we are not concerned here with double counting since the issue will be reconciled in the next step, our divisor makes the necessary adjustment for the double counting.). Thus, the cost savings attributable to A and B is $10,000 and the total cost savings quantity is $20,000 ($10,000 from each scenario). The cost savings attributable to each investor is determined as that investor's percentage of the total cost quantity multiplied by the societal benefit. That is:

$$Cost \text{ Savings Attributable to A} = \frac{\$10,000}{\$20,000} \cdot \$10,000 = \frac{1}{2} \cdot \$10,000 = \$5,000$$

$$Cost \text{ Savings Attributable to B} = \frac{\$10,000}{\$20,000} \cdot \$10,000 = \frac{1}{2} \cdot \$10,000 = \$5,000$$

Multi-Investor Case

The difficulty in the allocation process arises when there are more than two investors because the number of subgroups and required comparison calculations grows quite rapidly. In general, the total number of subgroups and comparison calculations can be determined from a combinatorial problem. The number of subgroups G formed from m-investors with each subgroup consisting of more than one investors is:

$$G = \sum_{i=2}^{m} \binom{m}{i} = 2^m - (m+1) \tag{10.16}$$

Table 10.7. FV by Subgroup

SUBGROUP	A	B	C	AB	AC	BC	ABC
Trave Value	$ 5M	$ 5M	$10M	$10M	$15M	$15M	$20M
FV (bp)	40bp	60bp	70bp	45bp	40bp	50bp	45bp
FV ($)	$20K	$30K	$70K	$45K	$60K	$75K	$80K

The total number N of comparison calculations is:

$$N = m \cdot \sum_{i=1}^{m-1} \binom{m-1}{i} = m \cdot (2^{m-1} - 1) \qquad (10.17)$$

Example 16. Three investors (A, B, and C) solicit principal bids from a broker-dealer through a blind-bid process. To provide the best possible bids for all parties, brokers price trade lists in aggregate (ABC), allocating the net savings via our cost allocation scheme. This encourages brokers to compute the FV for each investor and every subgroup. This information is in Table 10.7. Following the previous process, we compute the societal benefit of the aggregation to be:

Societal Benefit = ($20,000 + $30,000 + $70,000) − $80 = $40,000

Now we need to allocate the $40,000 across all investors. Since there are three investors there are four subgroups of investors (Equation 10.16): AB, AC, BC, and ABC and nine required comparison calculations (Equation 10.17). That is, we need to determine the cost savings that A brings to AB, to AC, and to ABC. For B we need to determine the cost savings that B brings to AB, to BC, and to ABC. And for C we need to determine the cost savings that C brings to AC, to BC, and to ABC. The allocation of the societal benefit is based on the percentage of the total savings each investor brings to all possible scenarios.

The process used to determine the cost savings allocation is depicted in Table 10.8. The first column (1) of that table lists investors currently being evaluated. There are rows for each of the investors. The second column (2) shows the subgroup that investors in column 1 are joining. There will always be one row for every subgroup that includes that particular investor. The third column (3) lists the costs that would be borne by all parties if investors in column 1 did not join the group. The calculation is the sum of the costs for investors alone plus the cost of the group minus investors. For example, the cost in column 3 on the first row is $50,000. It is calculated as the FV of A plus the FV of B, that

Table 10.8. Savings Allocation Methodology

Investor (1)	Subgroup (2)	FV Costs Separate (3)	Aggregated FV Cost (4)	Savings (5)
A	AB	A & B = $50,000	AB = $45,000	$ 5,000
A	AC	A & C = $90,000	AC = $60,000	$ 30,000
A	ABC	A & BC = $95,000	ABC = $80,000	$ 15,000
				$ 50,000
B	AB	B & A = $ 50,000	AB = $45,000	$ 5,000
B	BC	B & C = $100,000	BC = $75,000	$ 25,000
B	ABC	B & AC = $ 90,000	ABC = $80,000	$ 10,000
				$ 40,000
C	AC	C & A = $ 90,000	AC = $60,000	$ 30,000
C	BC	C & B = $100,000	BC = $75,000	$ 25,000
C	ABC	C & AB = $115,000	ABC = $80,000	$ 35,000
				$ 90,000
Total				$180,000

is, $20,000+$30,000=$50,000. The fourth column (4) shows the cost borne by the aggregated group in column 2. For example, the FV cost of the aggregated group of AB is $45,000 (see Table 10.7). The fifth column (5) is the cost savings from investors in the first column and is computed as the difference between the separate FV costs and aggregated FV cost, that is, (5) = (3) − (4).

From the information shown in Table 10.8 we can compute the cost savings attributable to any investor i as follows:

$$Attributable\ Savings(i) = \frac{Cost\ Savings(i)}{Cost\ Savings} \cdot Societal\ Benefit \qquad \textbf{(10.18)}$$

Thus in this example the attributable savings to investor A is:

$$Attributable\ Savings(A) = \frac{5,000 + 30,000 + 15,000}{180,000} \cdot \$40,000 = \$11,111$$

$$Attributable\ Savings(B) = \frac{5,000 + 25,000 + 10,000}{180,000} \cdot \$40,000 - \$8,889$$

$$Attributable\ Savings(C) = \frac{30,000 + 25,000 + 35,000}{180.000} \cdot \$40,000 = \$20,000$$

The broker would then provide each investor with a revised FV principal bid that incorporates the attributable cost savings that each investor brought to the group. The formula to determine the new FV principal bid is:

$$FV'_i = \frac{FV_i(\$) - Attributable\ Savings_i(\$)}{Trade\ Value_i} \qquad \textbf{(10.19)}$$

In this example the revised FV principal bid for each investor is:

$$FV'(A) = \frac{\$20{,}000 - \$11{,}111}{\$5{,}000{,}000} = 18bp$$

$$FV'(B) = \frac{\$30{,}000 - \$8{,}889}{\$5{,}000{,}000} = 42bp$$

$$FV'(C) = \frac{\$70{,}000 - \$20{,}000}{\$10{,}000{,}000} = 50bp$$

Investor A experiences a reduction in the FV principal bid from 40bp to 18bp, Investor B experiences a reduction from 60bp to 42bp, and Investor C experiences a decrease from 70bp to 50bp.

In this example, every investor is allocated some cost savings and is better with the group than individually. But, this is not always the case. There are some rare situations where investors add cost to the aggregated position without providing any risk reduction through diversification or hedging. Here, investors would realize an increase in FV. Additionally, in some situations where investors provide a large quantity of risk reduction their allocation of the cost savings results in receiving a payment for their list rather than being charged a fee. Here, investors would realize a negative FV, i.e., a net savings or profit.

CHAPTER ELEVEN

VWAP Trading Strategies

A VWAP TRADING STRATEGY IS an implementation strategy where traders participate with market volume in the attempt to achieve an average execution price equal to the VWAP benchmark price. It has become a very popular execution strategy over the years for passive investors. VWAP (pronounced vee-wop) is an acronym for *volume weighted average price* and is a measure of the average transaction price for all market activity in a stock over a period of time. It is believed by market participants to be an indication of "average" and "fair" price over that horizon. Traders execute lists via a VWAP strategy to minimize market impact, although this comes at the expense of increased risk exposure and at times higher price appreciation cost. The stock's VWAP is also a popular measure as a means to assess trader or broker performance, although in many cases it is not the most appropriate measure of skill. Performance analysis is discussed in chapter 13, Post Trade Analysis. In this chapter we focus on presenting insight into the statistical distribution of the VWAP statistic and introduce ideas for improving upon a VWAP strategy.

The VWAP is different from most other benchmarks and reference prices because it is a calculated value, not a price at a specified time (e.g., the market open, market close, high, low, etc.). The VWAP is most commonly computed for the primary market hours (9:30 A.M. to 4:00 P.M.) over one day.

The VWAP statistic is equal to a stock's total dollar turnover $\sum p_j v_j$ over the period divided by total volume $\sum v_j$ in the same period.

$$VWAP = \frac{\sum\limits_{j} v_j p_j}{\sum\limits_{j} v_j} \qquad (11.1)$$

Achieving VWAP Price

Theoretically, to achieve execution at the VWAP price, traders would have to participate in every single market transaction. For example, if the trader's order accounted for 5% of total volume in the period, the trader would need to participate with 5% of every market trade; if it is for 10% of total volume, the trader would need to participate with 10% of every market trade, and so on. But this is not possible. Even if this were possible traders do not know the total volume over a period in advance, thus they could not specify an appropriate participation strategy. The next best solution is to execute the order in proportion to the percentage of market volume that executes in specified trading periods (such as half-hour or fifteen-minute intervals). For example, if 10% of the total volume is expected to execute in a given trading period, then traders need to execute 10% of their order in the same period. This type of execution strategy has become known as a slicing strategy.

The solution to VWAP trading lies in finding an appropriate slicing scheme to allow traders to participate with market volume without prior knowledge of the day's total trade volume. This process consists of segmenting the day into time or trading intervals such as fifteen-minute or thirty-minute intervals and computing the average percentage of daily volume traded in each period (volume profile depicted in Figure 11.1). This chart shows the average daily volume traded in the market during August 2001 for stocks that comprised the S&P 1500 index on January 2001. The chart depicts the percentage of daily volume that trades on average in each thirty-minute interval. As shown in the chart there is considerably more volume traded at the open and close than during midday. Trading activity begins higher, tapers off through midday, then picks up again into the close. For example, approximately 13% of the day's volume trades in the first half-hour, 8% in the second half-hour, and decreases until the 12:30–1:00 P.M. and 1:00–1:30 P.M. periods where approximately 5.6% of the days volume trades in each period. These percentages then begin to pick up again into the close where 8.1% trades in the 3:00–3:30 P.M. period, and 12.5% trades in the last half-hour period from 3:30 P.M. to 4:00 P.M. A volume profile with this shape is referred to as a "u-shaped" trading pattern or "u-shaped" curve. While this u-shape pattern is consistent from month-to-month it does exhibit some deviations in percentages in each period. For best results investors should rely on the most recent data observations.

Figure 11.1   Volume Profile

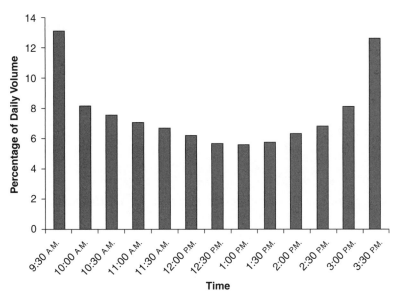

Derivation of VWAP Strategy

Many times traders are instructed to achieve an average execution price equal to the VWAP benchmark. Since there is no guarantee of prices in the market, traders often elect to execute an order with a strategy that has the best chance of achieving the VWAP. In these instances, the best execution strategy (i.e., the strategy that provides the highest chances of achieving VWAP benchmark price) is determined as follows:

The VWAP equation in Equation 11.1 can be rewritten as:

$$VWAP = \frac{\sum_j v_j p_j}{\sum_j v_j} = u_j \overline{p_j} \tag{11.2}$$

where u_j is the percentage of day's volume traded in the jth period and $\overline{p_j}$ is the average price in the jth period.

Then, if y is the specified slicing strategy, the average execution price of the order can be written as:

$$Avg\ Exec\ Price = \sum_j y_j \overline{p_j}$$

assuming that traders execute at (or at least close to) the average price in each period. Then the strategy that provides highest chances of achieving

VWAP reduces to that of finding the strategy y that minimizes the difference between the VWAP benchmark and the average execution price. Mathematically it is found by determining the strategy that minimizes the mean square error of the difference between the two measures, that is,

$$Min: \quad \delta = \left(\sum u_j \overline{p_j} - \sum y_j \overline{p_j} \right)^2$$

But this can be rewritten in vector notation as:

$$Min: \quad \delta = (u^t p - y^t p)^2$$

where u, y, p are nx1 column vectors and u^t, y^t, p^t are the corresponding 1xn transpose of those vectors.

Minimizing sum of square we get:

$$\frac{d\delta}{dy} = (y - u)^t p = 0$$

But this is an underdetermined system of equations since there is one equation and n unknowns indicating numerous solutions. However, since price is always positive, $p \geq 0$, one solution is $(y - u)^t = 0$ or simply $y = u$. Therefore, for traders to achieve VWAP, an appropriate slicing strategy is one where the order is sliced in accordance to the percentage of volume traded in the period. Further, this holds true over any trading horizon. Finally, the slicing strategy $y = u$ is also the strategy that minimizes variance between expected price and VWAP (discussed next).

The strategy y that minimizes variance between expected price and VWAP can also be seen from the fact that delta is always greater than or equal to zero, that is,

$$\delta = \left(\sum u_j \overline{p_j} - \sum y_j \overline{p_j} \right)^2 \geq 0$$

since $u, y,$ and $p \geq 0$. Then at the value $y_j = u_j$ we have $\delta = 0$, thus a minimum point.

Alternative Derivation of VWAP Strategy

A VWAP strategy does not necessarily protect investors from large price swings and high costs. For example, investors implementing an order utilizing a VWAP strategy will execute some shares at the close. Thus, buy orders will incur higher costs if the price has increased and sell orders will incur lower costs. A VWAP strategy does not minimize total cost, only temporary market impact. An alternative VWAP strategy can be derived as follows:

$$\underset{x_k}{Min} \quad I\sum \frac{x_j}{X} \cdot \frac{x_j}{x_j + \frac{1}{2}\hat{v}_j}$$

Solving we find,

$$x_j = X \cdot \frac{v_j}{\sum v_j} = X \cdot \mu_j \qquad\qquad (11.3)$$

Estimating Volume Profiles

The strategy that minimizes the expected difference from the VWAP benchmark is $y_j = u_j$. But how is u_j estimated? We have found the best way to determine u_j is from a historical moving average of period volumes from twenty to thirty days back. The exact number of days of data is dependent upon the stability of volume profiles. For example, the more liquid stocks require about twenty days worth of data because these volume profiles are the most stable. The less liquid stocks, however, require closer to thirty days of data. In any case, the results do not diminish using more data points.

The volume profile of the stock is estimated as follows:

Let,
V_i be the total volume that traded j days ago
v_{ij} is the volume that traded in the jth period i days ago

$$\hat{u}_j = u_j = \frac{1}{n}\sum_{i=1}^{n} \frac{v_{ij}}{V_i} = \frac{1}{n}\sum_{i=1}^{n} u_{ij}$$

for $n \geq 20$.

We denote the vector containing the expected daily percentages in each period as $u^T = (u_1, u_2, \ldots, u_n)$ where u_j = the percentage of daily volume that typically trades in the jth period, and of course $\sum u_j = 1$. To trade utilizing a VWAP strategy, traders slice their order X according to the volume profile u. In any given period the number of shares to trade x_j is $x_j = u_j \cdot X$.

There are several known facts regarding volume profiles throughout the industry. We highlight the more important ones for deriving the profiles for those readers who are not as familiar with the underlying structure of the market. They are:

▲ There is no statistical improvement found from using more than thirty days of trading data to estimate the volume profile of the stock. For the most part the trading patterns are stable, and unlike total volume amounts, which can change dramatically from one day to the next, the percentage of daily volume in a period is more consistent. The exception, of course, is those illiquid stocks when there are large block prints in a period.

▲ Having a lagged data set is not as detrimental to the estimation of the volume profile as one would think. Volume profiles are very stable, probably the most stable phenomena in trading. Therefore, using data from a month ago does not provide much different results than if one uses the most current month's data. In most cases there is no statistical difference between the two data sets. Therefore, analysts can realize the same level of accuracy from an older data set as would be realized from a recent data set. But as always, we do recommend usage of the most recent data set one has access because it would quickest reflect any structure change. However, to the extent that traders behave in the same manner today as they did last month and last year, we can say that the trading structure is stable.

Example 1. A trader is given an order to buy $X = 100,000$ shares of XYZ and achieve the VWAP price of the day. If the volume profile for XYZ is u, the number of shares to trade in each period most likely to achieve the VWAP price is $x_j = u_j \cdot X$. This is shown in Table 11.1.

Stock Specific or Generic Profiles?

An interesting question that arises regarding volume profiles is whether to use stock specific profiles (e.g., one profile for every stock) or some generic curves by market capitalization or sector. It is much easier to compute and maintain a data library of generic profiles over stock specific profiles. Our

Table 11.1

Start	9:30	10:00	10:30	11:00	11:30	12:00	12:30	1:00	1:30	2:00	2:30	3:00	3:30
End	10:00	10:30	11:00	11:30	12:00	12:30	1:00	1:30	2:00	2:30	3:00	3:30	4:00
u_i	0.132	0.080	0.075	0.071	0.068	0.062	0.056	0.056	0.058	0.064	0.069	0.082	0.127
$u_i \cdot X$	13200	8000	7500	7100	6800	6200	5600	5600	5800	6400	6900	8200	12700

research has found that generic volume profiles do produce results that are consistent with stock specific curves on average. However, in order to best develop confidence intervals and error bands surrounding these estimates, stock specific profiles are needed.

Why Do Traders Select VWAP Trading Strategies?

There are two main reasons why traders execute orders using a VWAP trading strategy. First, a VWAP strategy is the trading strategy that minimizes market impact cost. Traders executing orders utilizing VWAP strategies are interested in participating with market volumes so to cause the least disruption to the supply-demand imbalance in each period. Second, for many traders their execution performance is measured against the VWAP benchmark. An average execution price more favorable than the VWAP price benchmark is considered high-quality performance while an average execution price less favorable than the VWAP benchmark is considered inadequate performance. As we show next, both of these reasons for executing via a VWAP strategy may not be in the best interest of the fund and may cause the fund to incur higher than necessary trading costs.

A VWAP strategy is indeed the strategy that minimizes market impact cost. But it is not necessarily the strategy that minimizes total trading costs. Market impact cost is only one component of the total trading costs. During the implementation of the order traders also incur price appreciation cost and a large quantity of timing risk. A VWAP strategy minimizes market impact cost but not price appreciation. For example, a trader buying a stock in a rising market utilizing a VWAP strategy will incur a higher cost than necessary because that trader is forced to buy at the higher prices toward the end of the day. Similarly, a trader selling a stock in a falling market utilizing a VWAP strategy will incur a higher cost because the trader is forced to sell at the lower prices toward the end of the day. A VWAP strategy does not protect the fund from price appreciation cost. Also, recall that a VWAP strategy in the presence of price appreciation is not an optimal trading strategy since it is not the least cost strategy. Traders could find a lower cost strategy for the same quantity of risk, a lower risk strategy for the quantity of cost, or both a lower cost and a lower risk strategy. Investors electing to execute an order with a VWAP strategy in the presence of price appreciation are neither acting in a fiduciary manner nor making a rational trading decision.

This can easily be seen through the following formulation of cost,

$$\phi = \sum x_j j \Delta p + \frac{0.95 I x_j^2}{X(x_j + 0.5v_j)} + \frac{0.05 I x_j}{X}$$

Figure 11.2   Efficient Trading Frontier

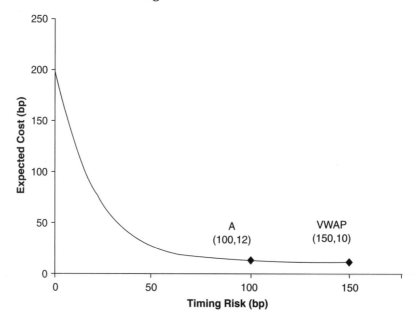

It can be easily verified that in the presence of price appreciation, trading cost ϕ is not minimized using a strategy $x_j = X \cdot \dfrac{v_j}{\Sigma v_j}$.

In situations where there is no anticipated natural price appreciation over the period a VWAP strategy is the lowest trading cost strategy since the only true cost component is market impact. Thus, in these cases a VWAP strategy is an optimal trading strategy and does lie on the efficient trading frontier. However, even in these cases the VWAP strategy does not best protect investors from timing risk. In comparison to those strategies on the ETF we find that the VWAP strategy is the riskiest of all the optimal strategies. While it might be the least cost strategy, it does not best protect funds from adverse price movement because it forces investors to accept whatever prices are in the market toward the end of the day.

Example 2.   A trader has using decided to execute a list of stock using a VWAP strategy. The equation of the ETF for the list is:

$$\phi = 190e^{-0.05\Re} + 10$$

The VWAP strategy (Figure 11.2) is the least cost of all optimal strategies. It has an expected cost of 10bp and a substantial quantity of risk of 150bp. But investors could quite easily determine an optimal trading strategy with a very small level of risk aversion such as $\lambda = 0.10$ or $\lambda = 0.05$ and better protect the fund from adverse price movement. A strategy such as this is shown as strategy A in the figure. It has expected cost of 12bp and timing risk of 100bp. Traders could achieve a 50bp reduction in risk for a relatively small increase in cost of 2bp. We typically refer to strategy A as a VWAP-hedge strategy, that is, a low cost strategy very correlated to that of the VWAP but with substantial less timing risk. A VWAP-hedge strategy is a trading strategy that executes the order following the volume profile of the stock but does not necessarily execute the order over the entire day. Smaller orders are executed over a smaller time frame such as hours, while the larger orders are executed over the entire day. The optimization algorithm determines exactly what orders should be executed over what periods following the volume profile of the stock. For example, while it may make sense to execute a 150,000-share order over the entire day to minimize market impact cost, a smaller order such as 15,000 shares should be executed over a shorter period of time to limit risk exposure.

A VWAP-hedge strategy does a better job than the pure VWAP strategy at protecting the fund from incurring a high trading cost brought on by adverse price. For example, the VWAP-hedge strategy has a 55% likelihood of executing better than 25bp compared to 54% for the VWAP strategy and a 65% likelihood of executing better than 50bp compared to 61% for the VWAP strategy. In fact, the VWAP-hedge strategy will always provide the same likelihood or higher of executing better than some specified cost C > 0. In this example C ≅ 16bp. If fund managers or traders are concerned about executing better than a cost of 16bp or more, they are better off selecting a VWAP-hedge over a pure VWAP strategy because it better manages cost and risk, and provides better protection from adverse price movement.

Figure 11.3 is an illustration of the cost protection afforded from the VWAP and VWAP-hedge strategies. This figure shows the cumulative cost distributions for each strategy and depicts the probability that each strategy will incur a cost less than that specified on the x-axis. Notice that the VWAP-hedge provides better cost protection for costs greater than 16bp. Thus, the VWAP-hedge is the better strategy for those investors interested in preserving asset value. The value of C* where the VWAP-hedge strategy provides more protection than the pure VWAP strategy is dependent upon the cost and risk profile of each strategy. The reader interested in determining this cost for different lists can plot the cumulative trading cost distribution of each strategy along side of one another. The point C* will be the cost value (x-axis) where the two cumulative distributions intersect one another.

Many investors use the VWAP benchmark price as the performance metric for traders and/or brokers. Their primary goal for the VWAP strategy is to achieve an average execution trade price equal to or better than the volume weighted average price (VWAP) of the stock. In this case it is not necessary to reduce market impact cost and it is definitely not to minimize timing risk or protect the fund from adverse price movement. A common

Figure 11.3   Preserving Asset Value

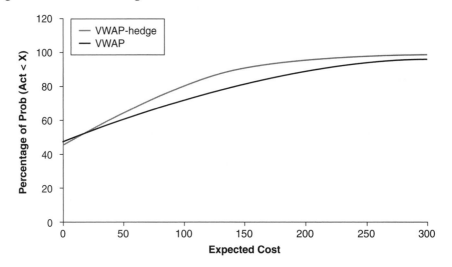

reason for the selection of this trading strategy is that the VWAP price benchmark is a good indication of the fair market price for the security over the day. Therefore, executions at prices less favorable than VWAP are deemed poor performance while executions at prices more favorable than VWAP are deemed superior performance. But one can easily see how these goals are at odds with investor's goals, namely, to preserve asset value.

There is a great inconsistency between the goal of implementation and the primary goal of achieving the VWAP benchmark price. Through this point we have described the process that investors can use to balance the trade-off between cost and risk, realize price improvement, and achieve best execution. But none of these strategies is centered around the VWAP strategy. However, a VWAP strategy is what many traders seek to achieve because it is how they are being measured. The inconsistency lies in the fact that many traders/brokers have their performance measured in a way that causes them to act and trade in a manner that is detrimental to the fund.

VWAP Strategy: The Good Side

There are many good aspects regarding a VWAP trading strategy. For example, a VWAP strategy minimizes market impact cost and in the absence of any expectations regarding price appreciation cost (i.e., $E(\Delta p)=0$) it is the least cost optimal strategy. A VWAP strategy also allows traders to disguise the order size and their trading intentions by always being surrounded by other buyers and sellers. By participating with market volume in the same percentage in each period, traders make it extremely difficult for the market to learn what traders want to accomplish. Many have stated that the speed of execution of a VWAP strategy is just right, not too fast and not too slow. To be fair to this argument, others have said that the execution rate of a VWAP strategy is too right and it allows sophisticated market participants to discover trading patterns. For example, quants could develop models to uncover the buy-sell imbalance in each period and, in theory, make very accurate assessments of the buying and selling pressure in the market that is likely to persist over the remainder of the day if the imbalance is due to a VWAP trading strategy.

A VWAP strategy could also serve as the basis for developing an optimal trading strategy based on a specified trading rate to balance the trade-off between cost and risk rather than a dynamic trade schedule would. Utilizing a trading rate as opposed to a trade schedule allows a trader to better adapt to changing market conditions. In times of higher trading volume the trading rate accelerates trading to protect against incurring a larger quantity of timing risk, and in times of lesser liquidity the trading rate decelerates the trading to protect against incurring too high a market impact cost. An optimized trading strategy using the trading rate is identical to the VWAP strategy in that it follows the volume profile of the stock. It differs in that the optimized trading strategy does not require the order to be traded over the entire day if it is not deemed necessary. The optimization technique will determine the appropriate time to execute an order following the volume profile of the stock. Depending upon the size of the order this time period could be minutes, hours, days, or longer. The exact optimization technique using volume profiles and the trading rate is fully discussed in Chapter 12, Advanced Trading Techniques.

Mathematical Analysis of VWAP

In order to understand the VWAP statistic we examine its distribution. A thorough understanding of the distribution is required in order to make better trading decisions going forward. The VWAP statistic consists of the random variables v_i and p_i (volume and price). It is commonly computed over the entire trading day during market hours (e.g., 9:30 A.M. to 4:00 P.M.), although it can be computed over any specified period such as a few hours or several days. For simplicity, we will use a one-day period where there are n trades. This statistic is defined according to Equation 11.1 and can be modified as follows:

$$VWAP = \frac{\sum\limits_{j=1}^{n} v_j p_j}{\sum\limits_{j=1}^{n} v_j} = \sum\limits_{j=1}^{n} \frac{v_j p_j}{V} \tag{11.4}$$

where v_j and p_j are the volume and price of the jth trade respectively, n is the number of trades during the period, and $V = \sum_{j=1}^{n} v_j$.

Alternative Computation

An alternative methodology for computing the VWAP focuses on segmenting the day into periods and computing the percentage of daily volume traded in each period and the average execution price in each period. This formula is likely to be more intuitive for traders who execute utilizing a slicing strategy and for occasions where an accurate assessment regarding the total number of trades on the volume over the period cannot be made. The process is as follows:

Segment the day into n groups, $n_1, n_2, \ldots, n_{(n-1)}, n_n$. Then the VWAP statistic in Equation 3 can be expanded as follows:

$$VWAP = \sum_{j=1}^{n} \frac{v_j p_j}{V} = \sum_{j=1}^{n_1} \frac{v_j}{V} p_j + \sum_{j=n_1+1}^{n_2} \frac{v_j}{V} p_j + \ldots + \sum_{j=n_{(n-1)}+1}^{n_n} \frac{v_j}{V} p_j$$

Then with the following substitutions:

$$\sum_{i=n_{j-1}+1}^{n_j} \frac{v_j}{V} p_j = \sum_{j=n_{j-1}+1}^{n_j} \frac{v_j}{V} \overline{p_j}$$

$$\sum_{j=n_{j-1}+1}^{n_j} \frac{v_j}{V} = u_j$$

where $\overline{p_j}$ is the average price in period j and u_j is the percentage of daily volume traded in period j ($\sum u_j = 1$), we have the VWAP statistic computed in terms of the average period volume and the average trade price. That is:

$$VWAP = \sum_{j=1}^{n} u_j \overline{p_j} \qquad (11.5)$$

Expected Value and Variance

The VWAP statistic is a function of two random variables: volume v_i and price p_i. While there is evidence of correlation between volume and price movement, there is very little correlation between the percentage of daily volume in any given period and price movement. A random variable is loosely defined as a variable that can take on many different values, described with a mean or expected value and a measure of dispersion around that expected value. Independence of two random variables is

Figure 11.4   Price Uncertainty

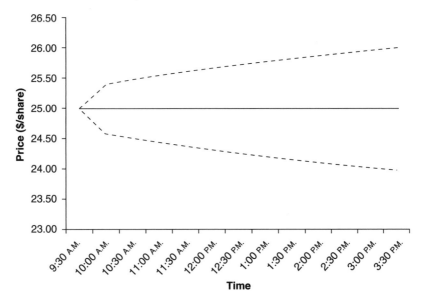

loosely defined such that the value of one of the random variables has absolutely no affect on the outcome of the other random variable. These conditions certainly hold for volume profiles and price movement. For example, on any day the total traded volume in any period can take on value greater than or equal to zero but will most likely be equal to the mean plus or minus its standard deviation. The same is true for price evolution in any period or over the day. The price evolution from period to period is also independent since a period with a higher than average percentage of daily volume may be accompanied with high price movement, either much higher or lower than average. Since it is equally likely that it could be higher upward or higher downward movement, the opposite signs (+, –) make the correlation of the two zero. However, the correlation between volume profiles and absolute value of price movement is indeed positive!

The expected values and standard deviation for our volume profile is shown in Figure 11.4. For every time interval (e.g., 9:30 to 10:00, 10:00 to 10:30) the exact percentage of daily volume is not known with certainty until the end of the day. But it is quite possible to state that the percentage of daily volume that will trade in the 9:30 to 10:00 period is between 10.5% and 16% of the daily volume. Similar forecasts can be made for the other periods during the day. The associated uncertainty in period volumes introduces uncertainty and/or errors in the VWAP estimate. For example, suppose one is planning that the period volumes will be equal to the

Figure 11.5   Volume Profile

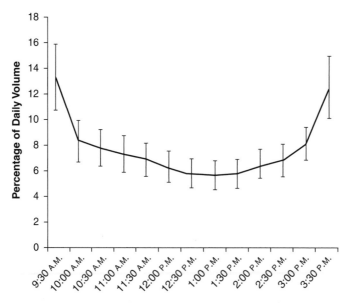

expected values, but what actually occurs is higher than average volumes in the morning and lower than average volumes in the afternoon. This change in volumes affects the VWAP price over the day. This error is exasperated further by price uncertainty. Notice the potential fluctuation in price movement in Figure 11.5. If traders are seeking to achieve the VWAP price for an order and the stock's prices trend and volumes differ from their expected values, traders can potentially incur an average price much different than the VWAP price. In addition, the result of this difference is due to market driven forces, not inferior trading performance. However, if traders understand the potential costs of the action they may be able to select an implementation strategy that is better suited for the fund. Hence, to critique a trading decision such as a VWAP strategy (e.g., costs or performance) it is necessary to have a thorough understanding of the VWAP distribution, its mean, and variance.

The expected value and variance of the VWAP statistic is determined in the following way. Let each v_j be i.i.d. distributed random variable with mean and variance as follows:

$$E(v_j) = \bar{v}$$
$$\sigma^2(v_j) = \sigma^2_v$$

But the price variable p_j itself is not independent. The price at time j is dependent upon all previous prices and trading activity. But if we define price at time j in terms of its successive increments or price changes time where Δp (expected trade-to-trade price change) is i.i.d. with $E(\Delta p_j) = \Delta p$ and $\sigma^2(\Delta p_j) = \sigma_p^2$ then we can write price at time i as:

$$p_j = p_0 + \sum_{k=1}^{j} \Delta p_k$$

where p_0 is the price of the stock at the beginning of trading and Δp_j is the change in price between trade j-1 and j. Then,

$$E(p_n) = E\left(p_0 + \sum_{j=1}^{n} \Delta p_j\right) = E(p_0) + E\left(\sum_{j=1}^{n} \Delta p_j\right) = E(p_0) + \sum_{j=1}^{n} E(\Delta p_j) = p_0 + n \cdot E(\Delta p)$$

$$\sigma^2(p_n) = \sigma^2\left(p_0 + \sum_{j=1}^{n} \Delta p_j\right) = \sigma^2(p_0) + \sigma^2\left(\sum_{j=1}^{n} \Delta p_j\right) = \sigma^2(p_0) + \sum_{j=1}^{n} \sigma^2(\Delta p_j) = n \cdot \sigma^2(\Delta p)$$

So we have:

$$E(p_n) = p_0 + n\Delta p$$
$$\sigma^2(p_n) = n\sigma_p^2$$

In the case where $\Delta p = 0$ (no price trend or momentum) we have $E(p_i) = p_0$. The variance, however, is dependent upon all previous trading activity regardless of the expected trend. It is proportional to trading activity and the standard deviation (volatility) is proportional to the square root of trading activity, for example $\sigma(p_n) = \sqrt{n \cdot \sigma_p^2} = \sqrt{n} \cdot \sigma_p$.

Often in the financial literature, price volatility reportedly increases with the square root of time, for example, $\sqrt{t} \cdot \sigma_p$. However, this is a simplification to our previous derivation and is based on the expectation that an average (or equal) amount of trading activity will occur in each trading period. For investors with a long-term horizon, scaling volatility with the square root of time is accurate as long as the higher trading activity days are offset by the lower trading activity days. While this simplification works well in the portfolio management phase of the investment cycle (where decisions are made with a long-term horizon in mind), it does not work well in short-term trading horizons because trading activity varies throughout the day. There is more volume traded at the open and close than during afternoon hours; therefore, we cannot assume that volatility scales exactly with time on an intraday basis. The better alternative is to have price volatility scale with the number of trades or volume rather than time.

This is again a simplification, but a mere one for VWAP trades. In actuality, one would find price volatility to be dependent upon order arrivals (volume) and correlation to general market movement (time).

Turnover Term (Numerator)

Now that we have specified the mean and variance of each of the random variables comprising the VWAP statistic we next examine the VWAP statistic as defined in Equation 11.3. We begin by calculating the expected value and variance of the turnover value of the jth trade—that is, the total dollar value of the jth transaction.

Let,
$z_j = v_j p_j$ with the pdf of z stated as $z \sim p(z)$ for all z_j

Then,
$E(z_j) = z \cdot p(z)$ and $\sigma^2 (z_j) = E(z^2) - (E(z))^2$

But these calculations require the distribution $p(z)$. To solve this we can make use of Theorem 1. For a more thorough explanation see (Meyer 1970).

Theorem 1

Let (x, y) be a two-dimensional continuous random variable with joint pdf f. Let $z = h_1 (x, y)$ and $w = h_2(x, y)$, and where h_1 and h_2 satisfy the following conditions:

  i. Let $z = h_1(x, y)$ and $w = h_2(x, y)$ may be uniquely solved for x and y in terms of z and w, that is $x = g_1(z, w)$ and $y = g_2(z, w)$.
  ii. The partial derivatives dx/dz, dx/dw, dy/dz, and dy/dw exist and are continuous functions.

Let $k(z, w)$ be the joint pdf of (z, w); then we compute as follows:

$$k(z, w) = f(g_1(z, w), g_2(z, w)) \cdot |J(z, w)|$$

where $J(z, w)$ Jacobian of the transformation $(z, w) \rightarrow (z, w)$.

By application of Theorem 1 we compute the distribution of the turnover term z as follows:
Let $z = vp$ where v and p are independent random variables (this is a very reasonable assumption since we are talking about individual trades).

If $v \sim g(v)$ and $p \sim g(p)$. Then, $f(v, p) = g(v) \cdot h(p)$

Let, $w = v$, and $p = v/w$.

Then the Jacobian transformation is:

$$J = \begin{vmatrix} 1 & 0 \\ -\dfrac{z}{w^2} & \dfrac{1}{w} \end{vmatrix} = \frac{1}{w}$$

And the distribution of turnover is computed as follows:

$$f(z) = \int\limits_{Real} (g(v)h\left(\frac{z}{v}\right)\left|\frac{1}{v}\right| dz$$

In many situations the distributions of the random variables, v and p, make the above integration extremely difficult to solve explicitly if solvable at all. For example, if v is chi-square and p is lognormal. In situations where no analytical solution exists or the computational process is extremely difficult one can gain insight into the distribution using Monte Carlo simulation and estimate the mean and variance empirically. Many times the graphical depictions from these simulations provide enough information to make an informed and educated trading decision.

Additionally, in cases such where no analytical solution exists it is possible to approximate the mean and variance using a Taylor series expansion and the use of characteristic (CHF) or moment generating functions (MGF). For a complete explanation of the process, see Dudewicz and Mishra (1988). This approximation formula is provided in Theorem 2:

Theorem 2

Let (x, y) be a two-dimensional random variable where x and y are independent. Let $E(x) = \mu_x$, $E(y) = \mu_y$, $\sigma^2(x) = \sigma^2_x$, and $\sigma^2(y) = \sigma^2_y$. If $Z = H(x, y)$ and the various derivatives of H exist at (μ_x, μ_y) we have:

$$E(Z) \cong H(\mu_x, \mu_y) + \frac{1}{2}\left[\frac{d^2H}{dx^2}\sigma^2_x(\mu_x, \mu_y) + \frac{d^2H}{dy^2}\sigma^2_y(\mu_x, \mu_y) \right]$$

$$V(Z) \cong \left[\frac{dH}{dx} \right]\sigma^2_x(\mu_x, \mu_y) + \left[\frac{dH}{dy} \right]^2 \sigma^2_y(\mu_x, \mu_y)$$

Then by application of Theorem 2 we compute the mean and variance of the turnover of the jth transaction as follows:

Let:

$$z_j = v_j p_j$$
$$E(v_j) = v \qquad E(p_j) = p_0 + j \cdot \Delta p$$
$$\sigma^2(v_j) = \sigma^2_v \qquad \sigma^2(p_j) = j \cdot \sigma^2_p$$

Then,
$$h(v_j, p_j) = v_j p_j$$

$$\frac{dh}{dv_j} = p_j \qquad \frac{dh}{dp_j} = v_j$$

$$\frac{d^2h}{dv_j^2} = 0 \qquad \frac{d^2h}{dp_j^2} = 0$$

Solving we get:

$$E(z_j) = h(v_j, p_j) + \frac{1}{2}\left[\frac{d^2h}{dv_j^2}\sigma^2(v_j) + \frac{d^2h}{dp_j^2}\sigma^2(p_j)\right]$$

$$= v_j p_j + \frac{1}{2}[0 \cdot \sigma_v^2 + 0 \cdot j \cdot 0_p^2]$$

$$= \bar{v} \cdot (p_0 + j \cdot \Delta p)$$

$$\sigma^2(z_j) = \frac{dh}{dv_j} \cdot \sigma^2(v_j) + \frac{dh}{dp_j} \cdot \sigma^2(p_j)$$

$$= p_j \cdot \sigma_v^2 + v_j \cdot j \cdot \sigma_p^2$$

$$= (p_0 + j \cdot \Delta p) \cdot \sigma_v^2 + \bar{v} \cdot j \cdot \sigma_p^2$$

Denominator

The next step is to evaluate the denominator term in Equation 11.4. Let

$$V = \sum_{j=1}^{n} v_j$$

Since v_j is i.i.d. we calculate the mean and variance directly. No tricks, approximations, or additional theorems are required. This calculation is as follows:

$$E(V) = E\left(\sum_{i=1}^{n} v_j\right) = \sum_{i=1}^{n} E(v_j) = \sum_{i=1}^{n} \bar{v} = n\bar{v}$$

$$\sigma^2(V) = \sigma^2\left(\sum_{i=1}^{n} v_j\right) = \sum_{i=1}^{n} \sigma^2(v_j) = \sum_{i=1}^{n} \sigma_v^2 = n\sigma_v^2$$

Quotient: Numerator/Denominator

The next step is to compute the quotient of the VWAP (turnover divided by the total volume). We can approximate $E(y_j)$ and $\sigma^2(y_j)$ through application of Theorem 2. The calculation process is as follows.

Let,
$$y_j = \frac{v_j p_j}{V} = \frac{z_j}{V}$$

$$E(z_j) = \bar{v} \cdot (p_0 + j\Delta p) \qquad\qquad E(V) = n\bar{v}$$

$$\sigma^2(z_j) = (p_0 + j\Delta p) \cdot \sigma_v^2 + \bar{v} \cdot j\sigma_p^2 \qquad \sigma^2(V) = n\sigma_v^2$$

Then,
$$h(z_j, V) = \frac{z_j}{V} = z_j \cdot V^{-1}$$

$$\frac{dh}{dz_j} = \frac{1}{V} \qquad\qquad \frac{dh}{dV} = \frac{-z_j}{V^2}$$

$$\frac{d^2h}{dz_j^2} = 0 \qquad\qquad \frac{d^2h}{dV} = \frac{2z_j}{V^3}$$

Solving for the mean we get:

$$E(y_j) = h(z_j, V) + \frac{1}{2}\left(\frac{d^2h}{dz_j^2}\sigma^2(z_j) + \frac{d^2h}{dV^2}\sigma^2(V) \right)$$

$$= \frac{z_j}{V} + \frac{1}{2}\left(0 \cdot \sigma^2(z_j) + \frac{2z_j}{V^3}\sigma^2(V) \right)$$

$$= \frac{\bar{v} \cdot (p_0 + j\Delta p)}{nv} + \frac{1}{2} \cdot \frac{2\bar{v}(p_0 + j\Delta p)}{(n\bar{v})^3} \cdot n\sigma_v^2$$

$$= \frac{p_0 + j\Delta p}{n} + \frac{p_0 + j\Delta p}{(n\bar{v})^2} \cdot \sigma_v^2$$

$$= \frac{1}{n}(p_0 + j\Delta p)$$

since $(n\bar{v})^2$ is very large causing $\dfrac{p_0 + j\Delta p}{(n\bar{v})^2} \to 0$. Now for the variance we get:

$$\sigma^2(y_j) = \frac{dh}{dz_j} \cdot \sigma^2(z_j) + \frac{dh}{dV} \cdot \sigma^2(V)$$

$$= \frac{1}{n\bar{v}}((P_0 + j\Delta p)\sigma_v^2 + \bar{v} \cdot j\sigma_p^2) - \bar{v}(p_0 + j\Delta p)\frac{1}{(n\bar{v})^2}n\sigma_v^2$$

$$= \frac{(p_0 + j\Delta p) \cdot \sigma_v^2}{n\bar{v}} + \frac{\bar{v} \cdot j \cdot \sigma_p^2}{n\bar{v}} - \frac{\bar{v}(p_0 + j\Delta p) \cdot n\sigma_v^2}{(n\bar{v})^2}$$

$$= \frac{1}{n}j\sigma_p^2$$

We are now ready to approximate the expected value and variance of the VWAP statistic based on $y_j = \dfrac{v_j p_j}{V}$. Let

$$E(y_j) = \frac{1}{n}(p_0 + j\Delta p)$$

$$\sigma^2(y_j) = \frac{1}{n} j\sigma_p^2$$

Then,

$$E(VWAP) = E\left(\sum_{j=1}^{n} y_j\right) = \sum_{j=1}^{n} E(y_j) = \sum_{j=1}^{n} \frac{1}{n} p_0 + j\Delta p$$

$$= \frac{1}{n} \sum_{j=1}^{n} p_0 + j\Delta p$$

$$= \frac{1}{n}[(p_0 + 1\Delta p) + (p_0 + 2\Delta p) + \ldots + (p_0 + n\Delta p)]$$

$$= \frac{1}{n}(p_0 + p_0 + \ldots + p_0 + 1\Delta p + 2\Delta p + \ldots n\Delta p)$$

$$= \frac{1}{n}(np_0 + \Delta p(1 + 2 + \ldots + n)) = \frac{1}{n}\left(np_0 + \Delta p \frac{n(n+1)}{2}\right)$$

$$= p_0 + \Delta p \frac{(n+1)}{2} \qquad\qquad (11.6)$$

$$\sigma^2(VWAP) = \sigma^2\left(\sum_{j=1}^{n} y_j\right) = \sum_{j=1}^{n} \sigma^2(y_j)$$

$$= \sum_{j=1}^{n} \frac{1}{n} j\sigma_p^2 = \frac{1}{n}\sigma_p^2 \sum_{j=1}^{n} j = \frac{1}{n}\sigma_p^2 \frac{n(n+1)}{2}$$

$$= \frac{(n+1)}{2}\sigma_p^2 \qquad\qquad (11.7)$$

Distribution

The actual distribution of the VWAP can be approximated using a generalization of the weak law of large numbers. This is, if $W = \sum_{j=1}^{n} x_j$ then the distribution $f(W)$ is normal with $E(W) = \sum_{j=1}^{n} \overline{x_j}$ and $\sigma^2(W) = \sum_{j=1}^{n} \sigma^2(x_j)$.

Thus,

$$f(W) \sim N\left(\sum_{j=1}^{n} \overline{x_j}, \sum_{j=1}^{n} \sigma^2(x_j) \right)$$

Therefore, the VWAP distribution is approximated as a normal distribution with mean and variance as follows:

$$f(VWAP) \sim N\left(p_0 + \Delta p \frac{(n+1)}{2}, \frac{(n+1)}{2} \sigma_p^2 \right)$$

Example 3. In a situation where there is expected price trend over the day, compute the expected value and standard deviation of the VWAP benchmark price at the end of the day assuming the following:

$$p_0 = \$25$$
$$n = 1000/\text{day}$$
$$\Delta p = 0$$
$$\sigma_p^2 = \$0.01/\text{trade}$$

Solution

According to Equation 5 and Equation 6 we compute the expected value and standard deviation of the VWAP as follows:

$$E(VWAP) = p_0 + \Delta p \frac{(n+1)}{2} = \$25 + 0 \cdot \frac{(100+1)}{2} = \$25.00$$

$$\sigma^2(VWAP) = \frac{(n+1)}{2} \sigma_p^2 = \frac{(100+1)}{2} \cdot \$0.01 = \$0.5050$$

$$\sigma(VWAP) = \sqrt{\sigma^2(VWAP)} = \sqrt{\$0.5050} = \$0.7106$$

In situations where there is no expected price trend over a period (i.e., $\Delta p = 0$) the expected VWAP price at the end of the period will be equal to the stock price at the beginning of trading (as is computed earlier). However, price risk is always present (i.e., market volatility) and will cause some uncertainty in the VWAP estimate. In instances where analysts are interested in the VWAP price at some future point in time after trading has already commenced, say 1:00 P.M., in the absence of price appreciation future VWAP is estimated as:

$$VWAP_n = (1 - \alpha) VWAP_t + \alpha P_t$$

where α is the expected percentage of daily volume to be traded through the close, $VWAP_t$ is the current VWAP and P_t is the current price.

Example 4.   An analyst is interested in examining the potential VWAP price at the end of the day and anticipates a positive price trend. This estimate is:

$$p_0 = \$25$$

$$n = 1000$$

$$\Delta p = \frac{\$1}{1000} = \$0.001$$

$$\sigma_p^2 = \$0.009$$

i.   Compute a one standard deviation confidence band for the VWAP price at the end of the day (i.e., after 1,000 trades).
ii. Compute the probability that the VWAP price will be less than \$27.
iii. Compute the probability that the VWAP price will be higher than the stock price at the beginning of trading (i.e., \$24).

Solution

i. A one standard deviation confidence band for the VWAP price is its expected value ± one standard deviation, that is, $E(VWAP) \pm \sigma(VWAP)$.

$$E(VWAP) = p_0 + \Delta p \frac{(n+1)}{2} = \$25 + \$0.001 \frac{(1000+1)}{2} = \$25.5005$$

$$\sigma^2(VWAP) = \frac{(n+1)}{2} \sigma_p^2 = \frac{(1000+1)}{2} \cdot \$0.009 = \$4.5045$$

$$\sigma(VWAP) = \sqrt{\$4.5045} = \$2.1224$$

Therefore, the one standard deviation confidence band for the VWAP price at the end of the day is:

$$=[E(VWAP) - \sigma(VWAP), E(VWAP) + \sigma(VWAP)]$$
$$=[\$25.5005 + \$2.1224, \$25.5005 - \$2.1224]$$
$$=[\$27.6229, \$23.3781]$$

There is a 67% likelihood that the VWAP will be between \$27.6229 and \$23.3781. Similarly, a 90% confidence interval is computed as:

$$= [E(VWAP) + 1.67 \cdot \sigma(VWAP), E(VWAP) - 1.67 \cdot \sigma(VWAP)]$$
$$= [29.04491, 21.95609]$$

And a 95% confidence interval is computed as:

$$= [E(VWAP) + 1.96 \cdot \sigma(VWAP), E(VWAP) - 1.96 \cdot \sigma(VWAP)]$$
$$= [29.6604, 21.3406]$$

ii. The probability that the VWAP will be less than any price (e.g., <$27) can be approximated from the normal distribution since the VWAP is approximately normal. Therefore, we need to standardize $27.00. This is as follows:

$$z = \frac{X - \bar{x}}{\sigma_x} = \frac{27 - 25.5005}{2.1224} = \frac{1.4995}{2.1224} = 0.7065$$

$$P(VWAP < 27) = P(z_i < 0.7065) = F(0.7065) = 76\%$$

iii. The probability that the VWAP price will be greater than some specified price is found as follows:

$$z = \frac{X - \bar{x}}{\sigma_x} = \frac{25 - 25.5005}{2.1224} = \frac{-0.5005}{2.1224} = -0.2358$$

$$P(VWAP > 25) = 1 - P(z_i < -0.2358) = 1 - F(-0.2358) = 59\%$$

Example 5. Compare the VWAP price benchmark to the underlying stock price. To completely address this question it is best to first examine the difference without price appreciation (e.g., $\Delta p = 0$) then with price appreciation term (e.g., $\Delta p \neq 0$). The expected value and standard deviation of each is shown in Table 11.2.

No Price Appreciation ($\Delta p = 0$)

In the case where there is no expected price appreciation, the expected VWAP price at time n will be equal to the expected stock price at time n. This is:

$$Price(n) = p_0 + n\Delta p = p_0 + n \cdot 0 = p_0$$

$$VWAP(n) = p_0 + \left(\frac{n+1}{2}\right)\Delta p = p_0 + \left(\frac{n+1}{2}\right) \cdot 0 = p_0$$

The ratio of the standard deviations is:

$$\frac{VWAP\ Undertainty}{Price\ Risk} = \frac{\sqrt{\frac{n+1}{2}} \cdot \sigma_p}{\sqrt{n} \cdot \sigma_p} = \sqrt{\frac{n+1}{2n}} \cong \sqrt{\frac{1}{2}} = 0.7071$$

Table 11.2

Statistic	Expected Value	Standard Deviation
Price(n)	$p_0 + n \cdot \Delta p$	$\sqrt{n} \cdot \sigma_p$
VWAP(n)	$p_0 + \left(\dfrac{n+1}{2}\right) \cdot \Delta p$	$\dfrac{n+1}{2} \cdot \sigma_p$

Figure 11.6   VWAP and Price Evolution

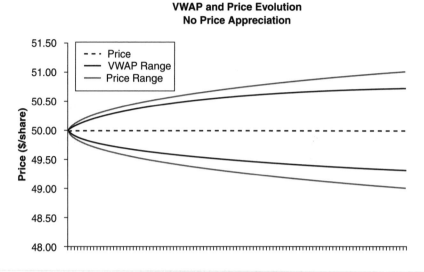

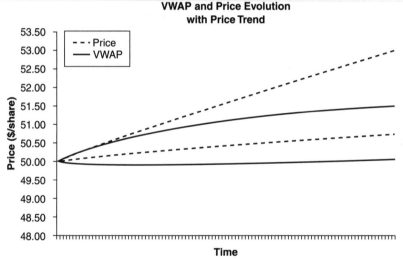

That is, the VWAP risk is approximately 70% of price volatility as n increases. This is shown in Figure 11.6.

Price Appreciation ($\Delta p \neq 0$)

In the case where there is anticipated price appreciation the expected VWAP price at time n will be different than the stock price at time n. The easiest way to understand this is to think of the VWAP price as a moving average. Then if the data series is growing (or falling), the moving average is always different from the most recent data point. Furthermore, there will always be less magnitude of movement (absolute price change) in the

VWAP price than in the stock price. This is best shown as the ratio of VWAP price to stock price as follows:

$$\frac{VWAP(n)}{Price(n)} = \frac{p_0 + \left(\frac{n+1}{2}\right)\Delta p}{p_0 + n\Delta p} = \frac{2p_0 + (n+1)\Delta p}{2p_0 + 2n\Delta p} < 1$$

since $n + 1 < 2n$ for $n > 1$.

The ratio of the standard deviation of the VWAP price and the stock price is the same regardless of the presence of price trend. However, in the case where there is no price trend, the confidence interval of our statistics will have the same center since the expected value is the same, but the VWAP interval will be smaller. In the case where there is a price trend, the confidence interval of our statistics will be different since the expected values are different, which causes the intervals to include different ranges. This is illustrated in Figure 11.6. The VWAP statistic changes at a slower rate than the underlying price similar to how the moving average changes at a slower rate than the underlying data points.

Alternative Scheme

It is also quite possible to compute the mean and variance of the VWAP statistic based on Equation 11.4 using our segmentation scheme. That is $VWAP = \sum_{j=1}^{N} u_j p_j$ where u_j is the percentage of daily volume in the jth period and p_j is the average trade price in the jth period (notice that we dropped the bar notation for the average price, $\overline{P_j}$). Then the average price can be written as:

$$p_j = p_0 + \sum_{i=1}^{k} \Delta p_j. \text{ If } E(\Delta p_j) = \Delta p \text{ and } \sigma^2(\Delta p_j) = \sigma_p^2$$

Then the expected price is:

$$E(p_j) = p_0 + j\Delta p$$
$$\sigma^2(p_j) = j\sigma_p^2$$

Now let,

$$E(u_j) = u_j$$
$$\sigma^2(u_j) = \sigma^2(u_j)$$

Then we can compute the expected and variance of the VWAP following Theorem 2. Notice the calculation process is much simpler because we only have two terms instead of three and no denominator. The process is as follows:

Let:
$$h(u_j, p_j) = u_j p_j$$
$$E(u_j) = u_j \qquad\qquad E(p_j) = p_0 + j \cdot \Delta p$$
$$\sigma^2(u_j) = \sigma^2(u_j) \qquad \sigma^2(p_j) = j \cdot \sigma_p^2$$

Then,
$$h(u_j, p_j) = u_j p_j$$
$$\frac{dh}{du_j} = p_j \qquad\qquad \frac{dh}{dp_j} = u_j$$
$$\frac{d^2h}{du_j^2} = 0 \qquad\qquad \frac{d^2h}{dp_j^2} = 0$$

Solving we get:

$$E(z_i) = h(u_j, p_j) + \frac{1}{2}\left[\frac{d^2h}{du_j^2}\sigma^2(u_j) + \frac{d^2h}{dp_j^2}\sigma^2(p_j)\right]$$

$$= u_j p_j + \frac{1}{2}[0 \cdot \sigma^2(u_j) + 0 \cdot j \cdot \sigma_p^2]$$

$$= u_j \cdot (p_0 + j \cdot \Delta p)$$

$$\sigma^2(z_j) = \frac{dh}{du_j} \cdot \sigma^2(u_j) + \frac{dh}{dp_j} \cdot \sigma^2(p_j)$$

$$= p_j \cdot \sigma^2(u_j) + u_j \cdot j \cdot \sigma_p^2$$

$$= (p_0 + j\Delta p) \cdot \sigma^2(u_j) + u_j \cdot j \cdot \sigma_p^2$$

The VWAP thus is written in terms of z_j as follows:

Let $VWAP = \sum_{j=1}^{n} z_j$ then,

$$E(VWAP) = \sum_{j=1}^{n} E(z_j) = \sum_{j=1}^{n} u_j \cdot (p_0 + j \cdot \Delta p) = \sum_{j=1}^{n} u_j p_0 + \sum_{j=1}^{n} j \cdot u_j \cdot \Delta p$$

$$= p_0 + \Delta p \sum_{j=1}^{n} j \cdot u_j \qquad\qquad (11.9)$$

$$\sigma^2(VWAP) = \sum_{j=1}^{n} \sigma^2(z_j) = \sum_{j=1}^{n} (p_0 + j\Delta p) \cdot \sigma^2(u_j) + u_j \cdot j \cdot \sigma_p^2$$

$$= \sum_{j=1}^{n} p_0 \sigma^2(u_j) + j\Delta p \sigma^2(u_j) + u_j j \sigma_p^2$$

$$= p_0 \sum_{j=1}^{n} \sigma^2(u_j) + \Delta p \sum_{j=1}^{n} j\sigma^2(u_j) + \sigma_p^2 \sum_{j=1}^{n} u_j j \qquad \text{(11.10)}$$

Thus we have,

$$VWAP \approx N\left(p_0 + \Delta p \sum_{j=1}^{n} j \cdot u_j, \ p_0 \sum_{j=1}^{n} \sigma^2(u_j) + \Delta p \sum_{j=1}^{n} j\sigma^2(u_j) + \sigma_p^2 \sum_{j=1}^{n} u_j j\right) \text{(11.11)}$$

Through the use of numerical approximation methods we can further simplify the variance term of the VWAP statistic so that it can be expressed in terms of the volume profile u_j and σ_p^2 in units per day. We do not provide the mathematical detail here but assure our readers that it is a very good approximation to the true variance, especially in situations where fluctuations in volume percentages do not vary widely from one period to the next and where traders do a reasonable job of participating with market volumes in the correct percentages. The approximation is as follows:

$$\sigma^2(VWAP) \approx \frac{1}{2} \cdot \sum_{i=1}^{n} u_j \cdot \sigma_p^2(day) \qquad \text{(11.12)}$$

Finally, when utilizing a slicing scheme we can approximate the expected value and variance of the VWAP statistic after m-periods as:

$$E(VWAP(m)) = p_0 + \Delta p \sum_{j=1}^{m} j \cdot u_j \qquad \text{(11.13)}$$

$$\sigma^2(VWAP(m)) \approx \frac{1}{2} \cdot \sum_{j=1}^{m} u_j \cdot \sigma_p^2(day) \qquad \text{(11.14)}$$

VWAP Convergence

Equation 11.13 and Equation 11.14 provide interesting insight into the potential VWAP range over a time period. The shorter the interval the less the VWAP price can change because there are less and less trades that can affect the VWAP price. This is very similar to potential price change where

Figure 11.7   VWAP Convergence

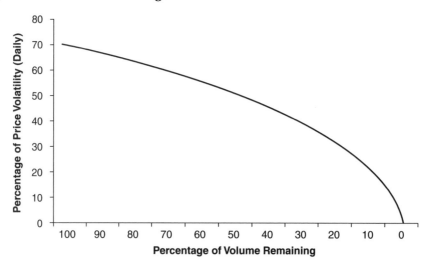

the potential price change over the day could be quite large, but the potential change over one-half the day is smaller, and the change over the next one-half hour is even smaller. For example, an analyst may compute the VWAP range over the day to be $1.50, but the VWAP range over the next one-half day to be $1.00, and the range over the next one hour to be $0.75. This point is illustrated in Figure 11.7. The chart in the figure approximates the VWAP uncertainty as a percentage of the daily price volatility using the remaining volume quantities. For example, at the market open there is 100% of the market volume that needs to be traded, so the VWAP interval is the opening price plus/minus 70% of the daily price volatility. If 50% of the volume remains to be traded, then the VWAP interval is the current VWAP price plus/minus 50% of the daily price volatility. When there is 25% volume to be traded the VWAP interval falls to 35% of the daily price volatility, and when there is 10% volume to be traded the VWAP interval falls to about 20% of the daily price volatility. The last important point to make with this chart is that price volatility on the day needs to correspond to the volume level on the day. If volume is higher than ADV price, volatility will be higher than average and opposite if volume is lower than ADV. Our calculation will provide a larger interval on those high-volume days and a smaller interval on those low-volume days.

A trader seeking to achieve or even beat the VWAP price can use these confidence intervals throughout the day to analyze trading activity. For example, suppose the current stock price is $50 and the daily price volatility is $1. The trader knows that a one standard deviation interval for the VWAP price is between $49.25 and $50.75. If the VWAP price at 12 P.M. is $50, then the one standard deviation VWAP interval falls to $49.40 and $50.40. Now, if the VWAP price is $50 at 2:30 P.M., the one standard devia-

Figure 11.8   VWAP Convergence

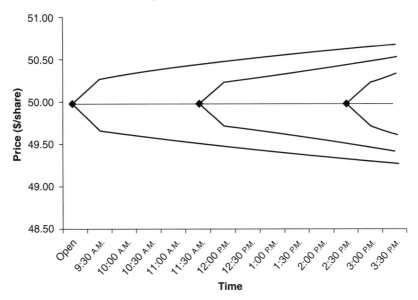

tion VWAP interval falls to between $49.60 and $50.40. The closer we get to the close the less the VWAP can change. This is shown in Figure 11.8. Notice the amount of uncertainty surrounding the price at different points in time during the day. Also, notice that even the scenario at 2:30 P.M. still has a large quantity of uncertainty surrounding the VWAP on the day because there is still a large quantity of volume that trades in the last few trading intervals, especially in the last interval.

This is important for a couple of reasons. Suppose that at 12 P.M. the trader's average execution price is $49.50 and the trader has a chance to execute the remainder of the order at that price. However, the trader is being evaluated against the VWAP price. If the daily volatility for the stock is $1 we can compute the standard deviation of the VWAP price over the remainder of the day to be $0.60. The trader computes the probability that the VWAP will be less than $49.50 and finds it is 20%. That is, 2 times out of 10 the trader will end up with unfavorable performance if they execute the order. Suppose that the trader does not like those odds and continues to trade. At 3 P.M. the trader has an average execution price of $49.50, which is less than the current VWAP at $50, and is once again asked if they want to execute the reminder of the order at $49.50. Hence the trader's average execution price will remain unchanged. Since we are closer to the market close there is less potential for change in the VWAP price and its standard deviation has fallen to $0.40. Now the probability that the VWAP will be less than $49.50 is 8%. So less than 1 in 10 times will the trader's performance be hurt. Hence, the trader should make the deal, complete the order, and go home early without any additional worries for the day.

Do Turnover Curves Improve Results?

We have mentioned that the best way to execute an order to achieve the VWAP price is the strategy where the order is sliced into smaller pieces based on the volume profile of the stock as follows:

$$x_j = u_j \cdot X$$

where x_j is the number of shares to trade in period j, X is the total number of shares of the order, and u_j is the average percentage of daily volume that trades in period j.

But is it possible to get better results using turnover profiles the percentage of dollar value executed in each period w_i rather than volume profiles u_i? Let us examine. In cases where $\Delta p = 0$ the profile curves for u_j and w_j will be exactly the same because $p_1 = p_2 = \ldots p_i = \ldots = p_n = p$. That is:

$$w_j = \frac{v_j p_j}{\sum v_j p_j} = \frac{v_j p}{\sum v_j p} = \frac{v_j p}{p \sum v_j} = \frac{v_j}{\sum v_j} = u_j$$

But in cases where $\Delta p \neq 0$ we have:

$$w_j = \frac{v_j p_j}{\sum v_j p_j} = \frac{v_j(p_0 + j\Delta p)}{\sum v_j(p_0 + j\Delta p)} = \frac{v_j p_0 + v_j j \Delta p}{\frac{n(n+1)}{2} \Delta p + \sum v_j p_0} \neq u_j$$

If $\Delta p > 0$ the turnover curve on the day will be tilted toward the afternoon, and if $\Delta p < 0$ the curve will be tilted toward the morning. But there are other cases of Δp that could arise where the price shoots up from morning to midday then shoots back down in sort of an upside down V or upside down U pattern on the day. The resulting turnover shape over the day could be flat. The extent that analysts use historical data to develop the w curve each day could have a different price trend, which could result in a turnover curve equal to the volume curve or even a turnover curve that is random.

For example, consider a situation where over the previous thirty days the price trend for the stock consisted of a rapid price movement through midday then a reversal back to the opening price by the close. That is, the trend was that of an upside down U or upside down V. The consequence of this movement would cause the dollar turnover in each period to be constant resulting in a thirty-day turnover profile that is flat. Now rather than following the volume profile of the stock to achieve VWAP the traders simply slice the order into equal suborders and execute throughout the day. Here since traders are not participating with volume they could realize an average execution price much different than the VWAP benchmark price, to mention a high market impact cost in the periods of lower liquidity. Other examples of this could result in turnover profiles with a ludicrous shape.

The reason behind these shapes is that price movement throughout the day is unstable from day to day. Even if there is a definite trend, the pattern on the day does not repeat itself from one day to the next. The easiest way to test this is to verify the unstable behavior of price movement by computing the correlation of price movement throughout the day from one day to the next. The result will show no correlation. In the case where price patterns arise they tend to be short lived because investors quickly learn to exploit the trend and turn the pattern into profit. Price patterns do not persist in the market. Volume profiles, on the other hand, are quite stable, and do persist. A definite trading pattern exists with more shares traded at the open and close than during midday. Furthermore, these patterns persist from day to day. If one were to perform a correlation analysis of the volume profiles in the market from one day to the next, last month compared to the current, or even last year compared to the current, we would find a strong correlation. These shapes persist in the market because without corresponding knowledge of price movement or knowledge of traders' intentions, there is no way to exploit this knowledge into profits. Traders are creatures of habit whereas prices evolve in an unpredictable way.

VWAP Tilt

Some traders believe they can accurately assess price movement over the day. Those traders could execute buy orders at the low of the day and sell orders at the high of the day and make a great deal of money. Moreover, those whose performance is measured against the benchmark can ensure that they will outperform the VWAP benchmark. But this is unlikely to be accomplished with any regularity.

Now let us consider a VWAP trader with good intuition regarding the price trend over the day. If this trader is willing to make educated bets regarding the true price trend, they could shift their VWAP strategy to take advantage of the changing prices. If the trader anticipates the price to be rising over the day and has a buy order, that trader will shift the trades to the morning to take advantage of the lower prices. If the trader has a sell order, they will shift the trades to the afternoon to take advantage of the higher prices. Conversely, if the trader anticipates the price to be falling over the day, they will shift more buys to the afternoon and more sells to the morning to achieve the better prices.

But how exactly should this shifting of trades be determined? The answer lies in first defining a trend line based on the expected price movement and the side of the transaction, then shifting the trades from morning to afternoon (and vice versa) based on the trend line. Two potential trend lines based on the current stock price p_0 and an intensity parameter k over an n period trading day are shown in Figure 11.9. The first defines

Figure 11.9   Morning and Afternoon Tilt

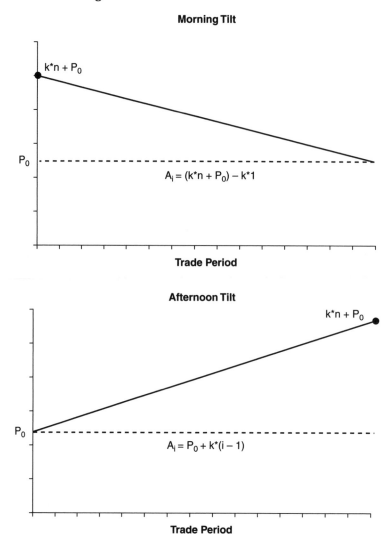

a trend line for a morning tilt that shifts trades from the afternoon to the morning. The second defines a trend line for an afternoon tilt that shifts trades from the morning to the afternoon. We provide the set of tilt equations by side (buy/sell) and expected price trend (Δp) in Table 11.3.

The VWAP tilt strategy w is then determined by incorporating this trend line A_i with the pure VWAP strategy u in such a way that the VWAP strategy is not permitted to change by too much.[1] The exact strategy w is

---

1. "By too much" is one of those mathematical phrases like "in the neighborhood of" that is knowingly vague but hoped to be understood in the context it is written.

Table 11.3

VWAP Tilt		*Δp > 0*		*Δp < 0*	
	Tilt	*Equation*		*Tilt*	*Equation*
Buy	Morning	$A_j = (p_0 + nk) - k \cdot j$		Afternoon	$A_j = p_0 + k \cdot (j - 1)$
Sell	Afternoon	$A_j = p_0 + k \cdot (j - 1)$		Morning	$A_j = (p_0 + nk) - k \cdot j$

found using the appropriate equation A_j and a specified value of $k>0$ as follows:

Let,

$$a_j = \frac{A_j}{\sum A_j} = \frac{A_j}{np_0 + \dfrac{n(n-1)}{2}} = \frac{A_j}{n^2 + n \cdot (2p_0 - 1)}$$

since, $\sum A_j = np_0 + \dfrac{n(n-1)}{2}$ for both equations.

Then,

$$w_j = \frac{u_j a_j}{\sum u_j a_j}$$

We depict two possible VWAP tilting schemes in Figure 11.10. The first chart shows these results for a morning shift and the second for an afternoon shift. The first data series in each chart is the pure VWAP strategy. Then we compare that to the VWAP tilt for values of $k = 3$ and $k = 10$. Notice that the parameter k behaves as a shift intensity factor. The higher the value of k the more assertive the shifting of trades becomes. This is shown in each chart with the tilt for $k = 10$ being more aggressive than that for $k = 3$. A shifting scheme such as this ensures that traders cannot completely deviate from the VWAP strategy. Furthermore, there is no distinguishable difference between the VWAP tilt strategies for larger values of k.

How Does This Work in Practice?

Suppose that a trader has a buy order and is expecting a positive price trend over the day, that is, $Δp > 0$. The trader could develop a VWAP tilt strategy to maximize the likelihood that they will outperform the VWAP benchmark by specifying the value of $k > 0$ to use in the derivation of w_i based upon their confidence of the trend. The higher values of k indicate more confidence regarding the price trend. The result is a strategy with a morning tilt for the buy order for an upward trending stock that allows the

Figure 11.10   Morning and Afternoon VWAP Tilt

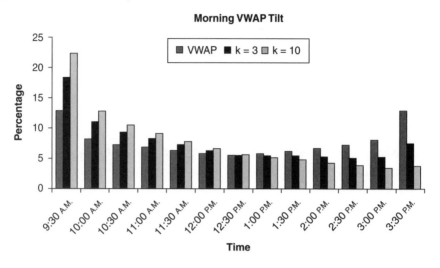

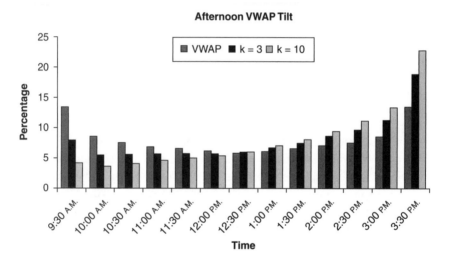

trader to take advantage of the better prices without allowing that trader to deviate from the VWAP strategy. The expected result is a positive comparison to the benchmark. The only problem is that if the actual trend is opposite what is expected, the trader will underperform the VWAP benchmark price. This effect could be dramatic. For example, if the trader defines a very high intensity parameter k (i.e., $k \geq 10$), the net result could be an exceptionally large underperformance.

But all is not lost. There is another alternative. The trader could actually set up an optimization routine that will determine the value of k that will maximize their expected performance compared to the VWAP benchmark price within a specified quantity of benchmark risk σ^*. (Benchmark risk is the potential difference between the average execution price of the order and the benchmark price.) This is written in vector notation as:

$$
Max \qquad \begin{cases} (u - w)^T p & Buys \\ (w - u)^T p & Sells \end{cases}
$$

$$s.t.,$$

$$
\sqrt{\sigma^2((y - w)^T p)} \leq \sigma^*
$$

where,

$$
p_j = p_0 + j\Delta p
$$

$$
A_j = (p_0 + nk) - k \cdot j \qquad (if\ morning\ tilt)
$$

$$
A_j = p_0 + k \cdot (j - 1) \qquad (if\ afternoon\ tilt)
$$

$$
a_j = \frac{A_j}{\sum A_j}
$$

$$
w_j = \frac{u_j a_j}{\sum u_j a_j}
$$

$$
k \geq 0
$$

A more general tilting scheme can also be found based on the prior technique but where p_0 is replaced by c and c is allowed to vary. The trend equation A_j is then defined by two parameters (c and k) as follows:

$$
A_j = c + k \cdot j
$$

The advantage of this form is that with the inclusion of the additional constraints $c > 0$ and $c + k \cdot n > 0$ we could eliminate the need for both a morning and afternoon tilt equation. These two constraints ensure that the resulting strategy w_j will never be negative. The resulting tilting strategy w would be better suited for our expected price trend. The disadvantage, however, is that it is more difficult to perform sensitivity analysis as in Figure 11.10 because analysts would need to tweak two parameters not one and time is usually quite limited for trading analysis. But if analysts and traders trust the optimization routine for the tilt strategy, they are better off using this more general formulation.

Finally, it is easy to see that for a shift intensity parameter of $k = 0$ there will be no difference between the tilted strategy w_i and pure VWAP strategy u_i since $A_i = A_j$ for all i, j, thus $a_i = 1/n$. The result is:

$$w_j = \frac{u_j \cdot \dfrac{1}{n}}{\sum \left(u_j \cdot \dfrac{1}{n} \right)} = \frac{u_j \cdot \dfrac{1}{n}}{\dfrac{1}{n} \sum u_j} = \frac{u_j}{\sum u_j} = \frac{u_j}{1} = u_j$$

If the trader selects a low enough value for the quantity of benchmark risk, the resulting optimization will be a strategy with a very small tilt and a very small value of k. Furthermore, if the value of benchmark risk is specific to be $\sigma^* = 0$, the resulting optimization will be $w = u$ since this is the only feasible solution for $\sigma^* = 0$.

CHAPTER TWELVE

Advanced Trading Techniques

Optimization Formulation Revisited

THE MAIN GOAL OF OPTIMIZATION is to determine the trading schedule x_k that balances the trade-off between cost and risk, (i.e., Min Cost + $\lambda \cdot$ Risk) However, formulation of this problem results in a complex optimization process, especially with the inclusion of real-world trading constraints. Even the optimization of the more simplified "trader's dilemma" (i.e., no anticipated price appreciation) and without participation or cash balancing constraints, the formulation is still highly complex.

Recall the formulation of the trader's dilemma:

$$\underset{x_k}{Min} \quad \sum_{i=1}^{m}\sum_{j=1}^{n} \frac{0.95I_i|x_{ij}|}{X_i} \cdot \frac{x_{ij}}{\left(|x_{ij}| + 0.5V_{ij}\right)} + \frac{0.05I_i x_{ij}}{|x_{ij}|} + \lambda\sqrt{\sum_{l=1}^{n} r_l^t Cr_l} \qquad (12.1)$$

$s.t. \quad i) \qquad \sum_{j=1}^{n} x_{ij} = X_i$

$\qquad ii) \qquad |r_{i,j+1}| < |r_{i,j}|$

where, $r_{ij} = \sum_{j=1}^{n} x_{ij}$

The formulation of this objective function results in many difficulties. First, the problem is not a linear programming (LP) or quadratic programming (QP) problem; there is no direct solution algorithm to solve the problem. The formulation is in the form of a non-linear or general programming problem (NLP), which requires search algorithms that could take considerable time to solve. Second, the objective function includes a decision variable in the denominator. Third, there are absolute value signs around the decision variable in the objective function and in constraint (ii). Fourth, there is a decision variable under the square root sign resulting in a much less direct convergence algorithm. Finally, in total there are m^*n decision variables, one for each stock and for each trading period. As the number of stocks in the trade list or number of allowable trading periods increases, the number of calculations and amount of time required to solve this problem increases dramatically.

The combination of all these nuisances coupled with lack of a direct convergence algorithm could work against traders. This is especially true for traders who are given orders or trade lists just before market opening or during the trade day. An important optimization requirement calls for solutions in minutes, anything longer may cause the trader to miss valuable trading opportunities.

In the remainder of the chapter we introduce short-cuts for solving the optimization without compromising accuracy. For example, we provide techniques to determine an exact solution to an approximate problem and an approximate solution to the exact problem.

Elimination of the Absolute Value Function

We easily eliminate the absolute value function in the objective function and in the constraint by converting the buys/sells problem into a buys only problem. It is important to note that this simplification process represents a transformation of data *not* an approximation (thus retaining accuracy). The technique simply consists of changing the signs of the order X_i, residual shares r_{ij}, and the entries of the covariance matrix c_{ij} to reflect the appropriate sides. Transformation is as follows:

$$Buys/Sells \leftrightarrow Buys\ Only$$
$$X_i \leftrightarrow |X_i|$$
$$C_{ik} \leftrightarrow sign\ (X_i)\ sign\ (X_k)C_{ik}$$
$$r_{ij} \leftrightarrow sign(X_j)r_{ij}$$

where,

$$sign(X_i) = \begin{cases} 1 & X_i > 0 \\ -1 & X_i < 0 \end{cases}$$

The introduction of the first two transformations results in an optimization problem where all shares and residuals are positive similar to that of an optimization that consists of buys only. The sells are reflected in the transformation of the covariance matrix. Once we determine the optimal trade schedule for the buys only problem, we can convert the trade schedule back to a buys/sells problem using the residuals schedule shown in the third transformation. In the case where one desires to solve the complete problem including price appreciation a similar transformation would be made surrounding Δp. That is

$$\text{Buy} \leftrightarrow /\text{sells} \leftrightarrow \text{Buys only}$$
$$\Delta p_i \leftrightarrow sign\ (X_i)\ \Delta p_i$$

Example 1. The transformation is computed as follows. Suppose that a buys/sells cost minimization is represented with trade vector X_i and covariance matrix C scaled for the appropriate trade period is as follows:

$$X = \begin{pmatrix} -1000 \\ 5000 \\ 2500 \end{pmatrix}, \quad C = \begin{pmatrix} 0.0009 & 0.0004 & 0.0003 \\ 0.0004 & 0.0016 & 0.0006 \\ 0.0003 & 0.0006 & 0.0025 \end{pmatrix}$$

Then the transformed matrices become:

$$\tilde{X} = \begin{pmatrix} 1000 \\ 5000 \\ 2500 \end{pmatrix}, \quad \tilde{C} = \begin{pmatrix} 0.0009 & -0.0004 & -0.0003 \\ -0.0004 & 0.0016 & 0.0006 \\ -0.0003 & 0.0006 & 0.0025 \end{pmatrix}$$

For simplicity in the notation we refer to the trade list and covariance matrix as X and C rather than $\tilde{X}$ and $\tilde{C}$. Finally, for those cases when there is a price appreciation term we constrict a similar transformation as follows:

$$\Delta P_i = \begin{pmatrix} -0.50 \\ .10 \\ .03 \end{pmatrix} \leftrightarrow \Delta \tilde{P}_i = \begin{pmatrix} 0.50 \\ .10 \\ .03 \end{pmatrix}$$

This results in a much simpler minimization in the form:

$$\underset{x_k}{Min}\ \sum_{i=1}^{m}\sum_{j=1}^{n} 0.95 I_i \cdot \frac{x_{ij}}{X_i} \cdot \frac{x_{ij}}{\left(x_{ij} + \dfrac{1}{2} v_{ij}\right)} + \frac{0.05 I_i x_{ij}}{X_i} + \lambda \sqrt{\sum_{l=1}^{n} r_l^T C r_l}$$

s.t.   i) $\displaystyle\sum_{j=1}^{n} x_{ij} = X_i$

        ii) $x_{ij} \geq 0$

(12.2)

This transformation also eliminates the absolute value in the second constraint since $|r_{i,j+1}| < |r_{i,j}|$ is always true providing $x_{ij} \geq 0$. Note, there is no difference between a constraint that is strictly less than $<$, or less than or equal $\leq$ since the optimization would solve the strictly less than problem with an extremely small value for the strictly less than case.

Elimination of the Decision Variable in the Denominator

The market impact term with the decision variable in the denominator reduces to:

$$\frac{x_{ij}}{x_{ij} + \frac{1}{2}v_{ij}} = \frac{x_{ij}/v_{ij}}{x_{ij}/v_{ij} + \frac{1}{2}v_{ij}/v_{ij}} = \frac{s_{ij}}{s_{ij} + \frac{1}{2}}$$

where s_{ij} is the trade size as a fraction of the period volume.

This expression is now in terms of one variable. The value of the expression over various values of s_i is shown graphically in Figure 12.1. Notice the strong relationship. It fact, we can find a good relationship between f(s) and s using a linear regression in the form:

$$f(s) = 1.71 - 1.2s = 1.71 - 1.2\frac{x_{ij}}{v_i}$$

Therefore, the prior market impact expression can be approximated with reasonably good accuracy in the regression equation:

$$\frac{x_{ij}}{x_{ij} + \frac{1}{2}v_{ij}} = (1.71 - 1.2s_{ij}) = 1.71 - 1.2\frac{x_{ij}}{v_{ij}}$$

Figure 12.1.   Adjustment Factor as a Function of Size

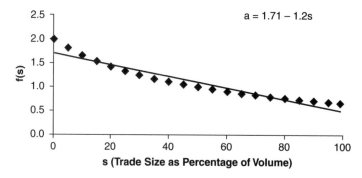

Finally, using the insight from the regression equation we can make an additional approximation to further simplify the equation by taking the average value for realistic order sizes. For example, the average value for order sizes $s_{ij} \leq 25\%$ is 1.65. Therefore, our market impact expression can be simplified to:

$$\frac{x_{ij}}{x_{ij} + \frac{1}{2} v_i} \cong 1.65 \cdot \frac{x_{ij}}{v_i}$$

for reasonable trade sizes and the objective function is then rewritten as:

$$\sum_{i=1}^{m} \sum_{j=1}^{n} \frac{0.95 I_i \cdot 1.65 x_{ij}^2}{X_i \cdot v_i} + \lambda \sqrt{\sum_{l=1}^{n} r_l^T C r_l}$$

Malamut (2002a) shows that an approximation with an adjustment factor of $a = 2$ yields accurate results over reasonable participation rates. Also, in the above formulation we omitted the permanent market impact expression since it is unavoidable.

Elimination of Square Root Sign in Risk Term

Unfortunately, the objective function is still in a complex form because of square root function in the risk term. However, if we eliminate the square root term we can get the format into an expression that can be solved using QP algorithms. This is accomplished as follows. Let,

$$\sqrt{\sum_{l=1}^{n} r_l^T C r_l} \approx \frac{\sum_{l=1}^{n} r_l^T C r_l}{\hat{\sigma}}$$

where $\sigma = \sqrt{\sum_{l=1}^{n} \hat{r}_l^T C \hat{r}_l}$ and $\hat{r}_l$ is a close approximation to r_l. This transformation follows directly from algebra where,

$$X = \frac{X^2}{X}$$

For example, for $\sqrt{2}$ we have

$$\sqrt{2} = \frac{(\sqrt{2})^2}{\sqrt{2}} = \frac{2}{\sqrt{2}}$$

Suppose,

$$X \approx \sqrt{2}$$

Then we can approximate $\sqrt{2}$ as

$$\sqrt{2} \cong \frac{2}{X}$$

Therefore, providing that $\hat{\sigma}$ is a close approximation to $\mathfrak{R}$ the loss of accuracy in the solution is minimal. The selection of $\hat{\sigma}$ above is as much an art as it is science and requires a thorough understanding of the trading environment. While a good approximation of $\hat{\sigma} \cong \mathfrak{R}$ simplifies the formulation an incorrect estimate of $\hat{\sigma}$ will worsen the results.

Quadratic Programming Solution

Using the previous numerical approximation for the risk term allows us to approximate the exact trader's dilemma formulation. The appealing aspect of this formulation is that we can compute an exact solution to an approximate problem. It in turn provides us with a very good approximate of the real solution in an acceptable amount of time that can be used by traders. Since only temporary impact is manageable via trading strategy we omit permanent impact from this formulation. This formulation follows:

$$\underset{x_k}{Min} \quad \sum_{i=1}^{m} \sum_{j=1}^{n} \frac{0.95 I_i \cdot 1.65 x_{ij}^2}{X_i \cdot v_{ij}} + \lambda \frac{1}{\hat{\sigma}} \sum_{l=1}^{n} r_l^T C r_l \qquad \textbf{(12.3)}$$

$$s.t. \quad i) \quad \sum_{j=1}^{n} x_{ij} = X_i$$

$$ii) \quad x_{ij} \geq 0$$

This can then be converted in to a QP formulation with the following notations:

$$z = \begin{bmatrix} r_{11} \\ r_{21} \\ \vdots \\ r_{m1} \\ r_{12} \\ \vdots \\ r_{1n} \\ \vdots \\ r_{mn} \end{bmatrix}, \quad b = \begin{bmatrix} \dfrac{-(1.65)^2 0.95 I_1}{v_{11}} \\ \dfrac{-(1.65)^2 0.95 I_2}{v_{21}} \\ \vdots \\ \dfrac{-(1.65)^2 0.95 I_m}{v_{m1}} \\ 0 \\ 0 \\ \vdots \\ 0 \end{bmatrix}, \quad A = \begin{bmatrix} -I_m & 0 & \cdots & 0 \\ I_m & -I_m & \cdots & \vdots \\ 0 & I_m & \cdots & 0 \\ \vdots & 0 & \cdots & -I_m \\ 0 & 0 & \cdots & I_m \end{bmatrix}, \quad c = \begin{bmatrix} -X_1 \\ -X_2 \\ \vdots \\ -X_m \\ 0 \\ 0 \\ \vdots \\ 0 \end{bmatrix}$$

$$
Q = \begin{bmatrix}
U_1 & D_1 & 0 & 0 & \cdots & 0 \\
D_1 & U_2 & D_2 & 0 & \cdots & 0 \\
0 & D_2 & U_3 & D_3 & \cdots & 0 \\
0 & 0 & D_3 & \ddots & \cdots & M \\
\vdots & \vdots & \vdots & \vdots & U_{n-1} & D_{n-1} \\
0 & 0 & 0 & & D_{n-1} & U_n
\end{bmatrix}
$$

where,

$$
I_m = \begin{bmatrix}
1 & 0 & \cdots & 0 \\
0 & 1 & \cdots & 0 \\
\vdots & \vdots & \ddots & \vdots \\
0 & 0 & \cdots & 1
\end{bmatrix}
$$

$$
U = \begin{bmatrix}
\dfrac{v_{11}}{\hat{\sigma}} + \dfrac{(1.65)^2 0.95 I_1}{X_1 V_{1j}} & \dfrac{v_{12}}{\hat{\sigma}} & \cdots & \dfrac{v_{1m}}{\hat{\sigma}} \\[2ex]
\dfrac{v_{21}}{\hat{\sigma}} & \dfrac{v_{22}}{\hat{\sigma}} + \dfrac{(1.65)^2 0.95 I_2}{X_2 V_{2j}} & \cdots & \dfrac{v_{2m}}{\hat{\sigma}} \\[2ex]
\vdots & \vdots & \ddots & \vdots \\[1ex]
\dfrac{v_{m1}}{\hat{\sigma}} & \dfrac{v_{m2}}{\hat{\sigma}} & \cdots & \dfrac{v_{mn}}{\hat{\sigma}} + \dfrac{(1.65)^2 0.95 I_m}{X_m V_{mj}}
\end{bmatrix}
$$

$$
D = \begin{bmatrix}
-\dfrac{(1.65) 0.95 I_1}{X_1 v_{1j}} & 0 & \cdots & 0 \\[2ex]
0 & -\dfrac{(1.65) 0.95 I_2}{X_2 v_{2j}} & \cdots & 0 \\[2ex]
\vdots & \vdots & \ddots & \vdots \\[1ex]
0 & 0 & \cdots & -\dfrac{(1.65) 0.95 I_m}{X_m v_{mj}}
\end{bmatrix}
$$

Hence, the cost minimization problem is represented as a quadratic programming (QP) problem as follows:

$$
\textit{Min:} \quad \frac{1}{2} z^T Q z + b^T z
$$

$$
\textit{s.t.,} \quad Az \geq c
$$

Malamut (2002b) provides an alternative QP formulation that is better tailored to the problem resulting in further speed improvements. Also, the formulation only accounted for temporary impact since we assume permanent impact is unavoidable.

Parametric Approach

Another measure we take to improve the computational speed of the algorithm is to express the trade schedule x_k in equation form using an exponential decay function. In this case, we compute an approximate solution for the exact problem. The number of shares of stock i to be traded in period j is computed as follows:

$$x_{ij} = \frac{X_i v_{ij} e^{-B_i(j-1)}}{\sum_{j=1}^{n} v_{ij} e^{-B_i(j-1)}} \tag{12.4}$$

Defining the trade schedule in equation form has many advantages over the solution with one decision variable for each trading period. First, this formulation only has a single parameter B_i for each stock. Contrast this to the dynamical model that requires $m*n$ decision variables in total. This results in a considerable reduction in computations and solution time, especially for larger lists and a longer time horizon. Second, expressing the trade schedule in terms of an exponential function provides many "natural simplifications" to the optimization algorithm. By our prior definition, we ensure that the number of shares traded in each period will be positive, that is, $x_k > 0$. By the inclusion of the denominator we ensure completion of the order, that is, $\sum x_{ij} = X_i$. This feature is quite appealing because in general the inclusion of any constraints in an optimization problem increases the amount of computational time required to solve the problem and increases the computational difficulty. Third, by including the market volume for each stock and period v_{ij} we ensure that the trade schedule will follow the volume profiles of the stock. This is a very desirable property because it will ensure that we trade more shares when there is more market volume.

The sole disadvantage of this formulation is that the problem cannot be written in QP form; therefore, there is no direct convergence QP algorithm available. But as we mentioned, this formulation only has one parameter to estimate for each stock regardless of the defined period. Large lists over a longer time horizon (e.g., days) results in a dramatic reduction in the number of decision variables. For example, the trade schedule has $m*n$ decision variables while this approach only has m. Also, there are no constraints to slow down the convergence.

In addition to having an optimization with only one parameter for each stock and no constraints, we can also increase the convergence of this optimization through the inclusion of the gradient and the Hessian. The gradient provides the optimization algorithms with an indication of the direction toward the minimum value so the search algorithm does not need to compute an additional step to determine which way to move. The Hessian provides the algorithm with an indication of the magnitude of

Figure 12.2. Comparison of Trade Schedule to Parametric Approximation

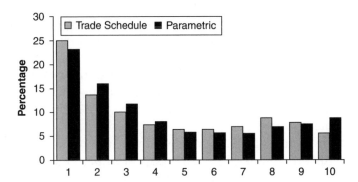

the appropriate step in such direction pointed out by the gradient. The flatter the surface around the current point (small Hessian) the larger the step (i.e., there is room to move). The more curved or sharp the surface (large Hessian) the smaller the steps need to be so to avoid "skipping" over and missing the minimum value. Brought together, the gradient and Hessian produce significant time improvement in GP problems. In fact, the fastest optimization algorithms include use of the gradient and/or Hessian in some form. The disadvantage of these expressions is associated with the difficulty of their derivation. If the incorrect derivation is incorporated in the model, there could actually be a significant increase in the solution time. In our case, though, the exponential function is very easily differentiable.

Figure 12.2 is a comparison of an actual trade schedule to an approximated schedule using a parametric equation. Notice how well the parametric equation approximates the actual strategy. This is even true for those periods with high trading activity and also for the later periods where the actual schedule is rather jagged.

Trading Rate Solution

Another measure taken to improve optimization speed calls for traders to participate with market volumes at specified rates rather than simply adhering to stated trade schedules. For example, for a given trading period j with total market volume v_j the number of shares that are to be executed is:

$$x_j = \begin{cases} \alpha v_j, & \text{if } \alpha v_j \leq R_j \\ R_j, & \text{otherwise} \end{cases} \qquad (12.5)$$

The utilization of a trading rate as an execution guideline as opposed to a trade schedule does have its advantages. First, it allows traders to better adapt to changing market conditions. Traders can accelerate trading in the presence of higher market volumes and decelerate trading in spells of less liquidity. This permits better control of market impact and risk cost components. Second, the trading rate also provides the means for improving the optimization speed because the algorithm relies on a single parameter α_i for each stock i. Third, the trading rate approach (or trading rate optimization) follows directly from the VWAP-hedge strategy from Chapter 11. Therefore, investors set on implementing and optimizing a VWAP strategy would find the trading rate useful.

The trading rate solution is not without drawbacks. First, a solution fails to take full advantage of hedging opportunities embedded in the list. For example, suppose a trade list consists of a buy order for 100,000 shares of ABC and a sell order of 100,000 shares of XYZ. If the stocks are well hedged, the trader could execute the list passively because the losses in one order caused by adverse price movement are offset (at least in part) by gains in the other order (favorable price movement). However, if one order contains 110,000 shares, the list is no longer well hedged because adverse price movement with more shares will result in a loss not likely to offset the gains in the other. In this situation, it would be in the trader's best interest to execute the order with more shares aggressively until residual amounts of each order are equal or close to equal (hedging advantage). The remaining residual shares could then be executed passively without incurring any unnecessary risk. In this example, the trading rate solution never allows residual orders to achieve the best hedge because it requires both lists to be executed according to a specific rate. Lastly, in times of low liquidity the trading rate may not provide sufficient opportunity for the order to be executed. For example, suppose that an order for 20% of the expected day's volume has an associated trading rate of 30%. If the actual volume on the day is one-half the expected quantity, the order would not be completed because the order comprises 40% of the actual day's volume. Traders utilizing a trading rate need to be mindful of liquidity conditions to ensure execution within the specified time.

An example of a trading strategy derived from a trading rate is shown in Figure 12.3. Here we show how an order that comprises 10% of the daily volume would be executed over the course of the day using a trading rate of 30%, 20%, and 10%. Notice each strategy follows market volume over the day, albeit at different rates and for different periods. As expected, the 30% rate is completed in the quickest time, followed by the 20%, and the 10% rate requiring the entire day to execute. If traders were to execute this list at a rate less than 10% the order would not be completed by day's end. Further if the actual volume on the day is less than expected traders would need to accelerate their executions in order to complete the order. If volumes were higher than expected traders could complete the order in a quicker amount of time.

Figure 12.3.   Trading Rate

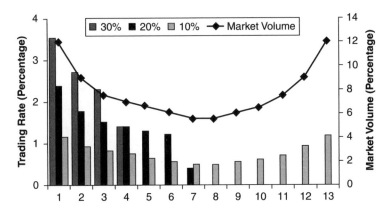

Trading Rate Cost Component Derivation

The solution of this transformed problem with the trading rate requires us to derive the cost components in terms of this new parameter. This can be determined directly using calculus and the notations.

Let,
V = expected volume over the period
t = time required to complete the order as a fraction of the day
s = order size as proportion of average daily volume

Then we have,

$$\alpha = \frac{X}{V}, \quad \alpha^* = \frac{\alpha}{(\alpha + 1)}, \quad s = \frac{X}{ADV}, \quad t = \frac{V}{ADV}, \quad \text{then, } t = \frac{s}{\alpha}$$

where, α represents the proportion of the order to the expected volume from all other market participants over the period and α^* represents the proportion of the order to all market volume including the order. For example, suppose that an order of 250,000 shares represents 25% of the ADV. If the order is executed over the entire day we have:

$$\alpha = \frac{25,000}{1,000,000} = 0.25, \; \alpha^* = \frac{250,000}{250,000 + 1,000,000} = 0.20$$

We can think of α as the ex-ante measure and α^* as the ex-post measure.

The trading time t is a measure of the time required to execute the order on a day with average volume at a rate of α. For example, if the order is for 20% of ADV ($s = .20$) and we are trading at a rate of $\alpha = .4$, the order will be completed in one-half day ($0.40/0.20 = 1/2$), a rate of $\alpha = .2$ will complete in one day, and a rate of $\alpha = .1$ will complete in two days.

Price Appreciation Expression

An order that executes at a constant rate will be completed by time $t = s/\alpha$. If we segment the trading interval t into n periods of equal volume then X/n shares will be executed in each period. If Δp is the one day price appreciation, then the price appreciation over the trading interval is $t\Delta p$ and the price appreciation per period is $t\Delta p/n$. The price appreciation cost is calculated as follows:

$$\mu(x) = \sum_{j=0}^{n} \frac{X}{n} \frac{t\Delta p}{n} j$$

where j represents the jth period.

As the number of periods n increases we have:

$$\lim_{n \to \infty} \sum_{j=0}^{n} \frac{X}{n} \frac{t\Delta p}{n} j = \lim_{n \to \infty} \sum_{j=0}^{n} Xt\Delta p z_n \, dz = \int_0^1 Xt\Delta p z \, dz = \frac{Xt\Delta p}{2} = \frac{Xs\Delta p}{2\alpha} = \frac{X^2 \Delta p}{2ADV\alpha}$$

Previously we used $z_n = j/n$ and $dz = 1/n$, for $j = 1, 2, \ldots, n$, so that $0 \leq z_n \leq 1$.

Notice that this expression is not dependent on the trading periods, only on the trading rate α. Therefore, the price appreciation cost can be written in terms of the trading rate:

$$\mu(x_k) = \sum_{i=1}^{m} \frac{X_i^2 \Delta p_i}{2\alpha_i ADV_i} \tag{12.6}$$

Market Impact Expression

An order that executes at a constant rate will be completed by time $t = s/\alpha$. If we segment the trading interval t into n periods of equal volume then we expect there to be V/n shares traded from other market participants and X/n shares traded from us in each period j. Then, temporary market impact cost is calculated as follows:

$$\kappa(x) = \sum_{j=1}^{n} 0.95I \frac{x_j}{X} \frac{x_j}{(x_j + 0.5v_j)} = \sum_{j=1}^{n} 0.95I \frac{X/n}{X} \frac{X/n}{(X/n + 0.5\,V/n)} = \frac{X}{(X + 0.5V)}$$

$$= 0.95I \frac{X}{(X + 0.5V)} \cong 0.95I \left(1.65 \frac{X}{V} \right) = 0.95\,I \cdot 1.65\alpha$$

For a list of stock the temporary market impact cost expressed in terms of the trading rate is:

$$\kappa(x_k) = \sum_{i=1}^{m} 1.57 I_i \alpha_i \qquad \text{(12.7)}$$

Note: This approximation as stated above works well for reasonable trading rates, e.g. $.05 \leq \alpha \leq .40$.

Timing Risk Expression

An order that executes at a constant rate will be completed by time $t = s/\alpha$. Segment the trading interval t into n periods of equal volume. Let σ^2 be the one-day variance of the stock. Then the variance scaled over the total interval is $t\sigma^2$ and scaled to the trading period is $t\sigma^2/n$. Let the residual shares at time j be:

$$r(j) = \begin{cases} X - \dfrac{X}{n} j & 0 \leq j \leq n \\ 0 & otherwise \end{cases}$$

Then the variance $\Re^2$ of the strategy is:

$$\Re^2(x) = \sum_{j=1}^{n} \left(X - \frac{X}{n} j \right)^2 \frac{t\sigma^2}{n}$$

Then as the number of trading periods increases we have:

$$\Re^2(x) = \lim_{n \to \infty} \sum_{j=1}^{n} \left(X - \frac{X}{n} j \right)^2 \frac{t\sigma^2}{n}$$

By using $z_n = j/n$ and $dz = 1/n$, for $j = 1, 2, \ldots, n$, we have that $0 \leq z_n \leq 1$ and then

$$\Re^2(x) = \lim_{n \to \infty} \sum_{j=1}^{n} \left(X - \frac{X}{n} j \right)^2 \frac{t\sigma^2}{n} = \lim_{n \to \infty} \sum_{j=1}^{n} (X - Xz_n)^2 t\sigma^2 dz = \int_0^1 (X - Xz)^2 t\sigma^2 dz$$

since $\displaystyle \lim_{n \to \infty} \sum_{j=1}^{n} f(z_n) dz = \int_0^1 f(z) dz$ when z_n varies from 0 to 1 (here,

$f(z) = (X - Xz)^2 t\sigma^2)$.

By solving the integral,

$$\Re^2(x) = \int_0^1 (X - Xz)^2 t\sigma^2 dz = \frac{t\sigma^2 X^2}{3} = \frac{s\sigma^2 X^2}{3\alpha}$$

The risk for the order is:

$$\Re(\alpha) = X \cdot \sigma \sqrt{\frac{1}{3} \frac{s}{\alpha}} \qquad\qquad (12.8)$$

Unfortunately, risk is not additive across stocks and there is no simple way to express the risk of the list in terms or the trading rate directly.

Advanced Trading Ideas

Uniform Slicing Strategies

Up to now, we focused on identical time trading intervals with differing volume. Constant time intervals have the advantage of being intuitive, for example, you perform the same task every fifteen minutes. However, we can construct trading intervals equal in volume having different time lengths predicated on volume traded in each period. This is shown in Table 12.1. Notice that each period in the equal volumes interval consists of 7.69% of the daily volume (e.g., 1/13th) but the time lengths of each period differ. For example, the length of the first period is seventeen minutes; the time length of the second period, twenty minutes and so on. The eighth interval takes longest lasting forty-one minutes. A transformation such as this allows traders to disguise their orders and intentions. Trades will enter the market at what appears to be random times and all sizes will be the same.

Table 12.1.

Trade Period	Equal Time Intervals				Equal Volume Intervals			
	Start	End	Minutes	Pct	Start	End	Minutes	Pct
1	9:30	10:00	30	13.2%	9:30	9:47	17	7.69%
2	10:00	10:30	30	8.0%	9:47	10:07	20	7.69%
3	10:30	11:00	30	7.5%	10:07	10:36	29	7.69%
4	11:00	11:30	30	7.1%	10:36	11:07	31	7.69%
5	11:30	12:00	30	6.8%	11:07	11:40	33	7.69%
6	12:00	12:30	30	6.2%	11:40	12:16	36	7.69%
7	12:30	1:00	30	5.6%	12:16	12:55	39	7.69%
8	1:00	1:30	30	5.6%	12:55	1:36	41	7.69%
9	1:30	2:00	30	5.8%	1:36	2:15	39	7.69%
10	2:00	2:30	30	6.4%	2:15	2:49	34	7.69%
11	2:30	3:00	30	6.9%	2:49	3:19	30	7.39%
12	3:00	3:30	30	8.2%	3:19	3:41	22	7.69%
13	3:30	4:00	30	12.7%	3:41	4:00	19	7.69%

Trade Rate Block Optimization

This optimization formulation uses a trade rate optimization for a single stock block trade. This is as follows:

$$Min: \quad \left(\frac{X^2 \Delta p}{2\alpha ADV} + 1.57 I\alpha \right) + \lambda \cdot X\sigma \sqrt{\frac{1}{3} \frac{X}{ADV} \frac{1}{\alpha}} \qquad (12.9)$$

$$s.t. \quad \alpha > 0$$

Recall that our definition for the trading rate was $\alpha = \dfrac{X}{V}$. Traders executing an order using the trading rate need to ensure that their order comprises $\alpha^* = \alpha/(1 + \alpha)$ of the total market volume (including one's own order). Therefore, α is not bounded by one whereas α^* is bounded by one.

Opportunity Cost

While we formulated our problems thus far to ensure completion opportunity cost did not exist. This was made certain through the completion constraint $\Sigma x_{ij} = X_i$. The objective function can be formulated to include opportunity cost.

First, recall the definition of opportunity cost. It is the forgone profit caused by not being able to fully implement the decision. It is equal to the residual shares multiplied by the natural price change of the stock. It is important to note here that opportunity cost should *only* include the natural price change of the stock caused by price appreciation and the permanent market impact caused by the order. It should not include any temporary market impact cost the order caused because this is only a payment the liquidity demands of the order and does not reflect the intrinsic stock price. Therefore, the opportunity cost at the end of trading is:

$$OC = \underbrace{\left(X_i - \sum_{j=1}^{n} x_{ij} \right)}_{\text{Uncompleted Shares}} \left(\underbrace{n\Delta p_i}_{\text{Price Appreciation}} + \underbrace{\frac{0.05 I_i}{X_i}}_{\text{Permanent MI}} \right)$$

Therefore, we can formulate the cost minimization to include the opportunity cost without the completion constraint as follows:

$$\underset{x_k}{Min} \quad \sum_i \sum_j x_{ij} \Delta p_i j + \frac{x_{ij}}{X_i} \frac{1.57 I_i x_{ij}}{v_{ij}} + \frac{0.05 I_i x_{ij}}{X_i} \qquad (12.10)$$

$$+ \sum_i \left(X_i - \sum_j x_{ij} \right) \left(n\Delta p_i + \frac{0.05 I_i}{X_i} \right) + \lambda \sqrt{\sum_{l=1}^{n} r_l^T C r_l}$$

$$s.t. \quad x_{ij} \geq 0$$

Evaluating Limit Order Prices

We discussed three main types of viable implementation strategies (cost minimization, risk aversion level, and price improvement) to achieve best execution for the entire list. For example, we showed how an optimal strategy could be developed to maximize the probability for price improvement for the entire list. But what if investors seek to maximize price improvement for one specific stock or a subset of the list?

Often investors' investment decisions will be conditional on share price as long as price is within some specified price range. For example, buy ABC as long as the price is less than $50 or sell ABC as long as the price is greater than $40. For these investors, the optimal trading strategy would provide the highest likelihood of executing these orders better than the specified cost. The strategy can be developed by the inclusion of an additional constraint where investors specify their desired percentage level α_i^* as follows:

$$Min: \quad Cost + \lambda Risk \tag{12.11}$$

$$s.t. \quad \sum x_{ij} = X_i$$

$$x_{ij} \geq 0$$

$$P(\varphi_i \leq L_i) \geq \alpha_i^*, \text{ or, } MaxP(\varphi_i \leq L_i)$$

However, this introduces another level of complexity into the optimization because the constraint is non-linear.

We can, nonetheless, find a direct solution by tackling this problem in two parts. First, investors determine the strategies z_i for all stocks that maximize the likelihood of executing better than the specified limit price C_i for all stocks with a limit price constraint. Then, investors run the optimization for the list by holding those strategies constant (fixed) and varying the strategies for all other stocks.

In the case where investors specify that the stock specific strategy satisfy $P(\phi_i \leq L_i) \geq \alpha_i^*$ for a given probability level there is no guarantee that the resulting strategy will be optimal, although it will be very close (the increase in computational speed in this approach more than offsets the loss in accuracy). However in cases where investors specify that the strategy be $MaxP(\phi_i \leq L_i)$, then the determined strategy will indeed be optimal.

Example 2

An investor is seeking to develop an optimal trade strategy for a list of m-stocks. The investor has further specified that for k of those names the strategy needs to provide the maximum chance of price improvement. Thus, the optimal strategy is determined as follows:

Step I: Determine the price improvement strategy for the specified stocks. Find z_i to be the strategy that maximizes for $P(\phi_i \le L_i)$ for $1 \le i \le k$

Step II: Determine the optimal strategy for the list by holding all z_i constant.

Let,

$$x = \begin{pmatrix} z_1 \\ \vdots \\ z_k \\ y_{k+1} \\ \vdots \\ y_m \end{pmatrix}$$

Solve the following,

$$\underset{y_k}{Min} \quad \sum_{i=1}^{m}\sum_{j=1}^{n} x_{ij}\Delta p_i j + \frac{x_{ij}}{X_i}\frac{1.57 I_i x_{ij}}{v_{ij}} + \frac{0.05 I_i x_{ij}}{X_i} + \lambda\sqrt{\sum_{l=1}^{n} r_l^T C r_l}$$

$$(12.12)$$

$$s.t. \quad x_{ij} \ge 0$$

This formulation will not allow the strategy z_i to vary. Therefore, we satisfy the stock specific price improvement constraint and still include the risk effect in the total cost calculation. This allows us to take advantage of the diversification and/or hedging opportunities those stocks may provide to further improve the cost consequence of the trade list.

Finally, while development of the strategy with the stock specific price improvement constraints provides better opportunities to execute the specific names, at least better than the limit price, the results are likely to increase a list's total cost. This could result in a total cost where each specified order satisfies the set limit prices that is higher than the total cost would have been had we allowed ourselves to accept market prices for all stocks (even if they were less favorable than the specified limit price). In other words, this technique could result in a "better off" position in some names but worse overall. Managers should be mindful of the overall cost consequences that limit prices could cause the fund to incur.

Crossing Order

Crossing systems provide excellent opportunities to reduce trading costs. The prime advantage is that investors execute at a known price without incurring market impact cost. However, execution is not guaranteed. Crosses will occur only if a match exists between buyers and sellers. A

Figure 12.4.   Efficient Trading Frontier

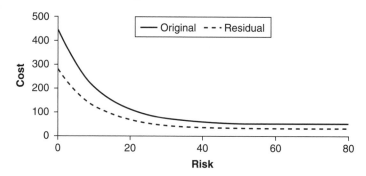

common misconception is that crossing systems provide benefit to investors. Even if no matches occur, then investors are no worse off. Keep in mind, though, if investors enter a list into a crossing system it is possible that the residual list will incur more risk than the original list. This occurs if investors entered a well-hedged two-sided trade list and only had executions of the buy or sell orders, but not both. Then if adverse price movement occurs, investors could incur a higher total trading than they would have had they not executed any shares on the crossing system. Therefore, investors should examine lists prior to entering orders into the crossing network to ensure any potential residual list will be less risky than the original.

Let us examine a situation where investors enter a hedged list into a crossing system that consists of an equal number of buys and sells. Before the matching session occurs, investors do not know what will trade or what the residual position will be. But what is certain is that list characteristics of any residual order will be different than the original list (unless of course nothing is executed). Suppose investors receive executions equally in buys and sells. Then, investors receive a large reduction in cost and, because the hedge is unchanged (or at least is not dramatically different), investors can utilize a passive strategy and further reduce cost without increasing risk. This situation is shown in Figure 12.4. Notice that the residual ETF is better than the original ETF for all values. This graph shows approximately a 40% reduction in cost for every quantity of risk. Clearly, crossing systems provide immense benefit to investors in cases where the residual list is less risky than the original.

Now let us examine a situation where investors receive the same number of executions but they are primarily on one side (either buys or sells). Therefore, the hedge of the list is damaged and the residual list is more risky. Investors receive a cost reduction. In fact, it is the same reduction in instantaneous cost (40%) as depicted in the previous example. But since the residual carries a higher risk, investors cannot utilize a passive strategy without increasing risk. Investors do not benefit from a cost reduction as in

Figure 12.5. Efficient Trading Frontier

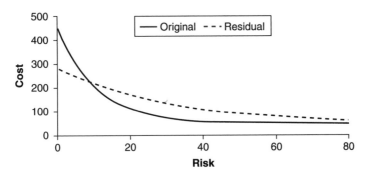

the previous case. In fact, for some strategies the quantity of risk surpasses the original list. This is shown in Figure 12.5. Notice residual list ETF carries a higher cost while the level of risk is identical to the original list. In short, if investors fail to manage their crossing list assiduously, overall trading cost will be adversely affected, sometimes dramatically.

It is important to note that many brokers guarantee investors they will cross a certain percentage of the list, say 30%, without commission. While this may seem like a good deal it often is not. In these cases, brokers choose shares from the trade list and thus receive a trade at zero cost, or select the most well hedged 30% of the list. In either case, investors are worse off. In the first case, investors failed to realize the full benefit of being a liquidity supplier and in the second case they were left with a riskier residual, which could easily result in higher costs.

Investors with a trade list X will seek a crossing strategy that determines the subset of shares Y so that regardless of the amount executed in the cross, Z will result in a less risky position. That is, investors want:

$$\Re((X - Y) + Z) \leq \Re(X)$$

This technique is further discussed subsequently.

Program-Block Decomposition

In order to take full advantage of natural diversification and hedging opportunities of the trade list, investors can decompose the list into two components: a program list and a block list. The program list entails those shares that reduce risk through either diversification or a buy-sell hedge. These shares can be traded passively throughout the day without incurring any incremental or unnecessary risk. The block list entails those shares that contribute positively to risk. This list defines those shares that need to be traded in an aggressive manner since a passive strategy will indeed cause investors to incur substantial incremental risk exposure. It also defines those shares where it is to traders' advantage to execute with immediacy as long as the price is right (e.g., through negotiations, large block executions, or via an intraday or end-of-day crossing system). For a list of stock the block portion is selected and traded in a manner such that for any residual list R the residual risk will be less than or equal to the original list, that is,

$$R^T\,CR \leq X^T C X$$

A perfectly hedged trade list (buying and selling the same dollar amount of two perfectly correlated stocks) should not be broken up for risk reasons alone. These names should be traded in conjunction with one another to reduce market impact cost without incremental risk. Utilizing this strategy, losses that may arise from adverse market movement in one name are offset by gains in the other name. Assume a trader obtains a negotiation to execute one of the names in full at the current market price. If the trader executes this order, the residual list (the order that did not execute) will no longer be protected. If an adverse price movement occurs, higher trading costs are incurred. An incorrect program-block decomposition scheme could potentially increase the cost of the list.

Example 3. We are buying and selling 100 shares of two stocks (ABC and XYZ respectively), perfectly correlated (hypothetically) with identical market price and volatility. As long as we buy the same amount of shares of ABC as we sell in XYZ throughout the day our transaction will be risk free (e.g., $R_j^T CR_j = 0$ for all periods j). Here we have "locked" in a transaction price that is independent of all potential market movement. However, if we do not execute these quantities in the same amounts, such as executing 50 shares of ABC and 25 shares of XYZ in the first period, the risk of the remaining shares (residual risk) will no longer be zero (i.e., have, $R_j^T CR_j > 0$). Here, adverse price movement could potentially hurt our overall trading costs.

Example 4. We are buying 150 shares of ABC and selling 100 shares of XYZ. Assuming the same risk characteristics as in Example 3 the list is no longer perfectly hedged because of the different number of shares. Define the block list to consist of 50 shares of ABC and 0 shares of XYZ. That is:

$$X = \begin{pmatrix} 150 \\ -100 \end{pmatrix}, Y = \begin{pmatrix} 50 \\ 0 \end{pmatrix}$$

If we trade the block list Y on some anonymous crossing or matching system, we can guarantee that the residual list will not be more risky than the original list. Recall that in a crossing system there is no guarantee of execution. If z_1 represents the number of shares of ABC executed in the crossing system $(0 \leq z_1 \leq 50)$, this can be shown mathematically as:

$$(150 - 50 + x_1, -100)C\begin{pmatrix} 150 - 50 + x_1 \\ -100 \end{pmatrix} \leq (150, -100)C\begin{pmatrix} 150 \\ -100 \end{pmatrix}$$

since the stocks are perfectly correlated at the same price with:

$$C = \begin{pmatrix} \sigma^2 & \sigma^2 \\ \sigma^2 & \sigma^2 \end{pmatrix}$$

Example 5. Now suppose the same situation and risk characteristics as Example 4 (buying 150 shares of ABC and selling 100 shares of XYZ) but the trader defines the block list Y to be $Y^t = (50, 25)$. Therefore, the unexecuted shares $Z^T = (z_1, z_2)$ needs to satisfy $0 \leq z_1 \leq 50$ and $-25 \leq z_2 \leq 0$. The residual risk is not guaranteed to be less than the risk of the original list. This is easily shown if $z_1 = 50$ and $z_2 = 0$, that is,

$$(150, -75)C\begin{pmatrix} 150 \\ -75 \end{pmatrix} > (150, -100)C\begin{pmatrix} 150 \\ -100 \end{pmatrix}$$

In Example 4, the choice of the 50 shares of ABC to be set aside for the block list is intuitive. However, in the general case, such a simple choice is not be available. Intuition collapses in cases with more than two stocks and in cases where the correlation across names is not perfect. Here, a more complex choice of a "sub-portfolio" is required if one wants to guarantee the residual list to never be more risky than the original list.

The trick of the program block decomposition is to determine the block list Y such that any potential residual list $(X - y + z)$ will be no more risky than the original. That is,

$$(X - y + z)^T C(X - y + z) \leq X^T CX$$

for, $0 \leq |z| \leq |y| \leq |X|$ for all i.

Ideally, one would prefer the block list to be as large as possible to maximize crossing opportunities.

Mathematical Formulation of the Program-Block Decomposition

Let $X \in \Re^m$ be a positive vector representing the number of shares invested in m stocks. Given a total number of shares S for all stocks combined, we want to determine the amount of shares Y to separate for a block list using a total of exactly S shares. $y \in \Re^m$ represents the number of shares of each of the m stocks such that, whatever residuals Z are not executed the portfolio formed by $X - Y + Z$ has the least risk among all possible choices of Y. By expressing the risk of a portfolio w as $\sqrt{w^T C w}$, our problem can be formulated as:

$$\min_y \left\{ \max_z [(X - y + z)^T C (X - y + z)] \right\} \qquad \text{(12.15)}$$

with

$$0 \le |z| \le |y| \le |X|$$

$$|y_1| + |y_2| + \cdots + |y_m| = S$$

$$sign(y_i) = sign(z_i) = sign(X_i), i = 1, 2, L, m$$

Note: The problem in Equation 7 is a QP problem. It is not hard to see that the problem's formulation is equivalent to a formulation without the absolute signs or the *sign* function. Indeed, replacing $|y_i|$ with y_i if X_i is positive and with $-y_i$ if X_i is negative (and the same for the other variables). Also, invert the direction of the inequalities when X_i is negative. The last constraint line, with the sign functions, becomes unnecessary. With the changes mentioned, which do not change the problem, the constraint set is linear and the problem is thus clearly a QP problem.

The optimization solution is indifferent to the specification of risk as the variance of standard deviation; therefore, we did indeed eliminate the need of the square root sign for risk to make the problem formulation that of a QP problem.

Even without the square root sign in the risk term this problem is extremely difficult. It is also important to point out the difficulty of enumerating all possible solutions in the search for an optimal solution for the problem in Equation 7. Suppose the shares are integers. Then the number of possible k-sized blocks taken from the S-sized list is $\binom{S}{k}$. For all sizes $k = 0, 1, \ldots, S$, the total is $\binom{S}{0} + \binom{S}{1} + \binom{S}{2} + L + \binom{S}{S} = 2^S$, a very large number. However, that number does not reflect all possible combinations of Y and Z from the S shares. We still need to take a subset Z of the subset Y. Since there are 2^y forms of choosing Z from each of the $\binom{S}{y}$ choices of y, we have a total of $s \sum_{y=0}^{S} \binom{S}{y} 2^y = 3^S$ combinations. This number is extremely

Figure 12.6. Residual Risk

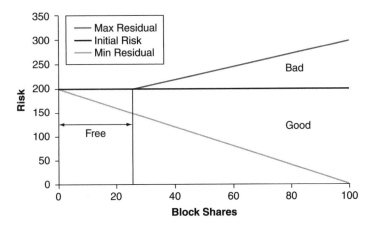

huge even for relatively small values of S. It could in fact take a super-computer hundreds of years in computational time to enumerate all possible subsets. In order to get a solution in reasonable time, we obviously cannot resort to enumerating all possible subsets of solutions; we need to find an alternative solution algorithm.[1] The prior formulation allows us to use optimization techniques to solve the problem in feasible time (and thus not by enumerating all possible solutions).

Graphical Interpretation

Figure 12.6 is an illustration of the mini-max optimization. The graphic depicts the residual risk of the total portfolio that may arise from a program-block separation as described earlier. Depending upon the number of shares S specified in the problem, the optimization algorithm will determine the program-block separation and state the minimum and maximum risk. The minimum risk is the quantity of residual risk that would exist if the entire block order were entered into a crossing system and executed in full. The maximum residual risk is the quantity of residual risk that would exist if the entire block order was entered into a crossing system and only the good risk were executed. Recall these shares provide the diversification and/or hedging benefits to the trade list. It could be an entire order or partial orders. Notice in Figure 12.6 how the minimum residual risk decreases as the block order increases in shares. The bottom line depicts the best case scenario and is the residual risk if the

1. The development of such an algorithm is beyond the scope of this book.

entire block were executed. Now notice how maximum risk does not change for the first 25 shares in this example. This is because the optimization algorithm first determines those shares that are only adding incremental risk to the trade list. These shares do not add diversification and/or hedging benefit to the trade list. Thus, if these shares are entered into a crossing system and executed either fully or partially (any subset), the residual risk will decrease improving the investor's position. The worse case scenario (where no shares are executed) is a resulting residual list identical to the initial trade list with original risk. The maximum shares where this phenomenon occurs defines a free block order for investors. It is the block position where investors will only be better off if there is any execution in a crossing system or if the shares are executed in bulk in the market. Investors have a free option to enter these shares into a crossing algorithm or offer to the market without worry of incurring a residual position more risky than the original. Hence, all trade lists are likely to contain a free-crossing option.

After this point, however, the addition of shares to the block order could result in increased residual risk if the wrong shares are executed. For example, suppose two stocks are correlated and trading at the same price. If the order is to purchase 150,000 shares of ABC and sell 100,000 shares of XYZ, the trade list is somewhat hedged because of the buy-sell list. Investors have a free option to enter 50,000 shares of ABC into a cross because any execution will only improve the residual position. Now suppose that investors enter 100,000 shares of ABC and 50,000 of XYZ into a cross but are only executed on the XYZ shares. Thus, the residual list is more risky, for example, 150,000 shares of ABC and 50,000 shares of XYZ. Investors need to understand and manage the potential risk of the program-block separation. An inappropriate allocation scheme can result in a residual position much worse than the initial position, thus leading to increased transaction costs and lower portfolio returns.

In cases where all shares in the list are perfectly correlated with one another the worse case residual risk will always be the same as the initial amount because none of the shares provide any diversification and/or hedging benefit. Thus, the free block option consists of the entire trade list. An example of a trade list where all shares perfectly correlate is a block order. When investors have only a single name to trade, it is in their best interest to submit the entire block to a crossing system; the residual risk will never be any worse.

Some traders may balk at this suggestion and bring up the possibility of adverse selection, which may result in a higher than necessary cost. While this may be true for list or basket trading, it does not apply to block trading with the goal of achieving a specified decision price. When investors desire to transact at a specified price and the crossing price meets that objective or better, it is in their best interest to utilize the cross. However, for investors who desire to achieve better than a specified price they may be better served by a slicing strategy over a period of time hoping for favorable price movement. The technique presented here pertains to investors seeking a specified price, thus adverse selection does not apply.

Use of Efficient Frontier to Understand Program-Block Decomposition

The benefits of the program-block separation are evident. By trading the block list in a low cost venue such as a crossing system or some other matching opportunity, investors achieve both lower residual risk and lower total trading costs since executed crossing orders do not incur any market impact cost.

The analysis in Figure 12.6 shows how residual risk can become higher than the original trade list. However, since investors achieve some cost savings it still may be beneficial for the residual risk to be higher than the original trade list risk, as long as their preferred execution strategy for the residual list is better than for the original trade list.

We can summarize this situation using the efficient frontier see (Figure 12.7). The figure shows the ETF for the original trade list along with two possible scenarios, one with lower residual risk and the other with higher residual risk. Notice how the ETF for the lower residual risk is always lower than the ETF for the original trade list, thus, total improvement. Regardless of investors' level of risk aversion they will always be better off with the lower residual trade list than the original. Now consider the higher residual list. Since the list consists of less shares, the instantaneous trading cost is lower than that for the original list. However, since the residual risk is higher, the ETF does not decrease at the same rate; cost here dissipates at a slower rate with risk than the original. Therefore, there

Figure 12.7. Residual Risk

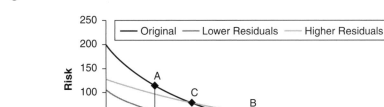

is some strategy "C" where the cost and risk are the same for both lists. To the left of this point investors are better off with the residual position with higher risk, and to the right of this point investors are better off with the original trade list. Therefore, if investors' level of risk aversion is denoted by point A, they are better served with the residual position with higher risk, implying that they can add more shares to the block list without hurting overall performance. However, if investors' level of risk aversion is denoted by point B, they would be better served with the original trade list over the residual position.

The moral of the story here is that even though a residual position may have higher quantity of risk, it may still be a viable option because the desired strategy is one with lower cost and lower risk.

CHAPTER THIRTEEN

Post-Trade Analysis

POST-TRADE ANALYSIS IS THE PERFORMANCE attribution of the implementation phase of the investment cycle. It is performed to measure the execution costs of the trade and distinguish between skill and luck of the trader and/or broker. Post-trade analysis measures the implementation of the investment decision to determine if best execution was achieved. It is performed in conjunction with portfolio attribution. Unlike traditional portfolio attribution, undertaken at specific time intervals (e.g., annually, semiannually, quarterly, and sometimes even monthly), post-trade analysis occurs after the execution of every trade list.

Post-trade analysis consists of two parts: transaction cost measurement and performance evaluation. Transaction cost measurement (TCM) determines the magnitude of costs and where these costs occurred. With TCM managers improve their understanding of the dynamics surrounding market microstructures and improve their asset allocation and stock selection processes. Performance evaluation consists of examining these costs to determine if they were justified. We determine if costs were a result of doing business, unavoidable due to market movement, or were the consequence of poor implementation decisions. This information is vital to managers' investment decisions, allowing them to dedicate more resources in areas where improvement is achievable (e.g., stock selection and execution decisions) and less in those areas where improvement is unattainable (cost of doing business and/or market risk). The goal: *Dedicate resources where they make a difference to improve portfolio returns.*

In this chapter, we provide a thorough account of procedures for measuring costs and evaluating trader/broker performance. We highlight advantages and disadvantages of each approach and present a recommended post-trade analysis approach for agency executions and principal bids. It is important to note that to evaluate performance one first needs to understand what managers hope to accomplish.

The Fundamentals of Post-Trade Analysis

The fundamentals of post-trade analysis deal with measuring costs, estimating (forecasting) cost as a distribution of expected cost and risk, and evaluating trader/broker performance. A measured cost represents an accounting of a past event. Estimated cost is a prediction about what is most expected to happen in the future, including the amount of uncertainty. A performance evaluation is a metric that attempts to determine if the actual incurred cost was reasonable given the actual set of market conditions, or if it was the consequence of good or poor decisions. Often managers, traders, and analysts confuse these measures, resulting in inappropriate investment and implementation decisions.

Measuring Transaction Costs

Why do we measure costs? The reason is simple. Managers need to know costs to improve investment decisions. Transaction costs are a cost of doing business and need to be included in the decision-making process. It is important for money managers to know their associated *doing business* cost. This is simply the difference between average execution price and the price of the stock at the time of the investment decision. Of course, there are numerous reasons differences occur, but the bottom line is that execution and decision prices are usually not the same.

We often see consultants and analysts tout the cost of doing business as the difference between the execution price and a benchmark price such as the VWAP. However, from the manager's point of view and investment goal of the fund this rationale makes no sense. Even if managers know beforehand that they are going to outperform or underperform the VWAP by −5bp, it adds zero value to the investment decision process because managers still do not know the price which they will transact. A cost measure is derived as the difference between the execution price and the decision price—this is a firm rule.

Example 1. A manager needs to decide between two stocks, A and B, both with a current market price of $50 and an expected annual return of 10%. Thus after one year, both stocks have an expected future price of $55. Which stock should the manager add to the portfolio?

Solution. For the manager to be able to make an educated choice regarding which stock to purchase he or she needs to know how much each will cost. If stock A costs 100bp and stock B costs 50bp, we can compute the realized return after one year as follows:

$$\text{Avg Exec Price} = \text{Current Market Price} \cdot (1 + \text{Cost})$$

$$\text{Realized Return} = \frac{\text{Future Price}}{\text{Avg Exec Price}} - 1$$

Stock A will be purchased for $50.50 ($50 plus 100bp) and have a net return of ($55/$50.50 − 1) = 8.91%. Stock B will be purchased for $50.25 ($50 plus 50bp) and have a net return of ($55/$50.25 − 1) = 9.45%. Therefore, it is obvious that the manager will prefer stock B over stock A because it has a considerable higher net return, 9.45% compared to 8.91%. But without accurate cost information, the manager is not able to make an educated decision regarding the best possible option. There is no debating this fact. The manager needs to know how much it will cost in addition to the current market price in order to make informed investment decisions.

Example 2. Consider the same situation from Example 1, but rather than having accurate cost information the manager has historical observations regarding average execution prices of each stock compared to the VWAP price. Suppose the average execution price compared to the VWAP for A is –5bp and for B is –20bp. That is, historical executions in stock A underperformed the VWAP benchmark by 5bp and stock B underperformed the VWAP by 20bp. How can the manager use this information to make an informed decision regarding which stock to purchase?

Solution. It is not possible for the manager to make any rational investment decision regarding which stock to add to the portfolio, knowing only that historical executions have under performed the VWAP price. Knowing that a stock has underperformed the VWAP by a certain number of basis points does not provide any insight into the actual cost or transaction price of the stock. The VWAP price may actually have been much higher for A than B, meaning that B was the lower cost stock and better investment even with a less favorable comparison to the VWAP benchmark. Even if the manager makes an assumption that the VWAP price for both stocks will be the same on the day, implying that A would incur a lower cost than B, these is still not sufficient information to make an educated investment decision. As we have shown previously, and highlight further subsequently, the size of the order and the execution strategy have a lot to do with the comparison of the execution price to the VWAP. As the order gets larger, its comparison to VWAP gets better and better, the execution price approaches the VWAP price. And as the order comprises 100% of the volume it becomes the VWAP price. Further, if the goal of implementation in the past has been different for each stock, there could be a considerable difference in VWAP comparisons. This would be true if the goal of implementation of A was to minimize cost (e.g., achieve the VWAP price) and for B to achieve price improvement. So if historical executions for A have been much larger in size than B and the implementation goal was to minimize cost while for B it was price improvement, A will have a better historical comparison to VWAP than B.

Still, managers do not know which stock is the better investment choice because they cannot accurately assess and compare realistic future returns. Having VWAP pricing knowledge does not help this point. The manager needs accurate cost information to make educated investment decisions.

Implementation Shortfall

The most common transaction cost measurement technique is the implementation shortfall (IS) methodology introduced by Perold (1988). The IS metric is defined as the difference between the actual portfolio return and its paper return benchmark. This measure accounts for *all portfolio costs* except for the management fees. The purpose of this measure was intended to measure one's ability to implement an investment decision and has since become the standard for transaction cost measurement.

$$\text{Implementation Shortfall} = \text{Paper Return} - \text{Portfolio Return} \qquad \text{(13.1)}$$

The implementation shortfall formulation decomposes cost into two parts: the execution cost component and the opportunity cost component. Execution costs comprise costs that arise due to actual market transactions such as commissions, transfer taxes, and price impact. In this case, Perold defines price impact to be the difference between the price of the stock at the time the investment decision was made and the price of the actual execution. As he correctly points out, price impact can be the result of many different factors: information leakage, liquidity demands, adverse price movement, market movement, or even the result of being a liquidity supplier, and so on. Perold's price impact definition includes our market impact, price appreciation, timing risk, and the delay cost. It does not isolate the change in price solely due to the trade. Thus, price impact does not have the same meaning as our market impact definition, which is the movement in the price of the stock due to the specific trade or order. However, what Perold defines to be price impact is exactly what we define as trading-related and investment-related transaction cost. The opportunity cost component of the IS relates to those transactions not completed in the market and is intended to measure the forgone profit of the missed trading opportunity. The main reasons for opportunity cost is lack of liquidity and/or unfavorable market prices.

The paper portfolio return over *n*-periods is defined as the difference between the portfolio value at time *n*, and the portfolio value at the time of the investment decision. The basic assumption of the paper portfolio is that unlimited quantities of stock are executed instantaneously at the current market price. Furthermore, the paper portfolio does not incur costs due to commissions, spreads, fees, or taxes.

The market price of the paper portfolio is taken as the midpoint of the bid-ask spread. It is important to note that the definition of the paper return requires all executions to occur at the midpoint of the bid-ask spread, otherwise the portfolio would incur one-half the spread cost on average. Assume an investor simultaneously buys and sells shares in a stock. If the paper portfolio recorded purchases at the ask and sales at the bid, the paper portfolio would record a loss equal to the bid-ask spread. But Perold's IS methodology specifically states that there are no transaction costs whatsoever associated with a paper portfolio. The actual portfolio return over *n*-periods, on the other hand, is defined as the difference in the portfolio value at time *n*, t_n, and the portfolio value at the actual execution prices less all commissions, taxes, and fees, and the associated opportunity cost. These calculations are shown next.

Let,

X_i = total shares of stock *i* to execute

x_{ij} = shares of stock *i* executed in period *j*

$X_i, x_{ij} > 0$ indicates buy; $X_i, x_{ij} < 0$ indicates sell

P_{id} = price of stock *i* at the time of the investment decision

p_{ij} = execution price of jth trade of stock *i*

P_{in} = price of stock *i* at the end of trading

Paper Return = $\sum_i X_i P_{in} - \sum_i X_i P_{id}$

Real Return = $\sum_i X_i P_{in} - \sum_i \sum_j x_{ij} p_{ij} + fixed$

Our notation specifically separates the non-transparent costs from those more visible costs (e.g., those costs that are unaffected by a specific trading strategy). Following these notations then we compute the implementation shortfall cost as follows:

Case i

In the first example, let us consider the case where there are no residual shares. That is, in cases where the order is completely executed by t_n.

$$\text{IS} = \text{Paper Return} - \text{Real Return}$$

$$= \left(\sum_i X_i P_{in} - \sum_i X_i P_{id} \right) - \left(\sum_i X_i P_{in} - \sum_i \sum_j x_{ij} p_{ij} \right) + \textit{fixed}$$

$$= \underbrace{\sum_i \sum_j x_{ij} p_{ij}}_{\textit{Execution Price}} - \underbrace{\sum_i X_i P_{id}}_{\textit{Decision Price}} + \textit{fixed}$$

Case ii

In the second example, let us consider a situation where there are unexecuted shares at the end of trading. In addition, as with Case i above, the IS calculation is always computed as the difference between the paper return and the real return even when the number of shares executed in each portfolio is different. Following this leads directly to Perold's opportunity cost definition. That is,

Let

y_i = unexecuted shares of stock i

$\sum_j x_j$ = executed shares of stock i

$\text{IS} = \text{Paper Return} - \text{Real Return}$

$$= \left(\sum_i X_i P_{in} - \sum_i X_i P_{id} \right) - \left(\sum_i \left(\sum_j x_{ij} \right) P_{in} - \sum_i \sum_j x_{ij} p_{ij} \right) + \textit{fix}$$

Since there are y_i unexecuted shares we have

$$y_i = X_i - \left(\sum_j x_{ij} \right)$$

$$\sum_i x_i P_{in} = \sum_i \left(\sum_j (x_{ij}) + y_i \right) P_{in} = \sum_i \sum_j x_{ij} P_{in} + \sum_i y_i P_{in}$$

$$\sum_i x_i P_{id} = \sum_i \left(\sum_j (x_{ij}) + y_i \right) P_{id} = \sum_i \sum_j x_{ij} P_{id} + \sum_i y_i P_{id}$$

and through substitution we get,

$$IS = \left[\left(\sum_i X_i P_{in} + \sum_i y_i P_{in} \right) - \left(\sum_i \sum_j x_{ij} P_{id} + \sum_i y_i P_{id} \right) \right]$$

$$- \left(\sum_i \sum_j x_{ij} P_{in} - \sum_i \sum_j x_{ij} p_{ij} \right) + visible$$

$$= \sum_i \sum_j x_{ij} p_{ij} - \sum_i \sum_j x_{ij} P_{id} + \sum_i y_i P_{in} - \sum_i y_i P_{id} + visible$$

$$= \left(\sum_i \sum_j x_{ij} p_{ij} - \sum_i \sum_j x_{ij} P_{id} \right) + \left(\sum_i \left(X_i - \sum_j x_{ij} \right) P_{in} - \sum_i \left(X_i - \sum_j x_{ij} \right) P_{id} \right)$$
$$+ visible$$

$$= \underbrace{\left(\sum_i \sum_j x_{ij} p_{ij} - \sum_i \sum_j x_{ij} P_{id} \right)}_{Execution\ Cost} + \underbrace{\sum_i \left(X_i - \sum_i x_{ij} \right)(P_{in} - P_{id})}_{Opportunity\ Cost} + visible$$

Thus, IS measure is separated into the execution cost, opportunity cost, and fixed cost component. It is important to note here that it makes no difference what time period the analysis is measured over just as long the period is equal to or longer than the trading period.

Case iii

Suppose that rather than specifying the number of shares to transact in each stock the manager specifies the dollar value D_i to trade in each stock where $D_i > 0$ indicates a buy and $D_i < 0$ indicates a sell. Here, determine implicitly the number of shares X_i the manager wishes to purchase at the beginning of trading, otherwise the ending portfolio value will be equal to the beginning portfolio value. Thus, the initial number of shares to transact in each stock i is computed implictly as:

$$X_i = \frac{D_i}{P_{id}}$$

Then the calculation of the implementation shortfall follows that of Case ii.

Expanded Implementation Shortfall Measure

The IS metric of Perold is exactly the measure required for managers to measure the implementation cost of an order. However, for portfolio attribution the IS metric is not as informative as it appears. Wagner has shown through numerous studies that the execution cost of an order can be further separated into a delay component and trading component. The delay cost is the forgone profit associated with the delay or from indecisiveness when managers wait to make execution decisions until traders release orders to the market. Trading costs represent the true cost of doing business. Having access to this information provides invaluable insight for money managers by identifying if costs are a direct result of fund management or a cost of doing business. The important issue is that by exercising proper transaction cost, management could easily reduce a large quantity of delay cost and improve portfolio performance.

By expanding Perold's measure into the terms specified by Wagner we can derive a formula that better identifies where these costs occurred.

Let,

t_0 = time the order was released to the market

t_d = time trading began

t_n = time trading ended

$t_d < t_0 < t_n$

P_{i0} = price of stock i at the time the order was released to the market

By expansion we have,

$$t_n - t_d = (t_n - t_0) + (t_0 - t_d)$$
$$P_{in} - P_{id} = (P_{in} - P_{i0}) + (P_{i0} - P_{id})$$

then we compute the execution cost and opportunity cost as follows:

$$\text{Execution Cost} = \sum_i \sum_j x_{ij} p_{ij} - \sum_i \sum_j x_{ij} P_{id}$$

$$= \left(\sum_i \sum_j x_{ij} p_{ij} - \sum_i \sum_j x_{ij} P_{i0} \right) + \left(\sum_i \sum_j x_{ij} P_{i0} - \sum_i \sum_j x_{ij} P_{id} \right)$$

$$\text{Opportunity Cost} = \sum_i \left(X_i - \sum_i x_{ij} \right)(P_{in} - P_{id})$$

$$= \sum_i \left(X_i - \sum_j x_{ij} \right)(P_{in} - P_{i0}) + \sum_i \left(X_i - \sum_j x_{ij} \right)(P_{i0} - P_{id})$$

Finally, by expanding the terms for the opportunity cost and substituting back into the IS measure we obtain:

$$\text{IS} = \underbrace{\sum_i \sum_j x_{ij}(P_{i0} - P_{id})}_{\text{Investment Cost}} + \underbrace{\left(\sum_i \sum_j x_{ij} p_{ij} - \sum_i \sum_j x_{ij} P_{i0} \right)}_{\text{Execution Cost}} \tag{13.2}$$

$$+ \underbrace{\sum_i \left(X_i - \sum_j x_{ij} \right)(P_{in} - P_{id})}_{\text{Opportunity Cost}} + Visible$$

with,

$$O.C. = \sum_i \left(X_i - \sum_j x_{ij} \right)(P_{in} - P_{id}) \tag{13.3}$$

$$+ \underbrace{\sum_i \left(X - \sum_j x_{ij} \right)(P_{id} - P_{i0})}_{\text{Investment-Related}} + \underbrace{\sum_i \left(X_i - \sum_j x_{ij} \right)(P_{in} - P_{i0})}_{\text{Trading-Related}}$$

The expansion of the IS in this format allows managers to better identify where and when the transaction costs occur. By exercising proper transaction cost control, traders and managers can work together to reduce delay and opportunity costs. In addition, by utilizing execution strategies developed in previous chapters managers and traders can reduce costs even more. Our expanded notation also distinguishes between the non-transparent costs (delay, price appreciation, market impact, timing risk, and opportunity cost) and the visible costs (commission, taxes, fees, and spreads).

The cost attributable to trading is thus:

$$\varphi = \underbrace{\left(\sum_i \sum_j x_{ij} P_{ij} - \sum_i \sum_j x_{ij} P_{i0}\right)}_{\text{Execution Cost}} + \underbrace{\sum_i \left(X_i - \sum_j x_{ij}\right)(P_{in} - P_{i0})}_{\text{Opportunity Cost}} \qquad (13.4)$$

While the expanded IS provides the proper transaction cost measurement calculation and does properly identify where the costs occurred, it has some limitations caused primarily by shortcomings of in-house and commercial order management and trading systems. For example, this methodology requires managers and traders to record the market prices at the time of the investment decision, the time of order entry, and the time of actual execution.

While managers obtain access to decision prices and traders/brokers have access to the price of every transaction (or at least the average execution price), the price of the stock at the time the order was entered into the market is often missing. While seemingly simple, there are times when these entry prices are not available. In these cases, reference prices such as the opening are often used as a proxy for the entry price making the exact identification of costs as investment or trading related a little less accurate, but it does not affect the accuracy of the total cost measure at all. Additionally, in order to account for the losses over a longer term period this methodology would require the manager to maintain two portfolios (one paper and one actual) on an ongoing basis increasing the administrative requirements of the portfolio.

In the formulation of Equation 13.2 it is easy to see that via proper transaction cost management, managers and traders can work together to minimize delay and opportunity costs. First, delay cost exists because traders need to examine lists to get a sense of their characteristics. Then traders should determine broker or execution venues best suited to execute the list. Often this causes traders to undertake research after receiving the list. Thus, continuously monitoring executions and knowing beforehand the brokers most capable of executing specific types of orders could reduce time delay. Another reason that delay cost exists is that traders are not always provided with sufficient information regarding the intentions of managers and/or how managers want lists executed, thus requiring more time-consuming research for traders. And in cases when managers give the list to traders just before or during market hours, potential for this cost becomes quite large. However, better communication between managers and traders would allow traders to begin implementation as soon as they are provided with trade lists.

Second, if managers and traders work together they could avoid opportunity cost. Recall that the opportunity cost of an order represents the foregone profit opportunity of a missed investment opportunity. However, the reason the order is unexecuted is because of inadequate liquidity or adverse price movement. It is quite possible for traders and managers to work together to identify these potentially unexecutable orders prior to trading so that managers would invest the funds in the next most attractive investment vehicle. In this case, utilizing the paper return of the portfolio to assess opportunity cost would not apply because realistically managers are not able to execute in those names. The best solution would be to turn to the economic definition of opportunity cost, that is, the missed opportunity of the most attractive alternative investment vehicle. With this in mind, it is quite possible to incorporate an economic opportunity cost measure into the implementation shortfall measure as long as managers track the next most attractive investment vehicle. This can be written as:

$$\text{IS} = \underbrace{\sum_i \sum_j x_{ij}(P_{i0} - P_{id})}_{\text{Delay Cost}} + \underbrace{\left(\sum_i \sum_j x_{ij} p_{ij} - \sum_i \sum_j x_{ij} P_{i0} \right)}_{\text{Execution Cost}} + \underbrace{\sum_k \alpha_k \left(\sum_i X_i P_{id} \right) R_k^*}_{\text{Economic Opportunity Cost}}$$

$$+ \; visible \tag{13.5}$$

where, R_k^* was the actual returns for the set of the next most attractive investment instruments over the period, α_k is the percentage of beginning dollar value invested in each alternative investment k, with $\sum \alpha_k = 1$.

The implementation shortfall methodology measures the cost of implementing an investment decision, but it does not provide any insight or guidelines for evaluating the performance of executing traders, brokers, or venue. To assess the performance of these market participants we need to use a different metric. This is discussed next.

Performance Evaluation

The main goal of performance evaluation is to assess the capability and performance of traders/brokers. The section above showed how to measure and identify where transaction costs occurred. But it did not provide a methodology to determine if those costs were reasonable. Proper performance evaluation will determine if the trader provided value in the process, resulting in lower costs or if the trader was counterproductive and contributed to the costs. Furthermore, performance evaluation will differentiate between a skilled and lucky trader. Regardless of the incurred cost, lucky traders will always be detrimental to the fund because their reactions will cause inferior performance as often as superior performance.

One of the more common, although, incorrect performance evaluation techniques is the benchmark comparison. Here, the average execution price is compared to a benchmark price such as the open, VWAP, or close and the performance is deemed superior if that execution price is more favorable than the benchmark and inferior if less favorable than the benchmark price. The benchmark approach is quite limited. It is difficult to compare performance across days and across stocks. Furthermore, it does not really address the question of good or poor performance. For example, it would be unreasonable to assess trading performance as inferior or inadequate simply because the average execution price is less favorable than a benchmark. This is illustrated in the case where a trader buys stock in a falling market where the closing price is the low of the day. Here all buys would be less favorable than the close but the difference is because of market movement, not because the trader did anything wrong. Traditional benchmark comparison will lead to incorrect conclusions because it does not account for market conditions, price trend, nor the specified implementation strategy. A better approach for evaluating performance is the *relative performance measure* (RPM), which gives a percentile ranking of the execution. This is a more intuitive methodology, and unlike the benchmark comparison, can be compared across stocks and across periods. Also, it *does* account for market conditions, price trend, and implementation strategy. It is discussed in a section below.

The performance measurement phase of post-trade analysis consists of determining if traders or brokers did a good job in executing the trade list. We seek to determine a performance measure for those parties involved in implementing the investment decision to determine if the cost was reasonable, or the result of superior or poor performance. As we show, it is quite possible for a low cost to be associated with poor implementation performance and a high cost to be associated with exceptional implementation performance. First, let us examine the current industry practices.

Current Practices

It has been stated often that there is no "one size fits all" performance measure and a correct performance measurement practice is quite vague and elusive. This statement, however, is wrong, made by those parties who confuse the difference between a cost measure and a performance. Industry participants involved in the trade implementation phase of the investment cycle have a strong interest in keeping the perception that the evaluation process is extremely complex because it consists of measuring a phenomenon (market impact) that cannot be readily observed. We believe brokers and traders want to maintain this impression so they can spin any incurred cost to make themselves look good. They do not want to be held accountable to any type of performance bogey. Furthermore, consultants have a vested interest in keeping this belief because it justifies their need and often high fees. Many have stated that transaction cost consultants have bullied their way into the transaction cost arena in much the same way that physicists bullied their way into the financial arena in the 80s and 90s. The justification of these physicists was that only they are best equipped to develop and understand stochastic calculus and complex derivative pricing models. In truth, most every graduate level science student has the (mathematical) background to understand, interpret, and expand those pricing models as well as understand the necessary stochastic calculus. Transaction cost consultants however, do play an important role in the industry. While they do not provide services that firms are incapable of doing on their own, they do serve as an important resource. Since these consultants have access to abundant data and numerous firms, only third-party consultants are capable of providing universe cost measures and performance metrics. This ultimately makes it possible to provide industry-wide broker and trader rankings.

Let us continue our discussion of performance measurement by referring to the expanded IS measure in shown in Equation 13.2. But now we are most interested in the performance of traders and/or brokers in the execution of the list; and can therefore exclude the delay cost and opportunity cost components from this analysis. In addition, proper transaction cost management techniques could reduce these costs to almost zero. In the performance measurement, we are only interested in the job done in the actual execution of the list. Finally, we do not incorporate the visible cost component into the performance measure since these costs are known in advance and already agreed to by managers and/or traders, and brokers and/or trading venue, they are not dependent upon trading strategy.

Benchmark Comparison

The current performance measurement practice in the industry consists of comparing the dollar value difference between the executed position and the position evaluated at some benchmark price. For an individual stock it is:

$$Performance_i(\$) = \sum_j x_{ij} p_{ij} - X_i P_b \qquad (13.6)$$

For a trade list it is:

$$Performance(\$) = \sum_i \sum_j x_{ij} p_{ij} - \sum_i X_i P_b \qquad (13.7)$$

with $x_{ij} > 0$ indicating a buy and $x_{ij} < 0$ indicating a sell, and P_b the benchmark price.

In this notation, a positive value indicates execution less favorable than the benchmark and a negative value indicates execution more favorable than the benchmark. It may be a little counterintuitive but this formulation does keep the calculation consistent with the cost measure. Recall that a negative cost is a savings. Readers uncomfortable with this notation can simply multiply by −1.

This dollar amount can then be converted to $/share or to basis point by dividing by the number of shares or market value at the time of order entry respectively. The rationale here is that performance is considered good if the average execution price is more favorable than the benchmark price (or at least within some reasonable range) and bad if the average execution price is less favorable than the benchmark price (or outside of that reasonable range). For example, if the execution price is better than 10bp compared to the benchmark price, it is considered good performance, and if it is worse than 10bp the execution is considered poor. But this line of reasoning does not typically work well and is in fact quite incomplete. It will also lead those participants who rely solely on these figures to make irrational execution decisions that are not within our best execution guidelines.

A survey of the set of benchmarks used in post-trade analysis shows that these benchmarks can be categorized as pre-, intraday, and post-trade. The pre-trade benchmarks include the prior night's close, the opening price. They also include, when available, the decision price and the price of order entry. They give a measure of trading costs. The intraday benchmarks include the VWAP and average of the open high low close (OHLC) price. They are intended to give a measure of how the execution price compared to the average market price over the day. The post-trade benchmarks include the closing price and a closing price sometime in the future (e.g., close+1 or close+5) as a measure of price reversion, poor execution, and/or adverse selection. But do these benchmarks really provide us with an unbiased measure as we hope?

Pre-trade. The pre-trade benchmarks in use serve as a cost measure, not a performance measure. For example, managers often make investment decisions after the market close; therefore, the decision price by default is the market close. These trade lists are given to traders who begin execution the next morning. Therefore, these benchmarks provide the delay cost and execution cost, not any particular performance. Even in cases where the decision price and price at order entry are known the measure simply provides a better cost measure, not a performance measure. The prior night's close and opening price are typically used as proxies for the decision price and price at market entry respectively. Pre-trade benchmarks provide proxies that can be used to compute the delay and execution costs but not opportunity cost unless combined with some post-trade price. Pre-trade benchmarks do not provide performance measures.

Intraday. The intraday benchmarks are the most consistent with a performance measure. The VWAP is a good indication of the fair market price over the day and the OHLC is believed to be a good proxy to this price. It is believed that the average of four prices is a good estimator of the average. The OHLC was a popular measure during the times when time and sales information was not readily available and VWAP calculations were hard to find. In the United States, this measure has been pretty much superceded by the VWAP but it is still very common in international markets where time and sales information and VWAP data are not readily available. The belief regarding intraday benchmarks is that if you performed more favorable than the benchmark you did a good job, but they do not incorporate the desired strategy in anyway shape or form. For example, if the goal of the implementation were to minimize risk exposure, any comparison to the VWAP is meaningless because the VWAP measure pertains to someone seeking to minimize cost not risk.

Post-Trade. Post-trade benchmarks are intended to measure market impact of orders. By comparing execution price to some future price, we determine if any mean reversion occurred. If mean reversion occurred then the order likely caused market impact. However, we all know that orders do cause market impact and there will be a disturbance to the price trajectory caused by permanent and temporary market impact, so this measure is only confirming what is already known. It can be argued that at least this comparison provides a magnitude of the price reversion, but it is still not any indication if that means reversion was reasonable given the market conditions or if it was caused by poor execution. Price evolution is caused by many factors. But even if the price evolution did result from just the order, the post-trade comparison would only measure temporary impact. It does not measure the total market impact cost from a temporary and permanent impact because permanent impact would be incorporated in future prices. And to the extent that the manager buys stocks that are rising and sells stocks that are falling, the post-trade measure often makes the trade look good. In fact, Perold highlighted these shortcomings. The post-trade measure, when used alone, does not provide any means of computing cost. The post-trade measure, however, provides a measure of the contribution to total tracking error for those index funds tracking a benchmark index, but by the same token underestimates the true cost of trading.

Hybrid Benchmarks. Many participants in the market insist on hybrid benchmarks for comparison such as a time-filtered VWAP or a composition of market activity and official prices. An example of a hybrid composite is one such as a 30-40-30 benchmark that is computed as 30% of the open plus 40% of the OHLC plus 30% of the close. But this measure is really the OHLC with different weights placed on each official price: 40%

Table 13.1.

Benchmark	Advantages	Disadvantages
Pre-	Good proxy to compute delay and execution cost.	Does not provide insight into opportunity cost unless coupled with post trade measure.
	Good for identifying costs as either investment related (delay) or trading related (execution).	Does not provide any insight into actual execution performance
Intra-	Good indication of fair market price over the day.	Does not provide a measure of performance for price improvement strategies, risk minimization, or for any strategy selected based on a specified level of risk aversion.
	Incorporates and account for market conditions and trading activity.	
	Serves as a good measure of execution performance for those circumstances where the manager elects to minimize cost.	Does not allow comparison of across different stocks or across different days
Post-	Estimates the contribution of the execution to the tracking error of the fund.	As a cost measure misses the permanent market impact cost.
	Can be coupled with a pre-trade benchmark to estimate the opportunity cost of an order.	Serves more as a measure of manager skill than trader performance.

open, 10% high, 10% low, and 40% close. It has been our experience that hybrid measures are only disclosed and used if they offer improvements over the more traditional benchmark comparisons and make the parties being evaluated look better. If they do not make the participant being evaluated look better, they are not shown.

Benchmark Comparison Limitations

Benchmark comparisons have some major deficiencies—they do not incorporate the specified execution strategy, they cannot be used to compare performance across stocks, and they can be gamed. This is true even when the performance is reported as $/share or basis points.

First, if managers and traders exercise fiduciary oversight, they will always specify implementation via an optimal strategy. But none of these benchmarks serve to determine if the strategy is optimal. It is possible that an optimal strategy specified ex-ante would result in costs with low benchmark scores (although, rare). Also, traders will specify the strategy to either minimize cost (e.g., VWAP), balance tradeoff between cost and risk, or to seek price improvement. The VWAP measure is a good estimate of the fair market prices over the day and is applicable to a cost minimization strategy. But it does not apply to a VWAP-hedge strategy (see Chapter 11, VWAP Trading Strategies), which in most cases is an improvement over the pure VWAP strategy. Furthermore, none of the benchmarks are good estimates of the fair price for price improvement and risk aversion strategies. While these strategies provide the best options for the respective goals, the variance between these average execution prices and the benchmark price will be quite large; they do not imply good or poor execution services.

Second, the benchmark comparison does not allow one to compare the performance across stocks on the same or different days, or even compare the performance in the same stock on different days. For example, suppose the benchmark comparison to the VWAP for stock A is 30bp and for stock B it is 50bp (both executions are less favorable than the VWAP). On the surface it would appear that the performance in stock A is better than stock B because of the lower number. But this could be due to a difference in the size of the order, the stock volatility, instability in trading patterns, or the result of a large single print at a very favorable price making the execution look worse than it really was. Furthermore, suppose that the benchmark comparison for stock A was 30bp yesterday but 50bp today. Even if the order size was identical, the values cannot be compared because both are dependent upon the actual market conditions and trading patterns, as well as the range of prices. For example, it is quite possible that the price range yesterday was less than 50bp; a comparison of 30bp implies that the order was executed at the least favorable prices of the day. Now if the price range in stock A today is 5% (ten times more than yesterday) a benchmark measure of 50bp indicates much better performance. Unfortunately, these benchmarks do not make comparison easy.

Third, there is always the possibility of gaming the benchmark. For example, if traders know they are being measured against opening or closing prices, they will concentrate all trades at these times causing the fund to incur unnecessary high market impact cost. In these situations traders look good but the fund is worse off. Also, if the order is sufficiently large and requires multiple days to trade, traders can accelerate or decelerate trades based on their performance and evolving benchmark score. For example, if traders are being compared to some benchmark and the market prices in the afternoon would cause the overall performance to become worse, traders could stop trading on the day and continue the next, thus increasing the timing risk. Furthermore, if prices make traders' performance appear more favorable, traders will increase executions on the day and incur more market impact cost, but in turn they would look better. Finally, for large orders and a VWAP benchmark, traders could cause their measured performance to converge to the VWAP by trading a larger percentage of the order on the day. This is because as the order size grows increasing larger, the execution price becomes the VWAP price. Because of these reasons, the benchmark comparison is considered a weak methodological practice.

Relative Performance Measure (RPM)

The relative performance measure (Kissell 1998) is a performance metric that computes the quantity of total activity that transacted in the market at a price less favorable than your own average price. It is similar to the VWAP benchmark in that it correctly adjusts for and incorporates actual market movement and trading activity. But it is an improved metric over the VWAP in that it can be used to compare and contrast trading performance across stocks and days. The RPM is modeled after the percentile ranking used in standardized academic testing. It provides a descriptive and meaningful measure that is consistent across days.

For example, let us suppose that one student scored a 52 on an academic exam and another student scored a 117 on a different academic exam. Without any other knowledge regarding the exams, it is difficult to assess any conclusions about the students' performance from the raw scores alone. But if we are told that the first student scored in the 95th percentile and the second student scored in the 10th percentile, we conclude the first student performed exceptionally while the second student did poorly. We do not need any other information to make this comparison.

The calculation process of the RPM metric consists of comparing the average execution price to all market activity over the trading period. The metric is computed as the percentage of all activity in the market that traded less favorably than your execution price. For example, for buy orders the RPM is computed as the percentage of all activity that traded at a price higher than your execution price and for sell orders it is computed as the percentage of all activity that traded lower than your execution price. We recommend computing the RPM based on market volume and number of trades in order to account for the potential skew of large block trades at extreme prices (e.g., large block trades with prices close to the high price or close to the low price). The RPM measure based on the number of trades weighs all activity equally. The calculation is as follows:

$$RPM(volume) = \frac{\text{Total Volume at a Price Less Favorable Than Your Execution Price}}{\text{Total Market Volume}}$$

$$RPM(trades) = \frac{\text{Number of Trades at a Price Less Favorable Than Your Execution Price}}{\text{Total Number of Trades}}$$

More specifically, if $P*$ was the average execution price of the order, the calculation of the RPM for buys is:

$$RPM(volume) = \frac{\text{sum(volume) for } P_i \geq P*}{\text{sum(volume)}} \qquad (13.8)$$

$$RPM(trades) = \frac{\text{sum(volume) for } P_i \leq P*}{\text{sum(volume)}} \qquad (13.9)$$

The calculation for sells is similar except that we evaluate all activity where $P_i < P*$. Hence, average RPM is:

$$RPM = \frac{1}{2}(RPM \text{ (trades)} + (RPM \text{ (volume)})) \qquad (13.10)$$

The RPM is a superior metric to the benchmark approach because it allows for comparison across stocks and days. Percentages can be used for cross-sectional comparisons whereas benchmark (magnitude differences) cannot. This makes the RPM a more robust measure. Suppose that a trader's performance measure using the benchmark approach was 30bp and 50bp in stocks A and B respectively. As we noted earlier, without any additional information we cannot conclude if this was good or poor performance or make any comparisons across each stock. However, if we are told that the RPM was 10% for stock A and 95% for stock B, we can easily determine that the performance was poor in stock A and excellent in stock B (even if A had a better benchmark score than B). This implies the trader did a better job with stock B than stock A. We only need the RPM to reach these conclusions.

Figure 13.1 is an illustration of the RPM calculation for a sell order with an average execution price of $25.75. The figure shows that 75% of activity traded at a price lower than $25.75. If the order had been for a buy, the process would calculate all activity higher than $25.75 and the RPM would be 25%. Graphically, the RPM is always shown by sorting all activity from lowest to highest price for sells and highest to lowest price for buys, and plotting the percentage of activity less than or equal to the specified price.

RPM of a Predefined Trade Strategy

Often managers will give traders specific trading instructions. In these cases it is not fair to examine the performance of traders using an RPM measure over the entire trading horizon because managers' instructions may cause traders to execute the majority of shares at times of the least (most) favorable prices. For example, an aggressive strategy will incur a low (high) RPM for buys in a falling (rising) market and a low (high) RPM for sells in a rising (falling) market. A passive strategy will result in the opposite. Thus, in order to distinguish between performance and manager

Figure 13.1. Relative Performance Measure

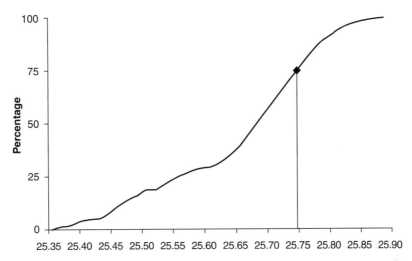

instructions it is necessary to calculate the RPM based upon the specified trading strategy as follows:

$$RPM_i^*(Strategy) = \sum_j \frac{x_{ij}^*}{X_i} RPM_j \qquad (13.11)$$

where RPM_j is the measure in period j and x_{ij}^* represents the actual execution strategy. This weighted RPM provides insight into the quality of prices achieved by traders during the times they are requested to trade.

RPM of Actual Trade Strategy

Assume an investor provides the broker with a buy order calling for complete execution by midday. As it turns out, the broker deviates from the prescribed strategy (for whatever reason) and trades the order over the course of the day. While the broker minimizes market impact cost, the decision also causes the fund to incur higher total trading cost by buying shares at the higher prices at the end of the day. Here it is quite possible for the broker's RPM to be around 50% or even higher indicating average (or above) price realization, but it does not communicate that the broker's action and decision to deviate from the prescribed strategy caused the fund to incur a higher cost.

To address this concern and quantify the decision-making ability of traders, let us define a new RPM metric to determine the quantity of value-added as follows:

$$Value\text{-}Added = \frac{RPM(x_i^*) - RPM(x_i)}{RPM(x_i^*)} = \frac{\sum_{j=1}^{n}(x_{ij}^* - x_{ij})RPM_{ij}}{RPM(x_i^*)} \qquad (13.12)$$

This value-added metric shows the percentage of the total RPM that is attributable to the deviation decision. If brokers/traders deviate from the prescribed strategy and obtain better prices, they will improve performance and have value-added > 0. But if their deviation causes them to obtain worse prices, then the value-added < 0. Moreover, this is exactly everyone's interest, e.g., measuring broker/trader performance. It is easy to see that if brokers/traders follow the prescribed strategy, then the value-added will be zero since $x^*_{ij} - x_{ij} = 0$. In this calculation for those periods where $x_{ij} = 0$ we compute the period RPM_{ij} assuming the trader achieves the average price in the period. For typical trading intervals such as fifteen or thirty minutes this assumption is a very reasonable assumption. This measure determines if the trader's real-time execution decision added value to the process or hurt overall performance.

There are market participants who make statements such as, "Why would anyone want to settle for average execution when they could get superior execution?" Of course, everyone would prefer superior execution over average performance as long as it does not come as the consequence of a gamble or incremental risk. Luckily, the quantitative RPM measure allows us to easily determine if traders or brokers are taking risks by simply analyzing the distribution of performance measures. Those traders who incur high metrics (excellent performance) as often as low metrics (poor performance) are those traders who are gambling and taking risk. A consistent trader is one who provides the best execution with little deviation in performance metric.

Qualitative Identification

Our performance measures up to now are based on a quantitative measure. But when it comes down to it, there probably is not much difference in the quality of performance between two measures that are close to one another (except for our value-added measure described below). For example, the actual execution performance is probably very close for those executions with RPM of 72% and 77%, or even 72% and 67%. Due to market noise, it is often difficult to distinguish between close percentiles. Now to make this a little easier it is possible to generalize the RPM into categories (e.g., good, average, poor) as long as the categorization is consistent across stocks and day (meaning, a good performance has the same meaning today as it did yesterday and will tomorrow and a good performance has the same meaning for all stocks). To address these concerns we can transform the quantitative RPM into a qualitative identification based on the average of the RPM volume and RPM trade measures.

The quantitative metric is converted to a qualitative label as follows:

Step i: Compute the average RPM.

$$RPM = \frac{RPM(volume) + RPM(trades)}{2}$$

Step ii: Convert to a qualitative label.

$$\text{Qualitative Label} = \begin{cases} Excellent & 80\% < RPM \leq 100\% \\ Good & 60\% < RPM \leq 80\% \\ Average & 40\% \leq RPM \leq 60\% \\ Fair & 20\% \leq RPM < 40\% \\ Poor & 0\% \leq RPM < 20\% \end{cases} \qquad (13.13)$$

This process makes it very easy for managers to judge traders. There really is no need to include any finer intervals or qualitative levels. We are certain that investors would be happy simply knowing their executions are consistently industry average or even better.

Comparison of RPM to VWAP

Of all the performance based measures mentioned, the VWAP is most similar to the RPM. They each provide a measure of how one's average price compares to all other market activity. In a way, the VWAP statistic is the expected or mean while the RPM 50th percentile is the median of all performance.

Both the VWAP measure and RPM suffer from the same disadvantages. First, as the order accounts for a larger percentage of the daily volume, the execution price converges to the VWAP and the RPM converges to 50% or average performance. And unfortunately, it is difficult to infer any information from these statistics. However, as we show next, if we couple the RPM with the expected cost, we can make very accurate judgments surrounding performance. Second, if the order is traded over a relatively short period of time, such as a couple of hours, any measure that incorporates the entire day's activity would include potential price movement not relevant to the particular execution. But it is quite possible to adjust each measure by using a time-filtered VWAP and an RPM calculation only over the actual trading periods.

The RPM has a few major advantages over the VWAP measure in the quantity of information contained in the statistic. First, as mentioned earlier, the VWAP measure provides the magnitude difference from the VWAP. But it does not provide any information regarding the dispersion of all other activity. This makes it difficult to compare the performance across stocks and in the same stock on different days. Furthermore, it makes it difficult to compare the performance between executions in the same stock on the same day. For example, suppose that one execution was 10bp compared to the VWAP and a second was 15bp. We know that the first performance was better, but was it a little better or a lot better? It is quite possible that because of market movement the 10bp measure is only slightly better than the 15bp. Also, just because a 10bp measure was good today does not guarantee that 10bp will suffice tomorrow. The RPM, not

Table 13.2.

Volume	Price	Pct. of Volume
20,000	$49.95	25%
20,000	$50.00	25%
20,000	$50.05	25%
20,000	$50.25	25%
VWAP	$50.0625	

the VWAP measure, is consistent across stocks or days. We know that if the performance was good, or say 65%, it has the exact meaning from one day to the next; it will not change.

Another advantage of the RPM measure over the VWAP is that the VWAP is not a symmetrical distribution since the majority of activity is likely to be on one side of the VWAP price. If the VWAP were symmetrical, 50% of prices and volume would be higher and 50% lower than the VWAP price. Therefore, it is not necessarily true that a loss compared to the VWAP benchmark necessarily indicates inadequate performance. It is possible for traders or brokers to underperform the VWAP but still outperform the majority of trades and volume in the market. The VWAP measure does not pick up on this.

Consider the following scenario. A stock trades in relatively small quantities in three price increments over the course of the day. But at the market close a large block (25%) trades at a price much higher than any of the previous price increments on the day. This is shown in Table 13.2. The result is a VWAP price that is higher than any of the price increments excluding the price of the block. Here, all market volume is at a price lower than the VWAP price except for the block trade. The resulting distribution is 75% of volume on one side of the VWAP price and 25% on the other side. It is a very asymmetric distribution. Now suppose that one of the market participants sold 10,000 shares at an average execution price of $50.05. This trader executes better than or equal to 75% of market volume but still underperforms the VWAP by 2.5bp. What should be considered as close to excellent performance is actually categorized as below the benchmark. The RPM does not allow us to make this oversight.

Goal of Implementation

To best understand appropriate techniques for performing post-trade analysis, understand the manager's goal for implementation. We briefly review the basics drawn from earlier chapters.

Let M represent the paper portfolio and P the real portfolio. Then if d represents the time of the investment decision and n represents the end of trading, the trading cost is calculated as:

$$\phi = (M_n - M_d) - (P_n - P^*) \tag{13.14}$$

where P^* is the portfolio evaluated at the average execution price. Visible fees are not included because they are not a consequence of trading. With this in mind we can state that the goal of implementation is to ensure that the value of the new portfolio is as close to the value of the paper portfolio as possible, for example,

$$Min: \delta = |(M_n - M_d) - (P_n - P^*)| \tag{13.15}$$

But the estimated trading cost ϕ cannot be forecasted as a single cost value. It is forecasted as a distribution of costs with a mean ϕ and standard deviation $\Re$ parameter that is dependent upon the implementation strategy x_k. Unfortunately, expected cost ϕ and risk $\Re$ are inversely proportional, meaning that as one component decreases the other cost component increases. Therefore, it is impossible to minimize cost without affecting risk, and vice versa.

Best Execution

Best execution is one of those expressions thrown around the industry and assumed to be understood and mean the same thing to everyone. In summary,

> Best execution is the practice of fiduciary transaction cost management before, during, and after each implementation; for example, it deals with process of evaluating alternative implementation strategies to determine the strategy that best maximizes the likelihood of preserving asset. The strategy, of course, needs to be assessed based upon the goals and objectives of the fund.

Whose Responsibility Is Best Execution? Best execution is everyone's responsibility. Managers need to perform best execution for plan sponsors and investors, traders need to perform best execution for managers, and the brokers need to perform best execution for traders. If any of these parties do not follow best execution procedures, the result is likely to be diminished returns.

How Can Best Execution Be Measured? The people who can realistically determine if a particular implementation strategy is a best execution strategy are those parties who are privileged to the goals or objectives of the fund for that specific trade list implementation. This is further complicated since each execution can be accompanied by a different set of objectives. Unless we know what managers were looking to accomplish for each specific implementation we cannot determine if a particular strategy was the exact strategy that maximized the likelihood of preserving value.

Best Execution Strategy

Even with these difficulties, determination of a best execution strategy is quite direct. It follows from our prior definition—best execution is a process that maximizes the likelihood of preserving asset value. In order for a strategy to best preserve asset value it must be an optimal trading strategy lying on the ETF. We consider any strategy not on the ETF an irrational trading strategy because an alternative strategy can be found with a lower cost for the specified quantity of risk, less risk for the level of cost, or both lower cost and less risk. If a strategy is not a rational strategy, it will fail to preserve asset value.

A best execution strategy is:

▲ An optimal trading strategy lying on the efficient trading frontier
▲ A strategy that will preserve asset value given the goals and objectives of the fund

The general consensus regarding the goal of implementation is to preserve asset value. We have previously identified three acceptable goals for preserving asset value:

▲ Minimize Costs Subject to Risk
▲ Balance the tradeoff between Cost and Risk
▲ Price Improvement

1. Minimize Cost Subject to Risk

The implementation strategy based on cost minimization is one where investors minimize costs via optimization based on a specified level of Risk exposure. This calculation is formulated as follows:

$$\text{Min} \quad \text{Cost}$$
$$\text{st.} \quad \text{Risk} \quad \leq \Re^*$$

where $\Re^*$ is specified by the investor.

The minimize cost goal is appropriate for an investor or fund that has internal risk constraints. This goal is often used by sell side firms and/or proprietary desks who have designated maximum levels of allowable risk exposure. For those investors who do not have any specified level of risk exposure or are unsure of this amount the next implementation goals may be insightful since it does not require one to specify a quantity of risk. This goal is also often selected by investors seeking to keep their trading risk consistent with their portfolio risk.

2. Balance tradeoff between Cost and Risk

The implementation strategy based on the level of a risk aversion parameter is one where traders specify their preferred trade-off between cost and risk. The strategy is determined via the following optimization:

$$Min \quad Cost + \lambda \cdot Risk$$

where λ specifies the level of risk aversion.

An investor with $\lambda > 1$ is more risk averse than price sensitive and would prefer an aggressive strategy over a passive strategy. An investor with $\lambda < 1$ is more price sensitive than risk averse and would prefer a passive strategy over an aggressive strategy. This strategy can also be interpreted as the strategy where investors are λ times more concerned about risk than cost. For example, an investor who specifies $\lambda = 2$ is twice as concerned about risk than cost. An investor who specifies $\lambda = \frac{1}{2}$ is one-half concerned about risk than cost, implying they are twice as concerned about cost as risk. And, an investor with $\lambda = 1$ is equally concerned about cost and risk. In economic terms lambda λ represents the marginal rate of substitution between cost and risk.

The strategy that minimizes the expected cost of the strategy is found through optimizing with a level of lambda $\lambda = 0$. This results in the following optimization equation:

$$Min \quad \psi = Cost$$

Here, the investor is completely risk neutral. This strategy will provide the same results as 1. Minimize Cost Subject to Risk where Risk exposure is set to be large. In situations where there is no anticipated price appreciation or where the net price appreciation is zero, the resulting strategy will be the VWAP strategy, i.e., minimize market impact. But as shown in Chapter 11, investors can usually offset a large quantity of risk for a relatively small increase in cost resulting in a strategy that better preserves asset value, e.g., VWAP – hedge.

3. Price Improvement

The price improvement strategy is the strategy that maximizes the likelihood of executing better than some specified cost L. It is found through the following maximization:

$$Max \quad Prob(\varphi < L) = \int_{-\infty}^{L} \frac{1}{\sqrt{2\pi}} \exp\left\{-\frac{(\varphi - \theta)^2}{2\Re}\right\} d\varphi$$

This can also be written (Almgren & Chriss) as

$$Max \; \frac{L - \varphi}{\Re}$$

where the solution is to draw a line from the specified cost L on the y-axis tangent to the ETF.

It is important that when we evaluate execution performance we keep in mind that each of these rational approaches results in a different optimal trading strategy. Therefore, the proper measurement of the performance first consists of knowing exactly what investors are looking to achieve.

The Post-Trade Analysis Process

The proper post-trade analysis procedure consists of much more than simply comparing the execution price to some benchmark price. It is necessary to first understand what managers and traders want to accomplish. Then we can measure costs and assess execution quality. Post-trade analysis should not be limited to agency executions only. It should also be performed for principal bid transactions. The recommended approach is as follows.

Post-Trade Analysis: Agency Execution

Step I: Evaluate the Implementation Decision

The very first step in post-trade analysis is to determine if the implementation decision was best execution ex-ante. Here we set out to answer two specific questions:

1. Does the strategy lie on the efficient trading frontier?
2. Does the strategy satisfy one of our acceptable implementation goals?

Does the Strategy Lie on the ETF? To determine if the strategy is optimal, we need only to determine if it contained the lowest cost for the quantity of risk and the least risk for the level of cost for expected market conditions at that time. Since managers and traders did not know exactly how market conditions were expected to turn out over the trading period, they needed to make this decision using their best expectations regarding the upcoming market conditions.

If, $E(\Omega)$ is the expected market conditions over the trading horizon (consisting of expected daily volume, buying and selling pressure, trading patterns, price trend, etc.), and $\theta_k = (\hat{\phi}_k, \hat{\Re}_k)$ is the cost profile of the specified strategy x_k, then we check to see if $\theta_k = (\hat{\phi}_k, \hat{\Re}_k)$ satisfies two conditions:

    i. Is $\hat{\phi}_k = Min \; \phi(x_k \,|\, E(\Omega), \Re(x_k) = \hat{\Re}_k)$,
    ii. Is $\hat{\Re}_k = Min \; \Re(x_k \,|\, E(\Omega), \phi(x_k) = \hat{\phi}_k)$

Figure 13.2. Efficient Trading Frontier

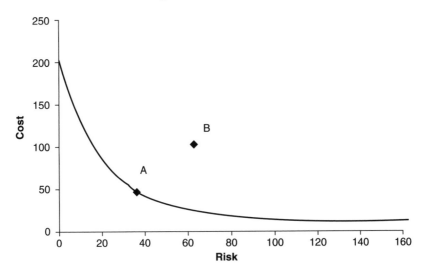

This analysis can be performed graphically by plotting the strategy on the derived ETF using expected market conditions at the time of the decision. In Figure 13.2 we show a plot of the ETF with two strategies, A and B. A is an optimal strategy but B is not. Investors selecting strategy B are neither making a good trading decision nor providing best execution regardless of the outcome of the implementation.

Did It Satisfy an Acceptable Goal of Implementation? The goal of implementation is to preserve asset value. But since the cost profile of the execution consists of a cost and risk parameter, investors are faced with managing two conflicting issues. We identified three potential tactics to preserve asset value given the uncertainty surrounding cost and risk. Therefore, we simply need to determine if the strategy x_k is a strategy that addresses one of the following concerns:

1. Minimize cost subject to risk
2. Balance tradeoff between cost and risk
3. Price improvement

In many cases, analysts performing the post-trade analysis will not know managers' specific intentions. Therefore, it would suffice to determine if strategy x_k were optimal and on the ETF.

The efficient trading frontier of Almgren and Chriss contains the set of optimal trading strategies and it is quickly becoming regarded as the proper framework for evaluating trading decisions. But what is little known about the ETF is that it is also an essential tool in performing post-trade analysis and determining best execution.

Step II: Measure Costs Using the Expanded IS Methodology

The next step of post-trade analysis consists of measuring the actual incurred trading costs and identifying where and why these costs occurred. There are no tricks, spells, or magic potions here. The cost is computed directly from our expanded implementation shortfall. That is:

$$IS = \sum_i \sum_j x_{ij}(P_{i0} - P_{id}) + \sum_i \sum_j x_{ij}P_{ij} - \sum_i \sum_j x_{ij}P_{i0}$$
$$+ \sum_i \left(X_i - \sum_j x_{ij} \right)(P_{in} - P_{id}) + Visible$$

and,

$$\varphi = \underbrace{\sum_i \sum_j x_{ij}P_{ij} - \sum_i \sum_j x_{ij}P_{i0}}_{Execution\ Cost} + \underbrace{\sum_i \left(X_i - \sum_j x_{ij} \right)(P_{in} - P_{id})}_{Opportunity\ Cost}$$

Step III: Estimate Costs Ex-Post

When the implementation strategy was developed, investors did not know exactly what the market conditions would be so they used the most likely expectations. But we know that the actual conditions will differ. Therefore, the specified strategy will have a different cost profile under actual market conditions than expected market conditions. So to accurately assess the execution performance we need to compare the actual costs to the estimated costs under actual market conditions; otherwise, it would not be fair to the participant being evaluated. For example, suppose that a specified best execution strategy ex-ante has an expected cost of 5bp and the trader follows the strategy exactly as prescribed by the manager. But because the actual market conditions are very illiquid the strategy actually incurrs a cost of 25bp. It would not be fair to the trader to compare the actual cost to the estimated cost with normal volumes and conclude that the difference was 20bp higher than expected because that estimated cost profile was never achievable. It is only fair to compute what the cost estimate would be with the actual market conditions. This process does not require any re-optimization, only a calculation of the cost and risk. We refer to these cost estimates as the ex-post cost estimates referring to cost estimates with known market conditions. These estimates are as follows:

$$E\lfloor \theta^*(x_k) \mid \Omega^* \rfloor = (\phi^*, \Re^*)$$

where Ω^* are the actual market conditions over the trading period.

Step IV: Compare Actual Trading Costs to Ex-Post Estimated Costs

We are now ready to compare the actual trading cost to the expected trading cost in the given market conditions. This is computed as follows:

Let,

$$\phi = \text{actual execution and opportunity cost}$$

and the ex-post cost profile be:

$$E\lfloor\theta^*(x_k)\,|\,\Omega^*\rfloor = (\phi^*, \Re^*)$$

Then, the difference between the actual and expected ex-post is:

$$\Delta\phi = Actual - Expected^* \tag{13.16}$$

and following our notation:

$$\Delta\phi = \varphi - \phi^* \tag{13.17}$$

In either equation a negative value indicates a cost that was less than the ex-post estimate thus indicating a savings. Since the cost and risk estimates are likely to vary greatly by stock, it is difficult to compare differences across stocks. Therefore, it is helpful to normalize the actual cost based on its expected cost and risk parameters. That is:

$$\delta_i = \frac{\varphi_i - \phi_i^*}{\Re_i^*} \tag{13.18}$$

This provides a normalized difference. For simplicity we assume it follows the standard normal distribution, that is, $\delta_i \sim N(0,1)$. At this point, however, we are still not sure if the under/overperformance was due to price volatility or if it was attributable to trader/broker quality. We determine this in the next step.

Step V: Measure Execution Performance Using RPM

The next step is to assess the performance of the trader or broker. As we mentioned earlier, the benchmark comparison technique commonly used is inadequate for our needs because it is an *inconsistent* metric. That is, a measure of 10bp can mean good performance in one stock and bad performance in another stock. It could also mean a good performance in one stock today but a bad performance tomorrow. Because of these reasons, the RPM is a superior measure to the benchmark approach. For example, if the RPM is greater than say 80% we are certain that the trader/broker obtained great market prices and if the RPM is less than 20% we are certain that the trader/broker received poor prices and hurt fund performance. There is nothing to debate here. We seek to determine if the trader achieved fair market prices and if the trader's ad-hoc execution decision added or subtracted value from the fund. This is accomplished using a strategy weighted RPM.

Were the Execution Prices Reasonable?

$$RPM_i(Strategy) = \sum_j \frac{x_{ij}^*}{X_i} RPM_j$$

where χ_k^* indicates the actual execution strategy.

Managers can be certain that traders realized fair market prices at times they were in the market if their RPM measures were in the 40–60% range. Those traders that execute better than 60% achieved the better market prices and those that execute less than 40% achieved the less favorable prices. Since this metric is a weighted average by strategy we account and adjust for price differences due to market movement.

Did the Trader Add Value?

$$Value\text{-}Added = \frac{\sum_{j=1}^{n} \left(x_{ij}^* - x_{ij}\right) RPM_{ij}}{RPM(x_i^*)}$$

where χ_k^* indicates the actual executor strategy and χ_k indicates the specified execution strategy ex-ante.

The value-added metric measures the actual decision-making ability of traders and/or brokers. Managers give traders specified strategies for implementation. Whenever traders deviate from the specified strategy they do so because they feel either that prices are better in the current period then they will be in a later period or that they will be better than they are currently. Thus, by comparing the deviation in strategy we can assess the value the trader's decision-making added to the process. A positive value-added metric indicates good decision-making ability (i.e., the decision achieved better prices and lower costs). A negative value-added indicates poor decision-making ability (i.e., the decision achieved worse prices and higher costs). It is important in analyzing traders' decision-making ability to use a sufficient number of observations to filter out decisions made in haste that turned out to be good.

A final note here is that if traders do not deviate from the prescribed strategy, for example, they do not make any deviation strategy, or better stated, their deviation decision to follow the prescribed strategy will achieve a value-added metric of zero. This indicates that they did not add to or take away from the implementation. This is intuitive since someone following directions can not be held responsible for higher costs or take credit for lower costs.

Step VI: Compare the Cost Difference to the Value-Added

Investors can perform a very accurate assessment of the overall contribution to cost attributable to the broker/trader's trading decisions (deviations) simply by plotting the normalized trading cost (x-axis) and the broker/trader value-added measure (y-axis) as an xy-chart. In this format, the data points in the upper half of the graph show the orders where the broker/trader added value and the points in the bottom half show the orders where the broker/trader hurt performance. The points on the right-hand side are those costs that were better than expected (lower cost), and the points on the left-hand side are those costs that were more than expected (higher cost). This illustration makes it easy for investors to identify the reason for over- or underperformance of the expected cost—that is, was the reason due to superior or poor executions or was it due to favorable or adverse price movement? Those data points with a high value-added were likely due to superior executions rather than just the result of favorable price movement, and those points with a very low value-added (negative) were likely lower due to poor executions rather than adverse price movement.

In Figure 13.3 we provide two examples of this illustration. The first graph shows the value-added of three brokers. Broker A deviated from the prescribed strategy, made the correct decisions, and provided superior performance (average value-added = 13%). Broker B also deviated from the prescribed strategy but made incorrect decisions and as a result had poor performance (average value-added = –13%). Broker C, however, followed the prescribed strategy and as a result had average or expected performance (average value-added = –0.06%). The average value-added for each broker is shown in parentheses. The second graph shows the executions for Broker D. This broker made good decisions resulting in improved costs and poor decisions that incurred cost. Overall the average value-added for Broker D was –0.32%, which would indicate average or expected performance similar to Broker C. But this is untrue; Broker D deviated from the strategy and made both good and poor decisions. We would expect the overall value-added for a broker who follows the specified strategy to also be near zero. To best distinguish the results, we recommend investors to analyze the standard deviation of value-added as well as the average of all values.

Step VII: Record Performance of Broker/Trader

It is important to keep a historical database of actual cost and performance by trader and broker. This way, managers and traders will have access to real and accurate cost and performance information. In return, this information can be used by investors to reduce the delay cost and better select the executing broker-dealer. The result will be improved portfolio returns. The exact statistics that should be recorded for each execution should include the following: order statistics (stock, side, shares), cost, normalized cost, RPM, and value-added by trader.

Post-Trade Analysis: Principal Bid Transactions

Principal bid transactions are a much different type of execution than the agency execution. Principal bids occur at a specified premium that is

Figure 13.3. Trading Cost Attribution Report

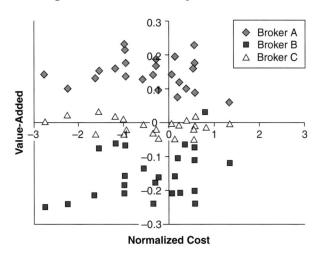

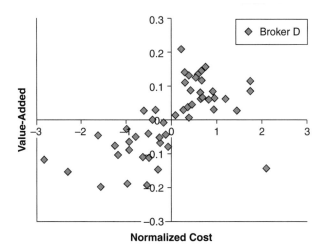

known exactly in advance. Because of this, many market participants state that there is nothing to measure and that the cost of the bid is exactly what they are told. But this is not completely true. Recall that in many principal bid transactions traders contact brokers during market hours and agree to the transaction at some future point in time (such as the close). The exact price of the bid then will include the market movement from the time of the solicitation to the close. If prices move adversely during that time, investors incur higher cost, but if prices move favorably, investors incur lower cost. The usual concern with a principal bid is that brokers will cause the prices to move unfavorably into the close by beginning to accumulate a position in the names. If this is true, the market impact cost of brokers will be factored into the closing price. With this in mind, we can write the cost of the principal bid in the expanded implementation shortfall notation as follows:

$$\text{IS(Principal Bid)} = \underbrace{\sum_i X_i(P_{is} - P_{id})}_{\text{Investment Delay Cost}} + \underbrace{\sum_i X_i(P_{in} - P_{is})}_{\text{Market Timing Delay Cost}} + Bid + visible$$

where,
P_{id} = the price of the ith stock at the time of the investment decision
P_{is} = the price of the ith stock at the time of solicitation of the bid
P_{in} = the closing price of the ith stock

In this notation it is easy to see that there are indeed incremental costs to the principal bid and fixed costs.

First, the delay cost is identical to the delay cost of an agency execution. Whenever there is a delay between the actual investment decision and the release of the order to the market there is the potential of adverse price movement. This delay cost, however, is caused by the fund and is not related to the actual execution. In theory, we would expect average price changes over the period of the delay to be equal to zero, but this is not the case. A large amount of empirical evidence exists revealing costs (rather than savings) associated with decision delays. The only explanation of this phenomenan (at least according to the money managers) is that managers are good at picking to buy stocks that are rising and choosing to sell stocks that are falling.

Second, there is the market timing delay cost. This is the cost associated with stock price movement over a waiting period—from solicitation and agreement of the bid to the actual bid execution (usually at the close). Again, in theory, we would expect this price change to be zero over the period. Therefore, if it is not zero (i.e., there is an associated cost) we can conclude that it was due to the price run-up the broker caused.

This can be conducted statistically using a Z-test and computing the normalized price change as follows:

$$Z = \frac{P_n - E(P_n)}{\sigma(P_n)}$$

Here we are simply conducting a confidence interval test of the normalized difference between the actual and expected price.

Our first example investigates price change when there is no expected trend. Here we simply determine if the price change from the time of solicitation of the bid to the close on the day is reasonable—that is, that the price falls within the expected volatility range. This test statistic is:

$$Z_i = \frac{sign(X_i) \cdot (P_{in} - P_{is})}{\sigma_i \cdot \sqrt{n - s}}$$

where $\sigma_i \cdot \sqrt{n - s}$ is the volatility scaled for the time period.
   Our hypothesis test is:

   H_0: No price run-up
   H_a: Price run-up results in a higher cost

Reject the null if

   $Z > 1.96$ (95%), or
   $Z > 2.32$ (99%)

   If Z is greater than the values we reject the null hypothesis and conclude that the broker did invoke price run-up. However, it is important that investors use a significant number of data points (orders and lists) before making any conclusions.
   Now to be fair to the executing broker we should incorporate into this statistic the expected price change over the period. In most cases there is no reasonable price forecast, especially for a few hours. But it is possible to assume that the same trend that has occurred from the time of the decision to the time of the solicitation, d to s, will persist from time s to time n. We would not want to incorrectly punish the broker for causing this natural price appreciation. In this case, we adjust our test statistic Z to account for the expected price movement as follows:

$$Z_i = \frac{sign(X_i)(\Delta P - E[\Delta P])}{\sigma_i \sqrt{\Delta t}} = \frac{sign(X_i) \cdot \left[(P_{in} - P_{is}) - \left(\dfrac{P_{is} - P_{id}}{s - d} \right)(s - n) \right]}{\sigma_i \cdot \sqrt{n - s}}$$

   H_0: No price run-up
   H_a: Price run-up results in a higher cost

   Reject the null if:

   $Z > 1.96$ (95%), or
   $Z > 2.32$ (99%)

   If $Z > 1.64$ for a 95% confidence interval or $Z > 2.32$ for a 99% confidence interval, then we conclude that the broker forced market impact into the price of the stock in order to increase the bid price indirectly.

REFERENCES

Achelis, S. B. (1995). *Technical Analysis from A to Z*. New York: McGraw-Hill.

Affleck-Graves, J., S. Hegde, and R. Miller. (1994). "Trading Mechanisms and the Components of the Bid-Ask Spread." *J. Finance* 49, 1471–1488.

Almgren, R. (2001). "Optimal Execution with Nonlinear Impact Functions and Trading-Enhanced Risk." http://www.math.toronto.edu/almgren/papers/nonlin.pdf

Almgren, R., and N. Chriss. (1997). "Optimal Liquidation Strategies." Original Working Paper.

Almgren, R., and N. Chriss. (1999). "Value Under Liquidation." *J. Risk* 12(12), 61–63.

Almgren, R., and N. Chriss. (2000). "Optimal Execution of Portfolio Transactions." *J. Risk* 3(2), 5–39.

Almgren, R., and N. Chriss. (2003). "Bidding Principals." *Risk*. Vol. 16, June 2003.

Amihud, Y., and H. Mendelson. (2000). "The Liquidity Route to a Lower Cost of Capital." *Journal of Applied Corporate Finance* 12, 8–25.

Arnott, A., and W. Wagner (1990). "Measurement and Control of Trading Cost." *Financial Analysts Journal*, Nov/Dec 1990.

Artzner, P., F. Delbaen, J.-M. Eber, and D. Heath. (1999). "Coherent Measures of Risk." *Math. Finance* 9, 203–228.

Atkins, A., and E. Dyl. (1990). "Price Reversals, Bid-Ask Spreads, and Market Efficiency." *Journal of Financial and Quantitative Analysis* 25, 535–547.

Barclay, M. J., W. G. Christie, J. H. Harris, E. Kandel, and P. H. Schultz. (1999). "The Effects of Market Reform on the Trading Costs and Depths of Nasdaq Stocks." *J. Finance*, 54, 1–34.

Barra (1997). *Market Impact Model Handbook.*

Basak, S., and A. Shapiro. (2001). "Value-at-Risk-Based Risk Management: Optimal Policies and Asset Prices." *Rev. Financial Studies* 14, 371–405.

Battalio, R. H. (1997). "Third Market Broker-Dealers: Cost Competitors or Cream Skimmers?" *J. Finance* 52, 341–352.

Battalio, R., J. Greene, and R. Jennings. (1995). "Do Competing Specialists and Preferencing Dealers Affect Market Quality?" Working Paper, Indiana University.

Beerbower, G. (1989). "Evaluating Transaction Cost," in *The Complete Guide to Securities Transactions*. W. Wagner, ed. New York: John Wiley and Sons, pp. 137–1500.

Beerbower, G., and W. Priest. (1980). "The Tricks of the Trade." *J. Portfol. Manage.* 6, 36–42.

Benston, G., and R. Hagerman. (1974). "Determinants of Bid-Asked Spreads in the Over-the-Counter Market." *Journal of Financial Economics* 1, 353–364.

Berkowitz, S., D. Logue, and E. Noser. (1988). "The Total Cost of Transactions on the NYSE." *J. Finance* 41, 97–112.

Berkowitz, S., and D. Logue. (2001). "Transaction Costs." *J. Portfolio Management*, Winter 2001.

Bertsimas, D., and A. Lo. (1996). "Optimal Control of Execution Costs." Working Paper, LFE- 1025-96, Sloan School of Management, MIT.

Bessembinder, H. (1998). "Trading Costs and Return Volatility: Evidence from Exchange Listings." *NYSE Working Paper 98-02.*

Bessembinder, H., and H. M. Kaufman. (1995). "Quotations and Trading Costs on Domestic Equity Exchanges." Working Paper, Department of Finance. Arizona State University.

Bessembinder, H., and H. M. Kaufman. (1996). "A Cross-Exchange Comparison on Execution Costs and Information Flow for NYSE-Listed Stocks. *J. Finan. Econ.*, forthcoming.

Bessembinder, H., and H. M. Kaufman. (1997). "A Comparison of Trade Execution Costs for NYSE and NASDAQ-Listed stocks." *J. Fin. Quant. Anal.* 32, 287–310.

Biais, B., P. Hillion, and C. Spatt. (1995). "An Empirical Analysis of the Limit Order Book and the Order Flow in the Paris Bourse." *Journal of Finance* 50, 1655–1689.

Bickel, P. J., and K. A. Doksum. (1977), *Mathematical Statistics: Basic Ideas and Selected Topics.* Englewood Cliffs, NJ: Prentice Hall.

Bloomfield, R., and M. O'Hara. (1996). "Does Order Preferencing Matter?" Working Paper, Johnson Graduate School of Management, Cornell University.

Blume, M., and M. Goldstein. (1992). "Displayed and Effective Spreads by Market, Working Paper 27–92, Rodney White Center, The Wharton School (December 23).

Blume, M., A. MacKinlay, and B. Terker. (1989). "Order Imbalances and Stock Price Movements on October 19 and 20, 1987." *Journal of Finance* 44, 827–848.

Blume, M. E., and M. Goldstein. (1997). "Quotes, Order Flow, and Price Discovery." *J. Finance* 52, 221–244.

Bondarenko, O. (2001). "Competing Market Makers, Liquidity Provision, and Bid-Ask Spreads." *J. Financial Markets* 4(3), 269–308.

Brown, P., D. Walsh, and A. Yuen. (1997). "The Interaction Between Order Imbalance and Stock Price. *Pacific-Basin Finance Journal* 5, 539–557.

Campbell, J. Y., A. W. Lo, and A. C. MacKinlay. (1997). *The Econometrics of Financial Markets,* Princeton, NJ: Princeton University Press.

Chakravarty, S. (2001). "Steath-Trading: Which Traders' Trades Move Prices?" *J. Financial Econ.* 61, 289–307.

Chakravarty, S., and C. W. Holden. (1995). "An Integrated Model of Market and Limit Orders." *Journal of Financial Intermediation* 4, 213–41.

Chan, L. K., and W. Fong. (2000). "Trade Size, Order Imbalance, and the Volatility-Volume Relation. *Journal of Financial Economics* 57, 247–273.

Chan, L. K. C., and J. Lakonishok. (1993). "Institutional Trades and Intraday Stock Price Behavior. *J. Financ. Econ.* 33, 173–201.

Chan, L. K., and J. Lakonishok. (1995). "The Behavior of Stock Prices Around Institutional Trades. *J. Finance* 50, 1147–1174.

Chase, R. B., N. J. Aquilano, and F. R. Jacob. (1999). *Production and Operations Management: Manufacturing and Services.* Irwin.

Chordia, T., and A. Subrahmanyam. (1995). "Market Making, the Tick Size, and Payment-for-Order Flow: Theory and Evidence." *J. Bus.* 68(4), 543–575.

Chordia, T., R. Roll, and A. Subrahmanyam. (2001). "Market Liquidity and Trading Activity. *Journal of Finance,* forthcoming.

Chordia, T., A. Subrahmanyam, and V. R. Anshuman. (2001). "Trading Activity and Expected Stock Returns." *J. Financial Econ.* 59, 3–32.

Chriss, Neil A. (1997). *Black-Scholes and Beyond: Option Pricing Models.* Irwin.

Chriss, Neil A. (2001). "Principal Bids and Basket Trades." Columbia Practitioners Conference, Columbia University, Sept 2001.

Christie, W. G., and R. D. Huang. (1994). "Market Structures and Liquidity: A Transactions Data Study of Exchange Listings." *J. Finan. Intermediation* 3, 300–326.

Christie, W., and P. Schultz. (1999). "The Initiation and Withdrawal of Odd-Eighth Quotes Among Nasdaq Stocks: An Empirical Analysis." *Journal of Financial Economics* 52, 409–442.

Coarse, R.H. (1937). "The Nature of the Firm." *Econometrica.*

Cochrane, J. (1993). "U.S. Equity Market Competitiveness." Working Paper, New York Stock Exchange, New York.

Cohen. K. J., D. Maier, R. Schwartz, and D. Witcomb. (1981). "Transactions Cost, Order Placement Strategy and Existence of the Bid-Ask Spread." *Journal of Political Economy* 89, 287–305.

Collins, B. M., and F. J. Fabozzi. (1991). "A Methodology for Measuring Transaction Costs." *Financial Analysis Journal* (March/April), 27–36.

Copeland, T. E. and D. Galai. (1983). "Information Effects on the Bid-Ask Spread." *Journal of Finance*, 38, 1457–69.

Coppejans, M., I. Domowitz, and A. Madhavan. (2000). "Liquidity in an Automated Auction." Working Paper, Pennsylvania State University.

Cox, B. (2001). "Transaction Cost Forecasts and Optimal Trade Schedule." Super Bowl of Indexing Conference, Arizona.

Cox, D., and D. Peterson. (1994). "Stock Returns Following Large One-Day Declines: Evidence on Short-Term Reversals and Longer-Term Performance." *Journal of Finance* 49, 255–267.

Cuneo, L., and W. Wagner (1975). "Reducing the Cost of Stock Trading." *Financial Analysts Journal*, Nov/Dec 1975.

Damodaran, A. (1994). *Damodaran on Valuation.* New York: John Wiley and Sons.

DeGroot, M. (1986). *Probability and Statistics.* Boston: Addison-Wesley, Publishing Company.

De Jong, F., T. Nijman, and A. Roell. (1993). "A Comparison of the Cost of Trading French Shares on the Paris Bourse and on Seaq International." *Eur. Econ. Rev.* 39, 1277–1301.

Domowitz, I. (1992). "A Taxonomy of Automated Trade Execution Systems," *Journal of International Money and Finance* 12, 607–631.

Domowitz, I. (1996). "An Exchange Is a Many Splendored Thing: The Classification and Regulation of Automated Trading Systems," in *The Industrial Organization and Regulation of Securities Markets*, Andrew Lo, ed. University of Chicago Press, Chicago.

Domowitz, I. (2001). "Liquidity, Transaction Costs, and Reintermediation in Electronic Markets." Working Paper.

Domowitz, I., J. Glen, and A. Madhavan. (1998). "International Cross-Listing and Order Flow Migration: Evidence From an Emerging Market." *Journal of Finance*, 53, 2001–2027.

Domowitz, I., J. Glen, and A. Madhavan. (1999). "Liquidity, Volatility, and Equity Trading Costs Across Countries." Working Paper, Pennsylvania State University.

Domowitz, I. and B. Steil. (1999). "Automation, Trading Costs, and the Structure of the Securities Trading Industry." *Brookings-Wharton Papers on Financial Services* 2, 33–92.

Domowitz, I. and B. Steil. (2001). "Automation, Trading Costs, and the Cost of Equity Capital." Working Paper, Pennsylvania State University, 22.

Dowd, K. (1998). *Beyond Value at Risk, The New Science of Risk Management.* New York: John Wiley & Sons.

Duan L. and W. L. Ng. (2000). "Optimal Dynamic Portfolio Selection: Multi-Period Mean-Variance Formulation." *Mathematical Finance*, Vol. 10, No. 3, July 2000.

Dudewicz, E. J., and S. N. Mishra. (1988). *Modern Mathematical Statistics* New York: John Wiley and Sons.

Dufour, A., and R. Engle. (2000). "Time and Price Impact of a Trade." Working Paper.

Dutta, P., and A. Madhavan. (1997). "Competition and Collusion in Dealer Markets." *J. Finance* 52, 245–276.

Easley, D., N. Kiefer, and M. O'Hara. (1996). "Cream-Skimming or Profit-Sharing? The Curious Role of Purchased Order Flow." *J. Finance* 51, 811–834.

Easterbrook, F., and D. Fischel. (1989). "The Corporate Contract." *Columbia Law Rev.* 89, 1416.

Elton, E. J., and M. J. Gruber. (1995). *Modern Portfolio Theory and Investment Analysis*, 5th ed. New York: John Wiley & Sons.

Ferstenberg, R. (2000). "Optimal Execution Strategies." Berkeley Program in Finance Conference, CA, April 2000.

Foerster, S. R., and G. A. Karolyi. (1999). "The Effects of Market Segmentation and Investor Recognition on Asset Prices: Evidence from Foreign Stocks Listing in the United States." *Journal of Finance*, 54, 981–1013.

Francis, J. C. (1980). *Investments Analysis and Management*, 3d ed. New York: McGraw-Hill.

Gallant, A., P. Rossi, and G. Tauchen. (1992). "Stock Prices and Volume." *Review of Financial Studies* 5, 199–242.

Gibbons, M., and P. Hess. (1981). "Day of the Week Effects and Asset Returns." *Journal of Business* 54, 579–596.

Glantz, M. (1994). *Loan Risk Management: Strategies and Analytical Techniques for Commercial Bankers*. New York: McGraw-Hill.

Glantz, M. (2000). "Scientific Financial Management: Advances in Financial Intelligence Capabilities for Corporate Valuation and Risk Assessment," AMACOM, Inc., New York.

Glantz, M. (2002). *Managing Bank Risk: An Introduction to Broad-Base Credit Engineering*. New York Academic Press, An Elsevier Science Imprint.

Grinold, R. C., and R. Kahn. (2000). *Active Portfolio Management*. New York: McGraw-Hill.

Handa, P., R. Schwartz, and A. Tiwari. (1999). "Quote Setting and Price Formation in an Order Driven Market." Working Paper, University of Iowa.

Harris, L. (1986a). "Cross-Security Tests of the Mixture of Distribution Hypothesis." *Journal of Financial and Quantitative Analysis* 21, 39–46.

Harris, L. (1986b). "A Transaction Data Study of Weekly and Intraday Patterns in Stock Returns." *Journal of Financial Economics* 16, 99–117.

Harris, L. (1987). "Transaction Data Tests of the Mixture of Distributions Hypothesis." *Journal of Financial and Quantitative Analysis* 22, 127–41.

Harris, L. (1990a). "Liquidity, Trading Rules, and Electronic Trading Systems." New York University Salomon Center Monograph Series in Finance, Monograph 1990–4.

Harris, L. (1990b). "Estimation of Stock Price Variations and Serial Covariances from Discrete Observations." *Journal of Financial and Quantitative Analysis* 25, 291–306.

Harris, L. (1994). "Minimum Price Variations, Discrete Bid/Ask Spreads and Quotation Sizes." *Review of Financial Studies* 7, 149–178.

Harris, L. (1995). "Consolidation, Fragmentation, Segmentation, and Regulation," in *Global Equity Markets: Technological, Competitive, and Regulatory Challenges*. Robert A. Schwarz, ed. New York: Irwin Publishing.

Harris, L., and E. Gurel. (1986). "Price and Volume Effects Associated with Changes in the S&P 500 List: New Evidence for the Existence of Price Pressures." *Journal of Finance* 41, 815–829.

Hasbrouck, J. (1995). "One Security, Many Markets: Determining the Contribution to Price Discovery." *J. Finance* 50, 1175–1199.

Hasbrouck, J., and R. A. Schwartz. (1988). "Liquidity and Execution Costs in Equity Markets. *J. Portfolio Management* 14 (Spring), 10–16.

Hasbrouck, J., and D. Seppi. (2001). "Common Factors in Prices, Order Flows and Liquidity. *Journal of Financial Economics* 59, 383–411.

Hastings, H., and R. Kissell. 1998 "Is the Nile Outflow Fractal? Hurst's Analysis Revisted." *Natural Resource Modeling*, Volume 11, Number 2.

Hiemstra, C., and J. Jones. (1994). "Testing for Linear and Nonlinear Granger Causality in the Stock Price-Volume Relation. *Journal of Finance* 49, 1639–1664.

Hill, J. (2001). "Transaction Costs and Liquidity in Evolving Markets." Superbowl of Indexing Conference, Arizona.

Ho, T., and H. Stoll. (1983). "The Dynamics of Dealer Markets Under Competition." *Journal of Finance* 38, 1053–1074.

Holthausen, R., R. Leftwich, and D. Mayers. (1987). "The Effect of Large Block Transactions on Security Prices." *J. Finan. Econ.* 19, 237–267.

Holthausen, R. W., R. W. Leftwich, and D. Mayers. (1990). "Large-Block Transactions, the Speed of Response, and Temporary and Permanent Stock-Price Effects." *J. Financial Econ.* 26, 71–95.

Huang, R. D., and H. R. Stoll. (1994). "What Does It Cost to Execute Trades? Evidence from the NYSE." Working Paper 94–05, Financial Markets Research Center, Owen School, Vanderbilt University (November 28).

Huang, R. D., and H. R. Stoll. (1995a). "Competitive Trading of NYSE Listed Stocks: Measurement and Interpretation of Trading Costs." Working Paper 94–13, Financial Markets Research Center, Owen School, Vanderbilt University (March 13).

Huang, R. D., and H. R. Stoll. (1995b). "The Components of the Bid-Ask Spread: A General Approach." *Rev. Financial Studies* 10(4), 995–1034.

Huang, R. D., and H. R. Stoll. (1996). "Dealer Versus Auction Markets: A Paired Comparison of Execution Costs on NASDAQ and the NYSE." *J. Finan. Econ.* 41(3), 313–357.

Huang, R., and H. R. Stoll. (2001). "Tick Size, Bid-Ask Spreads and Market Structure." *Journal of Financial and Quantitative Analysis*.

Huberman, G., and W. Stanzl. (2001). Optimal liquidity trading. Working Paper, Preprint.

ITG (2000), The Transaction Cost Challenge, 2000.

Jones, C., G. Kaul, and M. Lipson. (1994). "Transactions, Volume, and Volatility." *Review of Financial Studies* 7, 631–651.

Jones, C. M., and M. L. Lipson. (1999). "Execution Costs of Institutional Equity Orders." *J. Financial Intermediation* 8, 123–140.

Judge, G. G., W. E. Griffiths, R. Carter Hill, H. Lütkepohl, and T. C. Lee. (1985). *The Theory and Practice of Econometrics.* New York: Wiley.

Irvine, P., G. Benston, and E. Kandel. (2000). "Liquidity Beyond the Inside Spread: Measuring and Using Information in the Limit Order Book." Working Paper.

Kahn, R. N. (1993). "How the Execution of Trades Is Best Operationalized," in *Execution Techniques, True Trading Costs, and the Microstructure of Markets.* K. F. Sherrerd, ed. AIMR.

Karpoff, J. (1987). "The Relation Between Price Changes and Trading Volume: A Survey." *Journal of Financial and Quantitative Analysis* 22, 109–125.

Kaufman, P. J. (1998). *Trading Systems and Methods.* New York: John Wiley and Sons.

Keim, D. B., and A. Madhavan. (1995). "Anatomy of the Trading Process: Empirical Evidence on the Behavior of Institutional Traders." *J. Financial Econ.* 37, 371–398.

Keim, D. B., and A. Madhavan. (1995). "Execution Costs and Investment Performance: An Empirical Analysis of Institutional Equity Trades." *J. Finan. Econ.*, forthcoming.

Keim, D. B., and A. Madhavan. (1996). "The Upstairs Market for Large-Block Transactions: Analysis and Measurement of Price Effects." *Rev. Finan. Stud.* 9, 1–36.

Keim, D. B., and A. Madhavan. (1997). "Transactions Costs and Investment Style: An Interexchange Analysis of Institutional Equity Trades." *J. Financial Econ.* 46, 265–292.

Keim, D.B., and A. Madhavan. (1998). "The Cost of Institutional Equity Trades." *Financial Analysts Journal,* Jul/Aug 1988.

Kissell, R. (1999a). "Agency vs. Principal Implementation Strategies: Designing an Optimal Agency Trading Strategy and Evaluating the Economic Fair Value of a Principal Bid." Investors Press, CA, September 1999.

Kissell, R. (2000a). "Trading Strategies: Advanced Implementation Decision Tools." Berkley Program in Finance Conference, CA, April 2000.

Kissell, R. (2000b, 2001, 2002). "Understanding Transaction Costs and Designing an Implementation Strategy." University of Amsterdam, Faculty of Economics, Netherlands, Guest Lecturer, June 2001.

Kissell, R. (2000c), "Trading Strategies: Preserving Asset Value," Columbia Finance Practitioners Conference, Columbia University, October 2000.

Kissell, R. (2001a). "Improving Hedge Fund Returns Using Pre-Trade Analytical Techniques." Berkley Program in Finance Conference, CA, March 2001.

Kissell, R. (2001b). "Trading Strategies for Portfolio Re-Balancing and Manager Transitions." IMN, 4th Annual Asset Allocation Summit, Williamsburg, VA, June 2001.

Kissell, R. (2001c). "Trading Strategy Optimization: Preserving Asset Value." QWAFAFEW, August 2001.

Kissell, R. (2001d). "Developing Efficient Trading Strategies." Columbia Finance Practitioners Conference, Columbia University, Sept. 2001.

Kissell, R., and R. Malamut. (2002). "Optimal Trading Strategies: A Mathematical Framework for Estimating Trading Costs, Forecasting Market Impact, and Developing Optimal Strategies to Achieve Best Execution." Draft Research Paper.

Kissell, R., D. Zeevi, and L. Giordano. (1999b). "Agency vs. Principal Implementation Strategies: Designing an Optimal Agency Trading Strategy and Evaluating the Economic Fair Value of a Principal Bid." Investors Press, Inc.- Visionary Briefs.

Konishi, H., and N. Makimoto. (2001). "Optimal Slice of a Block Trade." Preprint.

Koski, J. L., and R. Michaely. (2000). "Prices, Liquidity, and the Information Content of Trades. *Rev. Financial Studies* 13, 659–696.

Kothare, M., and P. Laux. (1995). "Trading Costs and the Trading System for NASDAQ Stocks." *Finan. Anal. J.* (March/April), 42–53.

Kraus, A., and H. Stoll. (1972). "Parallel Trading by Institutional Investors." *Journal of Financial and Quantitative Analysis* 7, 2107–2138.

Kraus, A., and H. Stoll. (1972). "Price Impacts of Block Trading on the New York Stock Exchange." *J. Finance* 27, 569–588.

Kyle, A. (1985). "Continuous Auctions and Insider Trading." *Econometrica* 53, 1315–1335.

Lauterbach, B., and U. Ben-Zion. (1993). "Stock Market Crashes and the Performance of Circuit Breakers: Empirical Evidence." *Journal of Finance* 48, 1909–1925.

Lee, C. (1992). "Earnings News and Small Traders: An Intraday Analysis." *Journal of Accounting and Economics* 15, 265–302.

Lee, C. (1993). "Market Integration and Price Execution for NYSE-Listed Securities." *J. Finance* 48, 1009–1038.

Lee, C., and B. Radhakrishna. (2000). "Inferring Investor Behavior: Evidence from TORQ Data." *Journal of Financial Markets* 3, 83–111.

Lee, C., and M. Ready. (1991). "Inferring Trade Direction from Intraday Data." *Journal of Finance* 46, 733–747.

Leland, H. E.. (1996). "Optimal Asset Rebalancing in the Presence of Transaction Costs." Working Paper.

Lo, A., and Craig Mackinlay. (1999). *A Non-Random Walk Down Wall Street.* Princeton, NJ: Princeton University Press.

Lo, A., and J. Wang. (2000). "Trading Volume: Definitions, Data Analysis, and Implications of Portfolio Theory." *Review of Financial Studies* 13, 257–300.

Loeb, T. F. (1983). "Trading Costs: The Critical Link Between Investment Information and Results." *Financial Analysts Journal* 39, 39–44.

Macey, J. R., and D. D. Haddock. (1985). "Shirking at the SEC: Failure of the National Market System." *Univ. Illinois Law Rev.* 2, 315–362.

Macey, J. R., and M. O'Hara. (1999). "Globalization, Exchange Governance, and the Future of Exchanges." *Brookings-Wharton Papers on Financial Services* 2, 1–32,

Madhavan, A., and M. Cheng. (1997). "In Search of Liquidity: Block Trades in the Upstairs and Downstairs Markets." *Rev. Finan. Stud.* 10, 175–203.

Maginn, J. L., and D. Tuttle. (1990). *Managing Investment Portfolios, a Dynamic Process.* Boston: Warren, Gorham & Lamon.

Malamut, R. (2002a). "Multi-Period Optimization Techniques for Trade Scheduling." QWAFAFEW, April 2002.

Malamut, R., and R. Kissell. (2002b). "Multi-Period Trade Schedule Optimization." Draft Research Report.

Malkiel, B. G. (1996). *A Random Walk Down Wall Street.* New York: W. W. Norton & Company.

Mansfield, E. (1994). *Statistics for Business and Economics: Methods and Applications.* New York: W. W. Norton & Company.

Markowitz, H. (1952). "Portfolio Selection," *Journal of Finance*, March 1952.

Matytsin, A. (2000)."Valuation of Liquidity." Columbia Practitioners Conference, Columbia University, Sept 2001.

Meyer, P. L. (1970). *Introductory Probability and Statistical Applications.* Reading, MA: Addison-Wesley Publishing Company, Inc.

Mittelhammer, R. C., G. G. Judge, and D. J. Miller. (2000). *Econometric Foundations.* Cambridge: Cambridge University Press.

Murphy, J. (1999). *Technical Analysis of the Financial Markets.* New Jersey: Prentice Hall.

Murrin, J., T. Copeland, and T. Koller (2000). *Valuation: Measuring and Managing the Value of Companies.* New York: John Wiley and Sons.

Myerson, R. B. (1991). *Game Theory: Analysis of Conflict.* Cambridge: Harvard University Press.

Nalebuff, B. (2000). "Competing Against Bundles," in *Incentives, Organization, and Public Economics.* Gareth D. Myles and Peter Hammond, eds.

O'Hara, M. (1995). *Market Microstructure Theory.* Cambridge, MA: Blackwell.

Odders-White, E. R. (2000). "On the Occurrence and Consequences of Inaccurate Trade Classification." *Journal of Financial Markets* 3, 205–332.

Owen, G. (1982). *Game Theory.* New York: Academic Press.

Pagano, M., and A. Röell. (1990). "Trading Systems in European Stock Exchanges: Current Performance and Policy Options." *Economic Policy* 10, 65–115.

Paltrow, S. J. (1995). SEC Plans Charges in NASDAQ Probe, *L.A. Times,* July 7.

Perold, A. F. (1988). "The Implementation Shortfall: Paper Versus Reality." *J. Portfolio Management* 14 (Spring), 4–9.

Perold, A. F., and R. S. Salomon, Jr. (1991). "The Right Amount of Assets Under Management." *Financial Analysts J.* 47 (May–June), 31–39.

Petersen, M., and D. Fialkowski. (1994). "Posted Versus Effective Spreads: Good Prices or Bad Quotes?" *J. Finan. Econ.* 35, 269–292.

Pirrong, S. C. (1996). "Market Liquidity and Depth on Computerized and Open Outcry Trading Systems: A Comparison of DTB and LIFFE Bund Contracts." *Journal of Futures Markets* 16, 519–543.

Pring, A. (2002). *Technical Analysis Explained.* New York: McGraw-Hill.

Rickard, J. T., and N. G. Torre. (1999). "Information Systems for Optimal Transaction Implementation." *J. Management Information Systems* 16, 47–62.

Roell, A. (1992). "Comparing the Performance of Stock Exchange Trading Systems," in *The Internationalization of Capital Markets and the Regulatory Response.* Fingleton and Schoemaker, eds. London: Graham and Trotman.

Roll, R. (1984). "A Simple Implicit Measure of the Bid-Ask Spread in an Efficient Market. *J. Finance* 39, 1127–1139.

Roll, R., and S. Ross. (1984). "The Arbitrage Pricing Theory Approach to Strategic Portfolio Planning." *Financial Analysts Journal,* May–June 1984.

Ross, S. (1976). "The Arbitrage Pricing Theory of Capital Asset Pricing." *Journal of Economic Theory,* Dec. 1976.

Rudd, A., and H. K. Clasing Jr. (1988). *Modern Portfolio Theory, Principles of Investment Management.* Orinda, CA: Andrew Rudd.

Sall, J., and A. Lehman. (1996). *JMP Start Statistics: A Guide to Statistical and Data Analysis Using JMP and JMP Software.* New York: Duxbury Press.

Schack, J. (1999). "Cost Containment." *Institutional Investor,* (November) 43–49.

Schwartz, R. A. (1993). *Reshaping the Equity Markets: A Guide for the 1990's.* Homewood, Illinois: Business One Irwin, 1993.

Schwartz R. A., and B. Steil. (2001). "Controlling Institutional Trading Costs: We Have Met the Enemy and They are Us." *Journal of Portfolio Management.*

Sharpe, W. (1964). "Capital Asset Prices: A Theory of Market Equilibrium under Conditions of Risk." *Journal of Finance,* Sept. 1964.

Sheep, L. A. (1979). "The Joint Density of the Maximum and Its Location for a Wiener Process with Drift." *Journal of Applied Probability* 16, 423–27.

Shleifer, A. (1986). "Do Demand Curves for Stocks Slope Down?" *Journal of Finance* 41, 579–590.

Sias, R. (1997). "Price Pressure and the Role of Institutional Investors in Closed-End Funds. *Journal of Financial Research* 20, 211–229.

Spiegel, M., and A. Subrahmanyam. (1995). "On Intraday Risk Premia." *Journal of Finance* 50, 319–339.

Stoll, H. (1978a). "The supply of Dealer Services in Securities Markets." *Journal of Finance* 33,1133–1151.

Stoll, H. (1978b). "The Pricing of Security Dealer Services: An Empirical Study of NASDAQ Stocks."

Stoll, H. R. (1989). "Inferring the Components of the Bid-Ask Spread: Theory and Empirical Tests. *J. Finance* 44, 115–134.

Tobin, J. (1958). "Liquidity Preference as Behavior Towards Risk." *The Review of Economic Studies,* Feb. 1958.

Treynor, J. (1987). "The Economics of the Dealer Function." *Financial Analysts Journal,* 27–34.

Treynor, J.L. (1981). "What Does It Take to Win the Trading Game." *Financial Analysts Journal,* Jan/Feb 1981.

Vinod, H. D. (1982). "Maximum Entropy Measurement Error Estimates of Singular Covariance Matrices." *Journal of Econometrics,* Vol 20, 1982.

Wagner, W. H., and M. Banks. (1992). "Increasing Portfolio Effectiveness Via Transaction Cost Management." *J. Portfolio Management* 19, 6–11.

Wagner, W., and M. Edwards. (1993). "Best Execution." *Finan. Anal. J.* 49, 65–71.

Wagner, W., and S. Glass. (2001). "What Every Plan Sponsor Needs to Know About Transaction Costs," *Institutional Investor, Transaction Cost Guide,* 2001.

Wilcox, J.W. (1999). *Investing By The Numbers.* New Hope, Pennsylvania: Frank Fabozzi Associates.

Williamson, O. E., and S. G. Winter. (1993). *The Nature of the Firm.* Oxford: Oxford University Press.

Willoughby, J. (1998). "Executions Song." *Institutional Investor* 32(11), 51–56.

INDEX

Note: Italicized page numbers indicate illustrations.